Power, Prestige and Bilingualism

BILINGUAL EDUCATION AND BILINGUALISM
Series Editors: Professor Nancy H. Hornberger, *University of Pennsylvania, Philadelphia, USA* and Professor Colin Baker, *University of Wales, Bangor, Wales, Great Britain*

Other Books in the Series

At War With Diversity: US Language Policy in an Age of Anxiety
    James Crawford
Becoming Bilingual: Language Acquisition in a Bilingual Community
    Jean Lyon
Bilingual Education and Social Change
    Rebecca Freeman
Cross-linguistic Influence in Third Language Acquisition
    J. Cenoz, B. Hufeisen and U. Jessner (eds)
Curriculum Related Assessment, Cummins and Bilingual Children
    Tony Cline and Norah Frederickson (eds)
Dual Language Education
    Kathryn J. Lindholm-Leary
Foundations of Bilingual Education and Bilingualism
    Colin Baker
An Introductory Reader to the Writings of Jim Cummins
    Colin Baker and Nancy Hornberger (eds)
Japanese Children Abroad: Cultural, Educational and Language Issues
    Asako Yamada-Yamamoto and Brian Richards (eds)
Language Minority Students in the Mainstream Classroom (2nd edn)
    Angela L. Carrasquillo and Vivian Rodriguez
Learning English at School: Identity, Social Relations and Classroom Practice
    Kelleen Toohey
Language, Power and Pedagogy: Bilingual Children in the Crossfire
    Jim Cummins
Language Use in Interlingual Families: A Japanese-English Sociolinguistic Study
    Masayo Yamamoto
Learners' Experiences of Immersion Education: Case Studies of French and Chinese
    Michèle de Courcy
Reflections on Multiliterate Lives
    Diane Belcher and Ulla Connor (eds)
The Sociopolitics of English Language Teaching
    Joan Kelly Hall and William G. Eggington (eds)
Studies in Japanese Bilingualism
    Mary Goebel Noguchi and Sandra Fotos (eds)
Teaching and Learning in Multicultural Schools
    Elizabeth Coelho
World English: A Study of its Development
    Janina Brutt-Griffler

Other Books of Interest

Beyond Bilingualism: Multilingualism and Multilingual Education
    Jasone Cenoz and Fred Genesee (eds)
The Care and Education of Young Bilinguals
    Colin Baker
Encyclopedia of Bilingualism and Bilingual Education
    Colin Baker and Sylvia Prys Jones

Please contact us for the latest book information:
Multilingual Matters, Frankfurt Lodge, Clevedon Hall,
Victoria Road, Clevedon, BS21 7HH, England
http://www.multilingual-matters.com

BILINGUAL EDUCATION AND BILINGUALISM 35
Series Editors: Nancy H. Hornberger and Colin Baker

Power, Prestige and Bilingualism

International Perspectives on Elite Bilingual Education

Anne-Marie de Mejía

MULTILINGUAL MATTERS LTD
Clevedon • Buffalo • Toronto • Sydney

In memory of my parents

Library of Congress Cataloging in Publication Data
A catalog record for this book is available from the Library of Congress.

British Library Cataloguing in Publication Data
A catalogue entry for this book is available from the British Library.

ISBN 1-85359-591-8 (hbk)
ISBN 1-85359-590-X (pbk)

Multilingual Matters Ltd
UK: Frankfurt Lodge, Clevedon Hall, Victoria Road, Clevedon BS21 7HH.
USA: UTP, 2250 Military Road, Tonawanda, NY 14150, USA.
Canada: UTP, 5201 Dufferin Street, North York, Ontario M3H 5T8, Canada.
Australia: Footprint Books, PO Box 418, Church Point, NSW 2103, Australia.

Typeset by Archetype-IT Ltd (http://www.archetype-it.com).

Contents

Foreword

In most writing on bilingual education, the principal concern is with linguistic minority groups or with the development of language revitalisation programmes. This book opens a new window on bilingual education. It provides a wealth of information about elite or prestigious forms of bilingual (and trilingual) education provision in different parts of the world, including, for example, privately run international schools, the publicly funded European schools and different kinds of immersion programmes. It also shows how these and other forms of provision have developed in response to globalisation and to the increasing dominance of languages such as English within a globalised economic order.

Anne-Marie de Mejía is uniquely placed to write this book. She has been carrying out school and classroom-based research in English immersion programmes in Colombia for well over a decade now. She was one of the first to lift the veil on classroom processes in the context of research on the immersion experience of young children. Again and again, in her work, she has drawn our attention to the complexity of the bilingual routines and communicative practices that recur in daily life in such classrooms and has argued that these practices and routines need to be seen as embedded in particular cultural and historical contexts, rather than with reference to autonomous models of bilingual education. This argument is taken up again in this book.

Whilst developing her own empirical work in Colombia, Anne-Marie de Mejía has also been assembling a substantial body of documentation on different types of elite and prestigious bilingual education programmes around the world. Some of this material is difficult to get hold of because so little has been written about particular forms of provision, but, over the years, she has succeeded in building up a collection of material that is of considerable historical and contemporary interest. I know of no other equivalent set of resources and, over the past decade, I have found myself turning to her for advice whenever I (or one of my students) needed to know about a particular form of elite bilingual education provision. Now, with the publication of this book, others will also have access to her unique fund of knowledge.

The book will serve as an important new resource for both teachers and researchers in the field of bilingual education.

Marilyn Martin-Jones
University of Wales, Aberystwyth
November 2001

Introduction

Area Specification

This book represents an attempt to describe and demystify a particular type of educational provision which has been referred to in the literature as 'elite' or 'prestigious' bilingual education. These types of programme cater mainly for upwardly mobile, highly educated, higher socio-economic status learners of two or more internationally useful languages. Elite bilingualism is considered both as an international and an interdisciplinary phenomenon, which is increasingly valued in today's globalised universe, where proficiency in two or more international languages is becoming ever more necessary to efficient and effective processes of communication in business, in academia and in politics.

While the field of bilingualism in minority contexts has had a long and distinguished history (cf. work by Fishman, 1967, 1972, 1976, 1977, 1980, 1991; Cummins, 1980, 1986, 1989, 1991a, 1991b, 2000; Skutnabb-Kangas 1977, 1981, 1987; Romaine, 1988, 1989, 1992; Hakuta, 1986; Hornberger, 1988, 1989, 1990, 1997; Heller, 1994, 1999; Martin-Jones, 1989, 1995, 2000, among others) there has been relatively little written on bilingualism in elite contexts to date, with the notable exception of the well-known literature on immersion education. The reasons for this have not been discussed in any depth, but a few hypotheses may be advanced here. Firstly, bilingualism in minority communities has perhaps been seen as a more 'worthy' object of study than elite bilingualism, in that researchers may be conscious of their role of 'advocacy' (Cameron *et al.*, 1992) in writing about the inequalities of provision for development of the first or native language in those who speak minority languages.

Secondly, while many bilingual programes in minority contexts have received state or federal funding (cf. Title VII in the USA and bilingual support programmes in UK) and have therefore needed to be accountable to official bodies, elite bilingual programmes are generally offered by the private sector and rely on a certain competitivity in relation to other forms of educational provision. Thus, many institutions have been reluctant to share details of how they organise their language provision, for fear of benefiting potential competitors.

Thirdly, the historical traditions of many International Schools reveal that the development of bilingualism or multilingualism has not always been considered of prime importance for students. In many English International Schools, for example, which were founded in the first part of the twentieth century, it was taken for granted that the curriculum would be based on models used in British or North American monolingual schools (Carder, 1991). An 'English medium' rather than a bilingual education was offered. This was based on the view that the majority of students in International Schools in different parts of the world came from the expatriate communities, rather than the host nations, and therefore needed to return to the USA or the UK to complete their university studies. As Coreen Sears (1999, personal communication), for many years a teacher and Head of the English as a Second Language Department at the International School of Brussels notes, 'It is one of the problematic areas of English medium schools for those of us who are committed to producing students who function effectively in both the spoken and literacy areas of their two (or more) languages'.

Thus, this book aims, on the one hand, at charting the development of different types of bilingual or multilingual educational provision (which may or may not have been explicitly recognised as such) which cater for upwardly mobile students. On the other hand, it also purports to make an argument for the need to study bilingual education in majority as well as in minority contexts, in order to contribute to the field of bilingual studies in general.

Intended Audience

This book is intended for multiple audiences. It is aimed particularly at teachers, students and researchers working in the area of bilingual education, who have an interest in the development of programmes for majority language speakers, whether they follow the tradition of International Education, Immersion Education, or a European School model. The discussion of each of these modalities has been situated in relation to the historical, sociolinguistic and cultural context of implementation in order to show how specific forces have contributed to the creation of particular types of elite bilingual programmes in particular contexts. Provision of a number of case sketches and case boxes which illustrate ways in which individual institutions have coped with the need to provide bilingual programmes for specific populations, combined with examples of close analyses of bilingual classroom interaction, as well as the analysis of the discourse of International School brochures and language policy documents help to establish the grounded nature of the discussion, particularly in the second half of the book.

Content Overview

The first part of the book, Chapters 1–6, is entitled 'General Perspectives and Issues', and deals with notions of elite bilingualism and bilingual education as a world phenomenon. In Chapter 1, the emphasis is on the relationships of bilingualism and multilingualism with global international concerns, on the one hand, and the influence of specific contextual and historical factors in the development of different types of elite educational programmes, such as Finishing Schools, Language Schools, International Schools, European Schools and Canadian Immersion Programmes, on the other. Chapter 2 provides discussion and definition of key terms used throughout the book and relates these to the notion of different continua of bilingualism, biliteracy and bilingual education. Chapter 3 discusses sociocultural aspects of elite bilingualism in relation to three main areas: culture and bilingual marriage, multicultural and intercultural education, and cross-cultural communication in business. In Chapter 4 the emphasis is on aspects of bilingual classroom policy and practice, especially with regard to language use, content and language and cultural considerations. The chapter is illustrated by two extended examples of bilingual classroom interaction, one in Colombia and one in Hong Kong. Chapter 5 focuses on interrelationships between some of those who contribute to bilingual education programmes: parents, school administrators, teachers and students. The final chapter in this section, Chapter 6, summarises some of the main research carried out on elite bilingual programmes, particularly in the field of immersion education. The chapter ends with a description of a collaborative research project in the area of curricular design, carried out in Colombia, aimed at facilitating a process of empowerment among participants.

The second part of the book is entitled 'Overview of Elite Bilingual Provision in Specific Contexts of Implementation'. It contains eight chapters that deal with ways in which bilingualism and bilingual education have developed in different areas of the world. The first five chapters, Chapters 7–11, discuss developments in the field across the five continents. Thus, Chapter 7 focuses on two African nations, Morocco and Tanzania; Chapter 8 deals with the situation of bilingualism and bilingual education in three South American countries: Brazil, Argentina and Colombia; in Chapter 9 it is the turn of three Asian countries: Japan, Hong Kong and Brunei; while Chapter 10 is devoted to developments in four regions of Europe: Finland, Sweden, Belgium and Catalonia (Spain); finally Chapter 11 discusses developments in Australia.

Chapter 12 examines two discourse genres associated with elite bilingualism: International School brochures and language policy statements, from a critical perspective, with a view to showing how selected documents indirectly reproduce and legitimate existing power relations. In Chapter 13 the emphasis is on how practitioners who work in different types of elite bilingual education programmes around the world see aspects of their classroom practice. A series of cases reported by teachers are presented and commented on in the light of current developments in bilingual pedagogy. The final chapter, Chapter 14, draws together the main themes developed throughout the book, suggests further lines of enquiry and makes a series of recommendations for effective policy and practice.

Acknowledgements

There are many people who have contributed to the development of this book to whom I wish to acknowledge my gratitude here. First and foremost, I would like to thank very sincerely the two series editors, Nancy Hornberger and Colin Baker, for their enthusiastic support and insightful comments during the whole of the writing process. Largely due to their influence, this has proved to be a highly positive experience.

My deep thanks also go to Marilyn Martin-Jones who has been responsible, to a great degree, for interesting me in the field of bilingualism and bilingual education, and whose comments and observations have greatly influenced my ideas and perceptions in this area.

Another person who played a fundamental role in the genesis of this book is Marilda Cavalcanti, who by inviting me to a Round Table on Bilingualism and Bilingual Education at the University of Campinas (Brazil) in 1997 paved the way to meetings and discussions with Nancy Hornberger, and the subsequent invitation to contribute to the Multilingual Matters Bilingual Education and Bilingualism Book Series.

There are also many other people in different parts of the world who have generously provided information and comment on aspects developed in this book. I would particularly like to thank the following: Alatea Anderssohn (Morocco); Cristina Banfi (Argentina); Siv Björklund (Finland); Adriana Boogerman (Mexico); Martina Buss (Finland); Jayson Campeau (Canada); Ricardo Castañeda (Colombia); Andrew Cath (Brunei); Simon Colledge (Brunei); Eleanor Cosh (Colombia); Janda Cunha (Brazil); Kerstin Ekelund (Sweden); Sachiyo Fujita Round (Japan); Telma Gimenez (Brazil); Peter Gray (Japan); Gary Jones (Brunei); Angel Lin (Hong Kong); Peter Longcope (USA); Marina MacRae (Brazil); John Maher (Japan); Karina Mard (Finland); Peter Martin (Brunei); Sandra Miranda (Brazil); María Ester Navia (Colombia); Martha Pennington (Hong Kong); Stephen Ryan (Japan); Coreen Sears (Belgium); Ingrid de Tala (Colombia);

A special thank you is also due to all the teachers and parents who replied to the questionnaire on common problem areas in bilingual pedagogy. Their contributions form the basis of Chapter 13.

Thanks for help and support are also due to Bob Vassen, Mel Davies, JoEllen Simpson and to the members of the Bilingualism Research Group of Lancaster University (UK), particularly: Jo Arthur, María Pérez-Murillo, Kathryn Jones, Joan Pujolar, Mark Sebba, and Silvia Valencia.

I am also grateful to Marjukka and Tommi Grover and their colleagues at Multilingual Matters for their help, as well as Olga Patricia Ramírez for her assistance in aspects of diagramation. Finally, I would like to thank my family, Pablo, Natalie and Gabriel, for their patience and support throughout the whole of this venture.

Part 1
General Perspectives and Issues

In this first part, which comprises Chapters 1–6, the emphasis is on general perspectives and issues which may be of interest to teachers, students and researchers working in the field. Thus, although reference will be made to specific examples and contexts of implementation at times, the main thrust of these initial chapters is to situate the reader with respect to some of the more prominent issues relating to the theory and practice of bilingualism and bilingual education for students of elite or prestigious bilingual education programmes. Reference will be made to three main modalities of elite bilingual education provision: International Schools, European Schools and Immersion Programmes. There will also be illustration of two other more peripheral developments in this field: Finishing Schools and Language Schools.

In order to appreciate more fully how and why certain types of elite bilingual education provision have developed (the focus of Part 2) it is necessary to situate the discussion by referring to sociocultural and historical aspects of this phenomenon, as well as charting the evolution of research initiatives undertaken in the field. A focus on classroom policy and practice is complemented by an examination of the interrelationships between some of the different participants involved, with regard to the particular circumstances affecting students and their families in these types of programme. As Baker and Prys Jones (1998: 16) acknowledge, 'Among prestige bilinguals, there has historically not been a debate about the disadvantages and problems of bilinguals'.

Chapter 1
Elite Bilingualism as a World-wide Phenomenon

Globalism, Localism, Internationalism and Multilingualism

Any discussion of bilingualism or multilingualism today cannot be isolated from the consideration of globalising, international tendencies which have meant, in effect, that the world at the beginning of the twenty-first century is perceived as being far more interconnected than ever before. If we examine the last two decades of the twentieth century we can see that there has been a marked tendency to move from local, national concerns, towards a global, international perspective. According to Alistair Pennycook (1995: 34) 'the traditional boundaries of the world are slipping'. The emphasis in much current writing, planning and thinking is on globalisation in all its various facets – the world seen as 'the global village', global thinking, a global economy.

Along with this emphasis, there has been the extremely rapid development of international communications – 'the international technology revolution'. This has enabled global communication in all its electronic forms – fax, internet, tele-conferences, etc. – to have immediate repercussions all over the world. It is therefore now impossible to see international developments as distant or non-relevant, as evidenced by the British Prime Minister Joseph Chamberlain's famous appreciation in 1938 of the impending invasion of Czechoslovakia by Nazi Germany as 'a quarrel in a faraway country between people of whom we know nothing'.

One example of this interdependence can be seen in the currency collapse in South East Asia in 1997. This has had world-wide implications, not only in government or financial circles in South Korea, Japan and Indonesia, but also affecting many language schools in Australia and the United States which traditionally recruit their students from this sector. These institutions have had to start looking to China and Latin America as potential areas of diversifying their interests.

An increasing appreciation of internationalism is bound up with the growth of international organisations in the spheres of politics, business, academia and education. Thus, for example, we have the United Nations, the European Union, the Organisation of African States, and Amnesty International, to name a few. These organisations are generally based in key cities, such as Brussels, New York, London. They give rise to international, multilingual communities of employees which are characterised by a high degree of mobility. Frequently, job demands require that they and their families move to other international centres or back to their countries of origin at short notice. Thus, new generations of young people are growing up in a multilingual, multicultural environment, accustomed to interacting on a daily basis with speakers of several world languages and to constructing academic knowledge bilingually or multilingually. As Joshua Fishman so clearly observed in the 1970s, 'In a multilingual world, it is obviously more efficient and rational to be multilingual than not' (Fishman, 1978: 47).

However, these are not the only people eager for access to major world languages as a means of communication in the global marketplace. Tollefson (1991: 6) sees school-based language learning as a key means throughout the world of acquiring foreign or second languages for the purposes of further education, government service, political participation and employment. He notes the rapid expansion over the last 40 years of 'a new industry of language education' to cater to this demand. This, in turn, has led to a vast variety of courses for language teachers, textbooks, language laboratory technologies, as well as the development of a new theoretical discipline of Second Language Acquisition.

An interest in the use of international languages is often associated with positions of social prestige in societies which have a colonial history and the legacy of a colonial world language as in India, or in the newly independent nations of Africa. In these countries the use of world languages (especially English) is considered by many of the governing elite as vital to the modernisation of the economy and to the development of science and technology. Thus, bilingualism in English, French or Portuguese, in addition to use of indigenous languages, is officially encouraged.

In other contexts, such as Hong Kong, Japan and Malaysia in South East Asia, bilingual education is seen as a means of providing children of the influential middle and upper classes with the possibility of access to valued language resources. Angel Lin (1996: 2001) sees English in Hong Kong, even after return to Chinese sovereignty in 1997, as a key means of maintaining the region's privileged position in world markets. Bilingual or English medium schools are in high demand by parents who consider English as the language of educational and socio-economic advancement. The majority believe that mastery of this valued resource will enable their children to participate in the 'Hong Kong dream' of social prestige and economic advancement (Lin, 1996: 61).

Along with this globalising tendency discussed above, it is also important to recognise a counter concern with the influence of 'particular social, cultural and historical forces' in the development of our ideas about the world (Pennycook, 1995: 47). In the area of bilingualism, this is reflected in the growing emphasis on contextual factors which may influence bilingual learners' language acquisition and use, such as language use in particular societies, students' perceived language needs, and 'realistic' expectations of levels of foreign language proficiency.

Many researchers no longer believe that there is one model of bilingual education which can be applied universally. Instead, they argue for recognising that each individual programme is in some ways unique. The adopting of well-tried models which have been successful in other contexts, without modification to local needs, will not necessarily be effective (Paulston, 1980; Baetens Beardsmore, 1995). In addition, purely linguistic concerns, such as the order of language instruction, are no longer seen as the main factor in determining a successful bilingual programme. Instead, there is a growing recognition of the importance of decisions about policy and pedagogical matters related to specific situations (Tosi, 1990).

So, what can we conclude from this brief introduction to global and local tendencies in the area of bilingualism and multilingualism? On the one hand, we can see a rapid increase in the number of people who need to be bilingual or multilingual in one or more world languages because of job mobility, further education opportunities, socio-economic progress, or because they have to keep up to date with advances in the spheres of business, science and technology. On the other hand, there is a movement to recognise the influence of specific contextual and historical factors in the development of educational programmes which cater for the needs of such students in very diverse linguistic, sociocultural, political, economic and educational situations.

Another important conclusion has to do with the characteristics of the type of bilingualism or multilingualism which is increasingly valued in today's world and which has been referred to in the literature as 'elite bilingualism' (Paulston, 1975, cited in Harding & Riley, 1986; Skutnabb-Kangas, 1981). Taking into consideration what has been said above, it can be seen that this form of bilingualism is highly 'visible', in the sense that it provides access to prestigious international languages for those upwardly mobile individuals and their families who need or who wish to be bilingual or multilingual. Becoming bilingual for many students who come from higher socio-economic status groups means the possibility of being able to interact with speakers of different languages on a daily basis, and of gaining access to employment opportunities in the global marketplace. It also helps prepare them to become 'world citizens . . . in a world of growing interconnectedness' (Bingham, 1998: vi), and provides them with the experience necessary to understand cultural differences. (For further discussion of these ideas see Chapter 2.)

Educational Responses

In this part of the chapter, we will examine responses of different sectors involved in the provision of educational programmes in bilingual or multilingual settings. We will look first at two sectors, which may be classed as peripheral to most elite bilingual education programmes: Finishing Schools and Language Schools. However, these are included here as they both cater for the foreign language needs of students who wish to study abroad or who come from families who travel extensively, due to job requirements or socio-economic status. Then, we will examine three developments which have had an important influence in this area: The International Schools Movement, The European School Movement, and Immersion Education Programmes.

Finishing Schools

Traditionally, Finishing Schools cater for the daughters of wealthy families, who are sent to private, fee-paying colleges in places like Switzerland at the age of 15 or 16 to 'finish' or refine their education before entering society. *Websters' Third International Dictionary* (1986) defines a Finishing School as 'a private school that prepares young women for social life (as by emphasizing cultural accomplishments and social graces) rather than for a vocational or professional career'. This process of social preparation may involve acquiring sporting and cultural expertise, as well as paying attention to 'etiquette, cooking, dress-making, drawing and painting, history of Art', according to an advertisement for *Institut Chateau Beau-Cèdre* in Clarens-Montreux, Switzerland (1998). Finishing Schools also usually require students to attend intensive language courses in either French, English or German.

More recently, there has been a move to diversify the type of programmes offered, so that now students in Swiss International Schools and Colleges can take part in skiing trips, mountaineering expeditions, visits to European cultural centres and have the opportunity of participating in cultural enrichment programmes, as well as learning some of the foreign languages offered by the institutions. Below is an example of how students in one Finishing School near Montreux (Switzerland) spend a school day.

Text Box 1.1   *Surval Mont-Fleuri, Switzerland*

Surval Mont Fleuri is an international residential finishing school for young women in the Swiss Alps near Montreux. According to information sent out by the school a typical day would be structured in the following fashion:

7.0	*Get up*
7.15–8	*Breakfast*
8.0	*Tidying of room*
8.20–11.45	*French and English language classes/Cookery*
11.45–1.00	*Lunch*
1.00–16.20	*Foreign language classes and extra classes*
15.30–19.00	*Tea/Free time out*
18.30	*Dinner*
19.15–20.30	*Study time*
23.0	*Bedtime*

Summer and Winter Sports
Sport is very important at the school. In summer, students can partake in water-skiing,

---

swimming, sailing, table tennis, minigolf, tennis, riding and walking. In winter, skiing, tobogganing, skating and squash are offered.

Cultural Activities
A cultural trip is organised abroad at Easter for those students who do not return to their country of origin. Optional courses in photography and Art History are also offered.

Most of the Swiss colleges are characterised by a broad mixture of nationalities among their students. Some report that students from over 30 different nations are enrolled, while others cater for students from particular countries, especially the United States and Japan. In fact, one particular Swiss academy, the *Kumon Leysin Academy of Switzerland*, which was founded at the beginning of the 1990s, caters exclusively for Japanese students between 16 and 19 years old. It aims to enable them to experience Western culture and to develop their own potential to the full, either by following the Japanese education system or the US programme.

Finishing-type schools are not limited to Switzerland, however. Other countries provide programmes which are aimed at broadening students' linguistic and cultural horizons. As illustration, we will now examine in some detail a programme offered by the Graduate School of Education of the University of Pennsylvania which caters for young Japanese women from Kyoritsu University who wish to improve their level of English language proficiency and broaden their education.

Case Sketch[1] 1:1   The Kyoritsu Summer Programme at the University of Pennsylvania, USA[2]

Kyoritsu Summer Programms:	*Kyoritsu University (Japan) offers its students summer programmes at various international centres. In addition to the programme at the University of Pennsylvania (USA), students can also choose Thames Valley University in London (UK), the University of Geneva (Switzerland), and a university in China.*
Location of the Kyoritsu Summer Programme at the University of Pennsylvania:	*The programme at the University of Pennsylvania is offered annually during the month of August. For the first two weeks students stay in Bryn Mawr College, a prestigious women's college on the outskirts of Philadelphia. The site has been selected for student residence because of its beauty and safety. As there are other summer programmes running at the same time in the college for US students and for other international groups there are opportunities for social and linguistic mixing. The third week is spent with a host family (homestay) and students generally spend the fourth week in another location, such as Washington or New York City.*

Student Profile:	*Those who attend the Kyoritsu Summer Programme at the University of Pennsylvania are students either at Kyoritsu Women's University or Kyoritsu Women's Junior College. They are usually English Literature majors from the Literature Faculty or American Studies Majors from the International Studies Faculty. There are usually between 30 and 40 students a year who register and they are selected by means of an English listening comprehension examination.*
Study Programme:	*Two types of programme are offered: English language classes and US culture classes, generally in a 3: 2 ratio. The English language classes are generally structured round the notion of 'survival English' and such functions as 'how to order in a restaurant' and 'how to give compliments'. The US culture classes focus on such topics as: women's roles in US society, diversity in US culture, US family life. Guest speakers are also invited to address the students as part of the course.*
Extra Curricular Activities:	*These are generally scheduled for the afternoon. Students take part in field trips to local points of interest, such as historical sites in Philadelphia, and at Amish community centre at Lancaster County. They are given projects to complete during these trips, which the students report on and discuss in subsequent classes.*

Thus, it can be seen that this type of programme may be classed as a form of short-term finishing school, in that it caters for young women who come from families who have the means to send them on a residential course in the United States. The emphasis of the programme is on the learning of English, a prestige international language, and a cultural component is also included in the course.

Summary

Finishing schools differ from other types of foreign language programmes and summer schools in that they are aimed exclusively at young women, usually between the ages of 14 and 24, who come from wealthy families. There is generally an emphasis on culturally appropriate behaviour as well as foreign language proficiency, and most courses offered are residential. By their very nature, these schools are available to a very small segment of the population.

Language Schools

Language education today is a growing industry, focused mainly, though not exclusively, on a young, upwardly mobile population which includes the following groups: those who want to spend part of their school career abroad; those who want to pursue postgraduate study in another country; those who want to learn another language or improve their language skills during their vacations; and business people who need a command of other languages due to the demands of international clients. Traditionally, language schools are private institutions set up as business ventures to teach foreign or second languages to those who need or who wish to learn them. However, much language teaching is also carried out through university language institutes and official government bodies, such as the British Council in Britain, and the United States Information Agency in the USA, in the case of English.

In this section we will give a brief description of some of these types of language education provision offered in the area of English language teaching and learning. In each case one example will be given to contextualise the type of provision discussed.

Case Sketch 1.2 Private Language School (USA) (based on written information sent out by the school)

Name:	*The New England School of English, Boston (USA)*
Location:	*Next to Harvard University in Cambridge, Boston.*
Aims:	*'To provide the best in English language and culture training.' 'To provide an intellectually challenging program of the highest quality in a warm and supportive environment.'*
Programme:	*Intensive English language courses, American culture courses, TOEFL preparation courses, Business English, Legal English, Pronunciation, and University Entrance Preparation courses. Lectures by guest speakers.*
Staff and Students:	*The School Board of Advisors are drawn from Education, Industry and Science. Teaching staff all have university degrees. Students come from all of the world, particularly Europe, Latin America and Japan.*
Out of school environment:	*Students either live with local families as part of a homestay program, or they live in student dormitories nearby. The school offers excursions to local museums, theaters, historical sites and other places of interest. Weekend trips with American university and high school students are also available.*
Connections with University Programmes:	*The school has special relationships with Northeastern University and with Arthur D. Little School of Management and helps students who are interested in applying for admissions to programs offered by these institutions.*

Case Sketch 1.3   Private Language School (UK) (based on written information sent out by the school)

Name:	*The Bell Language School, Cambridge (UK).*
Location:	*A residential area of the city, not far from Cambridge University.*
Aim:	*According to Frank Bell, the Founder of the Bell Language Schools, the schools aim at 'encouraging international understanding through English language education'.*
Programme:	*Intensive English courses, English for Exams (First Certificate in English, Cambridge Proficiency in English, International English Language Testing System, TOEFL), English for Business, English for Academic Purposes, Teacher Training Courses, Young Learners' Courses.*
Staff and Students:	*Highly qualified teachers. Students from all over the world, particularly Europe, China, South East Asia.*
Out of school environment:	*Students live with local families through the homestay option. Students are offered a social programme which includes excursions to historical places of interest, cultural trips and shopping excursions.*
Connections with University Programmes:	*The school offers optional courses for those who wish to enter a university in the UK Students interested in business studies can take a course of two semesters which guarantees access on to a business degree course at Anglia Polytechnic University in Cambridge.*

As can be seen, there are certain similarities between both of these language schools. Both are situated in the vicinity of prestigious universities, Harvard and Cambridge; both offer intensive English language programmes and the possibility of taking international examinations; they offer an extended programme of cultural and historical excursions; and both have close connections with university programmes that might interest their students in the future.

Case Sketch 1.4   University English Language Institute (based on written information sent out by the Institute)

Name:	*Institute for English Language Education, Lancaster University (UK).*[3]
Location:	*Lancaster.*

Aim:	*As a Department of the Faculty of Education at Lancaster University the Institute offers high quality teaching and teacher training in the field of English as a Foreign Language.*
Programme:	*Open entry English language and teacher training courses; project-related training courses for specific institutional groups; an academic support programme in English for Academic Purposes free for students enrolled at Lancaster University, involving department workshops and a one-to-one tutorial service; overseas consultancies on behalf of international organisations.*
Staff and Students:	*Institute staff are highly qualified in the theory and practice of EFL and are involved in conducting research in the teaching and testing of English language teaching. Students come from all over the world, especially Europe and South East Asia.*
Resources:	*EFL Resource Centre and specialist library, Computer Laboratory, and Self Access Language Laboratory.*

Case Sketch 1.5 Total Immersion English Courses for Business and Cross-Cultural Relations (based on written information sent out by the Organisation)

Name:	*The East West Group, in conjunction with Monterrey Institute of International Studies, Monterrey, California (USA).*
Location:	*In the countries requesting the programme.*
Aim:	*To offer tailor-made English language programs and consultancy services in the field of Business and Cross-Cultural Relations which reflect the realities of the local contexts in which the programs are taught, the results of which can be immediately applied in particular work contexts*
Programme:	*Four-week intensive 'immersion' courses focused on English language proficiency and Cross-Cultural relations interspaced with work commitments over an eight-week period.*

Staff and Students:	*US teachers specialized in English as a Second Language. Students who have participated in the program have come from Indonesia, Germany, France, Switzerland, The Philippines and Colombia.*
Resources:	*Program designed by the Monterrey Institute of International Studies, including recognised pre and post course standardized tests.*

Both types of provision referred to above are situated within university establishments specialising in English Language Teaching and English for Academic Purposes. They focus on particular groups, such as students studying postgraduate programmes at a British university, and business personnel in particular companies. In the first case, the one-to-one tutorial service ensures that students can receive immediate feedback on specific problems. In the second, the fact that the course is offered 'on site' means that the specific needs of the target population can be catered for in the programmes offered. The intercalating nature of the programme also means that busy executives do not have to leave their offices for long periods of time.

Case Sketch 1.6 English Language Courses offered by a Governmental Organisation (based on written information sent out by the Organisation)

Name:	*The British Council.*
Location:	*The British Council works in 228 towns and cities in 108 countries.*
Aims:	*To promote educational, cultural and technical co-operation between Britain and other countries, and to advance the use of the English language. To establish long-term and world-wide partnerships and to improve international understanding.*
Programmes and Services:	*English language courses for adults and children, courses leading to British professional and academic examinations, international seminars and summer schools, advisory services for teachers and learners and university departments, resource centres.*
Staff and Students:	*Native speaking English language teachers servicing more than 100,000 students in more than 90 teaching centres around the world.*

As can be seen, the British Council, an official government organisation sponsored by the Foreign and Commonwealth Office and funded by the Departments for International Development and Education and Employment is active in the promotion of English Language Teaching throughout the world. As Pennycook (1994: 152) observes: 'The British Council is the main mediator of ELT projects from Britain, co-ordinating book publishing, teaching projects, video and television programmes'.

Case Sketch 1.7 International Student Exchange Programmes (based on written information sent out by the Organisation)

Name: *Aspect*

Location: *High Schools and Colleges in Washington State and New York State, USA*

Aims: *To offer final year school students the possibility to finish their High School in the United States.*

Programme: *10 months' study in a College in the United States, living with a local family and the opportunity to participate in an American way of life.*

These programmes are designed to appeal to young people who are finishing their studies and who wish to improve their English language skills in the United States. They are of special interest to middle-class families in Latin America, where it has become common practice for 16 and 17 year olds to spend a year abroad in an academic exchange programme, such as the one described above.

Summary

As can be seen from the different types of language programmes described in this section there is a lot of variety in the type of courses and facilities offered to cater for an increasingly diverse population of students who need to be proficient in more than one language. Due to the number of international students who apply for admission to postgraduate courses in English-speaking countries, such as the USA, the UK, Canada, and Australia, many institutions now insist that candidates either demonstrate an acceptable level of language proficiency before beginning their academic studies, or attend intensive study skills course or English for Academic Purposes (EAP) programmes. Thus, as higher education systems are becoming increasingly internationalised, language institutes are becoming a common feature of universities and colleges in many parts of the world.

International Schools

The term 'International Schools' refers to a variety of schools throughout the world which offer 'private, selective, independent education . . . mainly for the affluent' (Baker & Prys Jones, 1998: 533). Some schools are designed to be 'national schools away from home (French Lycees, German Gymnasia, English Grammar type schools)' (Hayden &Thompson, 1998: iii). Others are attempts 'to base an education on the emerging principles for global human development arising from, for example, the League of Nations and, later the United Nations' (Hayden &Thompson, 1998: iv).

Most of the International Schools which exist today are English Language International Schools, but there are also other languages represented, such as German, French, Italian, Portuguese and Spanish. In this section, however, we will be mainly concerned with English International Schools.

A historical perspective

Maurice Carder (1991) has traced the development of international schools to the growth and increasing mobility at international level of the following sectors international business, the United Nations, and the armed forces. Other typical family profiles are children of diplomats and missionaries. He sees these schools originally as a specifically Anglo/American initiative, where it was taken for granted by both administrators and teachers that the curricula used would reflect 'the cultural model of the country of the school language of instruction, i.e. British or American' (Carder, 1991: 2). Thus, these schools were characterised not so much by their 'international nature' but by the fact that they catered for 'displaced' students. In other words, they were aimed at providing education for 'students who found themselves in an institution which was in a culturally, if not educationally, different environment from that which they had experienced as part of their earlier education' (Hayden & Thompson, 1998: iii).

These views are seconded by Michael Matthews (1989), who divided the 'typical' student population of a medium-sized international school in Europe into three categories: (1) English-speaking members of the expatriate community who require an English language education as they expect to return to an English-speaking education system; (2) non-English-speaking members of the expatriate community who desire an English language education in order to facilitate future moves around the world, or because they wish to attend college or university in North America or the UK; (3) local nationals who want an English-language education for the same reasons as in (2) above.

Thus, it is clearly evident that international schools were initially conceived not explicitly as bilingual institutions, but as establishments which offered a particular educational and cultural model. The majority of students came from the expatriate community and the main aim of these schools was to prepare them for tertiary education in English-speaking countries. The first language of the non-English speakers was not emphasised, and proficiency in English was the overall linguistic goal. In the early 1960s it is reported that approximately 60 international schools existed (Hayden & Thompson, 1998).

However, things have changed considerably over the last 20 years. There is now greater diversity among the international school population. One reason for this change derives from the increase in prosperity among many of the industrially based economies of the developed nations and the subsequent demographic shift which involved the transfer of large numbers of commercial and business personnel around the world, 'creating a nomadic group of workers and their families' (Hayden & Thompson, 1998: iv). As a result, many international schools became market, rather than ideologically oriented.

In addition, international schools increasingly tried to attract pupils whose first language was not English 'in order to support slumping enrolment figures' (Murphy, 1990: vii). Similarly, more host country or local nationals started sending their children to international schools which they saw as having greater flexibility than schools in the national system.

In many schools (especially those catering for children of United Nations staff) only a minority of the students speak English as their first language. English as a Second Language (ESL) departments are now a common feature of many of these institutions who attempt to provide language support programmes to help students cope with handling content area instruction in a second or foreign language. There have been calls (Garner, 1990; Carder, 1991) to recognise international school students as bilingual or multilingual and to pay greater attention to the status of ' the bilingual students' mother tongue and mother culture' (Garner, 1990: 4).

Furthermore, there is also some recognition that the type of English spoken in international schools shows certain differences from standard varieties. One attempt to characterise International School English talks about 'a vaguely mid-Atlantic accent and particular quirks of expression and grammar, most of which come from the host country language' (Carder, 1991: 6). These 'quirks' reported by Carder are evidence of language contact phenomena, which until recently have been almost totally ignored in writing on international schools. The underlying assumption has been that International School students speak a standard 'uncontaminated' variety of either British or North American English.

Characteristics of International School participants

Students and their families

According to entries in publications such as *The European Council of International Schools Directory (ECIS)* and *The International School Services Directory of International Schools (ISS)* to date, there are more than 850 international schools in over 90 countries. These include names such as Geelong Grammar School in Victoria, Australia, famous, among other things, for its association with Prince Charles; The International School of the Sacred Heart in Tokyo, Japan; Machabeng International School of Lesotho in Maseru, Lesotho; Colegio Colombo Britanico in Cali, Colombia; and the American School of Bilbao, in Bilbao, Spain, to take a selection at random to cover the five continents. Some of these are religious schools, some are bi-national institutions, while others offer boarding facilities as well as day school. (For profiles of some individual international schools included in this book see the Casablanca American School, Morocco, and the International School of Tanganyika, Tanzania (Chapter 7); Graded School and Play Pen, Brazil, and St Andrew's Scots School, Argentina (Chapter 8); and Kungsholmen's Gymnasium, Sweden (Chapter 10)).

According to Murphy (1990), international schools can be classified as monolingual or as bilingual/multilingual. The former frequently cater for students from a wide range of nationalities but there is only one official language of instruction used in school. Bilingual or multilingual International Schools, on the other hand, can offer a type of dual track programme which enable children of the host country to learn about the language and cultures of other countries, while speakers of other languages, who are temporarily resident, can learn the language of the host country. Examples of such schools are the Washington International School and the Atlanta International School in the USA. In multilingual International Schools the students' first language is used as a medium of instruction for part of the school curriculum.

The diversity of student populations in these schools, linguistically, culturally and academically provides the schools with many opportunities for intercultural exchange, and this is attractive both to parents and to teachers in international institutions. At best, this can lead to an attitude of receptivity and lack of prejudice on the part of participants as a result of a process of questioning of cultural assumptions in company with classmates from widely different cultural backgrounds. The presence of native speakers among the students can also provide greater stimulus for language classes (Matthews, 1989).

However, this multicultural environment can also pose problems for both teachers and students as few shared cultural norms and attitudes towards such things as discipline, dress, modes of address and homework can be presumed. Furthermore, as Murphy (1990) reports, students may be puzzled by unaccustomed classroom teaching and learning styles. Students from the Middle East or South East Asia who are accustomed to a more formal relationship with teachers may find the informal and friendly style of teachers in other societies, strange and unsettling. For example, in Japanese educational philosophy children learn by listening attentively to the teacher, not by talking about their work or listening to other children, as is common in the UK. Interactive classes are therefore often perceived by Japanese students as 'playing' and not as serious study (Yamada-Yamamoto, 1997).

The effects of this process of intercultural contact are often most apparent when the international student returns to his home country. Asako Yamada-Yamamoto (1997) reports that researchers in Japan started taking an interest in young *returnees* in the late 1970s. They observed the process of readjustment of Japanese children educated abroad to the demands of Japanese society. An initial period of culture shock, confusion and conflict was common. Kobayashi (1986, cited in Matthews, 1989) also notes that these students were frequently ostracised because their social behaviour had lost some of its precision and nuance, with respect to mode of address or bowing. Some of them, although fluent in English, suffered low grades in their English classes back in Japan, until they had re-acquired the 'correct' standard school pronunciation.

Another common characteristic of International School students is an extremely high level of mobility. In many schools an annual turnover of 30% or more is regarded as normal. Thus, many students remain at one school for less than three years in total and must learn to adapt quickly to new surroundings. According to a study carried out by Harder *et al.* in 1987 (cited in Matthews, 1989) International School students were more concerned with social skills and mutual tolerance than their peers in the USA. They were able to cope better with stress and were more flexible in their attitudes.

Again though, mobility has disadvantages. Students and their families often require schools to provide skills and knowledge that will enable them to function in an international setting. They also need to find links with their own 'home' culture, to which most of them will return eventually. This contradiction sometimes leads to rather strange results. It is reported that one international school in Asia, with a minority of native born students from USA, has an obligatory high school course on the history of the United States.

In addition, many parents who move around the world are highly anxious about their children's education. They worry about how their children will cope with new school language and cultural demands. They are concerned about their children developing good academic standards. They often do not understand school communications and therefore feel unable to participate fully in school activities (Sears, 1990). Thus, the role of the teacher in International Schools is crucial to the success of the adjustment of both students and their families to the new situation.

Teachers

Teachers in International Schools are also often highly mobile. Indeed, one of the attractions of a career in international education is precisely the possibility of extensive travelling. Matthews (1989) has characterised International School teachers in Europe in the following ways: (1) Long-term teachers, who may move from school to school, or who have established themselves in the local community ; (2) expatriate wives, whose availability depends on their husbands' careers; and (3) so-called 'transients' who are often newly qualified teachers seeking a range of short-term experience and adventure in the early stages of their careers.

In addition to the advantages of easy travelling, there are also the attractions of small class size, motivated students and the challenge of trying to develop a vision of internationalism among their learners, which builds on the principles of tolerance, co-operation, justice and peace (Gellar, 1981 cited in Matthews, 1989). Teachers also often have more social contact with parents than in national schools, as they may participate in events organised by and for members of the educational community, and are generally held in high esteem.

Carder (1991) classifies teachers in international schools as ESL specialists, or content area teachers, reflecting the dual emphasis on language as a vehicle for the construction of knowledge in specific subject areas and content area teaching as a means of acquiring a high standard of linguistic proficiency. As most International School teachers see themselves as either subject or language specialists, rather than contributing to both areas, there is frequently a lack of contact and joint co-operation on students' learning difficulties and on the type of materials best suited to students' needs. There have been calls for closer links between the two areas, and a revaluing of the contributions made by ESL staff, who have sometimes felt 'undervalued and peripheral' (Carder, 1991: 26).

Curricular considerations

ESL programmes

The aim of ESL programmes is to provide language support for international students whose first language is not English, in schools where English is a medium of instruction. There are many different types of programme which have been classed as ESL support (Murphy, 1990). These include the following: *supported* or *sheltered* immersion, where ESL specialists work alongside class teachers in the mainstream classroom for part of the school day helping students who have language difficulties; *withdrawal* or *pull-out* classes where students with language difficulties are removed from the mainstream classroom for part of the school day for intensive English language tuition; and *transitional bilingual assimilation* programmes where students receive instruction in their own first language and also ESL classes. The ESL component is gradually increased until the whole curriculum is taught in English, with two or three periods a week set aside for first language teaching. Each of these modalities implies a different view of bilingual development, as will be discussed in Chapter 2.

Teachers and administrators participating in the *Fifth European Council of International Schools (ECIS) English as a Second Language Conference* held in Dubrovnik (Croatia) in 1991 noted that while withdrawal programmes seemed to be very common in many schools, there were serious objections to this type of ESL provision. Some of the disadvantages noted were: segregation of ESL students from the mainstream classrooms often led to a type of ghetto mentality and tended to foster negative attitudes by both mainstream students and the ESL learners themselves; being 'pulled out' of classes for varying periods of time also meant that ESL students missed valuable content lesson exposure; furthermore, denying ESL learners the possibility of interacting with their peers in the mainstream classroom for much of the day prevented them from forming relationships with students who spoke English better than they did and thereby improving their level of proficiency.

In contrast, participants felt that supported or sheltered provision had the advantages of not removing the students from the classroom situation and also enabling the ESL teacher to have more contact with the expectations and style of teaching of the content area specialist and therefore to be more effective in the help they gave to their learners. However, there was strong emphasis on the need for any type of ESL programme to have a high profile within the institution in order to be successful. It was felt that the status of ESL provision should be reflected in the size of the programme budget, quality of the staff employed and support from the administration.

International Baccalaureate examinations

In a report for the International Baccalaureate Office in Geneva (Switzerland) in 1986, Arturo Tosi defines international education as 'the education of a multinational population which studies a common curriculum for the preparation of the same examination programmes' (Tosi, 1986: 13). He traces the search of International Schools in the 1960s for an internationally co-ordinated and agreed curriculum to provide students with qualifications which were acceptable to as many universities as possible.

In 1962 the International School of Geneva, in collaboration with the Association of International Schools, and under the auspices of UNESCO, set up an initial project aimed at integrating History programmes. Working groups of secondary school teachers and university staff studied the feasibility of developing common programmes leading to a global examination, which would be recognised by universities and educational authorities in participating countries. The Ford Foundation, the Mountbatten Foundation and the Gulbenkian Foundation provided funds for the project. The result was the creation and ratification of the International Baccalaureate in 1967, after a General Congress held in Sèvres (Paris) with delegates from nine countries and observers from UNESCO, the Council of Europe, as well as representatives from the main Examination Boards – le Baccalaureat Français, The Oxford and Cambridge Board of the General Certificate of Education (GCE) (UK) and the Advanced Placement of the College Entrance Examination Board (CEEB) (USA).

In April 1974 another important congress was held, financed by the French government, to evaluate the project and to set up guidelines for the future. Representatives of 63 countries participated and agreed that the work of the International Baccalaureate Organisation should continue and that close contacts with the governments involved and with UNESCO should be maintained. From 1977 onwards the headquarters of the Organisation were established in Geneva and regional representatives were designated in North America (New York), Latin America, Europe (London), South East Asia, and Australia.

The International Baccalaureate Organisation is officially recognised as an international non-governmental organisation. Its legal status is that of a foundation under the supervision of the Swiss Federal Government. Currently, approximately 800 schools in 95 schools throughout the world have implemented International Baccalaureate courses.

The International Baccalaureate programme is a two year, pre-university course either leading to the award of the International Baccalaureate Diploma, or to separate subject certificates. This requires students to show proficiency in the use of two languages, denominated Language A and Language B. Language A is defined as the student's 'best language' (either their mother tongue or the main language used in the school), while Language B is considered 'the language the students choose as their second examination language . . . usually . . . a foreign language' (International Baccalaureate, 1986).

The examination requires candidates who wish to take the full International Diploma to present three subjects of the six curriculum areas at Higher level and three others at Subsidiary level, as well as studying certain compulsory core areas. It is also possible to take individual subjects, rather than studying the whole programme, and obtain a certificate. Table 1.1 shows the range of subject areas available.

Table 1.1 Components of the International Baccalaureate examination

Curriculum areas offered at Higher or Subsidiary level	
Language A	Experimental Sciences
Language B	Mathematics
Individual and Society	Arts and Options
Compulsory core areas	
An extended essay (4000 words)	
Theory of Knowledge	
Creativity, Action and Service Project	

Language A involves the study of world literature, while the courses provided for Language B are designed for students who have studied Language B as a foreign language for between two and five years and are concerned with language proficiency. The Theory of Knowledge course stimulates critical thinking on the origins, validity and value of beliefs and knowledge gained within and outside the classroom (St Paul's School, Sao Paulo, Prospectus, 1998). The Creativity, Action and Service Project aims at challenging and extending the individual student, in order to develop a spirit of discovery, self-reliance and responsibility in the service of the community in general and those who are disadvantaged, in particular (Northlands School, Buenos Aires, Prospectus, 1999).

The aim of the programme is to provide a sound preparation for university entrance, particularly in North America and Europe. According to reports from schools which have prepared Diploma candidates, it has the advantage of promoting autonomous learning, good argumentative writing and a high level of analytical skills. However, it also entails a heavy burden of preparation for students.

In a study carried out in 1989 for the International Baccalaureate Organisation at the Institute of Education of the University of London, Tosi evaluated the I.B. examination in relation to the spread of academic bilingualism. He surveyed all candidates who entered for the May 1988 I.B. Diploma examination, a total of 3438 students and noted that the vast majority of the students (51%) came from schools in Europe or in North America. He found that bilingual students (i.e. students who had two 'best' languages by the end of the I.B. programme, one of which was different from the language used in the school), constituted 49% of the total number of candidates.

In a general comparison of the academic performance of bilingual and monolingual pupils in the examination, he found that bilingual pupils scored higher than monolinguals. However, in spite of the variety of language options permitted, there was no evidence that the I.B. programme promoted bilingual teaching in general in international schools. According to the results of the survey, the spread of bilingualism was confined to non-native speakers of the school language, while native speakers of the school language did not achieve bilingualism within the programme. In general, English native speakers in international schools were the least likely of all the linguistic groups represented to become bilingual.

Tosi (1989) concluded that the model of language education promoted by the I.B. programme was essentially derived from a mononational and monolingual vision and called for the I.B. to take positive steps to promote 'bilingualism for all, in international education' (Tosi, 1989: 31).

Summary

To conclude this discussion on International Schools within the perspective of elite bilingualism, I would like to draw out some key points relating to this type of educational provision. First of all, it must be emphasised that the International School Movement was created to serve a basically monolingual student population, interested in tertiary education opportunities in North America and Europe. This emphasis is reflected in the large number of monolingual International Schools throughout the world, which currently use only one official language of instruction (usually a world language, such as English, French, German, Spanish or Italian). However, there are a growing number of bilingual or multilingual institutions, particularly in Central and South America, which offer two or more languages as a vehicle for academic content areas in their curricula.

Furthermore, much of the International School population is now bilingual, as either their first language is different from that of the school language or they are enrolled in bilingual International Schools. However, most of the schools cited in the current ECIS International Schools Directory offer programmes based either on the British or USA curriculum and sometimes both. A minority of the schools listed offer the opportunity for students to study a national curriculum.

There is thus a curious dichotomy. While many of the participants (teachers, students and administrators) are, in fact, bilingual or multilingual the emphasis in curricula and school language provision is monolingual and often monocultural. The opportunities for intercultural exchange, valued by many parents and teachers in such institutions seem to be almost incidental to official academic and institutional structuring. The question is, how far do International Schools see bilingualism or multilingualism as a priority, or how far are they content to offer their clients access to a world language (usually English) without taking into account local or individual language and cultural backgrounds within the curriculum?

European Schools

A historical perspective

The rise of the European School Movement has been amply documented by such scholars as Baetens Beardsmore (1990, 1993a, 1995), Baetens Beardsmore and Swain (1985), Tosi (1986) and Swan (1996). This movement has certain similarities with International Schools, but as it has certain historical and educational features which distinguish it from what has been said in the previous section, it will be considered separately here.

The initial network of European Schools grew out of a parental initiative in 1958 in response to the establishment of the European Coal and Steel Community in Luxembourg in 1951 and the foundation of the European Economic Community (the EEC, later the European Union) in 1956 (Baetens Beardsmore & Swain, 1985). The parents concerned were mainly foreign civil servants working for the European Coal and Steel Community who felt that their children's linguistic, cultural and academic needs were not being met within the Luxembourg school system (Housen, forthcoming). The first school was founded in Luxembourg. The curriculum was based on a synthesis of the curricula in operation in the six original states of the European Economic Community (France, Belgium, West Germany, Italy, Luxembourg and The Netherlands). This, in turn, led to the creation of the European Baccalaureate which aimed at giving successful candidates access to higher education in most countries in the world.

At present, there are 10 schools in the European network in six countries: Luxembourg (one), Belgium (three in Brussels and one in Mol), Germany (one in Karlsruhe and one in Munich), Italy (Varese), The Netherlands (Bergen) and Great Britain (Culham). These schools all follow the same programme and have the same examination requirements, though the languages offered in each case are different. (For a profile of a European School included in this book see Brussels I, Belgium – Chapter 10.)

Characteristics of European School participants

Students

As has been mentioned above, the students in European Schools are mainly sons and daughters of European civil servants, though non-civil servant children are admitted if space is available. They come mainly from the higher income bracket. Many European School students are 'highly mobile' children (Baetens Beardsmore, 1979), who because of their parents' employment reside in a foreign country for relatively short periods of time. Unlike International Schools, education is free for the children of European civil servants. At present there are approximately 17,000 pupils representing over 50 nationalities and more than 30 different language backgrounds currently enrolled in European Schools (Housen, forthcoming). Most students speak one of the official languages of the European Union as their home language.

In most schools, parent–teacher associations are strong and school communication with parents is carried out in their first language. Most of the families who send their children to European Schools speak one of nine European languages as a first language, Danish, Dutch, English, French, German, Greek, Italian, Spanish and Portuguese (Baetens Beardsmore, 1993a).

Within the schools, care is taken to mix students who have different first languages for many of the activities which are carried out as part of the curriculum, in order to develop a unified school population. This policy of 'social engineering'(Baetens Beardsmore, 1993a) leads to frequent contact between native and non-native speakers of different languages and thus provides for peer group interaction in promoting language competence and intercultural contact. It also helps to counteract linguistic and nationalistic fragmentation in order to promote multicultural awareness and to foster the development of 'a supra-national "European" identity' (Housen, forthcoming).

Teachers

Teachers and directors of European Schools are seconded from their respective national education systems and are officially appointed for a period of years, which varies according to the country concerned. They are native speakers of one of the languages used in the school and all are bilingual or multilingual. Most do not have qualifications in foreign language teaching, but on arrival, are assigned to a mentor who helps them adapt to the demands of working with what is, generally, a totally unfamiliar curriculum. The schools also provide special in-service programmes for newly appointed teachers. As in International Schools, there are teachers who work with students who arrive during the school year and whose level of proficiency in their second language is not sufficient to allow them to participate fully in classes carried out in this language.

Curricular considerations

Language distribution in the curriculum

Baetens Beardsmore (1993a) makes it clear that European School programmes cannot be neatly classified within existing typologies of models of bilingual education (cf. Baker, 1993), but include elements typical of maintenance, transitional and enrichment programmes (see Chapter 2 for a discussion of these distinctions). They are both multilingual and multicultural, not only in terms of the student population they cater for but also in their organisation, ethos and goals (Housen, forthcoming).

An important point to note is the status and use accorded to the student's *first* language, which is seen as the basis for the development of other foreign languages. At primary level, the pupils study mostly though the medium of their first language, although a foreign language, either English, French or German, is introduced at the same time as a *subject*, rather than as a medium of instruction. Parents choose what foreign language they want their children to learn. Then, in 3rd to 5th Grade this foreign language is used as medium of instruction in certain subject areas which are cognitively undemanding, such as physical education or so called 'European Hours', which are dedicated to ludic activities, including sewing, cooking and construction projects, such as puppets.

In secondary school the foreign language is increasingly used as a medium of instruction, while emphasis on the first language decreases. At this level, a third compulsory foreign language is introduced, again as a subject first in Grade 8. The third language may be used as a medium of instruction later during elective courses.

Thus, it can be seen that throughout the programme, both the first language and the foreign language (the student's L2) are taught as subjects, as well as used as media of instruction, in a gradual process of moving from context embedded activities in the L2 to more context reduced and cognitively demanding tasks (see Cummins, 1981). Furthermore, the use of up to eight different languages as first languages in the different subsections of the school leads to natural opportunities for students to interact with their peers in their L2 and provides them with possibilities of negotiating meaning inside and outside the classroom leading to the production of output which is precise, coherent, and appropriate, as well as being grammatically correct. Students are expected to reach a level of proficiency in their L2 by the end of their school career that they will be able to pursue further studies at university level in a country where the L2 is spoken as a native language. Therefore, the goal is linguistic enrichment 'through a transition from instruction in the pupil's L1 to instruction in both the L1 *and* the L2 (and sometimes the L3)' (Housen, forthcoming).

The same author has noted evidence of a developmental 'spurt' between 5th and 7th Grade, at the transition from primary to secondary school education and attributes this to two main factors. The first of these is the increase from Grade 6 onwards of the use of the L2 as a medium of teaching and learning, and the second involves the provision of analytic, form-focused activities, not emphasised at primary school level (see next section on Canadian immersion programmes for further illustration of this notion).

The fact that the European Schools' curriculum derives from the national curricula of the various European Union member countries means that students can be reintegrated into their school system of origin, or indeed the educational system of any other of the member states without too much difficulty (Housen, forthcoming).

European Baccalaureate examinations

As has been mentioned previously, the European Baccalaureate gives access to university education in most countries of the world. The final examination consists of a total of five written and four oral components and includes a written and an oral examination in the student's second foreign language, in which they are expected to reach a similar standard as in their first language. As in International Schools, emphasis in the Baccalaureate is concentrated mainly in the final years of the school programme. Baetens Beardsmore (1990) sees this as in line with the European School movement's primary goal as a response to educational rather than purely linguistic needs.

A high success rate (over 90%) is associated with the European Baccalaureate, and this in itself suggests that the multilingual environment of the schools does not impede students' academic and intellectual development but contributes to a successful outcome. However, it must also be borne in mind that many of the less academically able students may have to leave the schools before graduation if they do not meet educational grade goals on two occasions in secondary school.

Summary

Taking into account the particular characteristics of European Schools which distinguish them from the broad run of International Schools, we can see that European Schools are committed to a philosophy of first language maintenance and the promotion of academic multilingualism in at least two languages for *all* students during their school career. Thus, bilingualism is seen as a priority goal for these programmes. Furthermore, intercultural contact is actively encouraged as part of the institutional programmes by means of activities such as European Hours.

It must also be noted, that because of the multilingual and multicultural background of the students and because of the linguistic policy of the European network, there is not one lingua franca used by students and staff. This fact, together with the linguistic engineering policy of the European School programmes with their regular juxtaposition of different language groups, creates opportunities 'for justified and necessary communications' (Housen, forthcoming), which are not present in many of the Canadian immersion programmes (see following section).

In many cases, students are also able to use their L2 outside the school in interaction between friends and relatives and in recreational pursuits, such as reading magazines and watching television, as this language constitutes the language of the wider environment (e.g. French in Brussels). This leads to valuable reinforcement of L2 interaction in a wide range of non-academic contexts outside the classroom and helps to explain why studies carried out by Baetens Beardsmore and Swain (1985) in Brussels suggest that levels of French L2 achievement at the intermediate stage of schooling are comparable and even superior to those obtained in Canadian French immersion, in spite of lower amounts of classroom language contact.

There has been relatively little empirical research carried out on socio-cultural outcomes of the European School model, bearing in mind that one of this movement's main objectives is the developing of ' a complex multicultural identity that combines a pupil's own national and cultural identity with a supranational European identity' (Housen, forthcoming). However, a study conducted among 17 and 18 year olds in one of the Brussels' European Schools (Housen & Baetens Beardsmore, 1987) revealed that although during primary school most students chose friends in their own L1 section, by the end of secondary school relationships had become much more cross-linguistic, thereby increasing motivation towards other languages. Results of participant observations and interviews reported by Housen (forthcoming) revealed that older students seemed to equate European identity as 'the lack of a concrete or specific national identity' rather than a conscious awareness of what it meant to be European.

Canadian Immersion Programmes

A historical perspective

A combination of political and educational factors led to the setting up of the first voluntary immersion programme in an elementary school in St Lambert, Montreal (Quebec) in 1965. In a similar fashion to the creation of the European School movement, it was parents who prompted this initiative and were the driving force behind its development. In this case, the parents were middle class, anglophone residents of Quebec province, a predominantly French-speaking area of Canada, who were concerned about the increasing advantages, both politically, socially and economically that would accrue if their children grew up bilingual in French and English. They were also worried about the ineffective methods of foreign language teaching, then in vogue.

Even though it is important to recognise the important role of the parents in the creation of this famous educational innovation, it is equally important to recognise the political and socio-economic factors which were instrumental in ensuring the spread of what has been called 'The French Immersion Phenomenon' (Stern, 1984) and which help to explain its success. I will give a summary of some key developments below.

The British North American Act of 1867 created a Canadian confederation composed of Quebec, Ontario, New Brunswick, and Nova Scotia, and provided for the use of English and French in the Federal Parliament and in the courts. However, linguistic duality was only permitted in Quebec where two education systems based on religion were established. The majority of Catholic schools taught the curriculum in French, while most Protestant schools taught in English. (Rebuffot, 2000).

At the beginning of the twentieth century there was massive immigration to Canada, and English, which was spoken by the majority of Canadians outside Quebec, quickly became seen as the language of integration and the language of education in most parts of the country. French was generally seen as the language of social and family relations, even in Quebec where English was generally considered the language of prestige. Thus, a diglossic situation was established (Rebuffot, 2000). (For further discussion on the notion of diglossia see Chapter 2.)

The 'Quiet Revolution' of the 1960s involved changes in the material conditions of life for the inhabitants of Quebec Province. For a series of complex socio-economic and political reasons, analysed at length by Heller (1994), relations between anglophone and francophone groups began to shift and francophone groups were able to gain access to educational opportunities and middle-management and specialist jobs within the public and private sector, which up to then had been closed to them.

Traditionally in Quebec, only francophones had been bilingual; anglophones had always used English in their business dealings with other anglophones and with francophones. However, because of the increasing threat to anglophone economic control or participation in the public sector many English speakers began to see the need to learn French; in other words, they realised they needed to become bilingual. Their main concern was not to become bilingual themselves; they rather projected these aspirations on to their children who would have to participate in a changing linguistic, social and economic environment (Heller, 1990).

Furthermore, Quebec francophones became conscious that bilingualism was, in fact, threatening the survival of the French language in Canada. The fact that francophones rather than anglophones became bilingual was seen as *'la voie royale menant á l'anglicisation et á la assimilation'*[4] (Rebuffot, 2000: 5). Thus, a series of laws (Bill 63, Bill 22 and Bill 101) were passed by the Quebec government, aimed at protecting and promoting the French language and restricting access to English schools.

A further development on the political front was the passing by the federal government of the Official Languages Act in 1969. This decreed that both English and French were official languages in Canada and were given equal status in all aspects of federal administration. Thus, all federal employees had to be officially bilingual and all official communication had to be carried out in the two languages. Bilingualism was therefore given a high profile in key aspects of Canadian life and federal funds were set aside to be used to subsidise the teaching of French, both as a minority language and as a second language in the country. After various unsuccessful efforts to promote bilingualism among federal employees, the government decided to sponsor the so-called 'Youth Option' represented in French immersion programmes.

The first experimental immersion programme was set up to promote functional bilingualism by using French as a language of instruction as well as English, in order to enable anglophone children to acquire a high level of proficiency in French while maintaining their proficiency in their first language. Furthermore, it was also hoped that the immersion programmes would lead to better relationships between members of the anglo and francophone communities.

Two main distinctions in type of provision were established. The first referred to the age at which students enter the programme: early immersion (4–5 years old), middle immersion (9–10 years old); and late immersion (secondary or high school level). The second indicated the amount of time spent studying in the immersion language: total immersion (100% immersion initially in the second language leading to a 50% contact at the end of primary school); and partial immersion (50% immersion in the second language throughout the programme).

One of the first pieces of research into immersion education was conducted to investigate the outcome of this experimental programme (Lambert & Tucker, 1972). The type of bilingualism aimed at was additive (for further discussion of this term see Chapter 2) and the programme was directed at children from a middle-class community. The second language itself (French) had a rather ambivalent status, being both prestigious and stigmatised at the same time (Heller, 1993, personal communication). On the one hand, European French, the variety introduced in St Lambert, enjoyed high prestige as an international language. Canadian French, on the other hand, was stigmatised by the anglophone community who had no necessary interest in being taken for francophones, and this variety was not, in fact, included initially in the programme, in spite of the programme being aimed at improving community relations in Canada.

Since 1965 there has been a steady spread of French immersion programmes throughout Canada. In 1977–78 there were 37,835 students enrolled in immersion, while in 1998–99 the number had jumped to 317,351 students in around 2000 schools. At primary school level the Quebec Department of Education maintains that 60% of all students in the province are enrolled in immersion programmes (Rebuffot, 2000). While these statistics are impressive, it must also be borne in mind that in the whole of Canada only around 7% of the school-going population are in fact studying in a French immersion programme (Swain & Johnson, 1997).

Characteristics of immersion programme participants

As mentioned above, immersion programmes have been mainly developed with children from upwardly mobile middle-class families from the dominant majority in Canada. In some cases, school boards set minimum standards for IQ tests for children wishing to enter the programme (Olson & Burns, 1983), thus guaranteeing a high level of intelligence among the students accepted. Students are enrolled in the programme on a voluntary basis, in this way, ensuring a high level of parental support for the programmes.

Curricular considerations

Language distribution in the curriculum

A separation or 'sheltered' approach was incorporated into the programmes from the beginning. The principle behind this approach is that learners of the target language are kept apart from native speakers, 'at least until their linguistic skills are sufficient to permit them to learn academic content on a par with native speakers' (Swain, 1982: 84). However, the suggestion by Swain and Lapkin that French immersion students might eventually attend French language schools was in fact met with huge resistance by the francophones who feared being taken over by the anglophones (Heller, 1993, personal communication).

In addition to advocating a sheltered approach, Swain claimed that all children in programmes of this type should begin with the same zero level of target language skills. She recommended adopting three basic principles to achieve successful bilingual education. The first was the principle of 'First Things First' or ensuring a sound basis in the child's L1 for L2 learning. The second principle was 'Bilingualism through Monolingualism' by which she argued for the merits of a separation (rather than a concurrent) approach to classroom language use (see Chapter 4 for further discussion of these notions). She called her third principle 'Bilingualism as a Bonus' where she advocated letting the students know the advantages of bilingualism for them. This knowledge would in turn lead to a self-fulfilling prophecy (Swain, 1983).

The original programmes were of the early total immersion type – that is to say, teaching was carried out exclusively in the second language from kindergarten up to Grade 2. Here, the children had two 35 minute periods of English Language Arts

(Lambert & Tucker, 1972). They finished their primary schooling with approximately 50% immersion in the second language. However, later, different modalities of exposure (partial, middle, late) were introduced. There were also experiments with 'double' immersion programmes in Jewish day schools in Montreal (Adiv, 1984) where two second languages (French and Hebrew) were used as media of instruction.

In one type of double immersion provision, the curriculum was divided into religious and culturally related subjects taught in Hebrew, with the rest of the subjects taught in French from kindergarten onwards. English was introduced in Grades 3 or 4. In a second modality, instruction in all three languages started right from the beginning – with most time allotted to French and Hebrew (14 and 11 hours per week respectively). English was used for 7 hours a week (Adiv, 1984).

In 1997, Swain and Johnson drew up a series of core features which differentiate immersion programmes from other types of bilingual and foreign language provision. These can be summarised as follows:

- The second language is a medium of instruction.
- The immersion curriculum parallels the local first language curriculum.
- Effective support exists for the students' first language within the curriculum.
- The programme aims at additive bilingualism.
- Contact with the second language is largely confined to the classroom.
- Students enter the programme with similar (limited) level of second language proficiency.
- Teachers are bilingual.
- The classroom culture is that of the local community, not the target language community.

Thus, it can be seen that the Canadian immersion model is a language enrichment programme (see discussion in Chapter 2) designed to promote bilingualism in a largely *monolingual* environment, where the classroom is the main source of contact with the immersion language in many parts of the Canadian territory outside Quebec. In this sense it is very different from both the International and European Schools Movements which cater for multilingual and multicultural populations. Furthermore, contact with peer native speakers of the second language (French) is not common within the programmes or outside the school context. This has consequences for the development of L2 proficiency as will be discussed below.

In addition, there has been little attention in the past to the study of the second language as a subject within the curriculum, as well as a medium of instruction, as is the case in European Schools. More recently, however, this has been seen as an area for development, in an attempt to deal with the 'plateau' effect in oral French proficiency reported by Swain (1985) and Swain and Lapkin (1986). Harley *et al.* (1990) refer to the need to include both analytic (form focused) and experiencial (communication focused) classroom activities, while Kowal and Swain (1997) have argued for the need for more frequent opportunities for student output and the importance of consistent feedback on their language production. In addition, Rebuffot and

Lyster (1996) have advocated the adoption of a dual strategy in immersion peda-gogy, which includes a proactive (or planned) approach which is focused on an integration of both content and form, and a reactive approach in which immersion teachers react to formal aspects of their students' production in an attempt to help them to pay more attention to their utterances in the second language, to reflect on them and to correct them.

Examinations in immersion programmes

In Canada, there are generally no school-leaving examinations which are equiva-lent to the International or the European Baccalaureate examinations. However, during the initial stages of the immersion programmes students' proficiency levels in French and English were assessed, as well as their academic attainment in subject areas, such as Science and Maths. For this purpose standardised tests were used and results compared with children in regular (non-bilingual) programmes.

Overall, the results of these assessments are positive in academic terms. Student proficiency in listening and reading French has been seen as of native speaker stan-dard and there are no negative reports on academic achievement levels. Student proficiency levels in speaking and writing French were below native speaker level, yet higher than results from the regular programme. There was, however, no noticeable effect of a change in attitude of the students towards the francophone community in Canada.

Summary

As can be seen from the above discussion, immersion programmes differ signifi-cantly from both International and European Schools in the type of population they cater for and in the circumstances leading to their creation. They can be seen as a national initiative designed to support official bilingualism within the Canadian Federal Government Administration, rather than as a response to the needs of a highly mobile international student population. These programmes have received large amounts of research money from the government and may be described as one of the most thoroughly investigated educational innovations (Stern, 1984). In contrast, research in International Schools is still in its initial stages.

Moreover, the main contribution of immersion education has been in the peda-gogical school domain. There have been few initiatives to encourage contact between English and French-speaking Canadians as a result of the programmes. This lack of contact with native speakers of French is perhaps one of the reasons which account for the relatively low proficiency in students' oral French production noted by researchers. Again, this is another point of contrast with the situation in European and International Schools.

Conclusion

In this chapter, we have considered different educational responses to the requirements of middle and upper-middle-class students in different parts of the world who need to be bilingual or multilingual because of the international nature of their parents' occupations or because they have to interact with speakers of different languages on a daily basis. In some cases, we have seen how academic bilingualism enables students to gain access to university education in different parts of the world, particularly in the USA and in Europe. Furthermore, we have discussed how national bilingual policies in Canada have encouraged the spread of a particular type of bilingual educational provision, which has had subsequent wide influence on the setting up of elite or prestigious bilingual programmes in many different parts of the world, such as Sweden, Finland, Catalonia, Australia, and the USA.

In the development of all these initiatives, it is important to note that the languages used in the programmes are world languages of established power and prestige, which are recognised and valued by the international community as means of communication on an international level. However, each of the educational movements discussed in this chapter has been developed in response to a different constellation of particular historical, political and social factors. Thus, as we indicated at the beginning of this chapter, in discussing the spread of elite bilingualism we need to bear in mind the dynamic relationship between tendencies, such as globalism and internationalism without losing sight of the importance of local and specific contextual factors in the creation of different modalities of educational provision.

Notes

1. The term 'case sketch' derives from the notion of 'thumbnail sketch' introduced by Fishman (1976).
2. The author is greatly indebted to Peter Longcope for the information contained in this section.
3. In 2001 this Institute was integrated with the Department of Linguistics and Modern English Language of Lancaster University.
4. 'The highway leading to anglicisation and assimilation, author's translation.

Chapter 2
Definitions and Distinctions

Introduction

Any attempt to provide 'hard and fast' definitions of concepts such as bilingualism and bilingual education seems doomed to failure, especially if we take into account the fact that this field is highly interdisciplinary, a fact recognised by Joshua Fishman in 1976 when he wrote, 'Bilingual education itself is not a discipline, it is an interdisciplinary activity' (Fishman, 1976: 124). Thus, we have researchers such as Heller (1994, 1999) who see bilingualism and bilingual education in relation to political issues; scholars such as Coulmas (1992) and García (1995) who are interested in the economic aspects of bilingualism; linguists like Poplack (1980) who concentrate their attention on linguistic aspects of bilingual speech; sociolinguists like Fishman (1972, 1976, 1980, 1991) and Hornberger, (1989, 1991) who are concerned to relate bilingual phenomena to their context of situation; psycholinguists such as Grosjean (1982, 1985) and Cummins (1981, 1986, 2000) who are interested in how bilinguals acquire and process their languages; neurolinguists like Fabbro (1999), Paradis (2000) and Vraid (2001), part of a growing group of neurolinguists who have shown interest in bilingualism; those who take a historical perspective on the development of bilingualism and bilingual education, such as Lewis (1977, 1981); and educationalists like Swain and Lapkin (1982, 1986), Ovando and Collier (1986, 1998) and Baker (2001) who investigate how children and adults become bilingual in educational institutions. It is therefore no surprise that terms such as 'second language', 'bilingual proficiency' and 'identity' take on different connotations according to which tradition the particular researcher or author comes from.

As well as the interdisciplinary nature of the field itself, we must also bear in mind that there are individual researchers who try to incorporate an interdisciplinary dimension within their work. Thus, for instance, Cummins (1980, 1986, 2000) focuses particularly on educational, psychological and political aspects of bilingualism and their relation to educational policies and practices. This can be clearly seen in his recent writing where he states that one of the main themes discussed is 'the ways in which "language proficiency" is conceptualised and assessed in multilingual contexts and how policies and practices with respect to language teaching and testing are rooted in patterns of societal power relations' (Cummins, 2000: 5). Nancy Hornberger (1989, 1991) is another example of a scholar who works in an interdisciplinary framework, focusing particularly on the interrelations between sociolinguistics and education in relation to minority communities.

In one of the early works, seeking to define the range and scope of the field of bilingualism, Baetens Beardsmore (1982) attempted to come to terms with such diversity by providing a wide-ranging typology of bilingualism and bilinguals, in his introduction to the field. Drawing on published sources, this author discussed several fundamental distinctions, such as that between societal and individual bilingualism, receptive and productive bilingualism, and minimalist and maximalist definitions of bilingualism. The author acknowledged the complexity of the situation in the following commentary: 'The complex picture that emerges from any discussion of bilingualism, where individual language use is closely inter-related with social forces, brings into focus . . . that bilingualism is a relative concept with no clear cut-off points' (Baetens Beardsmore, 1982: 35–6). He considered that 'bilingualism is situated somewhere along a cline which ranges from non-diglossic monolingualism, through bi-dialectalism to the use of two distinct languages at varying levels of ability' (Baetens Beardsmore, 1982: 36).

More recently, Baker (2001) and Baker and Prys Jones (1998) have continued this tradition of trying to situate the reader in relation to the field by providing chapters and glossaries in their publications which are aimed at elucidating key concepts in the area. The reader is thus provided with information about the difference between such related concepts as 'elite' and 'prestigious' bilingualism, additive bilingualism and enrichment bilingual education, and international and intranational languages.

Although it is often easier to appreciate the difference in related concepts if they are defined in a contrastive relationship, it is probably truer to the nature of bilingualism to consider the multiple relationships between different types of bilinguals and their language use as part of a cline or a continuum. In this respect, Hornberger (1989, 1992: 198) in her pioneering work on biliteracy[1] postulated 'a framework that uses the notion of intersecting and nested continua to demonstrate the multiple and complex interrelationships between bilingualism and literacy and the importance of the contexts and media through which biliteracy develops'. She argues convincingly that rather than concern ourselves with 'polar opposites, . . . in order to understand any particular instance of biliteracy, be it a biliterate individual, situation, or society, we need to take account of all dimensions represented by the continua' (Hornberger, 1989: 273, 1992: 199).

This researcher makes reference in her original formulation to nine continua, relating to biliterate contexts, media and development, and in a later version to three more, relating to the content of biliteracy (Hornberger & Skilton-Sylvester, 2000). In this later version the original emphasis on sociolinguistic and educational aspects has been extended to political dimensions. Here we reproduce figures representing three of these sets of continua as illustration of the above notions.

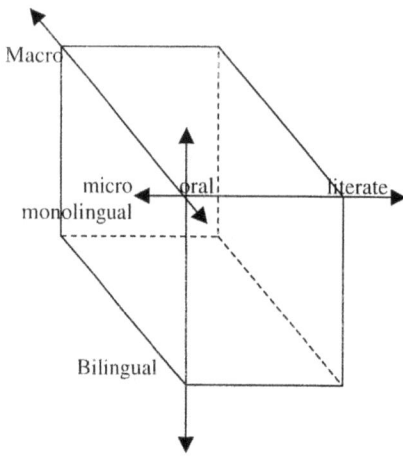

Figure 2.1 The continua of biliterate contexts (Hornberger, 1989: 273–274)

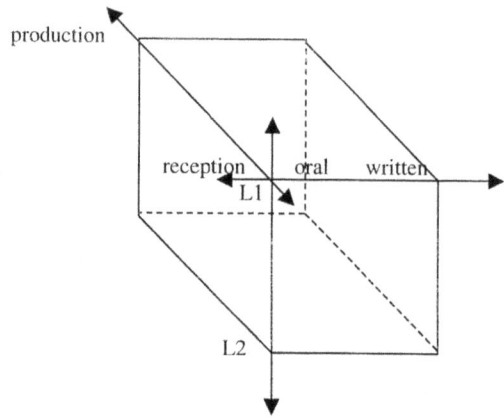

Figure 2.2 The continua of biliterate development in the individual (Hornberger, 1989: 273–274)

As can be seen in Figures 1–3, the author has represented the interrelated nature of the continua by means of the three-dimensionality of the individual figures depicted. Thus, for example in Figure 2 biliterate development in the individual is seen in terms of three continua: the reception–production continuum, the oral language–written language continuum and the L1–L2 continuum. It is important to note that this development does not occur in isolation. As Hornberger (1989: 281) observes, 'the development of biliteracy in individuals occurs along the continua in direct response to the contextual demands placed on these individuals', thus explicitly linking developments in Figure 2 with those in Figure 1.

Therefore, the emphasis is not on any particular points which may be identified on a continuum but rather that these are not 'finite, static or discrete . . . (but) inevitably and inextricably related to all other points (on the continuum)'

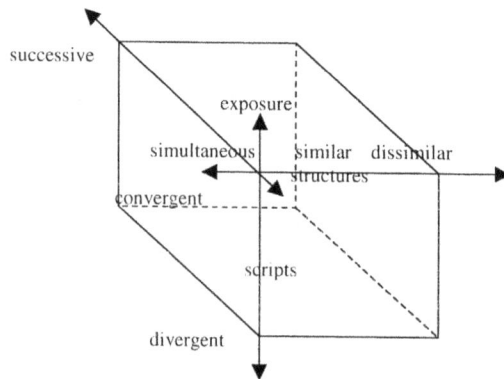

Figure 2.3 The continua of biliterate media (Hornberger, 1989: 273–274)

(Hornberger, 1989: 274). In this vision, the interrelatedness and complexity of the phenomena of bilingualism are foregrounded, rather than a focus on individual characteristics.

The different types of relationships between the continua are summarised in graphic fashion in Figures 2.4 and 2.5.

As may be surmised from the above discussion, it is exceedingly difficult to write clearly while at the same time trying to do justice to these multiple and complex interrelationships. Consequently, in this chapter we will adopt an approach which discusses key notions in relation to other ideas which have some type of incidence in

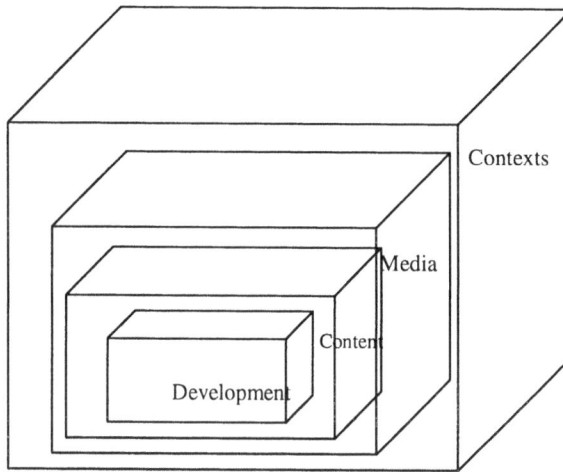

Figure 2.4 Nested relationships among the continua of biliteracy (Hornberger & Skilton-Sylvester, 2000: 97)

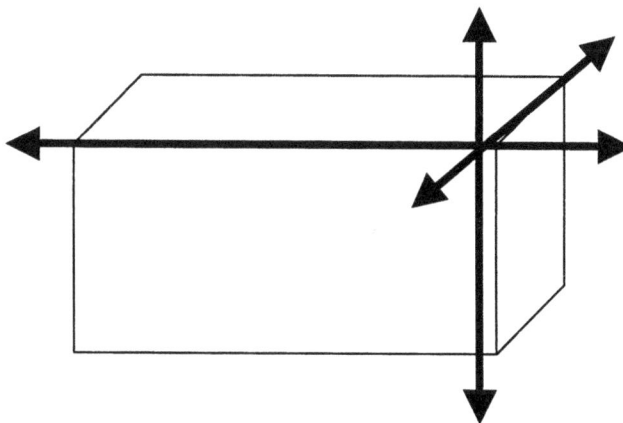

Figure 2.5 Intersecting relationship among the continua of biliteracy (Hornberger & Skilton-Sylvester, 2000: 97)

their formulation, in an attempt to define more clearly the concepts under discussion. Nevertheless, the reader should bear in mind that the distinctions and definitions arrived at should be understood ultimately as points of reference on a series of different continua relating to bilingualism and bilingual education; i.e. biliteracy. We will begin by situating our discussion with reference to Bourdieu's (1982) theory of language as symbolic capital, as this helps to explain how certain languages and types of educational provision are privileged as highly valued resources, at the expense of others which are considered less prestigious or less valuable.

Language as Symbolic Capital

In Bourdieu's (1982, 1991) sociological vision, language is considered a form of cultural or symbolic capital which is available to be exchanged in the 'marketplace' of social interaction. Thus, language may be seen as a symbolic resource which can receive different values depending on the market. The possession of symbolic resources, such as certain highly valued types of linguistic skills, cultural knowledge and specialised skills, helps to gain access to valuable social, educational and material resources. These resources, which constitute symbolic capital, in turn 'acquire a value of their own and become sources of power and prestige in their own right' (Heller, 1994: 7). An example of this can be seen in the case of Hong Kong, where the Cantonese/English bilingual elite have traditionally defined English as the most prestigious language used in education (Martin-Jones & Heller, 1996). It has thus been imperative for students in Hong Kong to have adequate English language skills as well as knowledge of the subject area and appropriate skills to succeed in such fields as Medicine, Architecture and the Law. Consequently, English in Hong Kong has been considered by students and their parents alike, as a highly valuable resource which will enable them to gain access to privileged situations of wealth and power (Lin, 1996).

Since 1997 and the return of Hong Kong to Chinese sovereignty, the language arena has become more complex. Official language policy now requires that most Hong Kong schools adopt Chinese as the medium of teaching and learning, while those schools who wish to make English the sole language medium of education have to satisfy the Education Department that their teachers and students are able to teach and learn effectively in English. This controversial measure, seen in relation to the historical and socio-economic development of the area, helps to explain why English medium education in Hong Kong has been so hotly fought over in recent times (see Chapter 9 for more details).

In her illuminating discussion of French and English as linguistic capital in Canada, Heller (1994) adopts Bourdieu's theory to trace the changes in the relative value of these languages from colonial times to the present. She notes that for most of the country's colonial and post-colonial history the two languages operated in separate areas. However, after the social and political changes which led to the mobilisation of francophone Canadians in the 1960s and 1970s this scenario changed radically. Increasingly, middle-class francophones and middle-class anglophones found themselves competing for the same political and economic resources. In this struggle the two official languages of the country, French and English, have taken on different values for the different communities. Bilingualism in these two languages, which had hitherto been the prerogative of francophones who wanted to succeed in the market controlled by anglophones, now became important to middle-class anglophones who wanted to compete in an integrated market. It was in these circumstances that the French immersion programmes had their origin, as we have seen in Chapter 1.

Heller (1994: 97) sees the greatest difference between middle-class francophones and anglophones who choose bilingualism as a means of gaining access to valued resources as 'the gap between the capital they possess and the capital they need to acquire, as well as the opportunities presented to them to acquire it'. For anglophones, opportunities to access French have mainly been provided through bilingual education (immersion) provision, which has received massive research funding in an attempt to provide scientific evidence for its viability.

Thus, it can be seen clearly in the two examples discussed above that education has been seen as a powerful means of providing access to valued symbolic resources, such as bilingualism or multilingualism in prestigious world languages. Parents believe that their children will be able to gain access to power by 'committing . . . (them) to particular media of instruction and ways of learning languages' (Martin-Jones & Heller, 1996: 6). In many cases, access to particular forms of bilingual education provision are restricted to those who can afford to pay (as in the case of International Schools) or those who demonstrate high levels of academic ability (as is currently the case of English medium schools in Hong Kong) thus conserving the notion of valuable linguistic resources as the privilege of certain powerful groups.

Diglossia and Triglossia in Relation to Bilingualism

In the following sections, as announced in the introduction to this chapter, we will take up various sets of terms which represent ways of talking about points along various continua relating to bilingualism and bilingual education. Reference will be made to Hornberger and Skilton-Sylvester's (2000) expanded continua model. Since each of these terms indexes an instance of biliteracy – whether at the societal, programme or individual level – each one, in fact, entails all 12 continua; for purposes of discussion, however, I will highlight only selected continua in relation to each set of terms. In this section the concepts of diglossia and triglossia can be considered in relation to the continua concerned with context, specifically macro levels of context, characterised along the continua of monolingual to multilingual, and oral to literate language use.

The characterisation of language as social capital in Bourdieu's (1982) terms has certain similarities with the notion of diglossia which has been widely referred to since its initial formulation by Ferguson in 1959. He defined the term as referring to a situation 'where two varieties of a language exist side by side throughout the community, with each having a definite role to play' (Ferguson, 1959: 1). He called these varieties High (H) and Low (L). Thus, in the German part of Switzerland Standard German (*Hochdeutsch*) would constitute the H variety and Swiss German (*Schweizerdeutsch*) the L variety.

These terms are not neutral. H varieties are prestigious, standardised, associated with traditions of literary heritage and used for formal functions, such as religious sermons, speeches in parliament and news broadcasts. They are usually learnt at school. L varieties, on the other hand, are often not standardised, lack literary heritage, and are not prestigious. They are associated with informal occasions, such as conversations with family and friends, folk literature and 'instructions to servants, waiters, workmen, clerks' (Ferguson, 1959: 5) and are usually acquired at home.

In 1967 Fishman made an important distinction between diglossia and bilingualism. According to this researcher, diglossia was associated mainly with work in sociology and bilingualism with developments in psychology. Thus, he considered diglossia as referring to the distribution of more than one language variety to serve different communicative tasks in society, whereas he saw bilingualism as relating to the ability of an individual to use more than one language variety. He constructed a typology of four possible relationships between diglossia and bilingualism illustrated in Figure 2.6.

	BILINGUALISM +	DIGLOSSIA –
+	Both diglossia and bilingualism	Bilingualism without diglossia
–	Diglossia without bilingualism	Neither diglossia nor bilingualism

Figure 2.6 The relationships between bilingualism and diglossia (taken from Fishman, 1967: 30)

An example of a country where stable diglossia and widespread bilingualism exist is Paraguay, where almost the whole population are bilingual in both Spanish and Guarani. Spanish, the High language, is used mainly in the domains of religion, education and government, while Guarani, the Low variety, is maintained for matters of intimacy and group solidarity (Fishman, 1967).

Situations involving diglossia without widespread bilingualism refer to contexts where there are two languages used within a specific geographical area. One language will be spoken by one group of inhabitants and the other language by another group, but there will be few who speak both languages. Examples given by Fishman (1967) of such situations range from the Romansch and Jura areas of Switzerland to distinctions between lower caste Hindus and upper caste Brahmins in India.

Bilingualism without diglossia, on the other hand, where most inhabitants are bilingual, usually obtains in situations of rapid social change such as in newly industrialised nations and 'dislocated immigrants and their children' (Fishman,

1972: 35) rather than in stratified societies,. This type of bilingual situation tends to be transitional as without the means of maintaining the functional separation of the two languages (as in a diglossic situation) contact between the two languages tends to lead to language mixing and later to language shift.

The final scenario, neither bilingualism nor diglossia, may take place in societies where there is little contact with other speech communities, and where mono-lingualism is the norm, such as in Norway, Japan and Portugal.

Fishman (1980) saw diglossia as contributing to linguistic stability. Other researchers, such as Eckert (1980) and Roberts (1987) argue that in fact that the very existence of varieties categorised as High (prestigious) and Low (less prestigious) implies conflict rather than complementarity in situations where the social and polit-ical relations between speakers who use these languages are not equal. Speakers of L varieties see H varieties, or symbolic capital, in Bourdieu's (1982) terms, as essential if they want to be successful socially, politically and economically and therefore struggle to have access to and to control these legitimised languages.

In the early 1970s a Tanzanian researcher (Abdulaziz-Mkilifi, 1972: 198) coined the term 'triglossia' to refer to a situation

> where there exists side by side (a) regional or vernacular languages whose basic role is in oral intra-group communication, (b) a local standardized lingua franca which is used extensively in the education system, mass media and in govern-ment administration but which is not developed enough to cover all settings of modern urban technological culture, and (c) a world language.

In the case of Tanzania the languages in play are English, Kiswahili and a variety of vernacular languages. The vernacular languages are acquired at home and are used in informal situations. Kiswahili, which is learnt at school, is 'the language of culture and communication at national level' (Abdulaziz-Mkilifi, 1972: 204). English, on the other hand, is used in higher education and is the means of access to world literature and technological information (Rubagumya, 1991) (see Chapter 7 for more information). In an interesting observation, Abdulaziz-Mkikifi (1972: 202) notes that in Tanzania triglossia constitutes 'an intersection between the two devel-oping diglossia situations, one involving Swahili and some vernacular and the other involving Swahili and English', a situation which has also been referred to as 'double overlapping diglossia' (Fasold, 1984).

Diglossia and triglossia, then, characterise the societal (macrolevel) context for individual (microlevel) bilingualism in terms of the degree to which one or more languages are in play (the monolingual to multilingual continuum) and the func-tions the language(s) perform(s), including those associated with primarily oral or literate domains (oral to literate continuum).

Additive, Elite and Prestigious Bilingualism

In the above discussion of language as symbolic capital, diglossia and triglossia we have foregrounded societal rather than individual bilingualism, as we have been concerned to show how different researchers in the fields of sociology and sociolinguistics have tried to account for the social values associated with different language varieties in particular contexts. In this section we will focus on how individuals see their ability to use more than one language in their daily lives. Here again, I will relate the ideas discussed to the continua of context, in this case at the more microlevels, and in relation to selected continua of content and media (Hornberger & Skilton-Sylvester, 2000). We will begin by considering the concept of additive bilingualism.

This term was first coined by Lambert in 1974. According to Baker (1996) there are two main uses of this concept in contemporary writing. Additive bilingualism refers, on the one hand, to the positive cognitive outcomes which result from being bilingual on an individual level, and on the other, to the enrichment of language, culture and ethnolinguistic identity at a societal level. In these cases, an individual acquires or learns a second or foreign language without detracting from the maintenance and development of his or her first language. The second or foreign language is seen as 'adding to' and enriching language experience, rather than replacing the first language. Being bilingual is associated with accomplishment and positive feelings. In other words, students acquire additional languages at no cost to their home language and culture. Generally, additive bilingualism is associated with the acquisition and learning of majority or world languages which are seen as being 'useful' for enhancing future opportunities. A well-known example of an additive bilingual educational environment are the French immersion programmes in Canada.

The opposite situation, where the acquiring of another language 'replaces' or undermines a person's first language, is referred to as subtractive bilingualism. Here, the second language is often a majority language which constitutes the dominant or official language of society, such as English in the USA. Because of perceptions of its prestige, use and status, this language gradually undermines the use of the first or home language (such as Spanish among Hispanic populations). The minority home language is often seen as low status, and being bilingual is associated with feelings of inferiority or punishment. This may lead to loss of cultural identity, with possible consequences of alienation and assimilation. Subtractive bilingualism is often associated with submersion education where a minority language speaker has to 'sink or swim' at school without any institutional language support.

The distinction between additive and subtractive bilingualism encompasses the contexts in which the individual acquires and uses the two languages, as well as the sequencing of that acquisition (simultaneous–successive media continuum) and the social meanings and identities (majority–minority content continuum) which accrue with that acquisition. This distinction leads us in turn to consideration of another pair of opposites, elite bilingualism and folk bilingualism, also relating to the context and content continua (in this case residing primarily in social class resources and identities). Elite bilingualism has been described as 'the privilege of middle-class, well educated members of most societies' (Paulston, 1975 cited in Harding & Riley, 1986: 24; Skutnabb-Kangas, 1981). This type of bilingualism has also been referred to as 'elective' bilingualism (Valdés & Figueroa, 1994) and includes 'individuals who choose to become bilingual and who seek out either formal classes or contexts in which they can acquire a foreign language . . . and who continue to spend the greater part of their time in a society in which their first language is the majority or societal language' (Valdés & Figueroa, 1994: 12).

Folk bilingualism, on the other hand, has been categorised as 'the conditions of ethnic groups within a single state who have to become bilingual involuntarily, in order to survive (Tosi, 1982 cited in Harding & Riley, 1986: 24; Skutnabb-Kangas, 1981). These have also been referred to as 'circumstantial' bilinguals (Valdés & Figueroa, 1994) We will now examine some of the characteristics of these middle-class, well-educated, 'elite' bilinguals.

As we have seen in Chapter 1, these individuals often come from families who travel extensively because of the international nature of their occupations and commitments or because of their socio-economic status. They are usually upwardly mobile and see the need to be bilingual or multilingual in order to have access to good job opportunities at international level. The languages that such bilinguals learn are world languages of established power and prestige, such as English, French, German, and Spanish.

Thus, it can be seen that 'elite' bilingualism is associated with additive bilingualism, in that it represents a definite advantage, socially and economically to speak more than one language for people who, because of lifestyle, employment opportunities or education, need to move frequently from one country to another, or who, because of the multilingual-multinational nature of the organisations they work for, need to interact with speakers of different languages on a daily basis.

As noted above, elite bilinguals usually come from higher socio-economic groups and thus their bilingualism or multilingualism is part of an ethos of social, cultural and economic advantage. As Baker and Prys Jones (1998: 15) note, 'Such families often regard bilingualism as a way of preserving family status and educational and employment advantage'. Children in such families may become bilingual initially as a result of having a nanny or governess who speaks another language to them. They may then go on to expensive International Schools or finishing schools where they have the opportunity of becoming fluent in one or more prestigious majority languages, or they may go to high status language schools for similar reasons. In all these cases, bilingualism or multilingualism is a 'planned and purposeful' (Baker & Prys Jones, 1998: 15) undertaking, where multilingual proficiency is regarded as a necessary attribute for those who wish to preserve or gain access to prized symbolic capital represented in attractive lifestyles and economic advantage. In this sense, elite bilingualism may be seen as a valuable personal possession which is consciously chosen and worked for. However, it is important to note that while reproduction of economic advantage may be a major factor in promoting this type of bilingualism, there may be also other motivations, such as wider enculturation and increasing tolerance of difference (Baker, 2000, personal communication).

However, the use of this term is not without its difficulties. As a teacher-researcher at an International School in Stockholm observes,

> I agree that our school is an elite school socio-economically and culturally, but I don't like to use the word since we have so many students who are not all from 'elite' groups. More and more families work abroad for a period of time. Some are sent out by their employers, some go back to the country they originally emigrated from, some get married to foreigners etc. The children always have to follow, whether they like it or not. I know that the children do not always feel 'elite-like' but just torn away from their familiar surroundings and friends. Learning languages to them is a means and not the goal. (Kerstin Ekelund, 2000, personal communication).

This observation points to the difficulty of using a socially loaded term like 'elite' to refer to a type of bilingualism which, while it is not a majority situation, is becoming increasingly common in an ever-shrinking globalised universe. In the Scandinavian countries, for example, it has always been necessary to speak foreign languages if people aimed at getting a 'decent middle-class job like bank-assistant, teacher, secretary, civil servant . . . Learning foreign languages has never been seen as a luxury, but as absolutely necessary' (Kerstin Ekelund, 2000, personal communication) as few foreigners take the trouble to learn Swedish, Norwegian, Danish or Finnish (see Chapter 10 for more details).

Furthermore, Harding and Riley (1986: 23) categorise as elite bilinguals 'parents who are abroad temporarily for educational or business purposes'. These authors are at pains to stress that this type of bilingualism is not rare and that 'the parents involved are by no means people who can afford private nannies and governesses or the fees of public[2] or international schools. They are likely . . . to be middle-class professionals' (Harding & Riley, 1986: 23). They point out that there is often the impression that researchers in this area are 'wasting (their) time on the imaginary troubles of a pampered minority'. However, this is very far from reality if we consider that the type of people who need to be increasingly mobile in today's world are likely to be teachers, soldiers, secretaries, translators and technicians, who while being relatively privileged if compared to most immigrants, are certainly not rich.

Perhaps for these reasons, researchers in the area of bilingualism have proposed other terms to refer to similar phenomena. Baker and Prys Jones (1998) talk about 'prestigious bilingualism' which they define with reference to bilinguals 'who own two high status languages' (Baker & Prys Jones, 1998: 15) as a result of regular travel abroad, in the case of diplomats and their families and bureaucrats in organisations such as the United Nations, the European Union, and the Council of Europe. Prestigious bilingualism may also result from exchange programmes, such as the ERASMUS programme in Europe which enables students to study for a semester or two at another European university as part of their course of studies. This term has wider coverage than elite bilingualism, in that it can be used to refer to the learning of languages which may be high prestige minority rather than majority or world languages which are associated with social mobility and political power, as in the case of Catalan in Catalonia (see Chapter 10 for more details).

Other terms used in this respect are 'voluntary', as opposed to 'involuntary' bilingualism, 'optional bilingualism', 'privileged bilingualism', and 'enrichment bilingualism'. The term 'voluntary bilingualism' relates to a notion introduced by Ogbu (1982) in the early 1980s when he distinguished between voluntary and involuntary minorities in the USA. The use of these terms refers to the idea that African slaves and Mexican and Puerto Rican minorities have a different ('involuntary') kind of relationship to the wider US society than do 'voluntary' immigrants, such as European immigrants in the early twentieth century, and Central American and South East Asian immigrants in the 1970s and 1980s. The use of this term highlights the idea that while it is one thing to 'choose' voluntarily to become bilingual from a position of privilege, it is quite another to have this imposed by circumstances such as war, conquest or slavery.

The concept of 'optional bilingualism' focuses in similar fashion on the element of choice involved in this type of bilingualism. Elite bilinguals consciously choose to become bilingual or multilingual due to a perception of the advantages that will result from this decision. This determination has a number of important consequences, such as the type of education programme selected and the consideration of actions taken to further incipient bilingualism or multilingualism in these individuals. The term 'privileged bilingualism' takes us back to Paulston's (1975) notion of elite bilingualism, referred to above, as being available only to a small number of individuals who have the means to gain access to it.

'Enrichment bilingualism', on the other hand, is a concept which has recently been associated with immersion education but which Hornberger (1991: 226) would like to see used in the broader sense that Fishman (1982) originally intended for it, 'extending it beyond its elitist origins' (see discussion on enrichment bilingual education below). There is also a sense in which it may be said that this notion refers rather to a process which covers both minority and elite bilingual education, while the terms 'prestigious' or 'elite' bilingualism emphasise the product of a particular type of educational provision (Baker, 2000 personal communication).

Transitional, Maintenance and Enrichment Bilingual Education

It is important to distinguish between three basic models of education recognised in the literature on bilingualism. These are: the Transitional Model, the Maintenance Model, and the Enrichment Model. The distinction between the first two of these is well known, whereas the latter term, although very valuable, is less frequently used (Hornberger, 1991). Like the terms discussed above, the terms discussed in this section refer mainly to selected continua of context, content and media in the Hornberger and Skilton-Sylvester (2000) model, in that they describe educational programme contexts (located along the micro to macro context continuum), programme goals with respect to the social identities and relationships of minority and majority language speakers (majority to minority content continuum), and the sequencing of the languages as (simultaneous to successive) media of instruction within the programme.

A transitional model refers to bilingual education programmes which are aimed at language shift, cultural assimilation and social incorporation (Hornberger, 1991). In other words, the emphasis in transitional programmes is to shift children from minority language communities away from the use of their first language towards the use of the dominant majority language or languages spoken in mainstream society. These students are taught initially through their home language and allowed to use this language at school until they are considered to be proficient enough in the dominant language to cope with mainstream (monolingual) education (Baker, 1996). An example of this type of programme is that offered for 'Limited English Proficiency' students in the USA where groups of students who are seen to have problems with English language proficiency are segregated from mainstream classes and are provided with content-area instruction in their native language as well as receiving tuition in English as a Second Language. Transition from the bilingual programme to mainstream classes generally takes place one to three years after children enter the programme (Freeman, 1998). In an influential policy statement about the role of bilingual education in the education of children in the United States, the TESOL organisation (*TESOL Matters*, 1992/3: 5) criticised the short duration of these programmes saying that 'it is not long enough to develop the cognitive and academic language proficiency needed for school success – typically a matter *of 5 to 9 years*'.

A maintenance model, on the other hand, refers to bilingual education programmes which aim towards language maintenance, the strengthening of cultural identity, and the affirmation of civil rights (Hornberger, 1991). In the USA this type of programme is less common than programmes relating to the transitional model and has as goals for minority language speakers, English language acquisition and native language maintenance. These programmes usually last longer than transitional programmes and work towards a situation of additive bilingualism where the new language is added to the speaker's first language. An example of this type of programme are Heritage Language Programmes in Canada for minority language speakers, where the students' first or home language is used as medium of instruction for 50% of the school curriculum (Baker, 1996). According to TESOL (1992/1993), a maintenance bilingual education programme uses content–subject instruction in both the home language and the second language (English) to achieve the goal of strong literacy in both languages.

An enrichment model of bilingual education shares certain characteristics in common with the maintenance model but goes beyond it by aiming not only at maintaining the speaker's first language but also developing and extending it. This model encourages cultural pluralism and the development of the social autonomy of cultural groups and refers to both language minority and majority speakers (Hornberger, 1991). Thus, immersion programmes in Canada and dual-language programmes in the United States are examples of this type of model, where both first and second or foreign languages are seen as important resources to be used and developed by the individual speaker. Hornberger (1991: 215) sees the enrichment model as offering 'the greatest potential benefit not only to language minority speakers but to the national society as a whole'.

The immersion programmes have already been discussed in Chapter 1. We note, however, that Fishman (1982) saw this type of programme as catering for students from 'the most fortunate socio-economic background' and as being 'a direct descendant of elitist' bilingual education (Fishman, 1982: 25). Dual-language programmes, however, differ from immersion in the sense that they cater for both majority and minority language groups, and in the fact that both languages are used in content area instruction. Thus, both majority (prestigious) languages and minority (less prestigious) languages are perceived as equal in status in dual-language education programmes (Freeman, 1998).

We can thus see, as Hornberger (1991) argues, that an enrichment model of bilingual education is not synonymous with immersion programmes, although the two have been closely linked in the past. For purposes of our discussion, elite or prestigious bilingual education may be taken as forming part of an enrichment model and may be defined as the whole range of programmes that provide bilingual education to highly educated, higher socio-economic status, usually majority-language-speaking groups. In spite of the negative connotations often associated with the term 'elite', these programmes make a unique and valuable contribution to bilingualism in many parts of the world, as will become clear in this book.

Language Intensification and Bilingual Education Programmes

Up to now, we have been referring to bilingual education programmes without having defined what we mean by the concept of 'bilingual education', assuming, perhaps, that its meaning is self-evident. However, as Cazden and Snow (1990) cited in Baker (1996: 172) warn us, bilingual education is a 'simple label for a complex phenomenon'. We will, therefore, briefly examine the difference between what is often referred to in certain Latin American countries as *intensificación* (intensification), and notions of bilingual education *per se*. As above, these concepts relate to the continua of context (at the programme level), media in terms of sequencing of the languages of instruction, and content (curricular knowledge) (Hornberger & Skilton-Sylvester, 2000).

In language intensification programmes, which some equate with bilingual education programmes, the emphasis is on foreign language instruction where these languages are taught as one more subject or area in the curriculum but with a higher number of hours (intensity) than is commonly assigned to this area. In language intensification programmes in Colombia, for instance, the number of hours of English (a foreign language) is often 10–15 per week, instead of the more usual 2–3 hours per week in schools which do not adopt a modality of language intensification. In this type of programme, the emphasis is on linguistic aspects of the foreign language, such as grammar, vocabulary, reading comprehension, etc. Although students may be required to study material related to specific content areas, such as Natural Science or Maths, the focus is linguistic and is not concerned with the students' conceptual development in academic curriculum areas.

In bilingual education programmes, in contrast, two languages are used as media of teaching and learning in educational contexts (Siguán & Mackey, 1987). This implies that both languages, the first language and the foreign or second language, are seen as vehicles for the construction of knowledge in different curriculum areas, such as Maths, Natural Sciences and Economics, as well as being used in Language Arts classes. Thus, the focus of language learning is not only linguistic but is also associated with academic achievement and communication within the educational institution. In this sense, we can talk about programmes of bilingual education, whereas in the language intensification programmes there is generally no integration of foreign or second language teaching and learning with the construction of knowledge in other content areas.

First Language, Second Language, Foreign Language, Other Language

The use of the term 'first language' suffers from similar difficulties in terms of meaning to the use of the term 'bilingual education'. First of all, it is based on a monolingual rather than a bilingual frame of reference in that it presupposes that an individual acquires one language *before* another or separately. This is obviously not the case if we are referring to simultaneous bilingualism, where a child acquires two languages at the same time. In this case, it is truer to think of Swain's (1972) designation of 'bilingualism as a first language'. The term 'first language' has also developed a number of different meanings, among which are the following uses: the first language acquired; the stronger or dominant language; the 'mother tongue'; or the language most used by an individual (Baker & Prys Jones, 1998). As we move away from discussing societal contexts for bilingualism and bilingual education programme structures and towards characterising the languages involved, our discussion of the continua relates more directly to the continua of development (first language versus second language) and content (mother versus other tongue), as well as context (foreign versus second language) and media (first/second language acquired) in the Hornberger and Skilton-Sylvester (2000) model.

A second language, on the other hand, is a language which has been defined as having 'official recognition or a recognized function within a country' (Stern, 1983: 16). Thus, in the United States the teaching of English as a second language to Hispanic children, whose first language is Spanish, aims at helping them gain full access to the political and economic life of the country they are living in, as well as enabling them to participate in the national educational system. As with the term 'first language' there are a number of overlapping meanings associated with this concept. According to Baker and Prys Jones (1998) these cover the following notions: the second language learnt (chronologically); the weaker or less dominant language; a language which is not 'the mother tongue'; the less used language. Moreover, researchers working in the field of language acquisition use the term 'second language acquisition' regardless of whether the language in question is used as a language of communication within the society or not.

The use of the term 'English as a Second Language' in connection with the International Schools movement has been justified by David Garner (1990: 2) in the following terms,

> ESL ... refer(s) to the situation in English-medium international schools around the world, where students from a range of different language backgrounds need to learn English in order to follow the school curriculum. For such students English is a 'second' language. 'Second' in this context ... indicates that whereas the language is not the student's mother tongue, it is needed for a substantial and essential aspect of the student's life.

When a language not used as a regular or frequent means of communication within a particular country is taught in schools, this is referred to as a 'foreign' language (Stern, 1983). This designation makes clear that the language is 'foreign' in the sense that it is the language of a community which is outside national boundaries. A foreign language is often taught in schools for instrumental purposes, such as access to bibliography published in a foreign language or visits abroad. As opportunities for contact with a foreign language are necessarily limited in the student's daily life, there is often need for higher level of formal instruction in order to develop an appropriate level of foreign language proficiency. At times, the teacher is the only model of the language that the student has access to on a regular basis. Thus, English as a Foreign Language (EFL) is taught in schools and language institutes in countries such as France, Spain and Germany where English is not used on an official basis.

In the European School context, Housen (forthcoming) sees the distinction between 'second' and 'foreign' language referred to above as problematic. He considers that the term 'foreign' language is inappropriate 'as a cover term for all languages in the European School context other than the pupil's first language' (Housen, forthcoming). He maintains that the terms 'second' and 'third' language should refer to the first and second foreign languages studied by pupils as part of their school curriculum.

The term 'other language' is associated mainly with the United States and Australia. In the USA the widely known acronym TESOL refers to a professional association of 'Teachers of English to Speakers of Other Languages', while official government documents in Australia refer to LOTE, (Languages Other than English). In both these cases, it can be seen that the notion of 'other' languages is defined in relation to the dominant language, which in both cases is English.

Dominant Language, Majority Language, World Language, International Language

In this final section, we will discuss different terms used to refer to language varieties which are considered prestigious or useful to be acquired or learnt. As we have seen above, elite bilinguals are usually individuals who are highly mobile at international level and therefore need to be bilingual or multilingual in languages which are widely spoken by the international community. As throughout, given our recognition that language is a form of cultural or symbolic capital in the marketplace of social interaction, the notions analysed in this section are again related mainly to the continua of context and in particular to relations of power at societal and global levels of context (Hornberger & Skilton-Sylvester, 2000).

According to Martin-Jones and Heller (1996: 5) the notion of 'dominant languages' in Bourdieu's (1982) terms is associated with

> the interests of certain groups that, because of the control they exert over a particular set of highly valued material or symbolic resources, are in a position to assign value to other forms of cultural and linguistic capital and to influence the operation of educational institutions that produce and distribute the most highly valued resources.

Thus, certain linguistic varieties which privilege dominant group interests are more highly valued than other indigenous or minority languages. These constitute dominant languages in terms of perceptions of their importance, power and prestige in global interaction. In developing countries, dominant languages are often the former colonial languages, such as English or French, which have been legitimised as official languages in many independent nations in Africa and Asia. In these types of situations, such as in the case of Burundi, while oral use of the vernacular language (Kirundi) is sometimes tacitly allowed in the classroom in the form of teacher and pupil code-switching, textbooks and all written work are required to be carried out in the dominant language, French, which is the language of the small educated elite in the country (Ndayipfukamiye, 1996).

The concept of 'majority language' is usually associated with a language that is spoken by a large number (the majority) of the population of a country, as opposed to minority languages, which are spoken by a relatively small percentage of the population. Thus, for example, in Australia, the majority language is English and in Japan the majority language is Japanese. There is, however, another sense in which a language can be classified as 'majority'. This is in terms of status or power in relation to the other language varieties used in the country. In this sense the term 'majority' language is similar in meaning to 'dominant' language as discussed above. Thus, for example, in Australia English would still be the majority language in status, while in Japan English as well as Japanese would also be recognised as majority languages.

The terms 'international language' or 'world language' are terms which do not foreground so explicitly as the relations of power implicit in the term 'dominant' language. They have been defined as 'high prestige, majority language(s) used as a means of communication between different countries speaking different languages (Baker & Prys Jones, 1998: 702). These notions are often explained in terms of the rapid rise in globalisation and internationalisation during the twentieth century which has meant that certain languages have become languages of international communication at world level in such fields as science, technology and international diplomacy (Baker & Prys Jones, 1998). The following languages of wider communication, that may be used as first or as second or foreign languages, are generally recognised: English, German, French, Spanish, Portuguese, Dutch, Arabic, Russian and Chinese. Many of these languages are used as official languages in meetings of such international organisations as the United Nations and the World Bank.

The term 'intranational languages' is a related concept which applies the notion of a high prestige language used as a medium of general communication between different language groups within one particular state or country (Baker & Prys Jones, 1998). Examples of intranational languages are the use of English in India, and Kiswahili in Tanzania (see Chapter 7).

In the above discussion we have been using the terms 'international' and 'intranational' language to refer to natural languages which have their origin in specific language communities. However, there have also been attempts to artificially create languages with simplified grammatical and pronunciation systems that can act as lingua francas. The most well-known of these is Esperanto which was created by Ludwig Zamenhof in 1887 in the hope that it would become a universal second language and thus contribute to global identity and global unity. These noble ideals have not, in fact, materialised, as after a rapid rise in the number of speakers of Esperanto between 1887 and 1970, there have been relatively few new learners of the language during the last 30 years. However, those who do learn Esperanto as a second or foreign language claim that it helps learners to have 'an enhanced awareness of language in general . . . (and) different cultures' (Lowenstein, 1995: 1–2).

Conclusion

In this chapter we have discussed some of the most important definitions and distinctions which underlie the developments described in this book. We have situated our discussion on such notions as diglossia, additive, elite, and prestigious bilingualism and bilingual education and dominant and international languages with reference to Bourdieu's vision of language as symbolic capital, as this helps to explain how certain language varieties and forms of educational provision are considered highly valued resources at the expense of others. This theory also helps to explain why these resources are not fixed but receive different values, depending on the state of the symbolic marketplace of social interaction, as can be seen in the current positioning of bilingualism in French and English as a valued resource for both of the principal language communities in Canada, in contrast to the situation in the first half of the century when bilingualism was seen as the prerogative of French Canadians.

We have also tried to show how one of the key means of access to these valued linguistic resources is through education. Certain powerful groups, such as those of higher economic status or high academic achievement, have more chance of being able to influence and participate in specific types of bilingual provision such as international education, and English medium schooling in the case of Hong Kong at the present time.

We have conducted our discussion of key notions in relation to ideas which have had some incidence in their formulation. These concepts have usually been presented in a contrastive relationship, as for example in the discussion of transitional, maintenance and enrichment bilingual education, or in the relationship between international and intranational languages. However, as stated in the Introduction and reiterated throughout, we wish to emphasise that it is important to situate all these concepts as points on nested, intersecting continua relating to bilingualism and bilingual education; i.e. biliteracy, where the emphasis is on the interrelated nature of these phenomina.

Notes

1. Hornberger and Skilton-Sylvester (2000: 96–8) define biliteracy as 'any and all instances in which communication occurs in two (or more) languages in or around writing'.
2. In Britain, this term refers to expensive private schools.

Chapter 3
Elite Bilingualism as a Sociocultural Phenomenon

Introduction

In the previous chapter we focused on key definitions and distinctions relating to the development of elite bilingualism and bilingual education in general. In this chapter we will continue this process of definition by initially examining various general concepts relating to the multiple relationships between language and culture such as intercultural relations, cultural relativity, biculturalism, cross-cultural communication, acculturation and deculturaltion. These concepts, while not exclusive to elite bilingualism, are important to a basic understanding of how language and culture are interrelated.

If we accept that elite bilinguals are generally well educated, upwardly mobile individuals who are proficient in two or more world languages, (see Chapter 1) then we can see how in many cases they have been in a position to forge a new global identity, due to their familiarity with different cultural systems. In the second part of this chapter, therefore, we will examine how increasing social mobility has led to an upsurge in intercultural marriages which, in turn, has resulted in increasingly complex processes of identity construction among elite bilinguals.

In the third part of the chapter we will go on to examine how the notions of multi-cultural and intercultural education have influenced the teaching and learning of foreign and second languages, to the point that there are strong arguments for adding intercultural competence to the list of linguistic, sociolinguistic, strategic and discourse competences that students of languages are now expected to acquire.

The final section deals with the relationships between culture and business, and examines how the notion of the global marketplace involves increasing levels of cross-cultural communication. Some examples of publications designed to help overcome potential difficulties in cross-cultural business and social encounters are discussed in the light of the insights these give into ways in which nationals of different countries are portrayed, and the type of advice provided about how to be successful in these types of interactions.

Definitions and Understandings

Most writings in this area begin by acknowledging that it is a wasted effort to try to provide an encompassing definition of 'Culture' (Ovando & Collier, 1987). However, there exists a large number of definitions and descriptions of cultural manifestations in different spheres: political, anthropological, psychological and economic. To give two examples, we can take a definition by Goodenough (1964) cited in Robinson (1985: 10) where he states that 'Culture does not consist of things, people, behavior or emotions. It is the forms of things that people have in mind, their models for perceiving, relating, and otherwise interpreting them'. In 1973, Geertz proposed a view of culture in the following terms, 'Believing, with Max Weber, that man is an animal suspended in webs of significance he himself has spun, I take culture to be those webs and the analysis of it to be therefore not an experimental science in search of law but an interpretive one in search of meaning' (Geertz, 1973: 5).

Wider, intercultural perspectives on world affairs are becoming increasing necessary, as recognised by Young (1996: 211) in the following statement, 'in most interrelated economies today, national affairs are international affairs . . . These are clearly problems which cannot be defined let alone addressed, without inter-cultural communication'. So, if culture is indefinable, at least in any global sense, how can we make sense of such terms as 'intercultural', 'cross-cultural', 'multi-cultural', 'bicultural', and the associated processes of 'acculturaltion', and 'deculturation' ?

For many monolingual and monocultural individuals, this does not constitute a problem. It is difficult (though not impossible) to see your own cultural practices as relative if you have nothing to compare them with. Usually, it is when people come into contact with different cultural conventions that they begin to question their 'common sense' assumptions. In a revealing discussion, Geertz (1983) argues that the actual notion of 'common sense' itself is not an absolute, but depends on what is culturally accepted as being sensible or practical within a particular community or society. Thus, for example, Geertz observes that, 'No one, or no one functioning very well doubts that rain wets; but there may be some people around who question the proposition that one ought to come in out of it, holding that it is good for one's character to brave the elements' (Geertz, 1983: 75).

The process of coming to terms with cultural relativism often causes distress or even trauma in the initial stages. This has been documented by various researchers who have postulated different types of 'stage' models of acculturation (Schumann, 1983; Wong Filmore, 1983; Acton & Walker de Felix, 1994, cited in Forbes, 1997). The latter refers to a four-stage model of acculturation to describe the reactions of adult bilinguals to new cultural experiences. First of all there is the *Tourist Stage*, where people are fascinated and attracted by their contacts with the foreign culture. This is also referred to as 'the honeymoon phase' (Sears, 1998: 12). Then comes the critical period, denominated by the *Survivor Stage*, where the individual experiences negative feelings of hostility, frustration, nostalgia, loneliness and resentment towards aspects of the new culture. This is also commonly known as a period of 'culture shock', where a person rejects aspects of the new cultural system and romanticises the positive merits of the former system. In International Schools (Sears 1998: 12) notes that parents of recent arrivals may appear 'demanding, anxious and, occasionally aggressive' during this period. The example in Text Box 3.1 vividly portrays the physical effects of culture shock.

Text Box 3.1   An Experience of Culture Shock (taken from Condon, 1993: 7)

My first experience of living abroad was in 1968 when at the age of 23 I followed my sister to 'the continent[1] where she had found her first job with a ballet company in Germany. I went to work for the Council of Europe in Strasbourg, Alsace, France . . .

Whilst in Strasbourg I did some part-time work helping an American Lay Minister from the World Council of Churches. It was in his home that I discovered the 'culture shock' syndrome and until that moment I had not realised that such a thing existed.

A young American university student was spending some time visiting Strasbourg and after some weeks she developed symptoms of tiredness and generally not feeling well. She ended up in bed with a fever. I have never forgotten that the doctor who examined her told us she was suffering from 'culture shock'. What was it? – many of us wondered. For most of us there has been a slight feeling of homesickness that had lasted until those who had been there longer took the 'newcomers' under their wings, so we had no experience to draw on to help in this new situation.

That might have been the end of the story for shortly afterwards I went back to England where I stayed for eight years. In 1980 I found myself applying, again, to work abroad. I came to Luxembourg in 1981 and, although it is very different from the part of France I knew and loved so well, I felt I had adapted to the change. It was not until two years ago that I suddenly began to feel isolated. I have a good and interesting job, wonderful husband, adorable children, nice home, even my fair share of very nice English friends, as well as lots of friends and colleagues of other nationalities, so why the problem? I couldn't put it into words – only that I felt 'shut in a cupboard', cut off and panicky. The 'culture shock' had finally caught up with me and I have only just realised it!

After a while, people will either reaffirm their previous cultural affiliation, and in this case never really accept their new situation, or they will adapt to the new system, modifying their cultural behaviour and perspectives accordingly. This stage is referred to as the *Immigrant Stage* and is followed by a final phase called the *Citizen Stage*, where the individual assimilates to a greater or lesser degree into the new culture.

As is clearly evident from the above, the development of cultural understandings is part of a process which necessarily takes time, involves change and is produced and reproduced through everyday practices in cycles of interaction. Thus, 'culture' is not, as is sometimes maintained, a possession of individuals, a tradition which is transmitted by a society to be handed down and learned by its members. As Young (1996: 208) argues, this static view of culture is unsatisfactory as it cannot cope with change. This author maintains, 'Members of all cultures have some possibility of autonomy in respect of them and it is this that makes it possible for them to see the possibility of intercultural spaces.'

In many cases, foreign language textbook writers include advice to students on how to avoid some of the more obvious cultural difficulties that may arise in intercultural encounters in relation to the interpretation of the meaning of casual invitations and the maintenance of the appropriate degree of social distance when greeting or referring to people, as can been seen in the excerpt in Text Box 3.2 which is targeted at Latin Americans in Britain or in the United States.

Text Box 3.2 Culture Shock (Taken from 'Goal International' McGraw-Hill, Book 4, Manuel Dosantos (1996))

The following are some points that Latin Americans should observe when visiting the United States, Canada and Northern Europe, or when inviting foreigners of those countries to their home or to eat out.

Invitations
When North Americans invite you to their homes that does not mean that you can take your entire family and friends with you. In Latin America, one extra guest is usually welcome. And don't take 'Come and see us some time' literally. It actually means 'Keep in touch'.

Hugging, Kissing and Keeping a Distance
In Latin America, it is common for people to kiss each other on the cheek. In Brazil, people kiss each other twice or even three times if they are young and unmarried. In other countries in the area one kiss is enough. People of Latin cultures like to touch and hug one another. The same does not occur among North Americans and North Europeans. They normally shake hands, and keep their distance. The acceptable distance is approximately 40 centimetres.

On First Name Terms
In Latin America, people are referred to as Mr, or Mrs so and so, Doctor so and so, or 'Licenciado' so and so. In the United States, it is becoming more and more common to call people by their first name immediately.

Bearing this in mind, we will now look at some of the concepts mentioned above to see how they relate to a developing understanding of the field of elite bilingualism. We will begin with the terms 'multiculturalism' and 'biculturalism'.

According to Grosjean (1993: 31), we all belong to a series of cultural networks (sub-groups and sub-cultures) even though we have had no contact with another majority or national culture, and we are all therefore necessarily 'multicultural'. He defines a bicultural individual as someone who 'participates, at least in part, in the life of two (majority) cultures . . . in a regular fashion'. In addition, this individual knows how to adapt his/her behaviour and attitudes to a particular cultural environment, and can synthesise cultural characteristics from both cultures.

Grosjean (1993) maintains that it is possible for a person to be bicultural without being bilingual, and also that someone can be bilingual without living necessarily in two cultures. As an example of the first statement he cites the case of a French Jew who participates in the life of Jewish and French cultures, without necessarily being bilingual in French and Yiddish. The writer illustrates the second case with an example of a Swiss German who speaks both Swiss German and High German and who is not bicultural. While this position is debatable, considering the close link existing between language and culture, and depends on the definitions of bilingualism and biculturalism used, it draws attention to the notion that both bilingualism and biculturalism form part of a continuum and may not develop in an exactly parallel fashion (see Chapter 2).

The terms 'intercultural' and 'cross-cultural' seem generally to be used as synonyms, though often in different domains. The term 'intercultural' is often associated with education, while cross-cultural training is usually related to business negotiations across different cultures and work carried out in psychology. Muñoz (1995: 230) sees the former as, 'an active process of communication and interaction between cultures for purposes of mutual enrichment'. The emphasis here seems on reciprocity. Both cultures benefit from the process. Cross-cultural communication, on the other hand, seems to highlight the idea of global connections which cut *across* cultural boundaries, rather than on the establishment of interrelationships. (See later sections on Culture and Education, and Culture and Business for further illustration of these terms.)

Mockus (1995: 4) maintains that those who come into contact with different cultures should value 'the tension' generated by the contact between these traditions and see this as 'a mechanism which forces one to a certain degree of universality'. Castañeda (1996: 7), on the other hand, warns against an over-emphasis on 'the foreign' as opposed to the 'native' as this may lead to the 'creation of false expectations and stereotypes in relation to the foreign culture'. However, he agrees with Mockus in that cultural understanding should result in the achievement of 'a higher degree of generality which transcends not only one's own particularity, but also that of the other' (Gadamer, 1972, cited in Castañeda, 1996: 11).

The terms 'acculturation' and 'deculturation' come from the field of anthropology and refer to the processes involved in cultural contact and change. Redfield *et al.* (1936, cited in Muñoz, 1995: 218) define acculturation as, 'phenomena which are a result of continual, direct contact between groups of individuals from different cultures and the changes that are caused in the original cultural patterns of one or both groups'. As it stands, this term is neutral and descriptive, rather than negative, though those who take a static view of culture may consider these changes threatening, as can be seen in the following statement taken from an article published in the newspapers *Clarin* and *The New York Times* (1997) by Roberto González-Echeverría which claims, '*Spanglish*, the mixed language of Spanish and English . . . constitutes a serious danger to Hispanic culture'.

Deculturation, on the other hand, refers to loss of the original culture. This term emphasises a static rather than a dynamic view of cultural change and is related to a subtractive view of bilingualism (see Chapter 2). This notion may help to explain the phenomenon of 'Global Nomads' reported by Sears (1998: 36), who describes a group of young people who have been educated at International Schools in foreign countries and who 'never entirely reintegrate into their home culture'.

Intercultural Marriage

As noted in Chapter 1, the world is becoming increasingly interconnected and people are routinely moving from one country to another for purposes of study, job opportunities, and language learning. This high level of mobility among students, business people and members of international organisations, in turn, leads to an increase in intercultural marriages between people who otherwise might have had fewer opportunities to choose their partners in an international setting.

If we take, for example, Japan, a country which for many years has considered itself monolingual and monocultural (see Chapter 9), according to a report in *The Japan Times* (29 June 1998), at the end of 1997 the number of registered foreign residents in the country totalled 1.48 million (1.18% of the total population). Over one million of these came from Asia, while the second largest group, 285,000, came from South America. Thus, foreign marriages are increasing, particularly between Japanese men and foreign women (75% of all international marriages in Japan), in spite of the difficulty that cultural differences often lead to initial friction with in-laws (*Daily Yomiuri*, 16 June 1998).

In order to illustrate some of the multiple differences which characterise international marriages, I will now present briefly two case studies; the first involving a North American man and a Japanese woman living in Japan, and the second, a Colombian man and a British woman living in Colombia.

Case Sketch 3.1   A North American-Japanese Family in Japan (adapted from Kamada, 1998b, 1999)

Jack is an American who first came to Japan over three decades ago as a member of the US Military. He remained stationed in Japan for some four years during that time. In the 1980s, he returned to Japan again as an English teacher with a company. He met Keiko by chance several years afterwards while conducting a business transaction for his company. After marriage, they have lived in a rural small town in a southern region of Japan . . . They have two children, Randy (13), an eighth grader in middle school l. . . and Katie (12), a sixth grader . . .

Jack and Keiko have their own English school where they both teach at two locations. Jack also teaches two lessons per week part-time at a nearby national university. Aside from this, he also does copy-editing for medical and other scientific papers intended for publication in such noted Western journals as Nature and Science. Furthermore, he is also a computer consultant to various local institutions.

Keiko mainly teaches . . . English to middle and high school students for the goal of developing their English skills for the entrance examination with a concentration on grammar and form. Keiko isn't required to use much English in conducting the class as most of her explanations are in Japanese, typical of such schools popular among the college track types. At home, Keiko speaks English with her husband and converses in Japanese with the children.

This case sketch involves a foreign husband living with his family in his wife's country, Japan. He has experience of his adopted country in a variety of roles: as a soldier, as a businessman, and later, as owner and teacher of an English school, and as a computer consultant. In spite of his long residence in Japan, some important cultural difficulties have recently surfaced as a result of decisions made about his children's education.

Keiko, reflecting current Japanese social attitudes, felt that it was most important for the children to be strong in their mother tongue, Japanese, as it is the language of the country where they were born and where they live. She did not agree with her husband that English should be used in the home. Furthermore, in accordance with cultural perceptions of the importance of homework in Japan, she would prefer the children to spend their time studying after they come home from school, rather than watching English videos, in order to improve their English language proficiency, which their father feels is important.

Jack disagrees with the Japanese cultural assumption that the school should have total responsibility for deciding what is best for the children in relation to all school-related matters. He has fought against what he considers the high levels of conformity exacted from children at school and feels proud that his eldest son, 'has been able to emerge with an open mind as one who can think and reason and has common sense' (Kamada, 1999: 16). He considers that cultural expectations of children in Japan do not allow them to enjoy life sufficiently, as many of them go straight from school to English classes, which they study until 9 or 10 p.m., after which they go home to carry on studying.

In the near future the family plan to move to the USA. Jack hopes that the differences in the US education system compared to what he sees as the difficulties his children have encountered with the Japanese system will help to ensure more enjoyment of life. As he says, 'I remember Randy was such a happy, smiling little boy, until he started going to school . . . I wonder what is the purpose . . . only to pass a test to qualify for some higher level of cramming'(Kamada, 1999: 16).

Case Sketch 3.2   A Colombian-Scottish Family in Colombia (based on information kindly supplied by Eleanor Cosh)

Juan Manuel is Colombian and his first language is Colombian Spanish. When he was 23 years old, he went to Italy in search of better job opportunities and lived there for eight years. He learnt Italian and was able to pursue university studies in that language and also start up a prosperous business based on glass in the building trade.

He met Eleanor during one of his holidays in Colombia. She is Scottish, her father was Scottish and her mother Colombian. Eleanor considers English as her first language. At the age of eight, when her family moved to Colombia from Britain, she learnt Spanish as a second language at school.

Eleanor and Juan Manuel got married in 1990 and settled in North Italy. Eleanor learnt Italian and she and her husband started using Italian as the main family language of interaction. Their two children, Paolo Andrés and Francesca were born there, and while Italian remained the principal family language, Eleanor decided to use English with the children as much as possible.

In 1994, the family moved to Cali, Colombia, because of family reasons and because of reports that the building business was booming. However, six months after their return, the property market collapsed and Cali with its drugs mafia property connections was particularly hard hit. Both Eleanor and Juan Manuel were forced to change jobs; she became a teacher in an elite British-Colombian bilingual school and he started up a food business.

When talking about some of the cultural differences she has experienced in her life, Eleanor emphasises the importance for her that her children are at the British bilingual school. She feels happy that they can 'experience cultural contact with British people and with teachers at the school'. In her own case, she admits, 'There is something in your heart . . . being far away . . . which makes you happy . . . to be able to start using your language all the time.'

There are two things that she finds particularly different about living in Colombia, after living in Italy, The first is the presence of live-in maids, and the second is the influence of the family. After Italy, where she was very independent and was accus-

tomed to finding things where she had left them in the house, she found it difficult to adjust to the presence of a maid, and the need to remember to lock things away. She understands that because of the great poverty that many maids live in, the things she owns must be a source of temptation for them. Yet, this puts constant pressure on her, as she's not used to having a relative stranger constantly in the house.

As for the family in Colombia, she notes that they expect to know about everything that happens in her life, which she finds rather difficult. Though there are compensations. The children are in constant contact with members of their father's family, such as aunts, uncles and cousins and this balances out the stress situation.

In general, Eleanor feels that living in Italy means contact with the Latin warmth characteristic of Colombia, without the difficulties of insecurity and lack of organisation which she complains of in Latin America. She feels that it is difficult to be aware of all these cultural differences before she actually experience them, though it very much depends on people's attitudes how they react to these changes. She knows that her husband is often tempted to get on a plane back to Italy, but the school situation of the children makes them think twice. Eleanor says that she doesn't want her children to suffer the constant cultural changes she experienced in her own childhood and concludes, 'You are always missing something. There's no perfect place where you could share both cultures'.

These two case sketches, to a certain extent, present opposite perspectives, in that in the first situation it is the man who is living in a foreign country, and in the second case, it is the woman. Both households have had to come to terms with different socio-cultural expectations of how families conduct their everyday lives in relation to the relative influence of the extended family, the inclusion of maids or servants within the immediate family situation, and different perceptions of schooling. In the first case, the difficulties resulting from these cultural differences have proved so great that the family feel that the solution is to move to the 'other' country (the USA). In the second case, although the temptation to move countries is great because of economic pressures, the perceived need for stability in the children's upbringing has made the parents think twice.

Children's names

The phenomenon of international or intercultural marriage and the subsequent establishment of intercultural families has led to a number of important implications. First of all, there is the question of children's names. This may seem trivial but, in fact, many parents think hard about the consequences of naming their children in one language rather than another.

In Morocco, Jane Griffiths[2] (1999, personal communication) relates how partners in mixed or 'interfaith' marriages between Muslims and Christians often prefer children's names which have common roots in both religious traditions. For girls, this is not too difficult, as there are such combinations as Maryam/Miriam, but many boys end up with names from Old Testament prophets, such as Yussef/Joseph, Yonas/Jonas and Ilyas/Elias.

According to Peter Gray (1998, personal communication), who is in the process of carrying out a survey on the naming of bilingual children, many parents often carefully choose names for their children with two languages and cultures in mind. In his own case (he being North American and his wife Japanese), the reasons he gives for his daughter's name are the following. Her name is Junko Gray. Her mother, Yoko, likes Japanese girls' names that end with 'ko' and because the family planned to live in Japan and send the children to Japanese schools Yoko wanted a common Japanese name which would not stick out. Peter wanted a name that would be easy for North American relatives to pronounce and felt that 'Junko' sounded like the English name 'June'.

The same author also reports the story behind the naming of an adopted Chinese girl by a North American couple who were temporarily resident first in China and then in Japan. The girl's name in Chinese is 芳佟 斯·布拉德利 ; in Japanese ブラッドリー ロランス キャサリン and in English, Laurence Catherine Bradley. Her mother explains that, as they planned to return to live in the USA, they chose names based on women relatives from both sides of the family. However, the resulting first name, Laurence, caused unexpected difficulties such that 'an American clerk in the Beijing embassy refused to believe it was a girl's name ... in a country where nearly every couple wanted a son as the only child they were allowed' (Gray, 1999: 5). The Chinese name is a transliteration of the English name, but has no actual meaning in Chinese, though it is four times as long as a 'real' Chinese name! When the family moved to Japan, Laurence's name was deemed unpronounceable and resulted in a nickname based on the first syllables of the word 'rollerskate' in Japanese, which she suffered for most of her primary education.

Other accounts in *The Japan Times* (June/December 1998) mention difficulties experienced by the wives and children of international marriages when they wish foreign names to be included in their Japanese passports. The Japanese Passport Law requires use of the *kunrei* spelling system, which closely reflects the nipponised pronunciation of names. Thus, Mrs Halliwell, the Japanese wife of a foreigner, was initially instructed to spell her married name *Hariueru* on her passport. She was then told that she could submit official documents if she wanted to change the spelling back to the original English version.

In Text Box 3.3 we have included a reflection by a graduate of an elite bilingual school in Colombia on the importance of her name as a reflection of her identity.

Text Box 3.3 Name and Identity (Based on information kindly supplied by María Ester Navia)

Back in my school they used to change my name. My real name in Spanish is María Ester, and they started calling me Mary Esther. So I got real mad, and when the chil-

dren started calling me the nickname of 'Miky', I just preferred to be called Miky Navia and that was my identity that I could rescue from my name . . . I was always fighting to be a Colombian, and not a Gringa,[3] like they wanted me to be. All my classmates were Colombians; we had very few American girls with us. But they were very identified with their structure of being a Gringa; it was better for them. It was easier to get along with everybody else, especially with teachers. So I was always a rebel and I wanted it to be my way and I still have a good sense of knowing that I learnt a lot things like my English, but I wanted to be Colombian; I wanted to be myself; I wanted to have an identity with my own name, not the name they were giving me. And they were transforming my name and that was the point. And Miky is a very American way of calling a person, but the children gave it to me in the sense that they liked to be with me, because I was always taking care of the small kids. And I thought that this was my identity and that it was me . . . but I didn't spell it like Mickey Mouse. I spelled it M I K Y and I always drew a little rose after the name and I still do it. And that's the only identity I had with my name and I didn't let them change it.

Identity and nationality

As we have seen in the previous section, children's names can be an important indication of how parents have projected their future linguistic and cultural identity. The question is though, how far children agree with their parents' projections. In order to examine the views of a bilingual/bicultural teenager, we will take the case of Tommi Grover, a 20-year-old Finnish-English bilingual.

Text Box 3.4   A Bilingual/Binational Teenager (based on Grover, 1997)

Tommi recalls that, although he was always torn between his two home countries throughout his childhood, it was only when he became an adolescent that this conflict became a real problem. Living in England, he acknowledged that between the ages of 16 and 19, he became almost fanatically pro-Finnish in everything and felt, 'a growing irritation at all things English and was annoyed at having to live in such a horrible country' (1997: 4), wishing he had 'normal' Finnish parents.

By 18, having read a lot of Jack Kerouac's books and feeling restless, Tommi decided to travel. He notes, 'Travelling was what finally resolved my identity crisis. Two months on my own in foreign countries with a one month break in Finland, made me realise that all countries have their good and bad sides, and that England isn't necessarily the living hell that I thought it was. I came to the unavoidable conclusion that I will always be somewhat of a foreigner wherever I am, but I will also be at home in two countries' (1997: 4).

This account clearly shows Tommi's strong emotional but unrealistic projection of

> *the country where he was not resident, Finland, as being an ideal paradise, and his gradual acceptance of his being, 'a valued member of the community with two different outlooks'. (Grover, 1997: 4).*

In a recent article about bilingualism and identity Kanno (2000: 2) following Taylor (1992) takes identity to mean 'A person's understanding of whom they are'. This understanding depends crucially on what others think of us. In other words, identity can be seen as socially constructed. In the case of bilinguals, as they inhabit different language communities, they often receive very different self-images from various cultural mirrors (Kanno, 2000). They are simultaneously involved in multiple discourses, thereby developing different identities that may contradict other identities which derive from other discourses (Peirce, 1995; McKay & Wong, 1996).

Nicola Küpelikilinç (1998), a British psychologist married to a Turk, working with bilingual children and teenagers in Offenbach, Germany, quotes a Czech proverb which says, 'Learn a new language and you will acquire a new soul' to express the close connection there is between language and identity. She sees enhanced self-esteem as a result of increased language skills and 'participation in different cultural worlds' (Küpelikilinç, 1998: 8).

Marc Sheffner (1998: 5), resident in Japan, criticises the traditional concept of nationality as 'bankrupt' because, 'it simply cannot handle the reality of (multi-lingual and multicultural) people's experience'. He suggests that the idea of being British, Japanese or French, etc. is a useful concept to some extent, but considers that it can also become restrictive and therefore dangerous. He argues that it is not because a person is Japanese that they can speak Japanese, use chop-sticks or appreciate cherry blossom, but rather because they are human. Thus, to talk about 'the Japanese smile' or 'the British stiff upper lip', or 'American indi-vidualism' may be a convenient label, but should not be taken as an absolute truth.

These appreciations are echoed in a more abstract formulation by Barbour (1996: 42) in a discussion of language and national identity in Europe. This author concludes that, 'Human beings often have complex, multiple identities – local, regional, familial, religious . . . In parallel to their complex multiple identities, indi-viduals also display complex and multi-faceted language use.'

These observations thus draw attention to the fact that multilingual and multi-cultural people, now and in the future, need to construct and display identities which reflect their complex everyday reality, taking into account an extra-national focus and that these may contrast with commonly accepted stereotypes. Further-more, they need to recognise that identities are not static but change and evolve over time in accordance with the influence of the different experiences they engage in.

Travel

Tommi Grover's solution to his identity crisis involved travel. Another member of a bicultural family, Robert Gee, notes that in bicultural families travel often becomes a way of life, as families try to maintain contact with friends and relatives living in different parts of the world. Travel is often considered necessary by parents of bilingual or multilingual children in order to maintain language proficiency in the less dominant language(s). As Gee himself notes, 'passive bilinguals quickly lose their inhibition to speak' (1998: 13).

As an innovative language and culture strategy, the same author recommends taking family holidays in multicultural hotels, such as those in Malaysia, which cater for guests from Singapore, Malaysia, Japan, Australia and Europe and provide child care facilities, mainly in English. In addition to children getting accustomed to interacting with a wide range of their peers from different countries in English, Gee maintains that the more relaxed service attitudes of Malaysian hotels provide a welcome change for the more time-conscious Japanese guests.

Interculture–Interfaith

Marriage to someone from a different country can sometimes mean marriage to someone of a different faith. This, as Alatea Anderssohn (1998) explains, can have minor implications, such as, what you eat for Christmas dinner, or major ones, whether you, in fact, celebrate Christmas at all.

Gender plays an important role in some interfaith marriages. For instance, in Morocco, while a Muslim man is free to marry a non-Muslim woman, provided she is Christian or Jewish, but not Buddhist, Hindu or Atheist, a Muslim woman is only supposed to marry a Muslim man. Case Sketch 3.3 shows clearly the difficulties some interfaith families have to pass through and the decisions they make as a result of differing family and societal religious and cultural influences.

Case Sketch 3.3   An Interculture–Interfaith Family (based on information kindly supplied by Jane Griffiths)

In Britain, religion is mainly a matter for the individual. Here (in Morocco) it is still a matter for the whole community. Even to speak Arabic convincingly you have to believe in God. You say, 'If God wills it', instead of 'I hope', and 'God reward you', instead of 'Thank you'. If you pay someone a compliment, you have to add 'God bless you', to make it clear that you are not jealous of the other person's good fortune.

This is an environment where little distinction is made between religion, ethnicity and culture: the word used to describe Westerners, Nasrani or Nasraniya, literally means 'Christian', and the word 'Muslim' is often used as equivalent of Arab. Unlike the Middle East, there are no native Christian communities: the only Christians are foreigners – mostly French, the former colonists. 'As a non-Muslim woman, and living in a small town, I felt for years as though almost everyone I came in contact with – my husband's family, our neighbours, my colleagues – was watching me and my children to see what my attitude was towards Islam', says Jane.

Jane is British, Abdelhaq is Moroccan. They met and married in France, where their two children were born, but moved to Morocco while the children were still small. Jane was brought up Protestant, with a very tolerant religious outlook. 'For me, the important values are tolerance, compassion, respect for others and for the natural world. People from all the great religions observe those values, and so do many people who do not consider themselves religious at all', she says.

As a student in France, Abdelhaq looked forward to returning to his home country, where he would be able to observe the Ramadan fast, for instance, in a Muslim environment. Jane was very sympathetic to Islam and interested in learning more about the religion, at least initially. 'I tried to make it clear that I was genuinely interested: but often people assumed that because I was a Nasraniya, I must be hostile towards Islam. When they talked to me about Islam they were often aggressively critical of the West and Christianity. At a rational level, I could understand them, because Islam is badly misrepresented in the West and it's reasonable for people to feel defensive. But it often seemed as though they were attacking me personally, and placing me in a false situation, where I instinctively felt forced to defend Christianity and Western culture.' Her initial sympathy towards Islam waned and she started identifying herself as Christian in a way she had never done before.

'It was very unnerving, because I'd always believed I was a very tolerant person, and now I was responding to intolerance by intolerance. I didn't want to react that way, but for a while I was stuck in it.'

Jane and Abdelhaq had agreed that the children would be brought up Muslim, in accordance with Muslim law, but that they would also learn to respect Christianity. The family has always celebrated Christmas at home, and the children know lots of Christmas carols. They have been to church services at Christmas and Easter in Britain, and enjoy the singing, although when they join in the prayers they are careful to leave out any words which are too specifically Christian.

When the children were small, Abdelhaq's mother and sisters were the vehicles for transmission of religious and cultural values to the children. Like many country women with little or no schooling, their understanding of Islam was heavily laced with superstition.

'They also used God to frighten the children – if they didn't say bismillah ('in the name of God') before starting to eat, God would send them to hell, for instance. I didn't want the children growing up believing in a God who punishes people for something like that, but I didn't want to criticise my husband's family to the children, or undermine the children's respect for them. Abdelhaq didn't play a large part in the children's religious upbringing when they were small, although he did sometimes intervene when his mother or sisters said things which were clearly superstitious rather than religious', Jane remembers.

In primary school the children were exposed to a more orthodox, educated view of

Islam. Some of their teachers taught a form of Islam which was tolerant, ethical and guided by respect for others. But in the older classes there was also anti-Christian and anti-Jewish prejudice, as teachers and children came to talk more about political and historical issues. The climate of post-colonialism, tension in the Middle East, and a perception that Western policy, led by America, is biased towards Israel and against the Arab states, contributed to a negative view of Christianity and Judaism.

The children themselves have not been victims of prejudice, and it is very rare for anyone to criticise them openly because their mother is Nasraniya. Jane has always tried to observe Ramadan, and she feels that this has made it easier for her children to be accepted. 'It makes it easier at home as well, as the whole household is living to the same timetable, instead of me trying to live to one routine and everyone else to another. It's also given me some insight into what the people around me are experiencing during this time – the sense that the month of Ramadan is special, the feeling of anticipation as sunset approaches and you are about to break the fast. Still, I can't really agree when people tell me that fasting is physically and spiritually beneficial.'

Some people think that the prospect for mixed-faith couples is poor, and that the longer the marriage lasts, the more rigid each partner's faith becomes. Or else that such couples succeed only when neither partner attaches much importance to religion. However, Jane disagrees.

'That hasn't been our experience. Certainly it was hard at first, because each of us took things for granted which seemed strange and irrational to the other. But as time goes on we have each learnt greater tolerance. I've learnt a lot about Islam, and I've learnt too that individual Muslims interpret their faith in a wide range of ways, some of which I can respect and some of which I can't – exactly as with individual Christians. I still identify myself as Christian because that is the tradition in which I grew up, and which gives my life an ethical and spiritual structure. Islam performs the same function for my husband and my children. The difference is that for them, Islam also provides a shared community identity. Christianity does not do that for me, partly because I know that many Christians would hardly consider me Christian at all. That doesn't bother me very much. I feel that I have been privileged to gain an insight into a different community. And the important things are still tolerance, compassion and respect for others.'

Culture and Education

We will now turn to a consideration of some of the issues involved in the relationships between culture and education in the context of elite bilingual or multilingual education. We will first examine differences between the use of the terms 'multicultural' and 'intercultural' education and then go on to discuss aspects of the current debate on the teaching and learning of culture in foreign language classrooms. Foreign language teaching and learning cannot be seen as equivalent to elite bilingual education, as the term has much wider coverage. However, for purposes of our discussion we may consider elite bilingual education as a subcategory of both foreign and second language teaching and learning, in that all three areas are concerned with students' learning of another language in addition to their first language.

Multicultural and intercultural education

According to Muñoz (1995), the first appearance of the term 'multicultural education' dates from 1969 when Jack Forbes published an article entitled 'The education of the culturally different: a multicultural approach' (Camilleri, 1985: 16, cited in Muñoz, 1995). Seven years later, the term 'intercultural education' was used in a declaration by the General Conference of UNESCO in Nairobi. Today, both terms are in common use in the area of bilingualism and multilingualism, particularly in relation to minority situations.

As Baker (1996: 382) has observed, the term 'multicultual education' has many different interpretations, ranging from 'awareness programs for majority language children to the sharing of cultural experiences within a classroom containing a variety of ethnic groups'. The National Council for Accreditation of Teacher Education in the USA has defined multicultural education in the following terms as,

> preparation for social, political and economic realities which individuals experience in human encounters which are culturally diverse and complex. This preparation provides the process by means of which an individual develops the competence to perceive, believe, and behave in situations which are culturally different. (Banks, 1981, cited in Muñoz, 1995: 229)[4]

This definition is interesting, as it does not restrict multicultural education to the relationships between minority groups and mainstream culture. Furthermore, it widens the sphere of multiculturalism to include social, political and economic realities and not only what are usually referred to as cultural practices.

Muñoz (1995: 229–30) contrasts the use of the prefix 'multi' or 'pluri' cultural, referring to the existence of various cultures in one society, with the use of the prefix 'inter', which he claims indicates 'a relation between various different elements . . . a reciprocity . . . and at the same time, a separation'. He thus considers intercultural education a more dynamic concept than multicultural education, a term which he considers is more popular with Anglo-Saxon researchers. He proposes that intercultural education may be defined as, 'the education of human beings in the knowledge, understanding and respect for the different cultures in which they live . . . (involving) reciprocity of perspectives'.

Teaching and learning intercultural communicative competence

While ethnic minority groups have had a long tradition of association with the notion of intercultural education (CCELA, 1989; Bratt Paulston, 1992; Baker, 1993), the concept has only fairly recently been discussed in relation to foreign language teaching and learning (see work by Kramsch, 1991; Kramsch *et al.*, 1996; and Byram, 1997).

Kramsch *et al.* (1996) in a study of language and culture in the United States and in France maintain that often language teachers are reluctant to go beyond language training, either because as non-natives they do not know enough about the target culture, or because as natives, they are unaware of what their students do not know. In their analysis of the situation in the United States, these authors note, 'frequent confusion about the notion of culture among US American youth' (Kramsch *et al.* 1996: 101) and maintain that, 'In the United States, culture has traditionally been viewed not in national terms, . . . but mostly as the characteristic of non-White, non-Anglo or non-English-speaking Americans'. They characterise the United States' viewpoint on the learning of foreign languages and the 'exotic' cultures of those who speak them as 'orientalist' and in a potentially controversial conclusion maintain that even though most US foreign language teachers would probably deny it, 'any relativisation of language and culture by foreign language educators would be seen as a threat to American education' (Kramsch *et al.*, 1996: 101).

In the case of France, while the teaching of culture in foreign language classes has never been completely absent from French state educational guidelines, it has only recently been officially recognised. In 1987, cultural enrichment (*'enrichissement culturel'*) was explicitly proclaimed as one of the three main aims of foreign language teaching at secondary school level. Kramsch *et al.* (1996: 102) give four main reasons to explain this late legitimisation of culture in language programmes.

First of all, the authors maintain that there is public prejudice and a general ethnocentrism, which is revealed in the widespread belief that language learning is easy and culturally unproblematic, if foreign languages are learnt early in life. A focus on the teaching of cultural aspects is usually viewed as, 'an expendable luxury'. Secondly, as foreign language teaching and learning is a mass enterprise with large classes and few curriculum hours, it is considered more worthwhile to teach linguistic 'facts' which are easily testable, rather than elements of culture, 'which require more interpretation'.

Another reason given for resistance to the teaching of cultural aspects in the French educational system are ingrained conceptions of disciplinary boundaries, and language teachers' fears of trespassing on colleagues' academic territories if they start including culture within their programmes. In addition, many French teachers are afraid that any reference to cultural matters in their teaching may lead to cultural conflict and ideological dissent in language classes.

However, in spite of these difficulties, which are in themselves cultural in origin, Byram (1997: 21) maintains that it is important for foreign language learners to prepare for 'inter-national interactions' by focusing on a critical and comparative methodology towards different cultural practices and beliefs. In this way, the researcher maintains that students will be helped to develop attitudes which reflect curiosity and openness to other cultures, a willingness to question accepted cultural values, and an awareness of factors which may lead to misunderstandings among interlocutors from different cultural backgrounds. He thus proposes the concept of 'intercultural speaker' to describe 'interlocutors involved in intercultural communication and interaction' (Byram, 1997: 32), and maintains that we should consider language learning, not only in terms of linguistic, sociolinguistic and discourse competence, but also in relation to intercultural competence.

Byram (1997) suggests that there are three main scenarios where intercultural competence may be acquired: in the classroom, in the pedagogically orientated experience outside the classroom, and in independent experience. Thus, it can be seen that these three scenarios constitute an outward looking, gradualist approach to the gaining of intercultural competence, where pedagogical guidance is progressively reduced so that students can finally confront the challenges of direct experience of intercultural communication with speakers from different cultural backgrounds.

In order to construct an appropriate curriculum for the planned development of intercultural communicative competence, the same author suggests six main stages of analysis and decision making. These involve the analysis of the geo-political context; the learning context; the development factor, both cognitive and affective; the identification of objectives; the determination of an intercultural communicative competence threshold or goal for the learners involved; and the sequencing and prioritisation of the identified objectives in the curriculum. If this type of process is followed, there is a greater probability that intercultural curricula will be appropriate for the needs of students in particular cultural contexts.

Finally, Byram (1997: 111) warns against the danger of an over-simplification of competences to what can be 'objectively' tested, as this may result in the trivialisation and 'the reduction of subtle understanding to generalisations and stereotypes' which have negative effects on the process of teaching and learning.

Culture and Business

Another area of life which is becoming increasingly internationalised today is business. The global marketplace is a literal as well as a linguistic reality and many companies and consultants are responding to the need to train selected employees, usually senior executives, in cross-cultural practices. Take for instance the following advertisement from JM Perry Corporation of Palo Alto, California which sells cross-cultural training to North American companies in terms of better performance management, higher quality and better customer service:

Text Box 3.5   JM Perry Corporation Helps You Meet the Challenge and Opportunity of Workplace Cultures

The Challenge
The American workplace is changing. More global companies are competing. Employees are now from all over the world. Today's organization must learn to utilize the knowledge and potential of their diverse populations to compete and succeed.

The Solution
Turn to JM Perry. Our training and consulting services are practical and targeted to your bottom line. We teach you how to:

- *Sustain your competitive advantage in an era of increased customer and market diversity*
- *Develop and refine skills, techniques and action plans for selling across cultures*
- *Find, hire and manage people from varied cultures internationally and within your organization*
- *Implement company policies and practices that recognize, value and profit from workforce and market diversity*
- *Establish successful international partnerships and alliances with suppliers and clients*
- *Effectively manage international projects and multicultural project teams*

The Bottom Line
By providing training that is focused, we are able to deliver impact and results immediately. You will see:

- *More effective communication*
- *Increased productivity from your workforce*
- *A higher level of job satisfaction – and even survival – requires innovative, global strategies in all areas of operation. JM Perry will help you leverage the benefits of cultural diversity.*

Our customised training program gets results !

Difficulties of cross-cultural communication are thus presented as a challenge, and an appreciation of the relativity of cultural practices is seen as an opportunity for successful business enterprises in multinational companies. Linguistic diversity and multiculturalism are recognised as advantages in today's business ethos rather than as threats to company or national loyalty, if this type of advertising is to be believed. However, the fact that this needs marketing also implies that it is not perhaps standard practice in much of the business world yet.

The elite group of senior management, to whom such advertisements are addressed, recognise that foreign language proficiency is not enough to conclude successful business deals. As one publication explains,

> While an Englishman's primary focus may be to conclude the business at hand, a Hong Kong Chinese will concentrate on first developing a personal relationship. Public praise is much enjoyed by North Americans, but it is a source of embarrassment for Japanese. Failure to recognize these inherent differences

will result in misconceptions and inappropriate responses that can doom a business relationship. (Engel & Murakami, 1996: 7)

There is now an increasing market for seminars and publications that can help to transcend these barriers; see for example, 'Getting Through Customs – training for international travelers' , and 'Intercultural Press' both available on internet. I will now briefly compare some of the information given in two publications in the Passport series, Passport USA and Passport Japan, published by World Trade Press, in order to provide evidence of the type of concerns which are seen as leading to cross-cultural difficulties, and the type of advice which is given to solve these problems.

According to the introductory information, this series is designed to provide 'detailed information about a country's business practices, negotiating style, etiquette, government, work environment, social mores, view of foreigners', etc. (Engel & Murakami, 1996: 96) and covers mainly countries in South East Asia: Hong Kong, Indonesia, Thailand, etc. as well as some European, African and American nations.

In both publications there are parallel sections on how nationals of each country see themselves and what business strategies are recommended to achieve success. We will begin by examining the self-images given of people in USA and people in Japan.

USA

Americans truly believe that the US is the best place on earth. If it wasn't, the thinking goes, why would everybody else be trying to get there? Why is it that everyone from Thailand to Iceland is hungry for 'American popular culture'? Americans see themselves as ambitious, hardworking, innovative and energetic. As evidence of this they will proudly point to their standard of living and America's pre-eminent role in world affairs. Democracy is equated with both freedom and a free-market economy. For better or worse, American foreign policy can largely be explained in terms of this belief.

Other basic assumptions are that individuals can control their circumstances (where they live, what their profession will be) and therefore their destinies; that competition (among individuals and groups is the basis for improvement and growth; that privacy is a guaranteed 'right' and that the laws and the actions of government officials, business enterprises or private persons can be openly criticized (hence their reputation for being litigious).

Americans place high value on what they call 'individual freedom' and they look with suspicion on authority ... Americans see themselves first as individuals, and only secondarily as members of a family, community, religion or organization. Children are encouraged to think for themselves and to strike out on their own (leave the nest) as soon as they're able. Students routinely choose a college or university far from home, and even those attending a college in their hometown prefer to live in school housing or in an apartment, as living with one's parents is considered an embarrassment. (Engel, 1996: 17–18)

According to this vision, by a North American author, the undoubted reputation of the USA for material success and its status as a world power has led to a tendency towards cultural arrogance in its dealings with the rest of the world, and a consequent difficulty of appreciating cultural beliefs and practices which run counter to this experience. Respect for individual rights and privacy may give the impression of a lack of solidarity and community concern, and a disrespect for authority. Accountability is valued in terms of responsibility for one's own actions. Ironically, these views are almost diametrically opposed to those of one of the US's closest trading partners, the Japanese, as evidenced in the following passage:

Japan

The Japanese see themselves as a people who are concerned about others, and whose business decisions take into account the personal needs of their associates and employees.

Harmony always takes precedence over individual desires. Accordingly, the Japanese value the ability to maintain an outward appearance of peace and unity even when the actual situation has neither. They rarely break ranks, and they certainly never do so with foreigners . . .

Japan's feudal era left an indelible mark on the culture; since then, Japanese identity, honor and, in some ways, survival have depended on membership in (and protection by) the local groups to which people belong. Today, the Japanese see themselves in terms of family, village, religion, university, company, ethnicity, etc.

They associate being part of (and dependent on) a group as a sign of maturity. Without a group affiliation, a Japanese feels very vulnerable and is likely to have difficulty fitting in. *Ippiki ookami* (lone wolves) are considered selfish and untrustworthy . . .

Group behavior is reinforced both in the classroom and in society. And while college students do receive some freedom, the dual institutions of company and marriage usually squash out most remaining individualism . . . It's been noted that today's adolescent Japanese act more independently than their parents; but it's also true that many of them choose to express their individuality in groups.

One's place within the group is also extremely important. Rarely do individuals approach a relationship as equals. If one is older (and, therefore, the authority figure) or more prominent in the business hierarchy, or of a higher educational or social status, he is treated with the respect due to such a position regardless of his talents or abilities . . .

The practice of subordination to group needs, combined with the extreme population density, has resulted in an absence of individual privacy. In fact, the language has no word for privacy. (Engel & Murakami, 1996: 15–18)

As can be seen in comparing these two self-images, there are fundamental differences revealed in such questions as: public and private lives, group and individual behaviour, authority and equality, and harmony and criticism. Such wide discrepancies make negotiating and consensus reaching more difficult than when groups have cultural expectations which are more similar. However, the fact that the USA and Japan have managed to work efficiently together in economic matters for the last half century points to the success of cross-cultural communication in business negotiations.

The type of advice given in these two publications to improve the chances of success in cross-cultural business negotiations includes the following recommendations:

USA

- Never let them see you sweat.
- Get it in writing.
- Issues, not positions.
- Win-win.

Japan

- Formality versus small talk.
- Opening protocol.
- Use of interpreters.
- Use of long pauses and silences.

These maxims refer to the different negotiating styles and tactics typically favoured by the two nations. The USA style advocates never revealing doubts about the position adopted or about the chances of winning; restating of agreements, preferably in writing, to ensure that both negotiating teams interpret things in the same way; separating personalities from fundamental points; and achieving deals which are advantageous for both sides.

Japanese tactics involve entering the meeting room and being seated in strict order of seniority and engaging in formal, polite conversation before negotiating begins; the delivering of initial speeches by the heads of both delegations; using interpreters to gain time for thinking; and using pauses and silences which sometimes disconcert foreigners.

While these recommendations reveal some points of contact, such as concealing individual doubts or differences with the common position, there is wide variation relating to issues of protocol based on seniority and the understanding of the time needed to conclude a successful deal.

The need for understanding of differing cultural and business practices is increasingly evident. If we take the example of trade between USA and Japan, we can see that although the USA has long been an exporter of mass culture, as seen in the presence of North American films, soap operas and satellite TV in such diverse parts of the world as Morocco, Colombia and the Philippines, Japan is not far behind. According to a report in *The Japan Times* (30 July 1998), after sushi, karaoke and Nintendo games, the latest Japanese mass cultural export is 'anime' or animated cartoon films.

The popularity of these films in USA has been put down to several factors. Firstly, they appeal to a wide age range, university students as well as small children. Secondly, there are a large number of female heroes, such as 'Sailor Moon', 'Nausicaa', 'Kiki', 'Otonashi' and 'Princess Mononoke', and these attract female viewers. Furthermore, high picture quality and a variety of storylines have made these films very popular with North American audiences in general. An interesting consideration is whether the original Japanese soundtracks, used together with English subtitles, will lead to a future increase in the number of Japanese loanwords in American English.

The negative consequences of business culture clashes have been reported recently in *The Washington Post/Guardian Weekly* (21 February 1999: 17). According to its correspondent in Tokyo, the defining characteristic of the Japanese economic system, protecting jobs, is now being undercut by global economic forces. Japanese employers, who traditionally think of their employees as friends, have been trying to introduce employment changes gradually, whereas 'American firms swooping in to take over such distressed firms often have no such patience or inclination', causing shock and distress among Japanese employees.

Bearing all this in mind, it is useful to reflect on the words of Sir Peter Parker, chairman of the UK National Languages for Export Campaign (Baker & Prys Jones, 1998: 261), who summed up the importance of cultural aspects in international communication in the following way,

> Communicating across cultural barriers means entering the mind set, and even the heart, of other peoples – understanding their language, not only in a narrow sense of the language of the mind, but what makes them tick, how and why they react.

Conclusion

In this chapter we have examined a range of issues concerned with the sociocultural aspects of elite bilingualism. After discussing different terminological distinctions, we have concentrated on three key areas where intercultural or cross-cultural understandings are becoming increasingly important: the areas of marriage, education, and business.

In the section on marriage, we have seen how different families react to the stresses caused by intercultural contact in family and school relationships. We have seen how stereotyped images of national characteristics are not appropriate to describe the complex, multiple, constantly shifting identities displayed by people brought up in multilingual and multicultural contexts. We have also noted the additional considerations that may have an influence on marriages which are not only intercultural but also interfaith, as in the case of Christian and Muslim partners.

In relation to education, we have seen how the concept of intercultural education is relatively new to foreign and second language teaching and learning in majority contexts. Thus, while foreign or second language tuition is generally seen as important, cultural considerations are often not recognised as classroom concerns, although there is a recent movement to redress the balance in this respect.

Finally, in the sphere of cross-cultural business relationships, we have examined the positions adopted by certain consultants and writers in helping to bridge cultural differences for the purpose of facilitating international trade.

However, a basic tension remains unanswered, which may be phrased in the following fashion: how far do the type of generalisations used in the construction of national self-images and typical ways of behaving and interpreting experience run the risk of leading to reductionism and trivialisation, as noted by Byram (1997)? We may question whether the type of national portraits supplied to travellers, foreign language students, prospective business people, etc. while undoubtedly useful on a short-term, instrumental basis, are an adequate representation of the complexity of the multicultural realities they purport to describe. We may also wonder about the possible long-term effects of simplifying and condensing complex realities into the equivalent of cultural phrasebook terms.

Notes

1. In other words, 'Continental Europe'.
2. Jane Griffiths grew up in Britain. She has studied and worked in France and Germany, and now lives in Morocco. She is a qualified translator with a keen interest in issues relating to family multilingualism and multiculturalism. She has contributed articles to *The Bilingual Family Newsletter* published by Multilingual Matters.
3. Popular term in Colombia and in other Latin American countries used to refer to US nationals, but also applied by extension to any foreigner.
4. Author's translation.

Chapter 4
Teaching and Learning in Elite Bilingual Classrooms

Introduction

Having considered aspects of elite bilingualism in relation to sociocultural issues, we will now turn to focus on aspects of classroom policy and practice characteristic of elite bilingual education programmes. We will begin by examining some general issues which characterise the debate in this area, such as: classroom language use; the relationship between content and language; and cultural considerations.

Interest in classroom language use has evolved from an initial focus on quantitative aspects, where attempts were made to establish the relative percentages of the use of the two languages in bilingual classroom interaction towards a more qualitative perspective which foregrounds the type of interaction involved and its relation to language choice. In this chapter we will document the reasons for these changes and how practices such as classroom code-switching need to be seen as a resource within the teaching and learning process rather than aberrant linguistic behaviour. We will also examine the development of the debate about the importance of comprehensible input and output in relation to a recognition of the need to develop closer relationships between an experiential approach (or a focus on content teaching and learning in two languages) and an analytic or linguistic-based focus (see Chapter 1).

In the section on content and language we begin by examining content teaching and learning as an instance of communicative-based foreign language programmes, where the demands of the subject area will determine the selection and sequencing of the curriculum rather than the language items to be taught. We will also examine different bilingual classroom methodologies which try to incorporate both subject area concerns and aspects of bilingual development within a coherent pedagogical framework for both teaching and evaluation of learning.

In our discussion of cultural considerations we will focus on the need to include the development of 'cultural competence' within elite bilingual education programmes and the importance of creating bicultural or intercultural policies at institutional level which will help to orientate individual pedagogic practices.

In the second part of the chapter, we will look in more depth at issues of teaching and learning in bilingual classrooms from two different, yet complementary perspectives: in relation to pre-school/primary level provision in elite schools in Colombia, South America; and with reference to Anglo-Chinese secondary schools in Hong Kong.

As those who have taught in bilingual programmes know, teaching and learning in two or more languages is very different to teaching and learning in only one. For one thing, the learner's languages are not confined to being considered subjects in the curriculum, but instead are used as media of instruction in curricular processes. In Britain, in a mainstream context, this type of approach is often referred to as 'language across the curriculum' and involves the use of first language instruction in all subject domains. In a bilingual context, both languages are used to construct knowledge. In some programmes, this is achieved by assigning different subject areas to different languages, so that Maths, Science and Economics may be taught in the foreign or second language, while the first language is used in the teaching of Social Studies, Physical Education and Ethics. In other types of bilingual programme, both languages may be used in the teaching of all subject areas, as in an alternate day approach, where different languages are used on different days of the week or at different times of the day. In all these situations, the relationship between language learning and content area teaching is brought to the fore.

Classroom Language Use

In her reviews of the development of research on bilingual classroom interaction, Marilyn Martin-Jones (1995, 2000) shows how, in the latter half of the 1970s, there was great interest in North American bilingual education programmes on examining the amount of time devoted to the use of the learners' two languages. Comparisons were made between those programmes which adopted a language 'separation' approach, i.e. where different languages were used on different days, or at different times in the day, or for different subject areas, and those where the two languages were used 'concurrently' by means of classroom code-switching on the part of both teachers and learners.

In the area of immersion education, this debate has been resolved traditionally, by advocating a separation rather than a concurrent approach. Merrill Swain (1983), one of the researchers who has been associated most closely with work in this area, has defended this position by postulating the principle of 'Bilingualism through Monolingualism', censuring the use of code-switching in the following terms, 'The mixing of languages that exists in most Hong Kong secondary schools serves neither the goal of academic achievement nor second language learning to maximum effectiveness' (Swain, 1986: 6, cited in Lin, 1996: 75).

Swain (1983) gives four reasons for her support of a separation approach. Firstly, she argues that if both languages are used to transmit the same content, there is no motivation for the students to make the effort to understand what is being communicated in the foreign language. Furthermore, she considers that a separation approach implies a greater effort on the part of both teachers and students to communicate effectively in the classroom. The third reason given is that a separation approach is more effective as, although it draws on the creative resources of the teachers to make themselves understood in the foreign language, it makes less demand on their linguistic resources, not forcing them to switch back and forth between languages, as in the process of simultaneous interpretation. Finally Swain (1983) argues that a separation approach ensures that an equal amount of time will be dedicated to the use of the two languages in the classroom, whereas a concurrent approach cannot guarantee that this will be so.

However, this position, based on educationally oriented work, has been questioned by researchers working in a sociolinguistic tradition. Heller (1990), Lin (1996) and de Mejía (1999) have argued that the direct application of *general* educational and linguistic principles to decisions involving classroom language use, without taking into account key aspects of the sociocultural, economic and political context of implementation, is insufficient to ensure an appropriate language development in specific bilingual classrooms. As Heller (1990: 81) succinctly explains in her discussion of the feasibility of considering immersion programmes in Canada as a model for Switzerland,

> My sense is that one can borrow from Canadian pedagogical models only in the broadest sense, since what is likely to work, and to be acceptable, is less a question of universals of language learning and more a question of the locally-defined social significance of language use and the socially and culturally constructed speech economy of a region.

An example of the above, as we have seen in our discussion about different modalities of elite bilingual provision in Chapter 1, is that the amount of reinforcement of the different languages in the immediate environment varies according to the different circumstances. Thus, an immersion type programme in Canada or USA may require a higher level of foreign or second language input than a European Schools programme in Belgium or Germany, where there is likely to be a much higher degree of language reinforcement in the immediate context. In these cases, a general recommendation of a 50% balance between the two languages may be inappropriate.

Furthermore, classroom-based research carried out in different educational contexts (Lin, 1990; Cambra Giné, 1991; de Mejía, 1994) has indicated that natural classroom code-switching[1] is quite different in essence to simultaneous interpretation, in that although there is evidence of some direct translation, much of the code-switching analysed relates to different classroom functions, such as explanations, paraphrases or reformulations, as well as the introduction of different 'voices' within the classroom arena. Thus, bilingual classroom discourse is 'much richer and wider than most teachers imagine' (Cambra Giné, 1991: 136). These researchers, therefore, argue against the banning of classroom code-switching in elite bilingual programmes, especially in the initial stages of second or foreign language learning, considering that the use of both the participants' languages as valuable resources in the teaching and learning process, along with other facilitating strategies, such as gestures, mime, and changes in intonation and stress.

Another key issue associated with discussions of language use in elite immersion programmes is the question of language input, or the type of language, either spoken or written, that the learner is exposed to, and language output, or the type of language that s/he actually produces. Lindholm (1990) characterises optimal input as having four characteristics: it is adjusted to the comprehension level of the learner; it is interesting and relevant; there is sufficient quantity; it is challenging. Thus, it can be seen that this is in line with the notion of 'comprehensible input' (Krashen & Terrell, 1983), in the sense of input that is a little beyond the current level of acquired competence of the learner, as a necessary factor in successful second or foreign language acquisition.

This obviously requires those who work in bilingual programmes to constantly monitor what they say or write, in relation to the developing language competence of the learners and to modify their own language use accordingly. The natural redundancy characteristic of classroom discourse in any situation, shown in the amount of repetition, reformulation and re-elaboration carried out by most teachers, takes on a special significance in bilingual contexts. Teacher re-elaborations and reformulations, in the second or foreign language, of students' contributions given in their first language serve the dual purpose of recognising and accepting student contributions to the interaction, while providing comprehensible input which is relevant and interesting to the learner as it relates directly to what he or she wants to express but is unable to formulate adequately.

As regards the development of output, as has been noted in Chapter 1, children in total immersion programmes generally approach native-speaker level in their receptive skills after five to six years but their productive proficiency is normally considerably below that of native speakers. This finding led to Swain's postulation of the output hypothesis which claims that students need to be provided with opportunities to produce discourse which is coherent, accurate, and socio-linguistically appropriate and thus to 'extend(s) the repertoire of the learner' (Swain, 1985: 252) so as to avoid the 'plateau' effect which prevents further progress in productive proficiency. Much of student output in bilingual programmes is restricted to one word answers or short responses framed by teacher initiations and feedback and this, therefore, does not help learners to extend their productive capacity.

Classroom strategies reportedly used to encourage student output range from teachers asking questions requiring more complex answers; waiting for student responses rather than supplying them quickly; asking for repetition; and involving students as peer teachers (Salomone, 1992).

A further strategy used to promote appropriate and coherent language production in immersion education is the provision of language arts instruction in *both* languages used in the classroom. As noted in Chapter 1, this was not a priority in the original immersion programmes, as it was assumed that if students received the type of language exposure similar to first language learning though content-based instruction, they would automatically develop native-like proficiency in their use of the second or foreign language. However, as a result of the evaluations of the early programmes, a closer relationship between content subject matter (an experiential focus) and linguistic skills (an analytical focus) was recommended. This means, for example, that the study of conditional verb forms might be based on mathematical subject matter and the use of the passive voice might be associated with the study of scientific texts, rather in the tradition of an English for Specific Purposes (ESP) approach. In this way, an explicit concern with linguistic skills in both languages complements student experience of language use in different content areas and helps to improve the quality of student output, particularly in the second or foreign language.

However, an important, but understudied issue is at stake here, concerning the status of classroom instruction in language learning. It has been suggested (Heller, 1990) that, in fact, it may not be possible to completely solve the 'plateau' effect noted in immersion programmes solely by means of pedagogic remedies. If students do not have the opportunity, or are not motivated to interact with speakers of the languages used in the school context, classroom strategies may have limited success in expanding students' overall productive capacity.

Relationship Between Content and Language

The relationship between academic content and language is fundamental to the concept of bilingual education in both majority and minority linguistic situations, as has been discussed in Chapter 2. Fishman (1976a, cited in Garcia, 1991: 7) recognised this many years ago when he observed,

> There is simply no way in which language teaching which focuses on language as a *target of instruction* can fully capture the total impact upon the learner which is available to language teaching which also capitalises upon language as the *process of instruction*.

More recently, Heller (1990: 73), has summarised this idea in relation to immersion programmes,

> The basic idea underlying immersion, a notion borrowed from communicative language learning theory, is that by using the target language as a language of communication in authentic situations, such as subject-matter instruction or any other form of teacher-student or student-student communication outside strictly instructional contexts, students' acquisition of the target language will be improved.

Thus, we can see that content instruction is seen as an example of a wider approach, that of language as communication and use in authentic, contextualised situations, where the attention of the learner is focused on meaning rather than on form. This notion can be linked to concepts such as task-based learning and activity-based syllabuses characteristic of many English Language Teaching programmes, where the emphasis is not directly on language learning *per se*, but rather, language learning results from carrying out tasks or doing activities which have been designed to promote language acquisition.

The materials used in these situations are 'authentic', in the sense that they have been created for a purpose other than language teaching. This means that the content matter in the area of Science or Maths, for example, will dictate the selection and sequence of language items to be taught and learnt, and not the other way round. Thus, content is used as the 'point of departure' (Brinton *et al.* 1989: 2) and teachers will usually be involved in modifying and adapting materials designed for teaching mathematical and scientific concepts for native speakers to the language demands of second or foreign language learners.

In an International School situation, where students often come from many different language, cultural and educational backgrounds, it is important to recognise both individual and national group differences in relation to achievement in different subject areas in the curriculum. In this respect, Sears (1998) has identified four different groups of students in International Schools who show markedly different characteristics in their mathematical formation.

A first group come from certain East Asian and European countries with a strong mathematical tradition. These students have a good background in computation, problem solving and mathematical process. Thus, they are able to use this to redress their weak English language skills and usually progress rapidly. A second group, mainly from the Indian subcontinent, have a history of numerical computation, but are not as skilled in problem solving or expressing mathematical principles through practical activities. Because of different cultural and educational expectations, many of these students' parents are concerned that the type of mathematical programme used in International Schools will not prepare their children for competitive entry into the national school system on return to the home country. The students themselves may question the relevance of what they are asked to do in their Maths lessons in an international context and need help in understanding the reasons for the differences they notice in relation to the type of teaching they have been accustomed to.

A third group may be behind in mathematical development because their home school system begins at a later age than International School programmes and they therefore have certain gaps in their learning. A final group show weaknesses in mathematical understanding. This means that the use of a foreign or second language as a medium of instruction in this area is an additional barrier to learning the meaning of mathematics. Both these last two groups may require intensive additional tuition in the structuring of mathematical concepts. Some of the worries expressed by parents of bilingual children in relation to their learning of mathematics are expressed in Text Box 4.1.

Text Box 4.1:   Bilingualism and Mathematics (taken from Bourjade, 2001: 6)

Do bilinguals manage to do mental arithmetic in both languages or only in the dominant language?

We moved back to France six months ago and although my children aged 8½ and 6 years old already spoke good French the majority of maths they have done has been in English. Both children know their number bonds in English and my eldest child has learnt her tables in English. Will there come a time when they will do mental arithmetic in French and if so how long will it take?

A concern with concept development in bilingual education programmes led to the creation of a bilingual classroom methodology called 'Preview-Review' which postulates an interactive yet sequential relationship between the learner's two languages to ensure optimal cognitive and linguistic development. In this three-phase, team-teaching approach, the introduction to the main concepts to be developed in the class is carried out by one of the instructors in the students' first language. Then, the second instructor develops and extends these concepts through activities carried out in the second or foreign language, without repeating what has been taught in the first phase. Finally, there is a phase of review and reinforcement of the class which may be carried out in either language, according to the aims of the class.

This methodology, which was created as part of a 'dual-language model' by González and Lezama (1976, cited in Ovando & Collier, 1987) in the USA, was evaluated in an elite bilingual context in Latin America in 1995. In a study carried out in Colombia related to the teaching of Mathematics with Fourth Year Primary School students (Marulanda, 1995), this methodology was found to be particularly effective with students who had difficulties with English (the foreign language). They reported that it was much easier for them to understand the mathematical concepts being introduced in a preview-review mode, than when the class was conducted wholly in the foreign language, as in previous years with the same teacher, and their course evaluation marks confirmed this appreciation.

Furthermore, according to parent feedback, this approach allowed many monolingual (Spanish-speaking) parents to share more easily in their children's achievements, as the students were able to refer to mathematical terms in both languages, and not just in English, as had previously been the case. This was felt to be especially important in the case of Mathematics, considering its traditional status in the school curriculum as one of the prime indicators of student success.

A team teaching approach is particularly relevant in a bilingual education programme which sees language learning and enrichment, and mastery of content knowledge as intrinsically interrelated. Language is a vehicle for the construction of knowledge in specific subject areas and, at the same time, content area teaching is a means of acquiring a high level of linguistic proficiency in two or more languages. This dual relationship has implications in the concerns of teachers who work in such programmes. They need to pay attention to aspects of language development in their students as well as their progress in learning of course content. In a team teaching approach, each of these aspects may be focused on at different times by the subject specialist and by the language specialist who can thus work together towards a common goal.

This dual relationship of language and content is also salient in the area of evaluation, where it is important to ensure that both language development and content development are adequately assessed on an ongoing basis. Some of the key considerations in this area are: (1) the selection of appropriate content matter in relation to the cultural and general background of the students in the design of tasks to assess language skills; (2) the adjustment of language demands in the evaluation of content knowledge, according to the present level of student linguistic proficiency; (3) the modification of scoring criteria depending whether the objective of the evaluation is primarily to assess content development, language development, or both; and (4) informed expectations as to the rate of acquisition of measurable language gains in specific skill areas (Brinton *et al.*, 1989).

All these factors affect the type of testing carried out in bilingual education programmes and have repercussions on the levels of achievement reported. Thus, for instance, if the subject matter used in an evaluation is familiar to the students, or if they know about the cultural conventions used for dealing with this type of topic, they will be more likely to be successful. In this respect, Peter Martin (1996) has shown, in a Bruneian context (see Chapter 9) how student difficulties in understanding the concept of 'plague' in Fourth Year Primary Science classes, conducted in general though the medium of English, compelled the teacher to explain and clarify this concept, by making an analogy with a prohibition of the Bruneian government to allow people from India to enter the country because of plague in India, as they had no other experience of this notion. Thus, we can see that if students in Brunei are forced to demonstrate their knowledge of English through a test based on the topic of 'plague', they are unlikely to do as well as they might do with more familiar subject matter.

The question of which language, which languages or which level of language should be used to evaluate content knowledge is also important. If this is not taken into account there is a danger that inadequate student language skills may hide the true extent of their content knowledge. Some ways in which this has been put into practice in different bilingual programmes in North America are: to use short-answers, less verbally demanding quizzes, rather than full length essays; to give examinations of content knowledge in the students' first language; to use a variety of tasks, such as related practice examples, guided library research, and production of drafts, for student evaluation rather than just one kind of task (Brinton *et al.*, 1989).

As indicated above, it should be made clear to the students whether a particular evaluation is content or language orientated and what criteria are to be used in the scoring procedures. This is not to say that both areas cannot be evaluated through the same material for different aims. Thus, a text on the water cycle can be used both for assessing understanding of key scientific concepts, such as evaporation and condensation, as well as the students' ability to recognise and identify examples of the passive voice.

Finally, the question of informed expectations of the rate of language acquisition in a given skill area depends greatly on previous experience in a particular area with particular groups of students, rather than on any generally accepted rates of progress. There are, however, certain very basic observations that indicate, for instance, that new topic-related vocabulary is learnt more quickly than, say, the use of discourse connectives, such as 'as a result', 'provided that' and 'bearing in mind the above'.

Cultural Considerations

The importance of cultural considerations in relation to elite bilingual education programmes has already been referred to earlier in this book (see Chapters 1 and 3). However, in the context of this discussion of teaching and learning it is important to focus on certain key aspects which influence classroom processes and which have a bearing on the results and rhythms of bilingual programmes in different parts of the world.

This is an area which, up to now, has been under-researched in elite contexts. Most of the work relating to discussions of biculturalism, interculturalism or multiculturalism is based on bilingual educational programmes for minority groups (CCELA, 1989; Paulston, 1992; Baker, 1993). However, the complexities and contradictions involved in the construction of identities, group loyalties and a sense of belonging to particular cultural traditions are also evident, though frequently unrecognised explicitly, in elite bilingual situations.

Skutnabb-Kangas (1987), in her discussion of cultural competence in bilingual development, postulates four components which she considers essential in this respect: knowledge, feelings, behaviour and metacultural awareness. Knowledge involves the transmission of information about language, history, traditions and institutions which are characteristic of different cultural groups. Feelings refer to attitudes towards and identification with certain cultures. Behaviour involves the capacity to act in culturally appropriate ways, while the notion of metacultural awareness refers to an understanding of the distinctiveness of different cultural groups. These four components attempt to identify the different facets involved in the development of cultural sensitivity, which is not only a matter of cognition but also involves key aspects of personal development, such as affect, understanding and the ability to act with tolerance and respect for cultural difference.

The first component, knowledge, is perhaps the easiest to identify in bilingual educational programmes. This is present in such events as cultural evenings, projects involving traditional festivals, ways of dressing, cooking, etc. However, this type of event may be in danger of celebrating the merely surface features of cultural difference, rather than considering the deeper sociocultural roots. This may, in turn, lead to the 'trivializations of biculturalism' which Fishman (1977, cited in García, 1991: 12) accused many bilingual programmes in the USA of promoting, by limiting their cultural coverage to 'show and tell' items or 'song and dance' routines. Through these type of activities, bilingual schools may feel that they are promoting a highly evident intercultural perspective among their students, while, in reality, they may be limiting their learners' ability to develop deeper affective, behavioural and metacultural awareness.

This difficulty in contributing effectively to the development of cross-cultural awareness can be seen in the Canadian immersion experience. One of the original goals of this education innovation was to improve anglophone attitudes towards their francophone neighbours. However, the early programmes led to no noticeable changes in this respect (Lambert & Tucker, 1972) and this aim was later dropped from the immersion agenda. Thus, today, immersion is mainly known for its educational and linguistic impact, rather than for its social or cultural consequences.

Nevertheless, whether they recognise it or not, all bilingual institutions have to contend with issues arising from the fact of their contact with two or more cultures in their day-to-day existence. In a study carried out in an elite bilingual context in Colombia, Hilda Buitrago (1997) set out to examine some of these key aspects, particularly focusing on how the issue of biculturalism was implemented both in institutional policy statements and in primary school classroom practices in one English–Spanish bilingual programme in the city of Cali.

She found that the school policy documents she analysed made no mention of the relative position and status of the cultures of the two nations involved, the United States and Colombia. This lack of policy direction was reflected in teacher classroom practices, which showed a high degree of improvisation and confusion as to whether the teachers should be focusing on key aspects of North American culture, or whether it was necessary and/or important to strengthen the students' awareness of their national heritage, especially in the area of Social Studies. An example of this confusion can be seen in the differing treatment accorded to North American and Colombian festivities in the school. Occasions like 'Thanksgiving', an eminently North American festival, were celebrated more elaborately than Colombian national days. The implicit message thus conveyed to the students, the vast majority of whom came from monolingual and monocultural Colombian families, was that US festivals were more important than their Colombian counterparts.

The researcher came to the conclusion that in a context such as Colombia, where English is a foreign language and access to cultural imput from the United States and Britain is restricted, it is impossible to implement a bicultural programme in the sense mentioned by Grosjean (1993: 31–2) which involves participation 'at least in part in the life of two cultures on a regular basis'. Instead, she recommended a position of interculturalism which would involve getting to know other cultural manifestations in order to enrich a sense of one's own reality and identity.

The importance of this study is that it shows that institutional bilingual policies which are limited to linguistic elements are insufficient. The processes of cultural construction and reproduction present in bilingual educational processes affect multiple aspects of the educational and affective development of the students concerned. It is, therefore, imperative that both administrators and teachers in elite bilingual programmes collaborate in developing clear and well-thought-out cultural policies which will help to guide both institutional decisions and individual practices.

Particular Instances

Teaching and learning in immersion type programmes at pre-school level in Colombia

Introduction

In this section we will look more closely at examples of classroom interaction in two pre-school immersion-type English–Spanish bilingual programmes in Cali, Colombia (Latin America) in order to illustrate how teachers and learners construct and negotiate meanings moment by moment in two languages, one of which (English) is not used as a means of communication in Colombian society. In order to contextualise what is said here, the reader is recommended to refer to the discussion of aspects of bilingual education provision in Colombia in Chapter 8.

The examples discussed in this section come from a wider unpublished ethnographic study (de Mejía, 1994) carried out over a period of five years (1989–1994) in which I examined aspects of bilingual classroom interaction in two types of classroom events: story-telling and the teaching and learning of vocabulary items in English. For reasons of space, the examples discussed here come from the story-telling events only (for further reference see de Mejía, 1998). I will begin by acquainting the reader briefly with key aspects of the institutional context.

The institutional context

In Colombia, there are an increasing number of private English-Spanish bilingual schools of the immersion type which cater for a mainly middle-class and upper-middle-class population who are anxious to send their children abroad to the United States or Europe to complete their tertiary education. These schools characteristically separate the two languages used as media of instruction in the curriculum across the different subject areas. Thus, Maths, Biology, Chemistry and Economics are typically taught in English (the foreign language) while Social Studies, Religious Education and Physical Education are conducted in Spanish (the first language).

Both of the schools which participated in the study are located in the same upper-middle-class, residential neighbourhood, on the outskirts of Cali, one of the three largest cities in Colombia. They are prestigious, private establishments, with a reputation for high academic achievement and ample facilities, such as well-stocked libraries with books in English and Spanish, gymnasiums and auditoriums. They cater for a mainly upper-middle-class population.

The two school entry year groups in the study consisted of 20–25 children between the ages of four to five. The majority of these came from upper-middle-class, monolingual (Spanish-speaking) homes where they had privileged access to

English, through films, videos and English-speaking friends and relations. It can be thus be seen that although English is not a language used as means of communication in Colombian life, many of the children in the two schools had a much higher degree of contact with the language, due to their socio-economic background, parental aspirations and lifestyle, than the majority of the population. Furthermore, it was established that most of their parents had not, in fact, attended bilingual schools themselves, but said that they wanted their children to grow up bilingual in English and Spanish because of the importance of English as a world language and its potential in their children's future success in the domains of work, international travel, tertiary education abroad and access to up-to-date information. The overriding concern of the parents was the development of English. As one of the teachers remarked, 'The parents' highest hopes are fixed on English . . . parents don't show any interest in the development of other skills' (de Mejía, 1994: 138).

Both pre-school programmes were of the Early Partial Immersion type with one important difference. In their first year of schooling the pupils had initially 80% of their teaching and learning in Spanish (the first language) and 20% in English (the foreign language). In their second school year, however, this ratio was reversed, so that the children had around 70% of their schooling in English and 30% in Spanish, thus approximating more to an Early Partial Immersion model. In one programme the mornings were mainly concerned with activities in English and the afternoons were reserved for the development of Spanish, thus showing evidence of a separation approach to language use in the curriculum according to time of day. In the other institution, there was an even more complete separation between the two languages in relation to time of day, physical space and teacher. A monolingual (Spanish-speaking) class teacher was responsible for all aspects of the curriculum taught in Spanish, while an English teacher (bilingual in Spanish and English) was in charge of the English activities which took place in the English room.

The two teachers responsible for English language input were bilingual, though each had a very different language background. One was a young Colombian woman who had studied English at High School in Colombia and had later taken ELT courses in Cali. The other, who was middle-aged, had been brought up in New York by Latin American parents, before settling in Colombia.

Both teachers were conscious that they code-switched during their teaching, but unlike many teachers in bilingual contexts, they did not feel guilty about this. They felt that code-switching helped to cushion their young pupils from an over-abrupt rupture with their monolingual home environment and possible feelings of anxiety or insecurity. They also saw the possibility of using two languages in their teaching as a positive resource in helping the children make the transition towards bilingual development, enabling them to revise concepts in Spanish before introducing them in English, so that the cognitive load might be lowered. They were thus influenced by both affective and pedagogic considerations.

These relaxed attitudes to a concurrent approach to classroom language use may be partially explained by a lack of official institutional pressure to implement a strict separation approach in the classroom. In both schools the teachers were expected to increase the amount of English used both by themselves and the children in the classroom during the school year, but this requirement was not imposed from above. The teachers were free to decide how best to implement this policy and to decide when it was appropriate to use which language in the classroom. This situation thus differs substantially from the generally accepted policy on language use in Canadian immersion programmes.

In the story-telling sessions, the children sat on a large rug in the middle of the classroom, facing the teacher. Both teachers told rather than read the stories, making reference to visual back-up material from the story books they were using. They also used their dramatic skills to enact parts of the tale for the children. This is in line with research carried out by Wolfson (1982) who noted that classroom story-telling, whether monolingual or bilingual, is a hybrid activity, having roots in both narrative, on the one hand, and performance or drama, on the other. When we tell stories we do not only answer the question 'what happened next?' we also create a fictional world by means of gesture, mime, changes in voice pitch and volume, exclamations and dramatisation. As one of the teachers explained, 'you never really follow a story the way it says in the book . . . you sort of go all round it' (de Mejía, 1994: 147).

Both teachers expressed highly favourable attitudes towards the use of stories in the classroom at this level, seeing them as a valuable motivating force, basically, because of their enjoyment value and also because of their potential in attaining a wide variety of aims, both linguistic and non-linguistic. In the non-linguistic domain, the teachers chose stories which reflected events in the lives of their young learners, such as the birth of a new brother or sister, or which helped them to consolidate a focus on the formation of values and behavioural practices. The linguistic aims that the teachers hoped to achieve through their story-telling consisted of such things as improvement of the children's listening skills and visual word recognition, as well as reinforcement of English language items previously introduced in other activities.

The two teachers were conscious of the multiple decisions they had to make to successfully carry out story-telling with children who were beginning the process of becoming bilingual in English and Spanish. The decision about which stories to choose depended on such linguistic and pedagogic considerations as how familiar the children were with the content of the story. In other words, whether the pupils already knew the story in Spanish; how easy it was to tell – in the sense of having a relatively simple plot; whether the illustrations were clear; and also whether the story was appropriate for introducing or revising items of English vocabulary. The teachers were very concerned to avoid frustration caused by the children not understanding the story and referred to the multiple facilitation strategies they used, such as dramatisation, gesture and mime, repetition of key vocabulary items, code-switching, and the use of questions both to act as a check on the children's comprehension and to involve the children in the construction of the tales, encouraging them to make associations with their own experience.

Performance and dramatisation

The element of performance and dramatisation was particularly evident at the beginning of the story-telling sessions, when the teachers were concerned to arouse the children's interest in the forthcoming event, as can be seen in the following extract where one of the teachers who participated in the study, Teacher A, is holding up the story-book as a means of attracting the children's attention:

Extract 1[2]

T	**Bueno** look what I have here {teacher speaks in a sing
	Well
	song tone} hahahaha
P	**Cuento**
5	*Story*
T	**Es el cuento más chistoso del mundo**
	It's the funniest story in the world
	ya lo saben
	you already know it

The teacher initially aroused the children's interest in the story by focusing their attention on the book she was about to use for the story-telling session (line 1). This was followed by a dramatic heightening of tone ('hahahaha'). Then, in line 6 the teacher built on the pupil contribution (line 4) with the utterance, '*Es el cuento más chistoso del mundo*' (It's the funniest story in the world). This utterance was accompanied by a code-switch into Spanish and the adoption of a tone reminiscent of that typically used at a fairground to attract the attention of passers-by from a distance. The teacher was, in effect, 'selling' the story.

As can be seen in the above extract, code-switching was used as an important means of achieving dramatic effect in the lead up to some of the story-telling sessions. It was also used as a means of distinguishing between the 'voices' of different personae assumed by the teachers at different moments in their story-telling. This can also be seen in the following extract taken from the introduction of a telling of 'The Three Bears' story using a flannel graph.

Extract 2

(The teacher is introducing the story by showing the children the flannel graph figures of the three bears.)

T	Do you know what animal family I have here
P	**Qué le van hacer allí**
	What are they going to do to him there
T	It's a **me da pena** {children laugh} it's a what
5	*I feel embarrassed*
P	Father
T	It's a bear family **una familia de qué**
	what sort of family

Ps   **De osos**
10   *Of bears*
T   **De osos** OK le the bear ahha
        Of bears
P   **Una familia de osos**
        A family of bears

The teacher first asked the children to produce a vocabulary item in English, which was one of the words that they would be expected to master in a later unit. However, she was also trying to create a sense of expectation, as can be seen when one of the children asked what was going to happen (line 2). This attempt at motivation was then heightened by a switch into Spanish in line 4. The 'I' that felt embarrassed was not the persona of the teacher, but the flannel graph figure, whose voice the teacher was momentarily projecting. The effect of this change in code, accompanied by an initial pause and by exaggerated stress and intonation patterns, was to create a comic, almost infantile voice which produced laughter in the children. The teacher then reverted to her pedagogic persona (line 7) to find out whether the pupils had understood the concept of 'bear family', checking this in Spanish.

In a further example, the use of different languages to distinguish between different voices takes on an added value. Here, the teacher was telling a story called 'Happy Birthday Moon', where one of the two characters, a bear, wanted to give the moon a birthday present, but did not know what to give. Later he found out, from an echo, that the moon wanted a hat, but unfortunately, after finding the present, the wind blew it away. In this case, it can be seen that the teacher used English consistently to convey the words spoken by the two characters in the story and Spanish to render the narration.

Extract 3

(The teacher is narrating the final reconciliation of the bear
and the moon. They are discussing the loss of the hat
and the bear's happiness when he finds out that the moon
still loves him, in spite of everything.)

T   I lost the beautiful hat you gave me **dijo el oso y**
                                said the bear
        entonces le contestó la lu(na) la moon I lost the
        and then the moon answered   the
5   beautiful hat you gave me **era el eco pero la luna**
                                it was the echo but the moon
        también le esta contando que se le había perdido el
        is also telling him that she had lost the hat
        sombrero that's OK I still love you **le dijo no no**
10   *he said no*

te preocupes luna yo tam(bién) yo todavía te quiero
don't worry moon I too   I still love you
entonces el bear **también le contestó ay** don't worry
and then the   also answered oh
15   I still love you **oo ay** {teacher speaks in a whisper}

In this extract, the voices of the two characters – the bear and the moon (the echo), although technically rendered through the use of reported speech, preserve the immediacy of direct speech because the teacher presented the actual words used by the bear and the moon as written in the story-book. The teacher's language choice for this was mainly English; however, she distinguished the voices of the two characters by means of reporting verbs in Spanish; *'dijo'* (said) and *'contestó'* (answered). In lines 5–9 she also code-switched into Spanish to provide an explanation of the role of the echo. In line 11, the teacher again switched to Spanish to provide a reformulation of the bear's previous statements given in English.

Through the use of code-switching in this example, the teacher was able to provide the children with an experience of the immediacy of the dialogue between the characters in the foreign language, presented in conjunction with explanatory comments and reporting verbs in the children's first language, which enabled the pupils to make sense of the episode.

Thus, we can see in the three extracts discussed above that the teacher used her two languages effectively to achieve polyphony and understanding within the stories she told at two levels. On the one hand, there were the 'pedagogic' voices of foreign language instructor and narrator. These voices were mixed with the 'dramatic' voices of street-sellers, shy animals and story characters, assumed briefly by the teacher during her story-telling sessions. These skilled pedagogic performances perhaps explain the almost 'hypnotic effect' that the stories created in the listeners, and their endless enthusiasm to hear more. As one of the teachers remarked, 'a story is the best thing that can happen to them' (de Mejía, 1994: 145).

Teaching and learning
    Although the teachers were conscious of the enjoyment value of the stories they told, they generally had other pedagogic aims in mind during these sessions. High on their list was the introduction or reviewing of key English vocabulary items, as can be seen in the following extract taken from a telling of the story 'Curious George Flies a Kite', where a monkey called George is returning a kite he borrowed to his friend Billy:

Extract 4

T   I'm going to take the kite to Billy my friend and
        he took the kite look at he took the kite to
        Billy and Billy look at how happy Billy was look
        how happy
5P   House
T   **Qué quiere decir** happy happy **quiere decir**
        What does   mean   means

P House
T **Que es(t) que está co-**
10 *That he's that he's* ha-
P **Alegre contento**
   Joyful   happy
P A house
T This ahha that's Billy's house
15P **Se siente muy contento porque salvaron a su amigo**
   He feels very happy because they saved his friend
T Ahha and his kite

After introducing the word 'happy' within the narrative (line 3), a word she expected the children to learn, the second teacher who participated in the study, Teacher B, asked the children to provide a translation in Spanish, to make sure they had understood the meaning. In line 11, a child came up with two possibilities: '*alegre*' and '*contento*'. The teacher then switched into English to pick up another child's contribution 'house', which she had previously ignored. Finally, in line 15, another child incorporated the discussion about the word 'happy' back into the narrative by providing an explanation for Billy's happiness, '*porque salvaron a su amigo*' (because they saved his friend). This contribution was then positively evaluated by the teacher in line 17 by use of the expression 'Ahha', indicating that this pedagogical sequence had been successfully completed.

Thus, it can be seen that the teacher's agenda of teaching and learning of vocabulary items was clearly demarcated from the telling of the story by the language used. The language of the narration was, for the most part, English. The concept and vocabulary checking were generally carried out in Spanish.

In the above case, the teacher required a Spanish equivalent for the word 'happy' and signalled this implicitly to the children by her code-switch into Spanish. Sometimes, however, the children had difficulty in recognising the cues for appropriate language use given by the teacher. This type of understanding is dependent, to a great extent, on the pupils' ability to recognise cues within the general flow of classroom discourse. This is something that students gradually acquire as they become more able to identify the tacit rules of interaction which govern the relationships between the participants in the particular classroom context in which they operate. However, initially, such requests may have to be made explicit, as can be seen in the following extract:

Extract 5

(In this lead up to the story of 'The Three Bears' the teacher is checking on the concept of 'family')

T Who live in the house
P **Los hermanitos**
   The brothers and sisters
T What

5Ps **Los hermanitos**
   The brothers and sisters
T   What
Ps   Mam pap
   Mu   Da
10T I don't understand Spanish you have to tell me in
   English

Here, the teacher tried twice unsuccessfully to indicate tacitly to the class that she required an answer in English, by repeating the word 'What' (lines 4 and 7). The pupils, however, understood this as asking them for content information, rather than a change of code and they repeated the term 'brothers and sisters' in Spanish. In view of this, the teacher was forced to explicitly formulate her request for a change of language (lines 10–11) with a statement which was not entirely true, but often used by teachers in bilingual contexts to indicate to their pupils that a change of language is required.

Later in the same interaction, it can be seen that the children were more successful in recognising this tacit form of request and responded appropriately during a discussion about where the three bears lived:

Extract 6

T   Where do they live they live in what
P   Garaje
   Garage
T   In a
5**P   Casa**
   House
T   In a what
Ps   House
T   In a house

There was no teacher uptake of the pupil contribution in line 2. Instead, the teacher expanded the prompt to include the indefinite article ('In a'), thus signalling simultaneously to the children that '*Garaje*' (Garage) was incorrect and that a noun was required to fill the slot. Again, there was no uptake by the teacher of the pupil response '*Casa*' (House), implying a negative evaluation of this contribution. The teacher further expanded the prompt (line 7) to implicitly request a change of language. Her positive evaluation in line 9, shown by her repetition and expansion of the pupil's answer, can be seen as terminating the pedagogic sequence, by establishing that a correct response (both from the point of view of content and language choice) had been provided.

This type of misinterpretation was not confined only to stories told in the early part of the school year. There is evidence of similar misunderstandings in stories told later on, thus confirming that the process of the internalising of classroom conventions was on-going throughout the year.

Teacher and student interaction

While both teachers considered that they had primary responsibility for the story-telling events, at times they either actively sought or at least allowed the learners to intervene in this process. In the following exchange, it can be seen that the teacher actively invited the pupils to participate in the joint construction of the tale:

Extract 7

(The teacher and children are discussing the fate of the hat given by the bear to the moon.)

T   What happened with the hat
P   **Se le cayó**
      It fell down
T   Very good the hat came down from the tree

Here it can be seen that although the teacher formulated her question in English the child replied in Spanish. The teacher gave this contribution an explicit positive evaluation ('Very good'), accepting it on the level of content. She then proceeded to reformulate it in English making the referents more explicit by replacing the pronouns used by the children by the nouns 'the hat' and 'the tree', providing the children with an appropriate form of comprehensible input, as discussed in the earlier part of this chapter.

Sometimes, however, the students spontaneously volunteered comments which were taken up by the teacher by being reformulated in English, but not acknowledged explicitly, as can be seen below,

Extract 8

T   Look at the Goochoo bird
P   **Está triste**
      He's sad
T   He's sad he's very sad

In line 2, a child volunteered the comment 'He's sad' in Spanish, after looking at the picture of the Goochoo bird as prompted by the teacher. The teacher did not acknowledge this contribution directly, but instead reformulated it in English in line 4. She thus indicated that the contribution was appropriate on the level of content.

At other times, only minimal uptake is provided by the teacher, as can be seen in the following example:

Extract 9

T   And she and she covered him up **para que no gritara**
                                    so he would not shout
      so he wouldn't yell

P **No podía mirar**
5 *He couldn't see*
T Ahha and put him inside

Here the teacher acknowledged the pupil's contribution to the developing discourse by saying 'Ahha'. However, she did not incorporate this in any way within the story. On other occasions, teacher uptake of pupil contributions was deferred, sometimes for quite a long time, when the teacher considered the intervention untimely, as can be seen in the following exchange where the teacher consistently ignores one of the children's references to the appearance of a wolf in the illustrations to the story she is telling about a hen and a baby alligator which she has hatched by mistake:

Extract 10

T Goodbye my little friend
P **El lobo el lobo el lobo el lobo**
  The wolf the wolf the wolf the wolf
T Goodbye she was crying look {teacher imitates
5 crying} goodbye alligator I was so happy with you
P **El lobo el lobo el lobo**
  The wolf the wolf the wolf
T Look the hen is crying   is really crying
P **El lobo**
10 *The wolf*
T And the alligator went inside the forest bye bye
  hen bye bye alligator and she was crying and
  crying
P **El zorro**
15 *The fox*
T And at this moment when the hen was going to come
  back to her house oh the wolf went out and catch
  the hen

Here the teacher ignored the child's contribution four times, even though the pupil changed the proposed item (from '*el lobo*' (the wolf) to '*el zorro*' (the fox) line 14). It was only in line 17 that the teacher included the child's contribution in the narrative in a translated form. Thus, it is evident that here the teacher was concerned with the narration of events on her terms and showed herself to be in control of the developing discourse.

Occasionally, however, the teachers suspended briefly their control of the interaction to allow the students to introduce their own concerns into the classroom arena. In the following extract the teacher is presenting a situation in which a strange bird – the Goochoo bird – renowned for its rudeness, has managed to escape from a dungeon in which it has been imprisoned. One of the children interrupted the narration in line 3 with a suggestion on how the escape succeeded, as can be seen below:

Extract 11

T	**Le dijo vaya usted y me lo trae**
	He said you go and bring me
P1	**Y yo yo sé cómo con con la cola el la saca**
	And I I know how with with his tail he takes it out
5T	Ahha
P	**Y y la**
	And and
P	**Y porque y porque se puede volar**
	And because and because he can fly
10P	**Y la y la mete y la**
	And it and he puts it and it
T	Fly well maybe
P2	**El se salió volando**
	He came out flying
15T	Maybe he came out flying
P	**No**
	No
P	**Se le quedó las alas**
	He left his wings behind
20P3	**El hace la cola mete la cola por un roto y y le**
	He makes his tail he puts his tail through a hole
	mete la llave y la y la abre
	and puts in the key and and opens it
T	**Ahh también pueda que sí** maybe **ahora ver lo que**
25	*that too maybe now you will see*
	pasó
	what happened

The teacher gave minimal uptake to the child's intervention which suggested that the bird had used his tail to effect his escape, using the expression 'Ahha' in line 3. Another child then took up the topic, introducing the idea of flying (one of the English vocabulary items introduced during the year). The teacher then code-switched to repeat the suggestion in English and gave a tentative positive evaluation, 'Fly well maybe . . . maybe he came out flying'. However, another child then came up with an alternative suggestion about using his tail as a key. The teacher again evaluated the suggestion positively, but rather tentatively, '*Ahh también pueda que sí* maybe' (that could be it too). However, she then clearly signalled to the children that this topic was now finished and brought the focus explicitly back to the main business in hand, the narration of the Goochoo bird's (the main story character) rudeness, '*ahora ver lo que pasó*' (now you will see what happened).

This practice is consistent with this teacher's views on pupil participation in group story-telling as revealed in the following observation:

> If (the children's comments) go with the story I don't mind it going on. If it starts to take them away from the story, then I kind of try to *disimuladamente* (in an un-noticed way) (say) 'Oh is that so?' and then go right back into the story . . . you have to do it in a gentle way because you really should be listening to them . . . and then letting them participate. (de Mejía, 1994: 242)

This clearly indicates the tension the teacher felt between letting the children participate and maintaining control of the on-going narration. As has been pointed out above, the teachers tended to adopt a teacher-centred stance in this respect, although they occasionally allowed the children to successfully introduce their own concerns within the story-telling sessions.

What is interesting about the different moments of bilingual classroom interaction discussed in this section in the context of two pre-school elite bilingual programmes in Colombia, is the creativity and resourcefulness shown by the two teachers in using a variety of communicative strategies to help their young pupils understand and participate in the construction of story-telling events. Changes of tempo, volume, voice pitch, visual dramatisation, gesture, along with the skilful and flexible use of both the children's languages provided the pupils with experiences of narrative construction which were enjoyable and meaningful.

An analysis of the different functions of the classroom code-switching shows that far from being a deficit strategy used to supplement imperfect linguistic proficiency on the part of the teachers, the use of two languages in teaching in these bilingual contexts demonstrates a sophistication and complexity often ignored by educationalists. Thus, pupils are enabled to see relationships between their two languages in use and to realise gradually that they can communicate in a bilingual speech mode with fellow-bilinguals. This is not to deny that they also need to realise that, in order to be able to communicate with monolingual speakers of their two languages in an appropriate manner, they will not be able to make use of code-switching.

Negotiation and boundary marking at secondary school level in Anglo-Chinese schools in Hong Kong

The institutional context

The second study of bilingual classroom discourse included in this chapter is based on research carried out in four different Anglo-Chinese secondary schools in Hong Kong by Angel M.Y. Lin in 1990. Extracts are included here to illustrate how bilingual classroom interaction is carried on between teachers and students in language classes at Junior High School level in an elite multilingual and multicultural context in South East Asia. As before, the reader is recommended to refer to the discussion of aspects of bilingual education provision in Hong Kong in Chapter 9 to get a fuller vision of the general sociolinguistic and educational setting.

The four schools in the study cover a range of Anglo-Chinese establishments. Two are well-established, prestigious, single-sex schools, while the other two are of more recent foundation, co-educational and of lower academic status. The five classes selected corresponded to Forms 1–3, where the students were aged 12–14. Four of the classes consisted of between 36 and 45 students. The other, a remedial English class, had 22 students.

The four teachers were female, which is the norm for most English language teachers in Hong Kong secondary schools. They were young, in their mid-20s. All had recognised teacher training qualifications and had taught for between two and four years. Furthermore, all were Cantonese-English bilinguals, though they varied greatly in their use of the two languages in their teaching. As explained in Chapter 9, the official language policy in Anglo-Chinese schools is monolingual English use. One of the four teachers subscribed completely to this norm; however, the other three all showed evidence of code-switching between Cantonese and English in their relations with the students, to a greater or lesser extent, even though they felt that ideally they should only use English in their work.

Class control

In this study, based on a Conversational Analysis approach, Lin (1990) shows clearly how communicative strategies, such as changes of stress and tone, pauses, facial expression and code-switching enabled the teachers to indicate to their students that they were changing topic. One very common reason for interrupting pedagogical topics was for purposes of class control. In some cases, this was achieved without changing language, as in the following example where the teacher is asking students questions about a character in a text they are studying.

Extract 12

{Students are talking and laughing noisily}

T   Shh ! {Loud sound of two knocks at a table} Respect, do you understand?
       Jyun-ging. Would you respect him?
       Respect
       {Some students are still talking}
5T   WOULD YOU PAY ATTENTION!! {in a loud and angry voice}
       {students become quiet}
T   Would you respect him if he is your manager ? {back to normal voice}

Here, the teacher marked off the utterance, 'Would you pay attention ! !' by changes of stress and tone from the other structurally similar phrases used by the teacher to focus the students on the topic under discussion (lines 2 and 7). These differences signalled to the students that this remark was not part of the on-going pedagogical interaction, but a brief, general attempt to control their behaviour and get them as a group to pay attention to what she was saying.

However, this signalling can be made much stronger if the teacher also includes a change of language and a change in addressee, as in the following extract. Here, the teacher was asking a student to give her some examples of plants:

Extract 13

T   Now tell me some of the plants. Grass, a kind of plant. . . flowers, a kind of plant.

S   {???}
    {Some student noises}

5T ANNIE! **Néih chóh fāan gwo làih yī bīn! Tùhng**
    Come back to   the   seat here! Sitting
    Lìhng-Ji_Chīu chóh sèhng-yaht kīng-gái hái douh! Chóh gwo
    with Lihng-Ji-Chiu you'll never stop talking!   Take the
    heui Rose gaak-lèih.
10 *seat next to Rose.*

T   Lily, tulip, okay now they are all flowers okay? Yes, they are plants.

In lines 5–10, the teacher singled out one individual student (Annie) for her disciplinary comment about too much talking. Furthermore, she switched into Cantonese and used an angry tone of voice. The combined effect of using these three different communicative cues shows that the teacher has temporarily suspended the pedagogical task of teaching English and has concentrated on criticising one particular student, while indirectly turning the rest of the class into 'over-hearers'. As Lin herself remarks, 'the effect is great. There is no room for negotiation and the reprimand is explicitly directed to the addressee' (Lin, 1990: 41).

Lin suggests that the bilingual teachers in her study made use of a range of communicative options for class control, which included change of language (English to Cantonese), using intonational accentuation, and changing addressee. She sees potential advantages in the use of these strategies. For example, if the teacher does not change language but uses intonational accentuation alone to regulate student behaviour, as in Extract 12, she has the advantage of using the foreign language (English) to 'soften' her authoritative stance of anger towards the students for their disruptive behaviour. She thus appears using a language which is not her own, as 'the Teacher in an English language lesson' (Lin, 1990: 44), an official enforcer of school regulations, rather than a dictatorial individual. Furthermore, as there is no change of language, there is also less disruption of pedagogical classroom interaction.

If, however, the teacher code-switches, as well as using intonational accentuation, and singles out one particular student (as in Extract 13), this clearly interrupts the pedagogic framework and focuses on one individual student, rather than the whole class, or a particular group. By using Cantonese, the teacher is no longer positioning herself as an 'objective' English language instructor enforcing classroom regulations. Instead, she is seen as someone who is more personally involved with the students and who communicates her displeasure about one particular incident in the language she shares with them as mother-tongue. She also isolates one individual student from the rest of the group, thus risking a potential loss of face of this student before the group. However, the strength of this position is mitigated, somewhat paradoxically, by the use of the first language. The teacher is seen as someone who has a personal interest in the well-being of the student (a parental figure), who is acting in his/her best interests.

Role relationships

These changes in position, referred to above, were also evident in other circumstances which were not connected with class control. In the following example, the teacher began in pedagogic mode by asking the students what they were going to do in the forthcoming Chinese New Year holidays. This came as a follow-up to a grammar lesson on the future tense. The teacher asked her learners to write five sentences about five things they planned to do. Some students protested, saying that they would not be doing so many things in the New Year holidays.

Extract 14

T   Alright, the whole class, would you take out a piece of paper. Would you take out–aah . . . no need to, just write it down at some blank, alright? Write down five sentences.
S1   **Waa ! Dím jouh dóu gum dō yéh aa?!**
5   *Exclamation particle ! How can I do so many things?!*
   {Some students} **Waa ! (? ?)**
   Exclamation particle ! (? ?)
T   **Néih m̀haih āak ngóh haih maah, sān nìhn jouh mh dóu**
   You must be kidding, during the New Year you can't
10   **m̀h yeuhng yéh? Neih jān-hūng gàah?**
   do five things   You are 'vacuum'?
S2   **Fan-gaau gaa jaa ngóh-deih.** {laughing}
   We'll just be sleeping.
S3   **Jān-hūng jauh jouh m̀h dóu m̀h yeuhng yéh gaa lāa.** {laughing}
15   *If we were 'vacuum' we would not be able to do five things.*
T   **Mh-léih néih jouh māt-yéh aa.**
   It doesn't matter what you do.
   {Students' voices (in L1)}
T   Quickly, five sentences, quickly.

Here we see the teacher switching to Cantonese in lines 8–11 to respond to the students' protest. She also changed tone from her serious pedagogic intervention in lines 1–3 to a 'jokey', light-hearted comment using a 'colloquial trendy L1 expression . . . '*neih jān-hūng gàah ?*' literally meaning 'you are vacuum ?' (Lin, 1990: 65). She, thus, adopted a bantering style characteristic of student talk, which positioned her momentarily on their level as their peer and enabled her to negotiate with them as equals. However, like the teachers in the Colombian pre-school study, this teacher in Hong Kong did not allow this change of role to last very long. Instead, she soon switched back to take control of the interaction, as shown by her change of language to English in line 19.

In another example, a similar negotiation strategy, involving one of the other teachers in the study, can be observed. Here, the teacher commented that many of the students had forgotten to bring their Chinese books for the immediately preceding Chinese History lesson. However, one of the students produced a rather irreverent comment which evoked student laughter.

Extract 15

T	Haa haa, just now you've got five . . . only, what happened?
S1	**Hóu dō yàhn m̀h gei dāk daai aa.**
	Many people have forgotten to bring it.
T	A lot of you did not bring your Chinese book, right ?
5	Chinese History, haa haa.
S2	**Mīsìh (? ?)**
	Miss
T	Pardon
S2	**Mīsìh néih sái-m̀h-sái (? ?)**
10	*Miss, do you need to*
	{sound of a student laughing}
T	**Néih nē jauh yuht lèih yuht dō yéh góng gaa laak . . .**
	You are getting more and more talkative . . .
	Alright, now let us start (our lesson). Page thirty two, page thirty-two.

Although the student comment in lines 9–10 was partially unintelligible, it caused another student to laugh and was potentially embarrassing to the teacher. The teacher changed from English to Cantonese (lines 12–13), apparently acceding to the student's implicit request for a continuation of the non-serious, casual talk about the Chinese books (lines 4–5) on the level of language choice. However, she rejected the student's behaviour as non-appropriate, as shown by her comment in lines 12–13. Lin interprets this outcome as a successful negotiation for good behaviour, 'without appearing too unapproachable and authoritarian' (Lin, 1990: 71).

Conclusion

In this chapter we have discussed some key aspects of how teachers teach and students learn in two or more languages in different elite bilingual programmes. We have seen that the debate about appropriate language use in bilingual classrooms is a topic which has generated a lot of controversy as regards the relative merits of language separation and language switching. Research which has been carried out from a psychometric tradition, particularly in Canada, has focused on the educational impact of bilingualism and has emphasised the advantages of adopting a separation approach to classroom language use. This is clearly seen in the development of the Canadian immersion programmes. On the other hand, sociolinguistic-orientated perspectives on bilingual education research in elite contexts have foregrounded the need to develop bilingual programmes which reflect the local speech economy. These views have led to calls to reconsider the merits of selective language alternation within bilingual schools.

What may be concluded from the above situation, then, is that there is an urgent need for more studies to be carried out in different bilingual programmes, showing how teachers teach and learners learn bilingually and what uses they put their languages to in their daily lives. Teachers, especially, need to be made aware of their own language practices and how they feel about using their two languages in the classroom arena. If the advantages and disadvantages of code-switching in the classroom can be discussed openly and be related to a wider vision about language use in specific sociocultural contexts, as well as its role in facilitating or hampering language acquisition in educational contexts, this may enable classroom language alternation to emerge from its present clandestine condition. In this way, classroom language use may be evaluated in relation to a wider language continuum which sees schools as a part of the communities they serve and not as self-contained, autonomous islands.

The complexity of the interrelationships between school and community also implies the need for more ethnographic research to be carried out, so that issues which have been considered primarily educational, such as the 'plateau' learning effect noted in immersion programmes, may be related to wider sociocultural and political factors, like for instance opportunities for interlinguistic and intercultural contact between different groups. This type of research, while not providing easily accessible statistical information for administrators and decision makers in elite bilingual institutions, helps to reveal the complex nature of bilingual educational processes. Moreover, ethnographic studies help to throw light on the multiple decisions, both conscious and unconscious, which underpin the interaction of the various participants involved, whether they be teachers, students, administrators or parents.

Notes

1. By the term *natural code-switching* I am distinguishing between language alternation carried out by bilingual speakers for different functional purposes, such as to emphasise a point, to facilitate learner understanding, or to distinguish between academic content and extra curricular concerns, and *planned* language alternation, such as Jacobson's 'New Concurrent Approach' discussed by Faltis (1989). In this second modality, teacher code-switching behaviour is regulated according to 16 pre-established cues, in order to ensure an equal balance in the use of both languages during pedagogical instruction and to avoid excessive alternation.
2. In all the extracts of bilingual classroom disourse cited in this chapter, use of the first language has been registered in bold and an English translation has been provided in italics. None of the mistakes noted in the original recordings have been corrected.

Chapter 5

Relationships and Participants in Elite Bilingual Educational Processes

Introduction

Up to now we have been considering elite bilingual education mainly in relation to the immediate classroom actors, teachers and students. However, these two groups, while important, are not the only participants in the process of education. We must not forget that politicians, parents and administrators are people that play a vital role in sustaining and supporting classroom participants. In this chapter, we will discuss how parents, administrators, teachers and students see their interrelationships and how the attitudes, expectations and viewpoints of the differing groups which together make up the educational community of each individual bilingual school, complement and at times conflict with each other. We will begin by considering the attitudes and roles of parents in different types of elite bilingual programmes, such as immersion programmes, European Schools, and International Schools (see Chapter 1 for a profile of these different types of bilingual education provision). The aim of this discussion is to show how parents have been influential in both supporting the bilingual and multilingual education of their children, and how, in some cases, they have been instrumental in helping to promote important educational and cultural initiatives which have led to fundamental changes in bilingual educational provision.

In the second section, we will go on to examine the multiple roles played by school administrators, such as principals and academic co-ordinators in the development of different types of elite bilingual education programmes, such as the highly centralised European School system and the more autonomous structures of many International Schools, whether bilingual or multilingual.

The final two sections of this chapter will focus on classroom participants – teachers and students – in relation to the different demands placed on them in international settings. The challenges involved in adapting to multilingual and multicultural classroom situations involve new responsibilities and new pressures for both parties. Teachers need to be able to help their students cope with a wide range of abilities and aptitudes which may be complicated by language and cultural barriers. Students often experience conflicting pressures, in that at times they are expected to adapt to new ways of behaviour and interaction at school, while their parents or grandparents may demand that they show evidence of conforming to established cultural and linguistic norms of their country of origin.

Parents

Although in writing about bilingual education there are frequent general references to the importance of the role of parents in these processes and to the influence that parents have in the construction of attitudes towards bilingual education in their children, until recently there was very little research carried out in this area. As Baker (1988: 91) states, 'Support for bilingual education is mostly from academics. We have negligible evidence as to the degree of parental, public or pupil support for the various forms of bilingual education.'

In the context of bilingual education programmes for minority children in the United States, Ovando and Collier (1987: 298, 1998) recognised the importance of the collaboration between teachers, administrators and parents in the success of these initiatives. In addition, they went so far as to say that parents should be considered partners in the educational process, stating, 'it is important for teachers and school administrators to avail themselves of opportunities to learn about parents and the community . . . One first step might be an assessment of parent' 'entry level' knowledge and opinions regarding bilingual education'. Thus, it can be seen that during the 1980s it was not common practice among teachers and school administrators to value parents' contributions to bilingual education. Parents, however, can provide important information about teachers' language use, as can be seen in the communication in Text Box 5.1.

Text Box 5.1   Teacher Pronunciation (taken from Anderssohn, 1996: 7)

I would like to ask for other parents' reactions to the following situation, which may arise in any family where children learn in school as a foreign language, a language which they already speak in the home, or which they have learnt during a period of residence abroad.

A teacher who is not a native speaker of the language in question corrects the child's pronunciation. The child, whose pronunciation is native or near-native, is confused and resentful. The teacher is probably better at grammar and spelling than the child, but diminishes his/her own credibility in the child's eyes by attempting to impose what is clearly incorrect pronunciation.

What is the best course for the parents to take, to maintain the child's self-confidence without undermining the teacher's?

Since then, things have changed somewhat. In 1996, Krashen wrote a defence of bilingual education programmes in the United States and dedicated a whole section of his argument to a consideration of parental and public opinion on bilingual education. His main conclusion, after studying the results of a series of polls of parents and other sectors of public opinion in the USA, was that there was widespread support for bilingual education programmes in which both the students' first language and the second language (English) were used in teaching and learning. In their *Encyclopaedia of Bilingualism and Bilingual Education*, Baker and Prys Jones (1998) refer to 'home-school relationships' in relation to language minority families and cite the work of authors such as Delgado-Gaitan (1990) and Moll (1992) in studying how parents can be empowered to become more actively involved in their children's education,

In her work, Delgado-Gaitan (1990) reviews research carried out on three levels of parent involvement in their children's education, which she terms: the family influence model, the school reform model, and the co-operative systems model. The first of these, the family influence model, involves research on ways of improving the family's capabilities of providing the type of home learning environment that enhances cognitive and emotional development, by encouraging positive attitudes towards education and high expectations of children's success. The assumption behind this model is that experts or books can provide parents with 'the right way' of bringing up academically successful children. While Delgado-Gaitan (1990: 50) recognises that 'when parents show interest in their children's learning (which is congruent with the expectations of the school), children's academic performance usually increases', she also notes that these types of studies do not include insights about family organisational structures, and tend to over-simplify an extremely complex phenomenon.

The school reform model, in contrast, 'shows how family and school influence shifts from the home to the school' and implies that 'parents may try to change the schools to make them more responsive to parents' (Delgado-Gaitan, 1990: 51). This model of parent involvement often means parent participation in the classroom and school, as well as serving as members of policy or advisory bodies. In general, work carried out in the light of this model (Irvine, 1979; Herman & Yeh, 1980, cited in Delgado-Gaitan, 1990) demonstrates that parents are a vital factor in a strong academic programme for students, especially those from working-class families. This points to the observation by Lareau (1987: 83, cited in Delgado-Gaitan, 1990) that while schools require very similar types of behaviour from all parents, regardless of their socio-economic status, 'not all cultural resources are equally valuable for complying with schools' requests'.

The third model analysed, the co-operative systems model, views parent-school involvement as a dual-directional relationship within the wider context of school and community interrelationships. In this model, parent education is seen not only in terms of how to help their children become successful at school, but also 'how parent involvement fits into the larger social scheme, including the parents' employment opportunities and their social position' (Delgado-Gaitan, 1990: 54).

Parents may play a variety of roles in this process, such as volunteer, paid helper, teacher at school, audience, decision maker, and adult learner. Studies carried out in this area (McConnell, 1976; Cochran, 1987, cited in Delgado-Gaitan, 1990) show that legislation can provide powerful support for parent involvement in schools and classrooms, and can lead to a gradual process of parent empowerment in their relationships with the educational establishment.

Although much of the research referred to above was carried out in monolingual rather than multilingual or bilingual contexts, it can be seen that it is highly important that parents who choose to send their children to schools providing elite bilingual education are closely involved with the school in order to help children cope with the extra demands of unfamiliar languages and educational and cultural practices. In immersion education, parents have been closely associated with the success of this initiative right from the beginning. In fact, in Canada, it was the parents who were one of the principal forces involved in the creation of the original St Lambert French immersion programme in 1965. As one school principal in the US Mid-West recognises, 'Parental support and involvement is an extraordinarily important component of the successful immersion program . . . Parents who choose such a program for their children have an additional vested interest in the success of the program' (Coffman, 1992: 167).

Most parent involvement in elite bilingual education programmes, as will be seen below, falls within the family influence model, with schools and teachers advising parents on how best to help their children adjust to the requirements of the new school and community environment. There is, however, some evidence that teachers in International Schools try to adapt their views on home-school relationships in the light of cultural differences in parents' expectations about their involvement with their children's teachers. Coreen Sears (1998: 30), an experienced International School teacher, advises teachers in this type of institution to 'put in place a range of strategies for formal and informal communication (between teachers and parents) and to plan for the regular involvement of all parents in class life' bearing in mind that 'the nature of expatriate life, with its separation from the wider family and the home culture, leads to greater demands on the school and on teachers from parents'.

Recently, there have been several studies carried out on parents of specific groups, such as European School students (Swan, 1996) the Japanese 'returnees' (Goodman, 1993), as well as Canadian and Australian immersion students (Gibson, 1984; Rebuffot, 1993; Johnson & Swain, 1997; Stevens, 1995; Fernandez, 1996). In Colombia, furthermore, there have been several theses devoted to this area, in relation to both English-Spanish bilingual schools and French-Spanish bilingual schools (Araújo & Corominas, 1996; Orejuela, 1997). We will examine each of these areas in turn to see the specific nature of parents' contributions in each case, as well as their differing expectations and attitudes towards the bilingual education programmes in which their children are enrolled.

Parents of European School students

As in the Canadian immersion programmes, parents were the initial driving force for the setting up of the first European School in Luxembourg in 1953. Since then, they have been involved both formally and informally in many aspects of European school life. They are formally represented on the supreme deci-sion-making body of the European Schools' system, the Board of Governors or the *Conseil Supérieur*, where they have the right to vote on educational matters. Further-more, there are regular informal meetings of delegates of the Parents' Associations of the individual European Schools, aimed at co-ordinating common activities among the schools and at preparing joint proposals for discussion by the Board of Governors (Swan, 1996).

Each school has its own Parents' Association which has the right to raise ques-tions and make proposals about day-to-day aspects of school life, as well as helping to organise extra-curricular activities. These associations are usually fairly strong and involve representatives in regular school contact, as institutions delegate such matters as school transportation services and meals provision to the parent body (Baetens Beardsmore, 1990). There are normally two class-parent representatives appointed to liaise between parents and teachers, 'on matters of common concern' (Swan, 1996: 78) and communication between the school and parents takes place in the language of the subsection in which the child is placed, i.e. in his or her first language. When general school meetings are called, the language used is the working language of the school, usually that of the host environment. As Baetens Beardsmore (1990) recognises, in a situation where different home–school lan-guages are used, it is vital for parents to be able to understand the working of the institution in order to be able to contribute fully to school objectives, and thus it is necessary for parent–school communication to take place in the language or languages they speak.

Although it is important to recognise the formal, institutional links of parents with the European School organisation, it is perhaps more illustrative of their immediate influence to examine their informal relationships with classroom partic-ipants. Depending which European country they come from, parents have differing expectations of their incidence in school affairs. Parents from Holland and Denmark are accustomed to being directly involved in the day-to-day running of their children's school, while in Britain and Ireland there has traditionally been a reluctance to involve parents in school decisions, though this has been reported to be changing recently (Swan, 1996).

Parents bring a wealth of different traditions and experience to the life of indi-vidual schools. They contribute among other things to 'the arrangement of school trips . . . the organisation of the school canteen, schoolbook sales and some school entertainment events' (Swan, 1996: 102). Headteachers report favourably on the 'concern and energetic interest of the parent body' (Headmasters' Report, 1984, cited in Swan, 1996: 103), expressed through parent-teacher meetings and parents' associations. This is not to say, however, that all is smooth sailing. In the words of one Brussels' school parent cited by Swan (1996: 87), 'The European Schools are fascinating, stimulating and superbly successful. Their advantages do outweigh their disadvantages. But there is much discontent'. Some of the main bones of contention for parents, expressed in an internal report in 1991 were: an exclusively academic orientation, inadequate guidance about higher education possibilities, teachers' different national styles of teaching, and insufficient help for pupils with learning difficulties.

Parents of Japanese 'returnees'

As we have seen in Chapter 1, Japanese returnees or *kikokushijo* generally belong to well-educated families in Japanese society, where the father, generally in mid-career, has been sent abroad by the organisation for which he works. These men usually work as diplomats, journalists, academics or as businessmen in large companies. Their wives and children generally accompany them as dependent spouses and minors. A definition provided by Goodman (1993: 15) categorises returnees as 'all Japanese children under the age of 20 who, because of one or both of their parents' jobs, have at some time in their lives spent at least three months overseas, and have returned to continue their education in the mainstream education system'.

While abroad, parents have to face a number of problems such as cultural and linguistic isolation (many Japanese families do not live near other Japanese families); fathers have to work long hours; mothers have to assume almost total responsibility for the education of their children in an unfamiliar system (Mitchell, 1998). Writing about her initial experiences as a Japanese mother of two boys (one six years old and the other, one year old) who attended school in England, Yumiko Shibata (1998) talks movingly about how important it is for parents to establish a high level of trust and communication with teachers and school administrators so as to be able to deal rapidly with linguistic and cultural misunderstandings.

She notes that on the third day of her elder son's attendance at his new school in London, she received a phone call asking her to meet the headmistress. To her astonishment, the headmistress complained that her normally well-behaved son had been shouting loudly, and kicking and punching the other children, many of whom were absolutely terrified of him. When the mother questioned her son about the incident, he readily admitted what he had done, but explained that he couldn't understand why none of the other children had understood what he had said to them when he spoke to them in Japanese. As he had heard them calling him 'Karate Man' he had started to behave accordingly so that he would attract their attention and be accepted. He told his mother, 'I didn't mean to hurt anyone, Mum. I just wanted to make friends' (Shibata, 1998: 114).

His mother immediately wrote a letter to the headmistress explaining what had happened. The head then apologised for her hasty judgement, taken without considering the child's cultural background. Shibata (1998: 114) concludes, 'What I learnt through this incident was how important it is for parents and teachers to trust each other and maintain good relationships. Presumably this would not be a problem for the English-speaking parents. However, we are likely to fail because of an inadequate command of English.'

In addition to problems of adapting to their new life, many parents are also very concerned about their children's eventual return to Japan. They want their children to improve their English but they also want them to maintain their Japanese identity. According to a survey cited by Goodman (1993: 164), '40 per cent of parents with children in elementary schools overseas were worried that their offspring would not be able to keep up academically when they returned . . . and about 70 per cent of the total surveyed expressed uneasiness (*fuan*) about the chances of their children entering good universities'. Thus, families are very concerned to maintain their children's Japanese language skills while abroad, so they either send them to Full-Time Japanese Schools (*Nihonjingakko*), or to Supplementary Schools (*Hoshuko*) which generally session on Saturday mornings, to provide classes in Japanese language and often Mathematics, in addition to their studies in local or international schools during the week. Thus, these children frequently feel pressurised both by their parents and by the amount of homework they receive from their English and their Japanese schools.

On their return to Japan from abroad, most *kikokushijo* are accepted in regular schools, while a minority, mostly girls, are sent to International Schools in Japan, which are extremely expensive, (see Chapter 9 for more details). There are three reasons which may account for the predominance of girls in International Schools, according to Goodman (1993): firstly girls tend to spend a longer period of time abroad than boys, due to the fact that many boys return to Japan alone around the age of 15, either going to boarding school or staying with relatives, so as to be able to finish their education in Japan, even though their families may still be abroad. The girls, who usually stay with their families for the whole of the time spent abroad by the family, often find it more difficult to adapt back to life in the regular school system in Japan when they finally return; secondly, the predominance of girls in International Schools may reflect the feeling among parents that they can take more risks with their daughters' education than their sons', who generally return to the state system which is the norm in the country; and thirdly, parents sometimes consider that returning to Japan for a girl can often be more traumatic than for a boy, as she has been exposed to images of female emancipation which differ considerably to what is traditionally expected of women in Japanese society and therefore choose to send her to schools which have a higher degree of foreign influence.

In an interesting commentary on the situation of returnees, the same author observes that these students face fewer problems than their parents expect on their return to Japan. A survey in 1982 suggested that parents' fears were rather exaggerated and that only 7% of returnee students were considered 'below average' by their teachers in Japan. This reality did not, however, deter an influential parent lobby from pressurising the authorities, with the help of the media, to provide special help for returnees. Thus, the majority view of returnees' problems, 'was the result of important and powerful groups creating an awareness of a social problem and bringing pressure to bear on the Japanese government to act upon that problem' (Goodman, 1993: 210).

However, another group of parents believed that it was not so much their children who needed help to adapt back into Japanese society, but rather that the Japanese educational system itself should adapt and internationalise to accommodate to the demands of this group. As Sato (1978: 222 cited in Goodman, 1993) argues, '*kikokushijo* should not be seen as a minority education case but must be seen as a key to a new education system in Japan'. Therefore, a very small number of Japanese students, backed by a large number of powerful interest groups, such as well-educated parents, private schools, the media, and commercial educational interests, have been at the forefront of a movement to create 'a new type of "Japanese internationalist" who will be able to carry on a dialogue with the outside world while maintaining his "Japaneseness"' (Goodman, 1993: 231).

This is, thus, another example of how parent pressure can be used to create educational and cultural initiatives which have long-reaching effects both on traditional pedagogical practices and also on the wider society.

Parents of Canadian immersion students

As noted in Chapter 1, parents were one of prime movers of the first Canadian immersion programme started in St Lambert, Montreal, in 1965. Some middle-class anglophone parents were anxious for their children to be successful within a Quebec which was becoming increasingly orientated towards the French language; others saw cultural, intellectual and social advantages if their sons and daughters became bilingual (Rebuffot, 1993). Thus, in 1963, 240 parents presented a proposition to the Protestant Schools Commission of Chambly which would authorise their children to be taught initial literacy skills in French during preschool (*maternelle*) and the first three years of primary school.

The petition was rejected, but the parents themselves decided to organise, at their own expense, '*un bain de langue francaise*'[1] for their children (Rebuffot, 1993: 13). They approached two professors from McGill University, Wallace Lambert and Wilder Penfield, to help them, as well as publishing articles in the press and lobbying during meetings of the School Commission. After two years of pressure, the Commission finally decided to open an experimental class in French immersion for preschool-age children.

This victory led to the first French immersion programme. By the end of the 1960s, 'the original goals of the St Lambert parents . . . were taken up by other parents across Canada where Anglophones constitute the majority population' (Swain & Johnson, 1997: 4). In 1977, 35 parents founded an organisation called 'Canadian Parents for French' (CPF), a voluntary association of over 6500 families pledged to support French second language opportunities, including immersion programmes (Gibson, 1984). This organisation provides pamphlets and leaflets on such topics as 'So you want your child to learn French' and 'How to be an immersion parent', as well as newsletters which keep parents up to date on news, research results and extracurricular enrichment activities, in addition to providing information about schools offering immersion programmes through the CPF Immersion Registry.

Some anglophone parents, however, choose to send their children to French Catholic schools catering for the francophone population rather than to anglophone French immersion programmes, although as Rebuffot (1993) notes many of the French school authorities were initially reluctant to accept a large number of protestant anglophone children in their schools. Case Sketch 11 provides a personal testimony to the success of this type of 'immersion' which is sometimes referred to as *'immersion sauvage'*[2] (Braun, 1991, cited in Rebuffot, 1993) in relation to children from a multilingual family background where French is one of the languages spoken by the parents.

Case Sketch 11   An experience of 'Wild Immersion' (based on material kindly supplied by Jayson Campeau who is trilingual in English, French and Flemish, and whose wife speaks Flemish, English and French, as well as some German and Spanish)

We are parents with three children in a French school in a small rural community in south west Ontario, Canada. My wife, Arlette, speaks mostly Flemish with the children, I speak English with them, and she and I communicate mainly in English. We are not overly involved in the school. We attend most parents' nights and get to as many school concerts as possible.

Our children need to take a school bus ride of approximately 30–40 minutes each way to school. Communication with the home is done mostly in French and English. The running of the school and the school board is done all in French.

We are extremely pleased with the quality of education our children are receiving. Benjamin is in Maternelle, Jacob in 1e and Sarah in 2e (of a 2/3 split). There is a very high standard at the school for discipline, spirituality and, most of all, academics. The teachers and educational workers work together with the administration and the church to deliver the latest curriculum. There is no apparent lack of resources for books or teaching materials. The parents' council is active in fundraising. Fundraising is necessary because money has been cut from education for the past 9 years.

The children are learning French almost exclusively at school. Our eldest is reading and writing in French beyond the norm. The middle child is struggling a little with reading and writing but manages well orally. The youngest seems to be taking it all in. He understands almost all the French but speaks very little so far. We were concerned that they might suffer and fall behind due to the choice of French school. In fact they have not. They are average compared to their classmates but well above the average of students in English schools. They are also managing to learn a third language (Flemish) at a slower rate, but it too seems to be unaffected by the French school. Actually, let me say, the French school is helping.

All in all we are extremely pleased and fortunate to have been able to send our kids to French school. We plan on staying with this system at least until the end of grade school (13 years old) and possibly beyond.

Parents of Australian immersion students

As discussed in Chapter 11, immersion education in Australia is a rapidly growing phenomenon, which has become a very popular option for middle-class families who want their children to add a foreign language to their academic achievements at school. In this section we will compare parent expectations and involvement in three of these immersion programmes: one early partial German–English programme that was started in 1981 in Bayswater South Primary School in the state of Victoria; one late partial Hebrew–English programme, set up at Mount Scopus College, Melbourne, in 1990; and another late partial immersion French–English programme developed at Mansfield High School in Queensland in 1991.

Parents of students at Mount Scopus (Jewish) College, when asked about their reasons for wanting their children to participate in the immersion programme referred to 'educational challenge' as being an important factor, as well as the reinforcing of their Jewish identity (Lorch *et al.*, 1992). Parents of students at Mansfield High School concurred in the importance of immersion programmes as providing educational challenge for their sons and daughters and added that they had encouraged their children to enrol in the programmes because of beneficial outcomes in terms of better career options and increased job opportunities; because of the quality conditions regarding teaching and class size, as well as the appeal of learning another language in an effective manner (Stevens, 1995).

This second group of parents had high expectations of the immersion programme. They expected their children to become bilingual in French so that they would be able to manage without difficulty in a French-speaking country. They also felt that this gain in foreign-language proficiency should not cause any adverse effect on the development of their children's first language, English. They expected the immersion programme to be harder than the normal foreign language provision offered, but that this would be offset by more frequent contact between teachers and parents during the school year and much greater parent involvement than in mainstream classes.

In the third school, Bayswater South, parents were closely involved in the programme right from the beginning. Initially, they began observing classes and then started helping out with class activities, such as reading (Fernandez, 1996). In 1984, immersion classes in German were offered to parents. These enabled them to share in their children's experience of learning a foreign language, as well as involving them more closely in the life of the school. For many parents this was a way of fostering their 'ownership' of the programme and of ensuring their enthusiastic support, as revealed in the following observations cited in Fernandez (1996: 53):

> The program seems to be such a natural part of the life of the school. At every school activity – whether it be the swimming sports, or even the school camp – the German teachers are there too, speaking German . . . it's just accepted. (Parent of Grade 3 child)

I'm really pleased that he is in the German program and is enjoying it so much. It's very important to our family that he can speak the language. (Parent of Grade 5 child)

These comments show clearly the high degree of satisfaction expressed by parents about the Bayswater South immersion programme in terms of children's motivation and the 'naturalness' of the experience.

Parents of children in the Mansfield High School immersion programme also revealed very positive appreciations about the experience as well as some elements of dissatisfaction, as can be seen in Table 5.1 based on Stevens (1995: 60–1):

Table 5.1 Parents' rating of Mansfield High School French immersion programme

Satisfaction	Dissatisfaction
Students coping well.	Negative attitude of teachers outside programme.
Students' enthusiasm.	Inflated expectations of some teachers.
Industrious application.	Problems associated with perceptions of 'elitism'.
Closeness of group.	Lack of total school commitment.
Settled behaviour.	Organisational matters.
Dedication of teachers.	Academic matters.
Willingness to recommend programme to others.	Teachers not up to expectations.
Nothing to be done differently.	Lack of post-programme options.

As can be seen, parents were happy with student motivation and the high level of co-operation and good behaviour among members of the group, which was supported and encouraged by the teachers. However, the very success of the immersion group also led to a perception of elitism and resentment by other teachers and people in the school. There was also preoccupation about teaching methodology and academic quality of the programme in general, with a concern about how their children's foreign language proficiency could be maintained at the end of the programme.

In an interesting conclusion Stevens (1995: 64) notes, 'It appears clear from this study that the powerful role assumed by Canadian Immersion parents cannot be expected of Immersion parents in Queensland, perhaps in Australia.' She bases this observation on the fact that parents had indicated that while they were keen to be involved they were unlikely to initiate this process. Most indicated that they would wait for the school authorities to make the first move to organise gatherings and meetings.

Parents of Colombian immersion students

In Colombia, there have been two recent studies carried out by teachers into parental attitudes and expectations towards elite bilingual education programmes,

Araújo and Corominas (1996) and Orejuela (1997). The first, focused on parents of children aged 5–6 years old, in the preschool section of four English–Spanish bilingual schools in Cali. The second was carried out in a French–Spanish bilingual school in the same city with parents of primary school children, aged 10–11 years old.

In the first study (Araújo & Corominas, 1996) the results of a questionnaire sent out to parents of the four schools included in the research showed that the main reason for parents' choice of school was the fact of its being bilingual in English and Spanish, as well as the quality, experience and recognised high academic level of the programme. However, parents' greatest interest was in their children's development of the foreign language, English, rather than in their progress in their first language, Spanish. For these parents, their children's bilingualism centred in the development of their proficiency in English, due to its importance as a world language, 'for study, work, travel, business and international communications' (Araújo & Corominas, 1996: 180). Progress in English was helped by the fact that most parents acknowledged that they could speak English and in many families there were other relations, such as uncles, aunts, brothers and sisters who had a knowledge of the language. This clearly shows the high degree of penetration of English in the lives of middle and upper-middle-class Colombian families.

In the second study (Orejuela, 1997) however, parents' reactions were somewhat different. While they were equally enthusiastic about their children becoming bilingual, in this case in French and Spanish, the role of culture was seen as more important than in the previous study. Parents gave as reasons for sending their children to a bilingual school the following: 'easier access to (French) culture'; 'a new culture opens the perspectives of one's own culture'; 'because French culture helps to create humanists and not technocrats' (Orejuela, 1997: 40, 70). It can thus be hypothesised that these parents (86% of whom are Colombians) have maintained an image of French culture which does not take into account more recent French scientific and technological advances in the modern world (Orejuela, 1997). This rather idealised vision of French culture and the French language is reinforced by the fact that most of the parents admitted that there were few opportunities for them to participate in activities related to French language and culture in Colombia.

Another of the results of this study had to do with the frequency of contact between parents and teachers, which has been referred to earlier in this chapter. While parents were generally satisfied with their contact with the school (62%), some of the teachers complained that they had little institutional time or space available to see parents. In addition, there was evidence that expectations of parents about the relationship with their children's teachers were different in France and Colombia, as reported by one of the teachers from France who thought that Colombian parents, 'were more worried about the type of affective relationship between teacher and student, while in France parents focused more on the academic development of the child' (Orejuela, 1997: 54).

One of the main ways that parents helped their children in relation to the school was in their homework, even though many of them did not speak French. They felt it was important that one of the parents had a good knowledge of the language so that the child 'would not feel so alone in his learning process and the intellectual gulf between parents and children would be reduced' (Orejuela, 1997: 60).

Thus, it can be seen that the parents of all these middle and upper class students have had great influence on the development of programmes designed to improve the foreign language proficiency of their children, with a view to increasing their chances of better career and study possibilities. In some cultures parents expect to be more highly involved in their children's education, while in others, they are accustomed to wait for the schools to take the initiative. In all the cases discussed in this section, however, it can be seen that parents have high expectations invested in these prestige bilingual programmes and have voluntarily chosen to send their children to these types of school, often at great personal expense. This shows clearly the importance they attach to their sons and daughters being able to become fluent in two or more international languages for their future success in an ever-shrinking world.

School Administrators

The roles played by administrators – headteachers or school principals, school boards, academic co-ordinators – in the development of elite bilingual education programmes, while fundamental to their success, are under-documented in the literature. As noted previously, the heterogeneity of the different institutions which may be categorised as both 'elite' and 'bilingual' makes generalisation difficult, yet there are certain differentiations which can be made if a comparative stance is adopted. We will thus talk first about the administrative structure characteristic of many independent bilingual schools and then contrast this with the corporate structure of the European Schools movement.

One common administrative structure in elite bilingual schools is exemplified by the Casablanca American School in Morocco (C.A.S.) (see Chapter 7), where a non-profit charter grants ownership of the institution to 'the full-time faculty and parents of CAS students, whoever they happen to be at any given time' (Blanton, 1998: 39). These constitute the Casablanca American School Association and are responsible for the election of six of the seven-member Board of Directors. The seventh (non-elected) member is the US Consul General, who is also the Head of the Board. The school has a Director and Deputy Director who are answerable to the Board for all matters pertaining to school life. There is also a business manager who is responsible for financial aspects. Although the Casablanca American School forms part of a loose association of American schools in Morocco, it is completely independent institutionally.

The European Schools Association, in contrast, form a single system, rather than a federation of autonomous institutions, where the emphasis is on central rather than local administration (Swan, 1996). The Board of Governors, or the *Conseil Supérieur*, is the supreme decision-making body of the organisation and enjoys great autonomy on all matters relating to academic, administrative and financial issues. It is made up of the directors of each of the schools, together with two teachers and two parents from each institution, as well as representatives of associated bodies. There are also a series of sub-committees, such as the Administrative and Finance Committee and the Teaching Committee, as well as the Board of Inspectors, who report back to the Board of Governors. In addition to this centralised structure, each school has its own director and two deputy heads. School directors are usually appointed by the Board of Governors for a period of seven to nine years and are usually of different nationalities from their predecessors.

As can be seen from the above, decision making is largely in the hands of the centralised Board of Governors and therefore individual school principals have little possibility of responding and adapting to local needs, or even appointing seconded teachers to their staff. Swan (1996) suggests that this leads to a high degree of rigidity and prescriptiveness in the type of curriculum offered by the schools, which may result in the creation of psychological distance between the different linguistic, cultural and educational traditions represented. There is also evidence of a considerable time-lag between the promulgation of new regulations and their implementation at local school and classroom level. However, one advantage of this system is that it ensures 'common standards and a common curriculum ... in order to ensure the "currency" value of the European Baccalaureate' (Swan, 1996: 83).

Principals' perspectives

In this section we will look at what type of issues are seen as important by principals of elite bilingual establishments. As an example, we will take a statement by the principal of the Bayswater South Primary School, near Melbourne (Australia) where a highly successful experiment in bilingual immersion education in German was undertaken in the 1980s (see Chapter 11). We will also refer to comments made by the school principal of a French immersion school, Glenwood Immersion, in the US Mid West.

According to the principal of Bayswater South Primary School, one of the most important issues confronting any headteacher is the question of contracting 'trained and talented teachers' (Fernandez, 1996: 45). The principal of Glenwood Immersion School concurred with this appreciation, as can be seen in the following comment, 'Finding competent, qualified classroom immersion teachers is, no doubt, the single most important and difficult challenge in building an effective language program' (Coffman, 1992: 158). In the case of a bilingual programme there are additional constraints relating to the choice of language to be offered, such that 'the supply of teachers may determine the language to be chosen and principals will walk the tightrope between what is seen as ideal and what is seen as possible' (Fernandez, 1996: 45).

Another important administrative problem to be solved relating to staffing is how to finance the extra teachers required for the bilingual programme. Rather than try to use existing staffing entitlement within the school, the principal maintains that it is important to ensure that bilingual teachers figure as 'supernumeraries', or in other words as additional staff so that they are seen as 'a bonus to the school and the bilingual program is seen as an addition to and enrichment for the school's curriculum' (Fernandez, 1996: 46) rather than as a financial burden.

As the principal of Glenwood School recognises, it is important to remember that the issue of staffing also includes support staff, i.e. secretaries, classroom aides, food service workers, who are generally monolingual rather than bilingual. An important part of a principal's role is to ensure that these people feel fully part of the school community and do not feel discriminated against, in the drive to use the school immersion language as much as possible in the institution.

Perhaps one of the most important aspects of a principal's work is to forge links between those involved in the bilingual programme and the rest of the school community, so that s/he can account for what is going on and also give up-to-date information to parents and prospective entrants and can facilitate a close level of co-operation and consultation between classroom teachers and bilingual staff. If this is accomplished effectively, potential resentment and suspicion of the bilingual programme will be minimised and support will be ensured. Another vital aspect involved in this liasing work is to establish contacts with the wider community which will help with the provision of both language resources and financial support. This means that 'the principal oscillates between the role of administrator and that of public relations officer' (Fernandez, 1996: 46). Below, the principal of an International School in Milan (Italy) gives some advice to parents who are interested in sending their children to an International School.

Text Box 5.2   A Principal's Recommendations to Parents on Choosing an International School Education for their Children (based on Haywood, 2000: 2)

The first factor to look for is a clear policy towards the different languages to which a student might be exposed. Sometimes the range is most impressive: English (the school's formal language), the home language(s), the host country language and other foreign language options. A real case I can think of involves a child with Portuguese and Japanese parents, living in Italy attending an international school which works in English but which offers from the age of eleven the choice of foreign language options. If such a child transfers to an International School at the age of nine, the family is going to need serious advice and support about how to operate and prioritize their language options. In this context, what is the school's perception of the host country language? Should the family continue to speak Japanese and Portuguese at home or should they start to use English? What if the parents don't actually speak English well? What can they do to encourage cognitive development and progress?

If the school has a consistent and clear approach to language, then it will be able to guide the family through these tough questions and through the transitional phase when the new student is facing personal difficulties in settling into . . . new surroundings. Language support in school is obviously of primary importance but this can be provided in different ways. Joining an ESL class is only one of them, and alternatives involve mainstreaming into regular classes with personal or small-group support. This can be costly in teacher time and that is why international education is never cheap. It should also be made clear that mastery of English takes time . . .

   This leads us to the second main factor in good practice: how can we use the languages that a child already knows, especially the mother tongue? There was once a time when it was fashionable to snub other languages and attempt to create an entirely monolingual English environment . . . But we have now learned that schools should actually take the opposite approach. They should really be encouraging continuing linguistic and cognitive development in the mother tongue as the basis on which to construct their work in English.

   This all goes to show that the support of the principal is vital to the success of the programme and demands careful planning and preparation. The rewards of this interest and dedication are multiple: the enjoyment and excitement generated by the children in their use of another language; an increased level of parental and community interest and involvement in the school; and the experience of being at the forefront of an educational innovation. In the perceptive words of the Bayswater South School principal it is the quality of the language learning experience intro-duced in the bilingual programme that is important,

   as a Principal one gains a great deal of satisfaction from watching the program in action and observing the children as they participate quite naturally in ac-tivities in which they are required to receive and convey knowledge, ideas and thoughts through the medium of a second language. This broadening of the language experience is what bilingual education is all about. (Fernandez, 1996: 50)

Teachers

   In this section we will focus on two main groups of teachers involved in elite bilingual education: those who teach in the European Schools Association and those who teach in International Schools, as these provide contrasting profiles of teacher recruitment and working conditions.

   As may be expected from what has been said earlier about the structure and philosophy of the European School Movement, most of the teachers employed in this type of school are seconded by the Education Ministry of the member state in which they have been working (Swan, 1996). The schools themselves have very little say in these matters. The duration of teachers' contracts was fixed in 1994 as not to exceed nine years in total, as it was felt to be important that they should share their experience of European education with their colleagues on their return to their home countries. There is also a second group of teachers in the European School

Movement who are called *chargés de cours*, recruited locally and employed on a temporary basis. Those selected are mostly qualified professionals. In addition to these two groups, there is a further category of teachers known as *conseillers d'education* who are responsible for some teaching, the supervision of recreation, and the preparation of end-of-term reports for the parents.

Teaching in this type of school is seen as a challenge which involves different types of skills from teaching in a national context. The European Schools' Staff Committee observed in 1986 that 'experience shows that an excellent national teacher is not necessarily a good European teacher' (cited in Swan, 1996: 92). There are various reasons for this statement. First of all, teaching in a multilingual, multicultural context where classroom norms on acceptable classroom behaviour, relative levels of formality and informality, and teaching styles may be very different to what the new European School teacher is accustomed to, often proves rather bewildering. Furthermore, the teacher is often the only cultural role model that the learners in a particular linguistic subsection have contact with and this places great responsibility on him or her to foster the students' developing sense of identity. In addition, many teachers are required to teach their mother tongue as a foreign or second language, rather than as a first language and lack the necessary training to do so.

Teachers who teach in bilingual International Schools will also have encountered several of these problems, especially if they work in the type of institution patronised by 'mobile, expatriate families' (Sears, 1998: 61) as well as host country families. According to this author, one of the most challenging aspects of a teacher's work in this context is the sheer variety of abilities, aptitudes and experiences to be found in the average International School classroom, added to the fact that few institutions provide support programmes to help students who are having difficulty. As she notes, 'New teachers in this situation may find the pressure of answering the needs of second language children almost overwhelming and certainly stressful. A major contributory factor to this stress . . . are the high expectations of both first and second language students' parents' (Sears, 1998: 14).

In the case of bilingual International Schools which cater basically for host country students the pressures are different. Here, the outlook, philosophy, and cultural practices are influenced by their geographical location and local teachers may not take kindly to any assumptions of superiority on the part of foreign teachers. Thus, 'Teachers from English-speaking countries in this situation need to recognise their role in the school. They have been hired to offer specific expertise in the use of English, not because they are representatives of an English-speaking culture' (Sears, 1998: 64).

This situation is one that needs to be handled tactfully if it is not to lead to a division between different members of staff along national lines, as is often the case in Colombia where there are at least three different categories of teachers who work in most bilingual schools. First, there is the privileged class of foreign (i.e. non-Colombian) teachers contracted abroad, usually in the USA or Britain, in the case of English–Spanish bilingual schools. Then there are foreign residents in Colombia, and finally there are a large number of Colombian nationals. There is a corresponding language continuum which goes from monolingual foreign language speakers, through bilingual speakers, to monolingual Spanish speakers. This differential in language proficiency is reflected in the areas the teachers work in. Generally foreign staff and national bilingual teachers teach Foreign Languages, Science, Maths and Economics in the foreign language, while Colombian monolingual staff teach Spanish language and literature, Physical Education, Art, Music and Religion in the first language.

Although many schools see foreign language monolingualism among the staff as an advantage, in that the teachers will not be tempted to use the students' first language in their classes, this can lead to difficulties of communication, especially with children who are in the initial stages of becoming bilingual. In general, school administrators value foreign language skills more highly in their staff than knowledge of the first language, and this is often reflected in differential rates of pay, a situation which is also potentially divisive.

Colombian Labour Law (Article 74C1) specifies that a maximum of 20% of teachers in any school may be foreigners brought into the country for the purpose of teaching in bilingual schools; the rest must be local. This ruling may be modified, by schools applying for permission to bring in extra teachers up to a limit of approximately 30% of the total staff. However, expatriate teachers living and working in Colombia are classed as local residents and therefore the numbers of foreign nationals working at any one time may be much higher than the 20% stipulated by the law.

It is important that schools which intend to become bilingual consider the implications of hiring foreign staff, whose presence, because of superior rates of pay and conditions, may cause division in the institution. While, as we have seen, foreign expertise is often highly valued by both parents and school administrators as a sign of school status and foreign teachers may bring advantages to the institution, such as new ideas on teaching approaches and methodology, they are, in general, a transient population, hired on two or three-year contracts, who often do not have time to identify with the institution or its wider aims. The financial burden involved in recruiting foreign staff often means that there are not sufficient financial resources for the professional and language development of local teachers. Furthermore, this dependence on foreign expertise has the disadvantage of potentially perpetuating a mentality of underdevelopment among host national teachers and administrators.

In this connection, it is interesting to note an Australian student's perception of the differences between native and non-native speaking teachers in his university level Japanese immersion programme. In contrast to the views expressed above, the student considers that native-speaking teachers can be problematic as they tend 'to forget that for the students, speaking Japanese is still only a second language and quite difficult at times', while he considers that 'non-native lecturers seem to have more tolerance and understanding of the student's position as a non-native speaker trying to speak Japanese' and that they provide 'a model and something to aim for' (Cross, 1995: 100).

Students

In line with the organisation of the previous sections in this chapter, we will now focus particularly on the situation and experience of students in European Schools as well as those who attend International Schools. As noted in the introduction to this book, both European School students and students who go to International Schools which cater for expatriate families are characterised by their linguistic, cultural and academic diversity as well as their high degree of mobility. These features often result in student profiles which are different in many ways from those who study in national educational systems.

Examples of some of these differences are provided by Swan (1996) and Sears (1998). They note that many students in these types of school enjoy a high standard of living and material resources, but often suffer the prolonged absence of at least one of their parents, who frequently have demanding jobs in international organisations or multinational corporations and cannot supervise their offspring as much as they may wish. On the other hand, parents may wish to cushion their children from a strange environment and go to the other extreme of trying to over-protect them from new experiences. This can result in children finding it difficult to achieve an appropriate level of independence and may lead to increased emotional difficulties and problems of adaptation.

Almost paradoxically, there are some parents who worry about their children adapting too well to foreign languages and cultures, in that they fear that this will change them radically and cause them to lose their national identity. In this respect it is interesting to note the experience of a Japanese mother whose son was attending an English medium International School in Brussels for the first time. At a parent discussion group, she recounted how the child's grandparents would phone from Japan every week to make sure that their six-year-old grandson was being brought up as 'a real Japanese boy' (Sears, 1998: 52) and how they were devastated when he refused to speak to them in Japanese, on one occasion. There is also the reaction noted by Margaret Pond, a teacher in an International School for girls in England who observes that 'A little girl who wants to have English friends may be ostracised by her Japanese friends who say, "Oh, you are not being Japanese enough, you are becoming English"' (Pond, 1999: 77).

The same author also recognises the need some international students feel for a refuge from the stresses involved in interacting in a foreign language with teachers and peers. The difficulty of not being able to communicate with others is movingly attested to by a Japanese pupil at the International School of Brussels (ISB) who recalled in her 6th Grade graduation speech how she had felt on her arrival at the school two years before,

> I came to ISB when I was in fourth grade. I couldn't speak any English at that time, everyone around me spoke only English. In Japan, I could talk and talk, shout and shout, but I said nothing here. Nothing was fun at first when I came, but when I began to speak, I felt that this school was great. (Sears, 1998: 55)

Other initial reactions to international education by new pupils may be seen in negative behaviour patterns, withdrawal (as in the example above), children talking in their first language to teachers and classmates (even though they know they will not be understood), and evidence of extreme tiredness or fatigue resulting from the effort needed to adjust to new language and educational demands.

One of the biggest dangers to new International School or European School students is a loss of self-esteem when they realise that they are not able to perform as well as they did previously in their countries of origin. This is often compounded by the fact that the grading or marking system used is different, so that the children do not recognise the parameters used in evaluation. For example, some children are used to school systems which penalise errors, rather than reward effort and find it difficult to understand a grading system which does the opposite. Also, children who are highly competent in Mathematics may find that their linguistic difficulties in the foreign language mean that they are placed in groups with less able students, thereby leading to frustration and resentment. Some of the difficulties involved in doing Mathematics in 'another' language is expressed by the mother of a bilingual student in Text Box 5.3

Text Box 5.3 Problems with Mathematics in Two Languages (taken from Bilger, 1997: 5)

I am English . . . My husband is German. . . Initially we communicated in French . . . Our daughter, Katrin, was born in 1985 . . . (We moved to Germany). At this point we made a conscious decision to drop the French . . . We started with the one parent one language approach . . .

Katrin made the transfer (to a German school) in August 1995. Prior to the transfer she had had no formal teaching in reading or writing German. She has coped extremely well with the change, although it was certainly difficult in the beginning and she needed much support. Interestingly, many of her problems are in Maths . . . Her teacher insists on speed but Katrin still has to translate the sum into English, do it and them translate it back into German – no easy task when one realises that German numbers are 'back to front' (24 = vierundzwanzig, 4 + 20). Her German spelling is improving rapidly, her vocabulary, accent and grammar structures have improved dramatically. She is no longer taking the easy option of reading for pleasure in English.

However, if students are supported and encouraged in their learning of the foreign language, this leads to renewed confidence and enjoyment, as evidenced by a comment made by an Australian university immersion student where he considers it vital to provide 'opportunities . . . which allow students . . . to see how much their language has developed over time . . . (as) language learning is an extremely gradual process and often one might not even realise the gains that have been made. . . . Tackling something as difficult as learning a new language needs lots of encouragement and support from those around them so the students can see that their efforts are being realised somehow or another' (Cross, 1995: 98).

Both Sears (1998) in the International School context and Swan (1996) in connection with European Schools make reference to the importance of friendship to ease problems of adjustment among new students. In European Schools there is widespread evidence to show that students do make friends across the different linguistic subsections and are able to communicate with speakers of other languages with increasing ease as they go up the school. In the case of International School students, Sears (1998: 102) notes, 'It is remarkable how children who do not share each other's languages are able to bridge the verbal divide'. She also observes that due to the fact that most international students move around a lot during their schooling, they often become adept at quickly establishing friendships with their peers and therefore acquire a range of social skills, which often gives the impression that they are fairly sophisticated and mature. However, this does not mean that they do not experience loss and disruption when their friends move on, and teachers and parents need to help these students come to terms with these difficult experiences. These feelings are aptly portrayed in Text Box 5.4.

Text Box 5.4   Help for a Teenager in a Foreign Country (taken from McTigue, 1998: 6)

My husband and I are both English and moved with our 7-year-old daughter, Jennifer, and our new born son Alex to Italy in 1992 . . .

After four years in Italy we all moved to our new home in Switzerland, and a very different lifestyle. Jenny spent her first eight months in a class for foreign children concentrating on the German language. Thanks to a very energetic and motivating teacher, she learnt very quickly and was moved to the local Swiss school. She entered at the 6th class level, which is already a more strenuous stage for Swiss children as it determines which type of school they will attend to finish their education. Here Jenny faces the additional problem of having formerly studied High-German, yet having to switch to studying in Swiss-German, practically a language of its own which she is 'learning as she goes along'.

A quick 13-year-old, she is adapting, making friends and trying to keep pace, but the stress of operating as a fledgling bilingual, coupled with the onset of puberty often leaves her tearful, prone to slight illnesses and unable to sleep at night. Thoughts of future gains are little comfort in the here and now for Jenny. Together with Jenny's teacher we are still trying out different ways of helping but I feel I lack any professional insight into how children manage a second language at this age and the emotional impact it can have. It has affected Jenny's self-esteem. Her competence in German effectively masks the effort she's required to make every school day.

Conclusion

In this chapter we have focused on how parents, administrators, teachers and students view their roles and relationships in the furtherance of elite bilingual education programmes in such diverse contexts as Canada, Australia, Colombia, Japan, USA, Belgium and England. We have noticed that the process of adapting to new linguistic, social, educational, and cultural norms inherent in these situations is often complicated by the different expectations, fears and presuppositions of the differing participants. Parents are concerned that their children settle well, but also do not 'lose' their cultural identity. Students are worried about making and keeping new friends, as well as working out what is expected of them in their new schools. Administrators, for their part, realise that they often need to act as public relations officers for the bilingual programmes offered by their institutions, as well as ensuring that the programme itself runs smoothly. Teachers have to get used to supporting and encouraging the children in their care to overcome the frustrations and difficulties of being educated in a different educational world to that in which they are used to functioning.

Thus, it can be seen that the roles assumed by these groups are different in many respects from the roles normally expected in monolingual settings, where cultural, social and linguistic norms are more homogeneous. In International or European Schools, administrators and teachers need to develop an understanding of the reasons why students and their parents may react in apparently unexpected ways to school demands. In national settings, such as the immersion programmes in Canada, Australia, and Colombia, although most of the school population comes from similar linguistic and cultural backgrounds, schools and families may have to come to terms with tensions generated between high expectations of the level of proficiency in two or more languages resulting from a bilingual education, and the realities of the process of learning a foreign language in a largely monolingual and monocultural context. It can thus be seen that it is important that all members of the school community, parents, teachers, students and administrators, are able to maintain close contact with each other, in order to obviate difficulties arising from misunderstandings based on linguistic, cultural or educational differences.

Notes

1. 'Immersion in French', author's translation.
2. 'Wild immersion', author's translation.

Chapter 6

Research Traditions and Trends, Partnerships and Empowerment in Elite Bilingual Educational Contexts

Introduction

In the first five chapters of this book we have discussed various general manifestations of elite bilingualism: as part of a world-wide globalising movement; in relation to a sociocultural dimension; in different educational contexts; and with respect to the different participants in elite bilingual educational processes. In this chapter we will examine the current state of research in the field of elite bilingual education from a historical perspective, in relation to three main areas of provision: English-medium International Schools, European Schools, and immersion programmes. We will then go on to discuss a recent collaborative research initiative in the area of bilingual curriculum construction which foregrounds the importance of facilitating processes of empowerment among participants if lasting, significant change is to be achieved.

Research Traditions

For anyone trying to make sense of the field of elite or prestigious bilingualism, one of the greatest difficulties is the current lack of research carried out in this area of study. There is one notable exception to this observation in the case of the well-documented literature on immersion research, not only in the Canadian context but also internationally, as demonstrated by Johnson and Swain (1997) (see below). In the field of International Schools, however, there has been little attention paid to the specificities of bilingual or multilingual educational provision which caters for students of higher socio-economic status from internationally mobile families, who are usually majority language speakers. Matthews (1989: 28), in a survey article on international education, refers to, 'the sparse literature of International School education', while Cristina Banfí (1999, personal communication) laments that as far as she knows there are no researchers working on aspects of elite bilingualism in Argentina (see Chapter 8). Moreover, Frances Bekhechi (2000, personal communication)[1] observes that in the International School of Brussels most of the teachers' work is based on 'our own observations and experience of working with internationally mobile children' due to the 'lack of a solid body of research on multilingualism in young children'.

Perhaps the most well-known publications in the International Schools literature with regard to English-medium International Schools have been two handbooks (Murphy, 1990; Sears, 1998) addressed to teachers and administrators in this type of school. These, as their designation implies, are aimed at helping those who work in international education understand and cope with the particular demands of a highly mobile population who need to adjust rapidly to different cultural and learning expectations. They were written by practitioners who have worked for many years in the field and who bring a wealth of practical experience to their writing. The value of the insights and perceptions of those who work in international education is undeniable. However, there is also a case to be made for the encouragement of research projects in this area which will provide a body of research evidence for some of the policies and practices currently advocated in International Schools.

Research in the field of European School education has been mainly concentrated in the hands of Hugo Baetens Beardsmore (Baetens Beardmore, 1990; 1993a; 1993b; 1995; Baetens Beardsmore & Swain, 1985; Baetens Beardsmore & Anselmi, 1991). Although some of his writings treat aspects of European schools in general, where he refers to 'European Models of Bilingual Education' (1993a and b), the main thrust of Baetens Beardsmore's later work has been in connection with the European School, Brussels I and the European School of Luxembourg. Initially, the emphasis was on comparing and contrasting European Schools with other types of bilingual provision, such as immersion education (1985, 1990), in an attempt to characterise the particular contribution of the European Schools movement to bilingual education. Later, these concerns changed into considering 'how different paths can lead to high levels of proficiency (and how) such proficiency is tempered by contextual variables more so than by programme variables' (Baetens Beardsmore, 1995: 147).

Together with Giulia Anselmi, Baetens Beardsmore (1991) has also conducted research into the process of code-switching among multilingual secondary school students in the Italian subsection of the Brussels I European School (see Chapter 10). This type of study is particularly valuable as it is one of the few carried out in an elite bilingual setting which focuses on informal language use outside the classroom and helps to show 'the significance of code-switching as an element in a language learning context, incorporating curricular and extra-curricular factors' (Baetens Beardsmore & Anselmi, 1991: 430–1).

In contrast to the relative dearth of research initiatives in these two areas, International School and European School programmes, the early experimental Canadian immersion programmes were conceived right from the start as integrally bound up with a process of systematic evaluation and research. The focus was on assessment of their impact on the linguistic, intellectual and attitudinal development of the children involved in the study (Lambert & Tucker, 1972). This type of extensively funded policy-driven research was specifically situated in a psychometric tradition, and was designed to have immediate educational impact on school planning (Tosi, 1989).

Although as Stern (1984) acknowledged, immersion is probably one of the most thoroughly investigated educational innovations, the actual lines of enquiry involved were largely restricted initially to a focus on educational outcomes. This has been explicitly recognised by Lapkin and Swain (1984) and justified by the perceived need to demonstrate to policy makers that immersion was indeed a viable educational alternative and to reassure anglophone parents that their children would not suffer either academically or in respect to their English language proficiency.

From the middle 1980s onwards the early, almost exclusive, focus of immersion research on educational outcomes was modified. Stern (1990) situates this change of emphasis within the general debate on communicative language teaching which began in the late 1970s. He charts the concern of immersion researchers, such as Harley and Swain (1978, 1984) and Harley (1991) to identify positive and negative aspects of proficiency development in immersion students and to identify problem areas in the development of the proficiency of immersion classes (Stern, 1990). Thus, a significant strand of immersion research began to concentrate on aspects of classroom practice which were seen to be associated with the development of L2 proficiency.

There were also calls for immersion research to investigate the nature of classroom processes. In an influential article in 1987, Tardif and Weber noted the shift in classroom research in first language contexts to a concern with, 'an understanding of classroom processes which take into account the setting of classroom interaction, the relationships between teacher and pupils and the socio-cultural knowledge that each brings to the situation' (Tardif & Weber, 1987: 71). They suggested that attention to processes of classroom interaction and to the ethnography of communication in the immersion classroom might illuminate some of the language acquisition processes at work.

In a similar vein, Handscombe (1990) argued for recognition of the need for classroom-based research involving close collaboration between researchers and practitioners, both in immersion programmes and in second language teaching in general. She highlighted the desirability of teacher involvement in establishing research agendas in collaboration with academic researchers and in carrying out the research programme itself (Handscombe, 1990: 186).

In a further development, Heller (1990) advocated looking beyond the immersion classroom and the immediate school situation in order to ascertain the realities of the learners' communicative needs and the issues of inter-group relations within the wider Canadian socio-political context. In this way, she feels that investigation into the impact of the social, economic and political consequences of immersion would help to illuminate language learning as a social, economic and political process, embedded in relations of power.

During the late 1980s, there was evidence of increasing interest in immersion research in new aspects within the pedagogical domain, such as curriculum design, teacher education and professional development (Harley *et al.*, 1990). The plateau effect, originally identified by researchers into bilingual proficiency (Swain, 1985; Swain & Lapkin, 1986), was also situated in a wider framework – that of the realities of communicative needs beyond the school (Heller, 1990).

In keeping with this change of emphasis there has been a corresponding shift in the type of methodological approach considered appropriate for research in the area. Heller (1990), like Tardif and Weber (1987), sees work of an ethnographic nature as fundamental to future developments in immersion education in Canada. She argues that, 'since so few ethnographic studies of immersion (whether of the classroom or its school and community environment) are available, it is difficult to pinpoint further the communicative constraints of the French immersion classroom which may be blocking further development, or whether it is possible in fact to do anything further in an instructional context of any kind' (Heller, 1990: 76). This appreciation points to the need to carry out detailed ethnographic observations both in the classroom and community context, which capture the nature of the processes involved more appropriately.

In the 1990s, more emphasis was given to process orientated work, as evidenced by an in-depth study of teachers and teaching in two immersion programmes, one French immersion and the other Spanish immersion, in the mid-West United States (Bernhardt, 1992). This two-year ethnographic research project focused on examining immersion teachers' beliefs and experiences as a way to understand how they approached their classroom practice. The researchers were also interested in examining 'immersion teaching' as 'a particular kind of teaching . . . not just language teaching' (Bernhardt, 1992: 3). There was thus an emphasis on pedagogical concerns rather than on the more widely discussed topics of the development and maintenance of student language proficiency.

This study is interesting, in that the focus is on teachers and classroom interaction, rather than the immersion programmes themselves, as seen through the eyes of principals, supervisors and teacher trainers. Moreover, the detailed discussions of classroom routines and aspects of contextualised student–teacher interactions provide a fascinating glimpse of how teaching and learning is accomplished moment by moment in different foreign language immersion contexts

In the late 1990s, there appeared another influential study (Johnson & Swain, 1997), this time highlighting immersion education as an international development, documenting advances in immersion programmes in countries such as Australia, Hungary, Finland, Spain, Hawaii, Hong Kong, Singapore and South Africa, as well as Canada and the United States. One of the interesting things about this compilation is not only the recognition of immersion as a world phenomenon, but also the differing conceptualisations of these programmes: as foreign language development; as minority language provision of majority language students; as language revival; as language support; and as contact with a language of power.

From the above discussion about research in immersion education certain tendencies can be noted. For instance, we may observe recognition of the importance of ethnography in providing insights into immersion teaching and learning processes both within the classroom and without; interest in curriculum design and teacher development; and calls for a closer partnership between academic researchers and practitioners.

Although research has been traditionally thought of as the prerogative of those who work in academia, well away from the stresses and strains of the chalkface, Cochran-Smith and Lytle (1993), in the field of teacher research in general, note the wide gap frequently established between academic researchers and teachers in the development of educational research projects. They point out that restricting teacher participation in research projects negates their role as generators of knowledge about their own pedagogical practice and leads to an undervaluing of their contributions to research. In this respect, the above authors make an important distinction between 'research on teaching' and 'teacher research'. They equate the former with university-based research. The latter they define as, 'systematic, intentional inquiry by teachers (which) makes accessible some of the expertise of teachers and provides both university and school communities with unique perspectives on teaching and learning' (Cochran-Smith & Lytle, 1993: 5).

Teacher research may involve collaborative research projects, such as action research, which involve both academic researchers and practitioners, thus bridging the traditional research–practice divide. In Latin America, Marilda Cavalcanti (1996) in her work in bilingual Amerindian community contexts has noted that in order to carry out this type of project, 'one has to look at oneself as both researcher and researched. As researchers, we are not usually very open to the opinions of the researched, when the researched is the *other* ... Research can be a tool for exploring what it means to listen to the *other*' (Cavalcanti, 1996: 187).

Cavalcanti assumes a similar position to that advocated by Cameron *et al.* (1992) in their considerations on how research in the field of language may help to empower the researched, and also to the position of the critical discourse analysts of the Lancaster University school (Clark *et al.*, 1987, 1990, 1991), who are concerned to help those who work in education become aware of the multiple links between language, power, and ideology, so that they may be able to assume a reflexive position with regard to their role and responsibility in these processes.

In this section, we have been concerned to trace the development of research traditions in the fields of English-medium International School provision, European School programmes, and Immersion Education. As we have noted, while there is a dearth of work carried out on aspects to do with International Schools and European Schools, the situation in immersion research is completely different. A wealth of studies document the development of research in this field and contribute to the high profile of this form of bilingual provision in contemporary educational thinking.

Having provided a brief research overview in the above section, we will now go on to focus on one particular collaborative research project, carried out during 1997–1998 in a school which was interested in becoming bilingual in the city of Cali, Colombia. The aim of our discussion will be to show in detail how a participative approach to the construction of a bilingual curriculum in an elite context has helped to foster a climate of empowerment among the participants in the project and in this way has pointed the way towards lasting, significant change.

An Experiment in Empowerment: The Case of *Gimnasio La Colina*, Cali, Colombia

Introduction

In Colombia and elsewhere in the world, this type of approach is relatively new in the area of elite bilingual education, and while interest has been expressed in the idea of empowerment, particularly in minority bilingual educational contexts (Cummins, 1989; 2000), there have been few research initiatives which have been specifically set up to study the process in bilingual curricular construction in elite situations. This case study, thus, offers insights which may prove of interest to other elite bilingual schools who are interested in promoting collaborative research projects in their institutions. We will begin by providing a short historical account of the school where the research took place and at the end discuss the importance of this type of initiative in the light of calls to promote processes of educational change from the grassroots upwards.

A brief history

Gimnasio La Colina is a small private school situated in the northern part of the city of Cali, founded in 1975. It caters for students from families of higher socio-economic status, from the ages of 2½ years old to 18 years old at three levels: preschool, primary and high school (*bachillerato*). At the time of this study, there were approximately 535 students and 63 teachers in the institution.

The school philosophy is based on promoting an integrated vision of education. It does not see itself only in terms of academic achievement, but aims at facilitating the development of 'all the personal, spiritual, social and cultural aspects of the students which will help them to live in harmony with themselves and with others in a constant search for happiness'[2] (School prospectus, 1996).

In recent times (1986–1996), the school implemented a policy of 'foreign language intensification', which meant that contact with the foreign language offered (English) was increased from 2 or 3 hours a week to 5 hours a week at preschool level, 11 hours in primary, and 5 hours in high school. However, the focus was on teaching language, rather than using English as a medium of instruction in different subject or content areas.

Towards the end of 1996, the school authorities decided that they wished to implement a programme of bilingual education, which would reflect the philosophy and educational approach of the institution, and at the same time allow the students to achieve a high level of proficiency in English. To this end they approached the School of Language Sciences at *Universidad del Valle* to request a consultancy (*asesoría*). In this way, two university researchers became involved in a novel participatory research project in the area of bilingual curricular construction.

In order to understand this experience appropriately, it is necessary first to sketch in some details of the specific educational and sociocultural context in which this study was carried out (for further details, see the profile on Colombia, Chapter 8.)

Educational and sociocultural context

During the past ten years, there has been great interest in the area of bilingualism and bilingual education in the whole of Colombia in general, and in Cali in particular. Very frequently new schools are opened which announce that they are 'bilingual', 'bicultural' or both. While there are some schools that may use these labels for the purpose of charging higher fees for their services, there are many serious institutions which are concerned about the need to respond to the changes brought about by the globalisation of the economy and new demands of increasingly complex multilateral international relations in a world which is becoming ever more interconnected and therefore in need of a lingua franca which, more often than not, is English.

There are also many monolingual schools in the country, mainly catering for an upper-middle-class population, which see the need to offer their students a bilingual programme. They see the advantages of developing a high level of proficiency in two languages as providing a good preparation for university education both in Colombia and abroad, better job prospects, a wider knowledge of the world, as well as increased opportunities for travelling and working abroad. However, up to now, there has been very little research carried out into bilingual education programmes in the country. Most schools either look to Britain, the United States or Canada to provide an appropriate model for bilingual education provision, or find out what other bilingual schools within Colombia are doing and copy certain practices. In both cases the results are often less than satisfactory, because there are no firm bases for decision making or criteria for curriculum development and the models have been developed in different sociocultural and educational contexts in response to other needs and circumstances.

When schools and university departments work together in the area of language education in Colombia, it is generally through a process of consultancy. In these cases, university professors are usually seen as outside experts, who are brought in to carry out an analysis. They observe, interview key personnel and write a report, detailing the results and recommendations for future implementation. They then leave and often have no further contact with the institution. The findings and recommendations contained in the report may be difficult to interpret without expert knowledge, and power and control are kept firmly in the hands of the consultants. Thus, there is an intervention, which may bring about some positive results, but there is generally little opportunity for learning on the part of the participants.

A process of empowerment

Right from the start, the bilingual curriculum project requested by *Gimnasio La Colina* was conceived by the university researchers as having a different emphasis. All participants, teachers, administrators, psychologists and researchers, were recognised as having different expertise, which would form the basis for the joint construction of the curriculum. Through a series of interactive sessions the participants would work together to draft, comment on, suggest and criticise the emergent proposals. No one person would be responsible for the final proposal, it would be a collaborative effort.

It must be emphasised here that in the initial stages of the project, the idea of construction of the project around the concept of empowerment came from the university researchers. The school participants were content to work in traditional fashion with the consultants whom they saw as 'the experts'. It was only gradually that they came to terms with the idea that all the participants in the project were jointly responsible for its successful development.

In the circumstances, we felt it was necessary to create our own working definition of empowerment which would reflect our second project aim (see next section for our first aim). We therefore proposed the following,

> Empowerment is the process through which the participants in the research become conscious of their capacities, potential, knowledge and experiences in the area, so that they can assume responsibilities in the development of autonomy and full participation in decision-making, not only during the research process, but also in the following phases of assessment and modification of the proposals in the light of the changes and new advances in national educational policies.

As can be seen, the emphasis in this definition is on *process* rather than product and therefore implies a longer time scale than is often considered in consultancies. The process of consciousness-raising was seen as leading to a greater degree of responsibility and participation in decision making both during the research and afterwards. Furthermore, everyone taking part in the project was considered a participant. There was no division into researchers, on one hand, and their subjects, on the other.

These ideas were greatly influenced by the work of Cameron *et al.* in their pioneering work on empowering research in the field of language, which implies a vision of research 'on, for and with' the participants (Cameron *et al.*, 1992: 22) and the use of interactive or dialogic research methodologies. This conception implies the redistribution of knowledge from academia to the community and vice versa. These researchers suggested certain provisional guidelines to help those interested in carrying out empowering research projects, which may be summarised in the following manner: '(a) Persons are not objects and should not be treated as objects; (b) Subjects have their own agendas and research should try to address them; (and) (c) If knowledge is worth having, it is worth sharing' (Cameron *et al.*, 1992: 23–4).

The use of interactive methodologies focuses on the need to involve the active involvement of all the participants in the project, and in order for this to happen they need to have a clear idea of the research objectives and procedures and be able to express their views about them. This should help to ensure a more equal relationship between researchers and researched, by reducing the imbalance of power normally associated in this type of relationship where it is usually the academic researchers who decide research agendas.

This new approach had repercussions on the way in which the project was carried out and how the university researchers acted in the meetings. For example, we refused to respond to demands on us as 'the experts' , which were common, particularly at the beginning of the project. At times, we decided to keep silent and not give our opinions, in an attempt to help others to take the floor. We also encouraged presentations and discussions of different aspects of bilingualism and bilingual education by members of the group. The written reports on each of the sessions were analysed, modified and approved by all participants.

In order to facilitate the process of curricular construction, diagnostic studies were first carried out to ascertain the current situation in the institution, both in relation to school philosophy, methodology, level of foreign language teaching and learning, profile of the bilingual student at the end of his/her school studies, human and material resources, and the expectations of members of the school community, particularly parents, towards the bilingual education project.

To document the process of empowerment, we collected three different types of data. First of all, we recorded the interactive sessions with a view to carrying out a later analysis of power relations within the group, examining such things as who initiated, who had the longest turn, who spoke most frequently, what type of speech acts predominated, etc. We also recorded our own observations as to the process of empowerment in an on-going research diary. In addition, we asked all the participants to reflect on their experiences in the project every three months, asking them how they felt about the process and mode of working as well as trying to find out how they felt they were contributing.

Results: Bilingual curriculum proposal

Our first aim in the project was to create a curricular proposal to convert a monolingual into a bilingual school programme, appropriate for the needs and wishes of the school community. The results of our discussions led to the formulation of a proposal based on an Alternate Day model, which incorporated a general ration of 40% contact in English in 1st Grade Primary to 60% Spanish, leading to a balanced level of contact with both languages at Secondary or High School level (see Table 6.1).

Table 6.1 Weekly language distribution

Grade	Monday	Tuesday	Wednesday	Thursday	Friday	Approx. %
1–2	Spanish	English	Spanish	English	Spanish	40E*–60 S
3	English	Spanish	English	Spanish	English	60 E–40 S
4–6	English	Spanish English	English	Spanish English	English	80 E–20 S
7–11	English	Spanish	English	Spanish	English	50 E–50 S

*E = English, S = Spanish

The proposal thus incorporated a modality of partial immersion in the foreign language, which differs from the Canadian immersion model in that there is a progressive increase in the contact with English in Primary, which reaches a high-point in Grades 4–6. The rationale behind the decision to have a greater emphasis on the first language (Spanish) in Grades 1–2 lies in the fact that the children are consolidating literacy processes in Spanish during this time and beginning to transfer these into English. This practice is based on the principle that it is important to work on new concepts initially in the first language (cf the Preview-Review Approach) before developing and expanding them in the foreign or second language.

In Grades 4–6 there is greater contact with English (80%) aimed at the consolidation and extension of concepts and academic content matter in the foreign language. In Grades 7–11 an equal linguistic balance is proposed to ensure that the first language is maintained and enriched at the same time as the foreign language is developed and extended.

In addition, we drew up a series of parameters, based on the results of the diagnostic study, to guide the implementation of the bilingual proposal. These included the following:

- The school philosophy and mission would be respected.
- An intercultural approach would be adopted, aimed at expanding students' horizons and helping to establish respect, tolerance and appreciation for both their own culture and the culture of other anglophone nations.
- The bilingual programme would not be the centre of the curriculum, but an important educational and linguistic support to such aspects as the teaching of values, and learning through project work.
- The bilingual programme would incorporate key educational elements characteristic of the school, such as the carrying out of projects at preschool level.
- Different areas of the curriculum would be subject to different linguistic treatment. Thus, initially the teaching and learning of Mathematics would be in Spanish, while Natural Science would be carried out in English with a Preview-Review orientation.
- Initial literacy skills would be taught in the first language and then transferred to the foreign language.

- There would be emphasis not only on the notion of using two languages as media of teaching and learning in the school, but there would also be time scheduled for study of linguistic aspects of both languages.
- The implementation of the proposal would be closely monitored and modifications would be made in the light of on-going changes in policy and practice.

Results: Empowerment (participant voices)

With respect to our second project aim, participant empowerment, the results of our analysis of the data indicate the following tendencies. Right from the beginning, the participants expressed satisfaction that everyone was able to participate actively in the project. One teacher noted, 'I think the way of working is excellent because it has encouraged wide participation, the expression of different points of view . . . and the opportunity of learning during the process of construction'. Another commented that, 'you feel an active part of the process, and it doesn't seem like something which has been imposed on you'; while a third said, 'I like the working dynamics and I think I have been able to contribute from my experience and knowledge as a teacher, even though I don't know much about bilingualism'.

Respect for the ideas of others was a central motif running throughout the observations of the participants. One of them observed, 'People in the group are very generous with their knowledge, respectful and patient'. Another recognised that, 'We have arrived at conclusions which have not been imposed (although some of them have been suggested or recommended)'.

There was also a general feeling in the group of a sense of challenge in that this was an initiative that would lead to the development of a new curriculum which would reflect the specific needs and wishes of *Gimnasio La Colina*, and that in this sense it would be a unique creation. As one of the teachers remarked, 'It is not the same to "make the path" (*hacer el camino*) as to find the path already made'.

However, these positive appreciations did not blind members of the group to certain difficulties inherent in the process of collaborative research, chief among which was the amount of time necessary for decision making. As one of the participants remarked, 'Although I agree with this process, it seems to me that it takes a long time, I mean it's slow with regard to all the needs there are'.

The perceptions of the university researchers strongly reflected the views of the school participants described above. Our conscious decision to adopt 'a low profile' and the initial group emphasis on discussing key concepts such as bilingualism, biliteracy, different modalities of bilingual education, biculturalism and interculturalism led to gradual changes in the ideas expressed by members of the group. At first, we noted a marked sense of resistance to some of these ideas, particularly in relation to cultural aspects. Many of the teachers felt threatened by what they saw as the prospect of a loss of cultural identity coupled with their fears that the implementation of a bilingual curriculum would mean dismissal for monolingual teachers.

Gradually, the discussion sessions based on readings taken from key texts on bilingualism and bilingual education helped to lessen these fears so that participants eventually came to appreciate the value and importance of understanding the contribution of other cultural perspectives in relation to their own. As we recorded in our field notes, 'it appears that the fear of "penetration" by "the other culture" and the threat to national identity is diminishing'.

Another key area of change related to empowerment was that of the new bilingual teachers hired for the preschool section who became involved in the bilingual curriculum project halfway through the first year, when they began teaching in the bilingual programme. At first, they asked many precise questions about practice, such as whether classroom commands should always be associated with the same classroom routines or whether these should be varied; and whether they should only talk in English, or when they could use Spanish.

Members of the bilingualism group reacted to these questions by recommending the teachers to adopt an experimental approach, often associated with Action Research. They suggested, for example, 'Try to vary your practice as you think best after this discussion and see how the children react'. This way of working was seen as helpful by the preschool teachers, as can be seen in their following insightful observation:

> Since September we have noticed a marked change, not only in activity but also in our attitude. We have found a lot of professional security in being able to share our experiences and knowledge, seeing how the group supports, discusses and enriches (these experiences). We have felt a lot of respect, understanding and listening to the different concerns. We feel more relaxed, realizing that this is an ongoing process.

Bearing in mind the guidelines traced by Cameron *et al.* (1992) with regard to the facilitation of empowerment in research, we can sum up the general agreement of the participants in this process (teachers, university researchers, co-ordinators, and psychologists) as to the high level of active participation of all the members of the group in the discussions and in the creation of academic, institutional and logistic proposals. Some of the reflections we have cited above show that the participants felt on an equal level and did not feel intimidated in contributing to the project. They also felt that the different interests of the group, pedagogical, administrative and research were catered for at different moments in the project.

The members of the group also demonstrated their capacity to assume responsibility for fundamental changes in the school, such as the implementing of an intercultural approach, the reconceptualisation of the Mission and Vision of the institution in the light of its characterisation as bilingual; and the design of bilingual projects integrating different areas of the school curriculum. Furthermore, they also felt able to contemplate the prospect of continuing the following stage of implementation of the proposal without the direct supervision of the university researchers.

For all these reasons, we feel that the process of empowerment of the participants in the project shows clear signs of progress throughout the study and that there is a good chance that this will continue into the following stage.

Implications and preliminary conclusions of this experiment in empowerment

Recently, various authors in the fields of Bilingual Education and English Language Teaching (ELT) (García, 1993; Auerbach, 1995; Ricento & Hornberger, 1996; Hornberger, 1997), have argued for recognising the importance of the role of teachers in promoting change, not only in the area of classroom practice, but also in such areas as curriculum development, language policy, and societal goals. These areas have traditionally been thought of as being the exclusive domain of so-called 'experts', as noted in the following observation by Ricento and Hornberger (1996: 417):

> In the ELT literature, the practitioner is often an afterthought who implements what 'experts' in the government, board of education, or central school administration have already decided. The practitioner often needs to be 'educated', 'studied', 'cajoled', 'tolerated', even 'replaced' by better prepared (even more compliant) teachers.

Teachers themselves have often been socialised into seeing themselves as passive recipients of ready-made curricula and policies, which they have little power to influence. In the field of curriculum development, Auerbach (1995: 13) sees what she terms the *ends-means* model as the dominant example of a process which usually begins with university-based researchers 'identifying the body of "knowledge". . . to be covered'. Once this has been established, curriculum content is then organised and sequenced into 'chunks' of knowledge to be covered in a particular space of time. Thus, 'despite the fact that it is couched in scientific terms, the ends-means approach serves as a mechanism of social control, disempowering for both students and teachers' (Auerbach, 1995: 14).

An alternative, empowering vision is to 'place the classroom practitioner at the heart' (Ricento & Hornberger, 1996: 417) thereby facilitating processes of educational and social change and institutional transformations from the grass roots, a 'bottom-up' perspective. García (1993: 36), in her work with bilingual teachers in New York, puts the onus for the development of this new perspective squarely on teachers themselves. In a strongly worded exhortation she claims:

> (The teacher) must stop being an instructor, accepting of orders, of curriculum planned, of material given, and must claim her role as an educator, empowering the community she teaches by providing it with the appropriate knowledge and resources it needs . . . Only then, will (teachers) feel empowered to transform practices that can, little by little, crack by crack, impact on societal goals.

García (1993) thus rejects a limited instructional role for teachers, which does not take into account wider sociocultural and educational influences. Her vision of a 'true' educator implies a critical commitment and active involvement in constructing knowledge which is valid for the wider community.

The difference in vision, advocated by these researchers, then, involves practitioners, school administrators and university researchers recognising that all members of the educational community have the right and the duty to contribute to processes of effective change and that change is not unidirectional. 'Top-down' policy proposals must be complemented and extended by 'bottom-up' initiatives and grassroots proposals must not be dismissed out of hand as inappropriate.

As we have mentioned in the analysis of the results of our case study, it is important not to underestimate the difficulties involved in processes of empowerment. One thing is recognising the need for this, another is actually facilitating its progress. As various authors have acknowledged, it is not a question of groups or individuals handing over power to others. Gieve and Magalhães (1994: 131–3) say that it is rather, 'about "voice" and allowing the subjects' own voice to emerge, indeed promoting it . . . Empowerment is the ability to value one's knowledge and meanings through a process of critical reflection on the meanings and knowledge of others'. Thus, one cannot empower someone else. The emphasis is on helping 'the other' to first become conscious of the need for empowerment and then facilitating the process.

In the bilingual curriculum project in *Gimnasio La Colina*, initially the participants did not ask to be empowered. In fact, they were quite happy to accept a traditional relationship of 'expert–inexpert'. It was because the university researchers decided to focus the project around the notion of empowerment that the school participants were, in a sense, forced to come to terms with the implications of assuming a much greater role and responsibility for decision making. There is, thus, a strange contradiction in the idea of 'forcing' people to recognise and accept the need for their own empowerment. There is also, of course, the necessity for the academic researchers to admit their own need for empowerment, which may not be immediately obvious.

Ivanic (1994: 118) maintains that collaborative research of the kind discussed above is usually advocated on ethical grounds, as in the case of Cameron *et al.* (1992). She lists some of these 'ethical' advantages as:

> the people who are being studied can learn a lot from the research; . . . decisions about methods are made jointly, ensuring that they will not constitute too much of a burden or an intrusion; . . . (and) knowledge is not the academic researcher's property . . . (but) should serve the needs of both the academic researcher(s) and those who are being studied.

However, Ivanic also advocates a collaborative approach in order to increase the quality of the research itself, in that research may be of greater interest and value, may develop 'richer' research methodologies involving the views and perspectives of the people being studied, and may lead to more reliable research findings, in the sense that the presence of the people who are being studied in the project helps to prevent over-interpretation of results on the part of the university researchers.

In the *Gimnasio La Colina* project we feel that we have gone some way towards exploring the ethical value of a partnership with school representatives in documenting the process of empowerment during the creation of an appropriate bilingual curriculum for the school. We also noted that the types of insights gained from the experience, not only while we were immediately involved in the project, but later when writing up the project, have greatly enriched the resulting discussion, in that our views as academic researchers have been contrasted with and complemented with the voices of our co-researchers, members of the school community, as can be seen in the above discussion.

Conclusion

In this chapter, we have been concerned to give an overview of the type of research initiatives which have been carried out on three types of educational programmes classified within the tradition of elite or prestigious bilingualism: English-medium International Schools, European Schools, and Canadian immersion programmes. As we have seen, there is a need for more research, particularly in the areas of International Schools and European Schools, both process and product orientated, to provide evidence of the specific nature of key aspects of programmes created to cater for the needs of highly mobile international students.

The case of research into immersion education is different, in that there has been a vast amount of money and research interest invested in this initiative over the past 30 years. We have shown how the orientation of research in these programmes has gradually changed from a quantitative, product-centred perspective, towards a more ethnographic, process-centred stance.

In the final section of the chapter, we have described, at some length, a study carried out in an elite school in Cali, Colombia, which documents a process of collaborative research, aimed at the construction of a bilingual curriculum for the school. Through this we have attempted to illustrate aspects of the process of empowerment of members of the research team. While it has been shown that there are certain undeniable difficulties in this type of approach, such as the length of time required for such projects, and a certain sense of lack of direction at times, there are also great advantages in adopting a collaborative stance. These advantages have been categorised as involving both ethical considerations and heightened research quality, as well as necessarily reducing the traditional gap between university researchers and practitioners by postulating a partnership of equality of expertise in the carrying out of research on teaching and learning in elite bilingual contexts.

Note

1. Frances Bekhechi is head of the ESL Department in the Early Childhood Center and the Elementary School at the International School in Brussels.
2. Author's translation.

Part 2
Overview of Elite Bilingual Provision in Specific Contexts of Implementation

This part, which comprises eight chapters – Chapters 7–13 and the conclusions chapter – will discuss how elite bilingualism and bilingual education have developed in various parts of the world in the light of different historical, sociocultural and educational influences. In the first part, Chapters 7–11, we will focus on two or three countries in each continent, and examine, in detail, how some of the tendencies discussed in earlier chapters in Part 1 have influenced the growth of different types of elite bilingual provision in situations which include post-colonial developing nations, state educational systems catering for upwardly mobile groups of higher economic status students, private International Schools which offer education in two or more world languages and state or national promotion of a favoured language.

In Chapter 7, therefore, we will focus on two former colonial African nations, Morocco and Tanzania. In Morocco we will chart the development of both French and English International Schools. In Tanzania we will look at how English is still seen as a language of power and prestige in spite of the growing influence of Kiswahili. In Chapter 8 we will discuss aspects of elite bilingual education provision in three South American nations, Colombia, Brazil and Argentina, in German and Spanish, and English and Spanish. The following chapter, Chapter 9, will foreground developments in relation to bilingualism in English in three Asian countries, Hong Kong (China), Japan, and Brunei. In Hong Kong we will focus particularly on the so-called 'Anglo Chinese' schools; in Japan on initial developments in bilingual education in immersion type schools; and in Brunei we will examine the *Dwibahasa* bilingual education policy and its incidence in the promotion of Malay–English bilingualism. In Chapter 10 we will examine four countries, first, two Northern European nations, Finland and Sweden, concentrating in the former on Finnish–Swedish immersion programmes, and in the latter on International School provision (Swedish–English). Then we will discuss developments in Belgium, focusing particularly on one European School, Brussels I. We will finish the European chapter by looking at how prestigious bilingual education programmes in Castillian Spanish and Catalan have helped to raise the profile of this prestigious minority language. In Chapter 11 we will discuss aspects of German–English immersion programmes in Australia.

In each context we will begin by giving a macro perspective on aspects of bilingual or multilingual development in the country concerned. Then we will concentrate on specific characteristics of bilingual programmes and bilingual teachers and learners, such as aspects of classroom interaction and pedagogy, curricular organisation, and attitudes and social relationships among participants.

The last three chapters in this part, Chapters 12–14, will look at the discourse of elite bilingual education from a critical point of view and then at key aspects of bilingual pedagogy as reported by teachers working in elite bilingual schools around the world, followed by a concluding chapter summing up and reflecting on elite bilingual education around the world.

Chapter 7
Africa: Multilingualism, Vernaculars, Intra- and International Languages

Introduction

In a conscious attempt to counteract the North American / Eurocentric imbalance evidenced in much writing on elite bilingual education, we will begin this half of the book by considering bilingualism and bilingual education provision in two countries in the African continent which represent, to some extent, opposing tendencies: Morocco, a North African Islamic nation which was a French protectorate for many years and also came under Spanish influence for a while, and Tanzania, a sub-Saharan country situated in the south-eastern part of the landmass, formerly part of the British Empire.

MOROCCO

General Perspectives

Morocco is a country situated on the northern coast of the African continent, which forms the gateway between Africa and Europe and a point of entry to the Mediterranean Sea. It has land borders with Algeria and Western Sahara. The population of present-day Morocco numbers around 28 million (according to 1994 figures) the majority of whom are of mixed Berber and Arab descent, as a result of intermarriage between native Berbers and Arab invaders who began arriving in the country during the eighth century AD. Approximately 65% of these speak colloquial Moroccan Arabic as a first language, while the rest are native speakers of one of a number of varieties of Berber which may be classified into three main divisions: *Tarifit* spoken in the north of the country, *Tamazight* in the centre, and *Tashelhit* in the south-west (Baker & Prys Jones, 1998; Blanton, 1998). While most Berber speakers are also bilingual in Arabic, which is the official language of the country, Arabic-speaking Moroccans do not usually develop fluency in Berber, considering this a language of limited use and prestige.

As a result of Morocco's status as a French protectorate between 1912 and 1956, the French language is widely spoken throughout the country. It was formerly particularly prominent in the educational system, until the 'Arabisation' of state education in the 1970s, and is still widely used in private schools. In the northern area of the country around Tangier, the use of another former colonial language, Spanish, is widespread, though not considered particularly prestigious outside this area. English, on the other hand, is taught as a foreign language in schools and in private language centres particularly in the large cities, and though popular, particularly among young people, is not widely spoken in the country (Blanton, 1998).

Thus, it is evident that present-day Morocco is a highly multilingual society where at least seven different language varieties, Berber (*Tarifit, Tamazight, Tashelhit*), Modern Standard Arabic, Classical Arabic, Moroccan Arabic, French, Spanish and English are in play in the linguistic market, though not all used in the same domains. A triglossic situation exists in relation to the use of the different varieties of Arabic noted above. Modern Standard Arabic is used in administration, the mass media, some government offices, and as a language of communication with other Arab nations, as well as being the language of literacy in Moroccan schools. Classical Arabic is the written variety used in ancient, religious or formal texts, such as the Quran, and thus characterises liturgical worship in the country. Moroccan Arabic, in contrast, is used in informal conversations, many television programmes and in education, particularly in classroom interaction. It is generally considered a dialect rather than a language, and consequently suffers from low prestige, even though it is the main language of communication within the country. In addition, as mentioned above, French is used in the education domain, as well as in government, business and commerce (Baker & Prys Jones, 1998; Blanton, 1998).

Many Moroccans go abroad to work or study, according to the US Department of State (Morocco Country Report on Human Rights Practices for 1998). In fact, tens of thousands of Moroccans hold more than one citizenship and travel on passports from two or more countries. Nevertheless, the number of Moroccans who marry foreigners is still very small, 1.5% of the population, according to statistics published in 1997 by the Centre for Demographic Study and Research; and 50% of these mixed marriages are to Europeans, particularly French nationals. A typical scenario (illustrated by Case Sketch 3.3 in Chapter 3) is of Moroccan men who do their university studies in France and who marry French women, subsequently returning to live and work in Morocco. Where possible, these families send their children to bilingual (French–Arabic) or French-medium schools, not only because these are seen as the passport to higher education and well-paid jobs but also because they help to maintain the children's links with their European culture. If this is not possible, such families may enrol their children on distance learning programmes from the mother's country of origin, thus enabling some of the children at the end of their school career to sit the French baccalauréat as independent candidates, in addition to the Arabic-language Moroccan baccalauréat (Jane Griffiths 1999, personal communication).

The complex social interrelations among these different linguistic and cultural groups may be illustrated by the humorous extract in Text Box 7.1 taken from a recent Moroccan publication (*La vie économique*, 30-8-96, 5-9-96, translation provided by Jane Griffiths).

Text Box 7.1   On the Problems of Bilingual Dinner Parties in Morocco

One piece of advice: never put Arabic and French speakers together . . . Faced with an Arabic speaker, French speakers get . . . rather a complex: at the first word of Arabic, they clam up for the evening, afraid of getting their pronunciation mixed up, mistaking one word for another which is probably its opposite, finding themselves saying something awful and ending up in very deep water.

Generally speaking, Arabic-speaking men occupy one end of the sitting room for themselves and leave the opposite corner to their wives, who ask for nothing better.

French speakers, on the other hand, divide into smokers and non-smokers. If one of the latter starts an argument about the evils of smoking, it will go on until midnight, at least.

The above extract exemplifies the linguistic and cultural divisions in the country, where on the one hand supporters of bilingualism argue for the maintenance of French, as well as Arabic, as an important means of communication, while others, on the contrary, support a policy of 'Arabisation', in other words, making Arabic the sole medium of instruction in education and promoting it as the language of wider communication. One of the repercussions of this policy in the area of education is that nowadays (unlike in the 1950s and 1960s), only children who come from wealthy families can hope to achieve better economic status and job opportunities as a result of their studies, as only their families can afford to send them to private bilingual schools which allow them to acquire a sufficiently high level of proficiency in French or English to cope with the demands of university education where these languages are the media of instruction.

Redouane (1997: 1) considers that bilingualism is developing without difficulty in Morocco, 'in a dynamic, evolutive and constructive perspective (where) [E]ach (language) occupies a certain place: Arabic, the language of culture and national identity is the centre, French, however, is (on) the periphery'. She thus considers that a 'bilingualism of rivalry' has been superseded by a 'bilingualism of complementarity', where French and Arabic co-exist side by side. However, judging by some of the articles which appear in the Moroccan press, with headlines such as *La politique d'arabisation au Maghreb* (*L'opinion newspaper*, 17 May 1996), and *De l'universel au spécifique: Conference sur le bilinguisme dans le systeme éducatif marocain*[1] (*Le Matin newspaper*, 25 June 1996), the language debate is still an important issue which continues to evoke strong reactions from both sides in the argument. In addition to the question of French–Arabic bilingualism, there is also debate on how far colloquial Arabic and the Berber languages should be used in schools in order to ease the transition from home language to Modern Standard Arabic, and on whether the Berber languages should be taught as languages in their own right.

Elite Bilingual Education Provision

Private bilingual schools

After independence from France in 1956, the state school system was decreed to be officially bilingual in French and Arabic, with a bias towards French. Arabic was only used in the teaching of Islamic studies, Arabic language and literature. Later, however, during the 1970s, as a result of the increasing influence both politically and socially of the policy of Arabisation, primary and secondary education became exclusively Arabic medium, while French continued to be used for the study of scientific or technical subjects at tertiary level. This meant an abrupt change of language for university students who chose to study in the field of natural science or technology, which often proved traumatic and prevented many monolingual Arabic-speaking students from continuing their tertiary education (US Department of State Morocco Country Report on Human Rights Practices for 1998). This was one reason for a sudden proliferation of private French–Arabic bilingual schools, aimed at parents who were afraid that their children would not have access to good job opportunities in business or commerce if they could not speak French (Jane Griffiths 1999, personal communication). Another, was the growing perception by parents that state schools used outdated methodological practices and relied largely on rote learning and oral recitation, without taking into account advances in computer literacy and multilingualism (Blanton, 1998).

In many such private, bilingual schools at primary level, in a similar fashion to so-called private 'bicultural' schools in Argentina (see Chapter 8), a separation approach based on time of day and teacher is implemented so that children are taught the full Moroccan curriculum for half the school day by an Arabic-speaking teacher, and the French curriculum by a French-speaking teacher for the other half of the day. However, standards vary widely among schools and very often no concessions are made in this dual curriculum to co-ordination of the two different syllabuses so that students have to study the same subjects at different times in each language, often becoming overloaded in the process.

At secondary school level things are slightly different, as students have to prepare for the Moroccan baccalauréat in Arabic. One approach is for each subject area to be taught by a bilingual subject specialist who uses both Moroccan and French course books and who follows a policy of language alternation, teaching one lesson in French and the following in Arabic. In practice, however, most subject specialists tend to code-switch extensively and generally use more French than

Arabic, as they have done their university studies in France and are therefore more familiar with the use of French scientific terminology. As an illustration of this, we can cite the example of one particular teacher at a private bilingual school who told the parents at an official meeting that when he introduced a new topic in the syllabus, he taught the lesson in Arabic and then used French for the discussion and examples. However, feedback from the students revealed that although this teacher generally began the class in Arabic, he very soon switched to French for most of the lesson (Jane Griffiths 1999, personal communication).

Moroccan International Schools

In addition to the French–Arabic private schools described above, there are also a number of International Schools (ECIS Directory, 1997/8). The majority of these are French schools teaching a French curriculum and often supported by the education authorities in France. There are also a number of English-language schools, almost exclusively North American in orientation, which cater for the needs of upwardly mobile students and their families. Most of these are found in the larger cities, such as Casablanca, Rabat and Tangier, and offer either a US-based or international curriculum, which enable students to do their university studies abroad, particularly in the USA. The main teaching and learning medium in the majority of these schools is English, though instruction is also offered in French and Arabic in many of these institutions. As a general rule, Moroccan pupils at all foreign-language schools must study Arabic.

One of these schools, the Casablanca American School, was recently the object of a study on language and literacy learning practices by one of the teachers who worked at the school in the late 1980s (Blanton, 1998), who has provided a rare glimpse of how teaching and learning practices are constructed in specific multilingual and multicultural International School settings. I will base the descriptive analysis in Case Sketch 7.1 on material from this book as well as referring to information supplied by the school to prospective parents, in order to show in more detail how official school policies and statements in relation to education in bilingual and multilingual educational contexts are implemented in practice.

Case Sketch 7.1   The Casablanca American School

The school was founded in 1973 to meet the needs of the growing business and diplomatic community located in Morocco's financial and industrial centre. It caters for around 400 students, half of whom are host country nationals from wealthy Moroccan families who can afford to pay the very high tuition fees, which are the equivalent of those characteristic of elite private schools in the United States. The other 200 students are drawn from around 20 different countries: Indian families resident in Morocco for generations, employees of multinational companies, such as Goodyear and Siemens which include their employees' children's school tuition as part of a benefits package, children of diplomatic families, and children of teachers who work at the school.

The school receives a small annual subsidy from the US government as an over-seas school educating US nationals, but is not officially registered as a US school. It is run by a board of directors elected by the community of parents and headed by the US Consul General. It is also part of a loose federation of US schools in Morocco, which include the Rabat American School and the Tangier American School. These schools foster inter-institutional links through joint sporting events and professional or educational encounters on topics such as curriculum development.

According to Blanton (1998), the reasons Moroccan parents choose to send their children to an English-medium school which is culturally associated with the United States, are based on a combination of political, social and educational factors. Politically, the US is not associated, as is France, with colonialism in the country and therefore some Moroccan parents feel that treatment of host nationals would not be as discriminatory as it might be in a French-medium school. Socially, North-American education is seen as prestigious and there is also the additional status value of sending children to a school associated with other socially and politically prominent Moroccan families. Furthermore, from an educational point of view, US education is perceived as centred around critical thinking, which is not associated with Moroccan education. In addition, as in many other parts of the world, English is seen by many parents as the language of future economic success.

An intercultural vision

In its statements of philosophy and objectives, the school maintains the following official position towards cultural awareness:

> *The Casablanca American School recognises the richness of the world's racial, ethnic and religious diversity. It shall be receptive to learning about and appreciating American cultures and all other cultures and their interrelatedness. While reflecting American educational values, the School must involve itself in the host country environment. It shall enhance awareness of Moroccan cultures among our community, and maintain lines of communication between the school and the host country. (Admissions Information, 1997–8: 4)*

The explicitly worded appreciation of cultural diversity contained in the above statement is manifested in school practices. Although the majority of the teaching staff are non-Moroccan (out of a total of 54, only 9–17% – are host country nationals), there is a conscious effort by the institution to encourage a comparative cultural perspective, in which Moroccan and North American holidays are cele-brated; Moroccan dignitaries and visiting North American guests, such as the world heavyweight boxing champion, Mohammed Ali, are invited to speak at school events; and all Moroccan citizens are required to attend Arabic language classes, as well as completing their studies through the medium of English

(Blanton, 1998). Thus, we note that for 1997–1998 the following festivities are recognised in the school:

Casablanca American School Festivities

Festivity	Date	Type/Country
Yom Kippur Day of Atonement	Oct. 11	Religious (Jewish)
Columbus Day	Oct. 13	USA
Green March Day	Nov. 6	Morocco
Independence Day	Nov. 18	Morocco
Thanksgiving Day	Nov. 27	USA
Christmas	Dec. 25	Religious (Christian)
Ramadan begins	Dec. 31	Religious (Moslem)
Declaration Day	Jan. 11	Morocco
Martin Luther King Jr. Day	Jan. 19	USA
Aid el Fitr – Ending of the Fast	Jan. 29	Religious (Moslem)
President's Day	Feb. 16	USA
Throne Day	March 3	Morocco
Aid Al Adha – Feast of the Sacrifice	April 7	Religious (Moslem)
Pesach – Passover	April 11	Religious (Jewish)
Easter Sunday	April 12	Religious (Christian)
First Muharram – Moslem New Year	April 27	Religious (Moslem)
Labor Day	May 1	Morocco
National Day	May 23	Morocco

Another very important manifestation of an intercultural position in school policies and practices has been adopted by the school in the payment of equal salaries and benefits to both foreign-hired and locally hired teachers (Blanton: 1998). This is not the case in many elite bilingual schools in other parts of the world, such as in Colombia, where staff are often divided by a two-tiered system of privilege associated with outsiders at the expense of insiders.

Language policy

The school prospectus states that, 'English is the language of instruction, and the school will make every effort to develop the students' interpersonal and academic proficiency in English while encouraging development of his/her first language skills as well' (Admissions Information, 1997–8: 5). Thus, though the main teaching approach adopted is total immersion in English, Arabic and French classes are offered to children who speak these as their first language, and all children have to learn French as a second language in Grades 2–12. In addition, the school offers the International Baccalaureate Programme in the final two years of secondary education, where students study English, Arabic or French as a second or foreign language.

The vast majority of graduates from the school go to university in the United States, but there are also former students who have studied in Europe (Switzerland, France, UK, Belgium, The Netherlands, and Spain), as well as at universities in Morocco itself.

Language and literacy development in early Primary school

At Nursery and Kindergarten level (3–4 years old) the emphasis is on the children acquiring oral fluency in English, before the curriculum requires literacy to be taught through the medium of English (Blanton, 1998). In the years that Blanton (1998) conducted her study she noted that out of the 121 children in Kindergarten, Pre-First Grade and First Grade, only two were monolingual speakers of English, and only a handful of the others came into contact with English at home.

To cater for this situation, the school provided the services of an English as a Second Language (ESL) teacher, who operated mainly on a pull-out basis, i.e. she withdrew a group of children who were considered to be most in need of English language reinforcement from the mainstream classroom. An interesting observation about language use at this level is given by Blanton (1998: 58–9), when speaking about the ESL specialist, Eileen:

> *Eileen – herself fluent in three languages, English, German, Arabic – is not a linguistic purist; and this is one of the many keys to her success with the kids. For her, language serves communication . . . and if, in a given situation, English, German or Arabic won't do, she'll try a little of Edward's French or Luis's Spanish.*

Thus, it can be seen that this teacher encouraged code-switching when working with young children who were beginning the process of becoming bilingual, in order to facilitate classroom communication and to encourage the pupils to use what they already know as a bridge towards their learning of a new language (cf. discussion in Chapter 4).

In addition, the teachers interviewed stressed that an integrated curriculum was necessary to contextualise language and concept development for their multilingual learners. They considered that the introduction of thematic units, such as 'All About Me' or 'The Solar System' helped the children to interrelate aspects of knowledge from different disciplines, such as Science, Music, Social Science, Maths, etc. Teachers also maintained that it was essential to focus constantly on English language development within this integrated framework and not to isolate it as a separate lesson at a specific time of day, as it is 'simultaneously the framework, the object and the medium of learning and teaching' (Blanton, 1998: 97). It is thus the language needs of each individual child which dictate the type of adjustment that the teachers need to make in the presentation of the different curriculum areas. Furthermore, as the great majority of the children do not speak English at home, their only contact with the language is at school and therefore the teachers considered that English language development should be a priority.

Perhaps the most important aspect of this in-depth ethnographic study, as noted by Shirley Brice Heath in her Foreword to Blanton's (1998) book 'Varied Voices', is the opportunity it provides for the reader who is familiar with developments in US classrooms to adopt a comparative perspective, or in other words 'to see the research done in the United States as it is played out in a classroom of multiple languages, cultural backgrounds and needs' in Morocco (Blanton, 1998: vi).

Higher education

As noted previously, the policy of language use at university level is that Arts subjects are taught in Arabic and Science and Technology are taught in French. According to Jane Griffiths (1999, personal communication), the practical result of this is that weaker students often have a tendency to choose an Arts subject, so that they will not have to change over from using Arabic at school to using French as a teaching-learning medium at university. Thus, as noted by the US Department of State Morocco Country Report on Human Rights Practices for 1998, this language policy automatically prevents many students from pursuing Higher Education in studies leading to well-paid jobs. However, the alternative, involving transforming science teaching at university level into Arabic, would imply a long-term trans-national project together with other Arabic-speaking nations in order to develop an appropriate database of scientific terms which would be recognised internationally and the subsequent production of Arabic language scientific text-books.

In addition to the above, there is one Moroccan university opened in 1994, which constitutes the only English-medium university in francophone North Africa and which offers courses in the areas of Engineering, Humanities and Commerce. *Al Akhawayn* University in Ifrane is based on a North American model and requires a high level of initial student English language proficiency for admission, based on TOEFL scores. An interesting research project from the point of view of bilingual education studies, led by researchers in the university language centre is in the process of investigating aspects of student foreign language proficiency in English in relation to general academic achievement. Researchers are also interested in establishing how far the intensive English courses run by the centre affect overall academic achievement, or whether, in fact, students acquire their English as a result of pursuing their studies through the medium of English, rather than through attention on linguistic aspects *per se* (Peter Hardcastle, 1999, www.alakhawayn.ma/~P.Hardcastle/researc.htm).

Summary

As can be seen, Morocco is a highly multilingual and multicultural society where language contact and language alternation is almost inevitable in any type of social interaction. In order to make the most of this linguistic diversity, many Moroccan parents have opted to send their children to bilingual schools where they can pursue their studies through the medium of French and English as well as Arabic, in the hope of future advantage in the spheres of Higher Education and in the national and international job market. Many of these families come from upper-middle-class backgrounds, especially those who choose to send their children to North American-type International Schools.

In the period after independence in 1956, it was possible for students from families of low economic status to compete at school on equal terms with students from families who were better off. All were taught through the medium of French, and opportunities for further education were equal, at least in terms of language. As a result, a significant number of students, mostly men (fewer women, mostly from the major cities) had the opportunity to study abroad and improve their social status when they returned to Morocco. Their children now go to French–Arabic bilingual schools and aspire to tertiary education, often outside the country. Their cousins, however, are often still submerged in poverty, and this situation often leads to difficult family relationships with pressure put on the more socially mobile members to support the others. Opportunities for children from poor families to 'make good' through education are now far more limited, partly because the social situation has stabilised in recent years, but also because of the language hurdle at university level.

This social complexity is mirrored in the ambiguous attitudes expressed by many Moroccans to the conflicts engendered by the confrontation between 'traditional' values, and values associated with Western societies. While on the one hand individuals may profess to hating North Americans, on the other hand, they may also state that the country they most wish to visit is the United States. The fact that these sets of cultural values are often seen as incompatible, leads many children from mixed marriages to find it difficult to accept their differences in a positive fashion. Yet, it is not only children of mixed parentage who face these conflicts. To varying degrees they affect almost all Moroccans, whether they live in the country or abroad.

Education too has to meet conflicting demands. On the one hand, state education has to provide education for all children in Arabic, the language of the country, in a country with relatively high illiteracy rates (43% in 1994). On the other, private education aims to satisfy the demands of a rapidly modernising society, in which knowledge of French and English is essential for educational and economic development, both for individuals and for the country as a whole.

TANZANIA

General Perspectives

This East African nation, in common with much of the rest of Africa, had a history of European colonisation during the nineteenth and first half of the twentieth century. The Germans ruled the country from 1885 to 1919, followed by the British from 1919 until independence in 1961. These periods of colonial rule have had a great effect on the current language debate which centres on the issue of which of the two official languages, Kiswahili or English, should be used in the educational system.

The majority of the Tanzanian population (28.7 million, according to 1995 figures) are bilingual, speaking a vernacular ethnic language as their first language, and Kiswahili (a local lingua franca) as a second language. English is used only by about 5% of the total population, generally when they are communicating with foreigners. Abdulaziz-Mkilifi (1972, cited in Rubagumya, 1990) describes language use in Tanzania as a triglossic situation, where the 120 or so vernacular, mainly Bantu, languages are associated with oral use in informal or family situations, Kiswahili is used as the language of national public life, in parliament, commerce, religious services, and in the administration, and English is reserved for the language of higher education, the High Court, diplomacy and foreign trade.

The relationship between the domains of use of vernacular languages and Kiswahili appears to be relatively stable in the sense that the former have been left in a state of almost complete official neglect while the latter has been promoted as the national language of wider communication within the country and in the East African region. The reasons given for official neglect of the vernacular languages appears to stem from the fear that emphasising their use might give rise to 'divisive ethnic groups at the expense of national unity' (Batibo, 1995 *et al.*, cited in Baker & Prys Jones, 1998).

In the case of the relationship between Kiswahili and English things are very different. As Rubagumya (1990: 10) notes, 'The trend is that many domains where English was used are now being taken over by Kiswahili'. The reason given for this trend is practical necessity, considering that nowadays only a very small percentage of the population have any knowledge of English, whereas about 90% are bilingual in Kiswahili and a vernacular language (Abdulaziz-Mkilifi, 1971; 1972, cited in Rubagumya, 1990). Therefore when people have to communicate in official institutions, such as the law courts and in education, most will use Kiswahili rather than English.

Kiswahili is increasingly being used in the lower courts or when court officials are dealing with plaintiffs, defendants and witnesses who do not speak English. However, judges, prosecutors and defence counsels continue to conduct sessions in the High Court in English, even though the majority of lawyers and judges also speak Kiswahili. The reasons for this practice are mainly historical. The Tanzanian legal system is based on the British system and judges have to refer to English cases for precedent. Furthermore, all lawyers are trained in a legal system which is basically oriented towards English and therefore are more accustomed to using this language in their professional life (Rubagumya, 1990).

The situation in the educational domain shows similar tendencies. Kiswahili is used as the medium of instruction for the seven years of primary education, with English being introduced as a subject in 3rd Grade, for about four hours a week. Then in secondary school there is a sudden switch to English as the teaching–

learning medium, with only Kiswahili language classes and political education being given in Kiswahili. The effect of this sudden change in school language is further complicated by the fact that English has shown unmistakable signs of a shift from being a second language to a foreign language for the majority of Tanzanians, having ceased to be used in daily communication and largely restricted to being 'a language for writing reports in government and parastatal organisations' (Yahya-Othman, 1990: 47). Thus, many students at secondary school are being taught through a language which they only hear used at school.

The reasons for this shift away from English towards Kiswhahil have been alluded to by several authors. Batibo (1995, cited in Baker & Prys Jones, 1998: 124) has explained the change by referring to the perception that English has 'divided society into English-speaking elites and lower status speakers of national, ethnic languages' and therefore has become politically unacceptable for many people. Trappes-Lomax (1990) and Rajabu and Ngonyani (1994) have also referred to the nationalist sentiments prevalent in the mid-1960s which culminated in the Arusha declaration of 1967 and the establishing of the National Swahili Council for the purpose of promoting Kiswahili in all spheres of national life.

In spite of this shift in the position of English in the country, however, there is still evidence that underlying attitudes towards the language have remained positive in that, 'English = education = a good job' (Rubaguma, 1986: 5). In Tanzania, therefore, English is in the interesting position of being a minority language, spoken only by a very small number of the population, and enjoying enormous symbolic power and status, unlike most minority languages which face discrimination and negative reactions. At the same time, English is 'being protected from Kiswahili' (Ruba-gumya, 1991b: 73, cited in Barrett, 1994: 6), the other official language, particularly in the educational system. In turn, English acts as a powerful gate-keeper for the small percentage of students who are able to continue their education at secondary school and at university level in Tanzania, thus ensuring their access to positions of power and prestige in the country.

The debate regarding the language medium for education is still in progress, showing evidence of signs of conflict, rather than complementarity (Eckert, 1980), (see previous section on Morocco). The reasons given for maintaining the use of English at post-primary level may be summarised as: (1) English is widely used as the language of academia; (2) English is seen as the language of scientific and tech-nological development; and (3) English is the language of international trade (Barrett, 1994).

While these instrumental justifications of the need to retain English in the educa-tion system are those commonly given, they also reflect a deeper, more general vision of what Rubagumya (1990: 2) has called, 'the very elitist nature of education in Africa'. Citing Ngalasso (1986: 15) in translation, Rubagumya (1990: 2) states that the use of a European language in Africa maintains this elitism as this language is seen as, 'a magic key to social prestige and power. Its use rarely corresponds to real need. It is usually used to show that one has reached a level of linguistic competence which entitles one to a legitimate claim to power, and eventually to mystify (those who don't speak the language)'. This perceptive interpretation of reasons for the continuing hegemony of English in the educational system in Tanzania helps to explain the government's apparent indecisiveness in replacing English by Kiswahili as the language of education, in spite of frequent national policy statements over the past 20 years which call for the use of Kiswahili as medium of instruction at all levels of education (Trappes-Lomax, 1990).

A further perspective on the discussion refers to wider political interest served by the retaining of English as a medium of instruction in the educational domain. As Barrett (1994) has argued, in an age when countries such as Germany and Japan are economically in the ascendant, it is vitally important for Britain to retain strong trading links with its ex-colonies. An increasing use of English in Tanzanian society, perpetuated in the educational system, helps to ensure that these links are continually reinforced and that UK expertise and publications are granted privileged access in the country.

The supporters of Kiswahili-medium education, led by a group of influential Tanzanian linguists based at the University of Dar es Salaam, present arguments for the replacement of English by the native lingua franca in education which are more educationally and nationalistically oriented. These centre on such premises as: (1) Kiswahili is an African language and thus appeals to a sense of national identity; (2) Tanzanian children find Kiswahili easier to learn than English because of having more contact with this language in their daily life, as well as because it is a Bantu language like most of the vernacular languages spoken in the country; (3) Kiswahili would be a more effective medium of teaching and learning than English because of the lack of trained teachers, adequate teaching materials and professional incentives available for the development of English in Tanzania at present.

As yet, the debate on language in education has not been resolved, though the recent commissioning of an official study on this topic by the Tanzanian Ministry of Education and Culture in 1998 entitled 'Language for Teaching and Learning in Tanzania: Language Issues Consultancy for the Educational Sector Development Programme' shows that interest in these issues is on-going.

Elite Bilingual Education Provision

State secondary schools

The situation analysed in the previous section clearly shows that secondary education is available to only a small sector of the population (3.3%, according to Mosha, 1990, cited in Rubagumya, 1991a). These students officially carry out their studies completely in English both at secondary school level and most probably at university level for the reasons outlined above. However, this situation is far from satisfactory as can be seen from the conclusion reached by a report commissioned by the Tanzanian government in 1984 which stated, 'The level of English in Forms I–IV is currently so low that English medium is not possible' (Criper & Dodd, 1984: 38). This dictate was reinforced five years later by the results of a survey conducted to ascertain the level of reading competence in English of secondary school students. The researchers concluded that, 'up to 90% of the secondary school population are unable to read and communicate in English . . . As a result they . . . gain very little knowledge in the four years that they spend in secondary school' (Qorro, 1989: 4).

It can thus be seen that for the majority of Tanzanian secondary school students the use of English as a medium of instruction results in submersion rather than immersion, where students are left to 'swim' or 'sink' without any kind of linguistic support, and where the linguistic goal is, in fact, monolingualism in the school language – English. In practice, teachers and students cope with the difficulties of the situation in various ways. Sometimes teachers separate language use for oral and written communication. In this case, Kiswahili is generally used unofficially for classroom talk, while teachers insist that all note-taking and written work should be done in English (Barrett, 1994), or else participants make use of extensive code-switching to facilitate classroom communication (cf similar situations reported in following sections on Hong Kong and Brunei).

This phenomenon, also referred to as 'the bilingual medium of instruction' (Mbise, 1994: 99), has led to adverse effects on student learning, according to some researchers, in that, 'the two language processing styles, which are culturally different, conflict creating confusion in students' knowledge' (Mbise, 1994: 100). However, other researchers (Rubagumya, 1994a; Ndayipfukamiye, 1994 in Burundi; and Arthur, 1994 in Botswana) see code-alternation in African classrooms in a much more favourable light, considering that 'bilingual or even trilingual code-switching is employed in subtle and skilful ways by both teachers and students to manage difficult teaching and learning situations' (Rubagumya, 1994a: 2).

The reactions of secondary school students to the use of English as a medium of teaching and learning are ambiguous. Most of them admit that they have problems learning through English, but maintain that they prefer being taught through English rather than Kiswahili (Rubagumya, 1991a). This ambiguity may be seen as symptomatic of the struggle to control or have access to the legitimised language, in Bourdieu's (1977) terms. Many parents, especially in Dar es Salaam and other big cities, are ready to pay for extra private English classes, particularly in the evening, to help their children with their school studies and thus ensure their access to privileged resources.

International Schools

Considering the high profile of English as key to higher education opportunities and future economic success within Tanzania, many parents of higher socio-economic status try to by-pass the difficulties of state school education by sending their children to private or International Schools. Indeed, Samoff (1990, cited in Rubagumya, 1991a) reports a 'mushrooming' of private secondary schools all over the country, many of which are established through the initiatives of parents' associations.

Furthermore, those who can afford it often choose to send their children to study abroad or to International Schools within the country. These are mainly based in the big cities, such as Dar es Salaam, the capital, Iringa, in the southern highlands region of the country and Moshi, on the slopes of Mount Kilimanjaro.

Case Sketch 7.2 shows in more detail how one particular International School in Dar es Salaam operates.

Case Sketch 7.2   The International School of Tanganyika (based on written information supplied by the school)

Name of School:	*International School of Tanganyika*
Date of Foundation:	*1963*
History:	*The school began as a private co-educational school designed to provide an educational programme for the international community in Dar es Salaam. It is now the largest International School on the African continent.*
Number of Students:	*1226 students, from 4 to 19 years old, representing 62 different nationalities.*
General School Aims:	*To develop individuals who are confident, compassionate, responsible citizens of a global society, with a passion for knowledge and self-development.To provide an outstanding educational programme that is academically rigorous and stimulates intellectual and personal development.*
Language Aim:	*To develop effective communication skills in more than one language*
Curriculum:	*International curriculum based mainly on UK and USA curricular models.*

The admission policy of the school states that children of expatriate parents, (defined as those having foreign passports) resident in Tanzania, may have priority over host country citizens if this is seen as necessary to preserving the international character of the institution.

The language of instruction in the school is English and a support programme at all grade levels is offered for the majority of children whose first language is not English. French, Spanish, German and Kiswahili are offered as foreign languages at International General Certificate of Secondary Education level. The school also offers the International Baccalaureate Diploma during the final two years of secondary schooling. Teachers are mainly recruited from Europe, particularly the UK, North America and Tanzania and most have experience in teaching in international education.

As can be seen, the school explicitly caters for an international clientele, though including children of Tanzanian citizens. It also states as one of its 14 general school aims 'that all students develop a positive attitude, understanding and knowledge of the host country, Tanzania' (Secondary School Parent/Student Handbook, 1998/99), thus recognising the importance of the students' understanding of the local context. This policy is implemented particularly in the final two years of schooling when students are expected to participate in a personal programme of Creativity, Action and Service (CAS) as part of the International Baccalaureate requirements. Some of the projects organised by the school include working with children at the Mother Theresa orphanage or with leprosy patients in the Kindwitwi Leprosy Village.

Although the school is not explicitly bilingual in nature, in that the language of teaching and learning is English, the composition of the student body implies a general necessity of being bilingual in English and the student's home language. Furthermore one of the school aims is communicative competence in two languages, which is stimulated by offering a choice of foreign languages within the school curriculum.

Summary

As can be seen from the above discussion, Tanzania has certain similarities with other post-colonial nations, such as Brunei and Hong Kong (see Chapter 9) in that the former colonial language is now an official language of communication within the country. An important difference, however, stems from the fact that an African language, Kiswahili, also has official status and is in fact encroaching on many of the domains where English has been traditionally used, such as the lower courts and the education system. In spite of nationalistic and educational arguments for the official recognition of Kiswahili as an appropriate language for teaching and learning throughout the whole of state education, there is reluctance to remove English as a prestigious status symbol at secondary school and university level.

The low level of achievement reported for state school students contrasts sharply with the success of students in private or International Schools who mostly aim at higher education in the United States or in Britain. However, the importance of social, economic and cultural factors cannot be underestimated in explaining these differences. As Barrett (1994) observes in her comments on English in Tanzanian secondary schools, the Canadian immersion programmes were parent-initiated, involved children from an urban middle-class background and consisted of small classes, 26 or so. In Tanzania, in contrast, most parents who send their children to state (public) schools have little say in the type of education their children receive, most students come from rural areas, and classes are generally large, around 50. It remains to be seen how the current debate develops in the future.

Conclusion

These two African nations, while both showing very different processes of historical and cultural development have certain things in common with regard to their linguistic and educational situation. Both nations are highly multilingual. In the case of Morocco, this is largely a result of different external factors, such as the Arab influence in North Africa and periods of foreign domination. In the case of Tanzania, the large number of vernacular languages spoken in the country are associated with tribal and community concerns.

In both countries a former colonial international language, French in Morocco and English in Tanzania, plays an important role in the linguistic ecology, particularly in the domain of education, where secondary education (in some cases) and higher education in general is mediated through these languages. Proficiency in these languages thus acts as a prerequisite to higher education opportunities in both nations.

There is also another prestigious language in play in the linguistic arena in both cases. In Morocco, Arabic is the official language of the country, and a strong policy of Arabisation, particularly in education and in the media, has strengthened links with other Arab nations in North Africa. In the case of Tanzania, Kiswahili, one of the two official languages, is a language of wider communication within the East African coastal area. Thus, bilingualism in minority community languages, such as the Berber languages in Morocco, and the Bantu-based vernaculars in Tanzania, and these linguae francae, are indispensable for progress at national and international level. However, bilingualism in French–Arabic and Kiswahili–English is available to only a small elite and is considered to be a source of power and prestige which will open up future opportunities for those who are fortunate enough to be able to develop proficiency in these languages. Middle-class parents thus often make considerable sacrifices to help their children learn French or English. In some cases they pay private school fees in order to guarantee their sons and daughters the possibility of competing for highly valued resources, such as tertiary education and future job opportunities.

Notes

1. Author's English translation 'The policy of Arabisation in Islamic North Africa' and 'From the universal to the specific: Conference on bilingualism in the Moroccan educational system'.

Chapter 8

South America: From Provision for Expatriates to Bilingual Education for Host Country Nationals

Introduction

In this chapter we will focus on the situation of elite bilingualism and bilingual education in three South American countries which form part of the American continent: Brazil, Argentina and Colombia. Although the situation of elite bilingualism in other parts of the Americas – Canada and the US particularly – has received widespread coverage, the three Latin American nations discussed here have been largely ignored in published studies on elite bilingual education provision available on the international market.

In spite of a tendency among North Americans and Europeans to generalise across Latin America, each of the three countries examined here shows very particular patterns of development, as well as some general similarities which may be accounted for, to some extent, by a common history of European colonisation in the fifteenth and sixteenth centuries. Thus, Argentina and Colombia both have Spanish as the first language used by the majority of the population as a result of the arrival of the Spanish conquerors (*conquistadores*). In Brazil, however, the official language spoken by the majority of the population is Portuguese, stemming from the influence of the Portuguese colonisers. In all three countries there is particular emphasis on the teaching and learning of international foreign languages, especially, English, French and German. As in the previous chapter on Africa, we will first consider the general sociolinguistic situation of each country and then focus on issues relating specifically to elite bilingual education.

BRAZIL

General Perspectives

Brazil is the largest country in Latin America, covering 47.3% of the South American subcontinent. Since the colonisation of the country in the sixteenth century by the Portuguese there has been a lot of migration both from Europe, mainly from Italy and Spain, and from Africa, as a result of the slave trade. In the nineteenth century, the British came to Brazil to build railroads, to operate mines and shipping companies, as well as to set up prestigious import–export businesses.

More recently, after the Second World War, large numbers of German-speaking Protestant Mennonites from Russia and the United States settled in the country. Thus, the population of Brazil today (estimated at 135.5 million people in 1995), is highly heterogeneous: 55% are of European origin, 38% of mixed white and African origin, 6% of African origin, and 1% comprising Arabs, Amerindian, and the largest Japanese community outside of Japan (British Council, 1997a).

The official language of the country is Portuguese, which some people maintain should be renamed 'Brazilian' as it shows considerable differences in pronunciation and lexis from the European variety and other varieties, such as Mozambican Portuguese. German, Italian, Polish, Ukrainian, Japanese and Amerindian languages are also spoken, mainly in the communities referred to above.

In spite of this evidence of community bilingualism, the Brazilian government has emphasised the 'myth of monolingualism' (Cavalcanti, 1996: 188), promoting Portuguese as the only language spoken in the country and the only language legally permitted for primary education, though in 5th Grade a foreign language chosen by the school must also be taught. This may help to explain why elite bilingual education is not as popular here as in other South American countries, such as Colombia and Argentina.

Although not widely spoken as a language of daily communication outside the Anglo-Brazilian communities, almost paradoxically perhaps, English, particularly American English, may be seen as Brazil's 'second language' (British Council, 1997a) in terms of its importance in the global market. According to MacRae (1997) English language proficiency undoubtedly opens doors to social mobility and privileged status. Thus, private English language schools are increasing rapidly all over the country and in 1996 Brazil ranked as the world's fastest growth area in the use of internet, mainly in English.

However, there is also an interesting increase in the demand for Spanish as a foreign language due to the recent creation in 1990 of Mercosur, the Southern Cone Common Market, which includes Brazil, Argentina, Uruguay and Paraguay, and possibly Chile in the future. According to a recent report in the Colombian newspaper *El Tiempo* (9–7–00), between 30 and 40% of secondary school students in Brazil (over 10 million students in total) are currently learning Spanish at school. Twelve years ago, in contrast, most learners of Spanish were middle-aged executives who needed Spanish because of job demands. In 2001, Brazil and Argentina signed a bilateral agreement whereby 4000 Argentine teachers would go to Brazil to teach Spanish for one or two years, while Brazilian teachers would go to Argentina to teach Portuguese.

The Brazilian Education and Language Travel Association in 1997 reported that Spanish was rated the second most popular foreign language in Brazil, in contrast to the traditionally popular French. Furthermore, English and Spanish are the two working languages currently used in diplomatic relations in the country.

During the nineteenth century Anglo-Brazilians were in a position of power and influence within the country, controlling postal, transport and financial services. They formed a tight-knit community who tended to intermarry and send their children to be educated in Britain. Since then, however, the position of this community has declined due to restrictions on immigration and a subsequent opening up to outside influences. Mixed marriages between members of the community and Brazilians or other nationalities are on the increase and consequently the use of Portuguese in these families is much higher than before. As illustration, it is noted that the numbers of Anglo-Brazilian students at St Paul's British School in São Paulo have dropped considerably from around 40% of the school population of 800 students in 1991 to 20% in 1997 (MacRae, 1997). Up until the 1980s a large number of such students had to travel regularly to Britain for higher education, as the school was not recognised by the Brazilian authorities for entry into Brazilian universities. Now, however, government recognition has meant that few Anglo-Brazilians go to the UK to study any longer. Thus, links with Britain are becoming ever more tenuous and Anglo-Brazilians are being increasingly incorporated into mainstream Brazilian life.

Since the 1950s it has been the USA which has been in the ascendant in Brazil. The majority of Brazilians who travel to English-speaking countries choose the USA, rather than Britain, due, in part, to the strong cultural influence of the US media and business enterprises, such as McDonald's, and also to a perception that fares and cost of living are cheaper in USA than in Britain or Australia. Furthermore, a number of exchange schemes allow teenagers to spend up to a year studying at high schools in the US free of charge, before returning to their university studies in Brazil. This experience often influences where Brazilian students choose to apply for subsequent postgraduate degrees.

Elite Bilingual Education Provision

Bilingual schools

Bilingual schools in Brazil, as in Argentina and Colombia, are found in the big cities, such as the capital, Brasilia, the former capital, Rio de Janeiro, and São Paulo. Most of them offer Portuguese–English bilingualism, though schools like the Liceu Pasteur in São Paulo and the Escola Francesa in Brasilia offer French and Portuguese, Colegio Humboldt in São Paulo offers German and Portuguese, and Colegio Miguel de Cervantes in São Paulo, Portuguese and Spanish. The French bilingual schools, particularly the one in Brasilia, cater mainly for French-speaking children from the diplomatic community, but they also accept children whose parents have some type of link with France (academics, for example).

The North American schools, in contrast, have a more diversified population. Besides English-speaking children and children who have ties with the English-speaking world, there are also children from internationally mobile families (Janda Cunha, 1999, personal communication). As in Colombia, there are also bilingual schools which show a greater national orientation. In the following section, I will present a brief contrastive portrait of two English–Portuguese bilingual schools in Sao Paulo, one international in origin and one national, in order to exemplify some similarities and differences between them.

Case Sketch 8.1   Two Brazilian Bilingual Schools (based on material supplied by Karin Leme, Paticia Avanzi, Alicia Godoy and Maria Cristina Lagreca de Oho, by kind permission of Marina MacRae)[1]

Name of Schools:	*Graded School*	*Play Pen (Associacao Escola Graduada)*
Date of Foundation:	*1920*	*1980*
Type of School:	*private, co-educational, non-denominational preschool – Grade 12*	*private, co-educational non-denominational preschool – Grade 6*
Population:	*Brazilian (40%) North American (38%) Other nationalities (22%)*	*Brazilian (95%) Other nationalities (5%)*
Languages Used:	*English only up to Grade 1. 1 hour per day Portuguese from Grade 2 onwards*	*Emphasis in English in preschool. Emphasis in Portuguese from Grade 2 to Grade 6*

As can be seen, while the schools are apparently similar in type and language influence, in reality there are substantial differences between them: Graded School is a well-established school, founded initially by the American Chamber of Commerce for Brazil as a North American day school and authorised since 1949 to confer the American high school diploma, as well as the Brazilian high school diploma and the International Baccalaureate. In contrast, Play Pen School was founded by a North-American–Brazilian couple who, seeing how easily other monolingual friends acquired some basic English while playing with their bilingual children, decided to set up a place of recreation where children could learn English through ludic activities. Later this became a small school situated in an upper-class neighbourhood of the city.

While the children in Graded School in 1st Grade use English almost exclusively both within the classroom and in the playground, in Play Pen School the morning is dedicated to activities in Portuguese with one teacher and the afternoon to activities in English with a different teacher. Moreover, the children use Portuguese to interact together in the playground. Thus, there is a language separation established according to time of day and location, i.e. whether the children are inside or outside the classroom. These patterns of school language use reflect both the differing student populations of the two schools seen in Case Sketch 8.1, as well as differences in their creation and philosophy.

While Play Pen School has a Brazilian emphasis to its curriculum, which although bilingual in nature is taught entirely by Brazilian nationals, in Graded School approximately 50% of teachers are North Americans. Perhaps for this reason, the school does not celebrate any of the national Brazilian holidays, such as Carnival, Tiradentes or Republic Day, instead, in 2nd Grade they are discussed by the Portuguese speaking teachers. The North American festivity of Thanksgiving is celebrated with a Thanksgiving meal in the classroom, as are Halloween, St Valentine's Day and St Patrick's Day.

Thus, it can be seen that these two institutions, while both qualifying as bilingual schools, have different orientations and philosophies. One is a large official educational establishment catering for a multilingual, international student population who intend to gain entry to prestigious universities in the USA, as well as in Brazil. English is the primary language of instruction and is used by both native and non-native speaking teachers. The other is a small, national institution which aims to help Brazilians who are monolingual in Portuguese achieve a high level of proficiency in a foreign language, English which will help them to be successful in study and work contexts within the country. The school tries to maintain a balance between the two languages, by adopting a policy of different language emphasis according to both time of day (Portuguese in the morning, English in the afternoon) and age group (preschool emphasis in English and Primary emphasis in Portuguese). English is used by non-native speaking teachers. It is thus evident that the experience of bilingual education offered by the two schools is different and proves once again the need for caution when generalising about the effects of bilingual education programmes in a particular national setting.

Private English Language Teaching provision

One important difference between Brazil and other South American countries is the huge number of private English Language Teaching (ELT) institutes established in the country (British Council, 1997a). While these are not officially bilingual institutions, their very existence points to a strong desire on the part of the students to develop proficiency in English as well as in Portuguese, or, in other words, to become bilingual. ELT institutes in Brazil may be divided into three main groups:

the US Binational Centers, the *Cultura Inglesa* Group, and the LAURELS schools. I will briefly describe each of these below.

US Binational Centers

There are 39 US Binational Centers in Brazil, although only 18 of these have the status of recognised US Binational Centers, which have a Board of Directors as well as a library. The main center is the *Casa Thomas Jefferson*, in Brasilia. The centers receive a certain amount of moral, technical and material support from the US Information Service (USIS), though less now than in the past and are linked to other institutions through the Association of Latin American Binational Centers (ABLA). According to a survey carried out by USIA in 1995, 39.55% of students in the US Binational Centers in the country were secondary school students, while only 23.9% were adults. This emphasises the current demand for English among young people in Brazil.

This trend is also reflected in the large numbers of candidates who register each year for the United States examinations in Brazil, particularly the Michigan Certificate examinations and the Test of English as a Foreign Language (TOEFL). In November 1996, a total of 2001 candidates took the Michigan exams and 6500 candidates sat the TOEFL in the same year. Since 1998, the larger binational centers have implemented a new computerised version of TOEFL, which has allowed many thousands of candidates to take the test in 12 Sylvan Technology Centers.

The *Culturas Inglesas*

Some of the *Cultura Inglesa* institutes (those in Rio de Janeiro, Sao Paulo, Belo Horizonte and Curitiba) date from the 1930s and 1940s. They have a strong link with the British Council, sponsoring British Council arts events in Brazil and participating in joint management and training projects. Since the 1980s, they have been grouped together as the Association of Latin American British Cultural Institutes, and since 1991, the Association of Brazilian *Culturas Inglesas*. Most of the *Culturas* recruit some of their staff from Britain, though this practice has tended to decrease in recent years. Recently, some young Brazilians who are waiting to begin their university studies, work at the *Culturas* as volunteer conversation assistants, as well as doing social work in the community.

Responding to a survey carried out by *ELT News & Views* (June 1999b Year 6 (2)), a newsletter for teachers of English who work in the 'Southern Cone' countries of Argentina, Brazil, Chile, Paraguay and Uruguay, Carmen Lucas, Superintendent General of the *Culturas* in the cities of Rio de Janeiro, Brasilia and Espirito Santo, sees the most important current concern in Brazil as the need to 'constantly prepare teachers for the challenges and demands of the future . . . in terms of the technological needs of the classroom process' and the increasing importance of cultural awareness and multiculturalism in relation to ELT.

The LAURELS Schools

The Latin American Union of Registered English Language Schools (LAURELS) was set up as an independent organisation in 1987 by eight independent Brazilian

ELT and two Uruguayan institutes to exchange ideas and information with each other and to organise ELT conferences with international speakers. They are committed to teacher training and development, as well as the provision of modern educational facilities, such as self-access centres and computer assisted learning facilities (British Council, 1997a).

Since 1990, the Brazilian LAURELS chapter has achieved a solid reputation, based on the quality of the international conferences it has organised, often in co-operation with the British Council, and on the adoption of a common code of practice, which helps to ensure homogeneity of standards to monitor existing schools and potential new members. Several of the institutions recruit teachers from English-speaking countries on two-year contracts.

Over the last 10 years, along with the explosion of private ELT provision within the country, there has also been a great expansion in the field of professional development of foreign language teachers. The most well-known teachers' organisation is BRAZ-TESOL, founded in 1986, which is the Brazilian representative of TESOL International (USA). There is also the smaller International Association of Teachers of English as a Foreign Language (IATEFEL), which is UK oriented.

There are regional BRAZ-TESOL chapters in six states, representing a total of 2000 English language teachers and considerable enthusiasm is generated among teachers who often travel long distances to attend conferences and workshops. In the word of a regional chapter official in the southern state of Paraná, 'This is a promising region, which is hungry for information and knowledge' (*BRAZ-TESOL Newsletter*, June 1998: 6). The organisation publishes a quarterly newsletter and holds a major national convention every two years, which is attended by international and national presenters.

In the business sector, many companies encourage their staff to participate in in-service ELT courses. Among these are the Central Bank of Brazil, *Thermo King do Brasil* (the Brazilian branch of a large multinational refrigeration company), *RTZ Mineracao Ltda* (the Brazilian office of a British mining company), and the Brazilian Stock Exchange Commission. Most of these organisations spend a considerable amount of their training budget on in-house English language classes, provided by private teachers and courses abroad. In some companies too, English language proficiency is now a requirement for incoming senior managerial staff. Thus, as Sidney Pratt responding to the *ELT News & Views* (1999b: 10) survey says, 'English is being seen as a tool, perhaps *the* tool, to career improvement' and emphasises the creation of a 'point and click' mentality among busy language-learning executives.

Summary

It is interesting to note that in Brazil, while there is official emphasis on monolingualism and the use of Portuguese by the majority of Brazilians, there is also great emphasis on the need to learn foreign languages, such as English and Spanish for purposes of study and work. Thus, while there are relatively few bilingual schools which cater for Brazilian nationals, the number of English Language schools is increasing extremely rapidly. In contrast to the situation in Argentina and Colombia, it seems that Brazilians currently see the learning of foreign languages mainly as an extra curricular activity rather than as an intrinsic part of school education.

Furthermore, as noted in this section, while American English is in the ascendancy at present, there are interesting indications that considerations of the role of English language teaching in the context of globalization has led to a shift from a focus on EFL (English as a Foreign Language) to a focus on EIL (English as an International Language), with a corresponding questioning of the role of culture (North American, British, etc.) in the classroom (de Moraes Menti, 1999).

ARGENTINA

General Perspectives

Geographically, Argentina, along with Chile, is situated in the southern peninsula of the South American subcontinent. The country shows a similar pattern of development to the other two Latin American nations discussed in this chapter, in the sense that many of the original Spanish colonisers married indigenous women and initially *mestizos,* people of mixed European and American Indian ancestry, constituted a majority in the country (Baker & Prys Jones, 1998). The situation in Argentina differs, however, from the situation of Brazil and Colombia, in that during the nineteenth and twentieth centuries there was large-scale immigration from Europe, particularly at the turn of the century. Thus, French, German, English, Welsh and Italian were quite widely spoken as community languages at the beginning of the twentieth century, as well as the Amerindian languages used in the various indigenous communities. Up to 1994, Spanish was the official language of the country, and although the Constitutional Reform of 1994 abolished this status, Spanish continues to be the first language of the majority of the population and is overwhelmingly the language of administration and education (Banfi[2] 1999, personal communication).

The current linguistic situation is complex. While some of the communities referred to above, such as the German and Welsh communities, have maintained their native languages into the third generation, there are other communities, the Italians for instance, who although statistically more numerous, have shifted to using Spanish as their main language of interaction. Furthermore, in recent years, new immigrant groups have arrived from Vietnam, Korea and Eastern Europe and these still use their native languages, with varying degrees of support in the educational system (Banfi, 1999, personal communication).

In terms of foreign languages, English is the most popular language in Argentina, in spite of temporary negative effects resulting from the South Atlantic Conflict involving Britain and Argentina in 1982. Many middle and upper-class Argentines in Buenos Aires still see their political and economic future in relation to the First World, rather than to developments within Mercosur. An interesting corroboration of this can be seen in Section 25 of the present Argentine Constitution which states explicitly that 'The Federal Government shall foster European immigration' but makes no reference to the immigration of other national groups.

A knowledge of English is, in many cases, a basic requirement for jobs in executive or skilled professional spheres in the country. Historically because of connections with Britain especially during the nineteenth century in relation to the construction of the Argentine railway system, British English has been the preferred variety. Many older members of the Anglo-Argentine community feel a great sense of loyalty towards what they still consider their 'mother' country and this influence is reflected in some of the names of the associations in Buenos Aires listed in 1997 – 'The Argentine–British Scholars Association', 'The British Engineers' Society' and 'The Pickwick Club', (British Council, 1997b).

However, since the subsequent temporary withdrawal of the British Council after the South Atlantic Conflict (1982–1990), there has been a new official emphasis on the need for English for International Communication, rather than either British or American varieties. Business companies, nevertheless, show a marked tendency to prefer North American English as a model and most postgraduate students in the areas of Business and Management choose to study in the United States (British Council, 1997b).

The influence of Mercosur, noted in the section on Brazil, has meant that Portuguese is increasingly seen by many Argentines as an important language to be used in commercial relations with Brazil, and the Argentine government is currently funding a distance learning project, and training for thousands of teachers of Portuguese. Furthermore, in the northern border province of Misiones, where Portuguese is a contact language, there are proposals for the use of both Portuguese and English in secondary schools (British Council, 1997b). In addition, Argentina is co-operating with Brazil on a bilateral agreement which will involve Brazilian teachers teaching Portuguese in Argentina in the near future (see previous section on Brazil).

Traditionally English and French, and occasionally Italian, have been taught as foreign languages at secondary school, usually for two or three years. In 1992, the state began an overhaul of the national educational system, which introduced foreign language learning (English and French) during the primary school (age 9) and 'new' foreign languages, such as German, in technical schools (Banfi, 1999, personal communication). A federal agreement, *El Acuerdo Marco de Lenguas,* currently under debate, was drawn up to define the legal status of all languages involved in the educational system. This document clearly distinguishes between the status of second and foreign languages in the country, and establishes that with the exception of Portuguese, the languages currently used in education have foreign language status (British Council, 1997b).

Elite Bilingual Education Provision

General panorama

Bilingual education provision involving world languages, such as English, French, German, Italian and Hebrew, has a long history in Argentina. Some of the oldest institutions date from the 1820s. However, the term 'bilingual' to describe the type of programme offered by these schools is very recent, stemming, in fact, from the South Atlantic Conflict of 1982 (British Council, 1997b). Before that, English–Spanish bilingual schools, the vast majority of bilingual educational institutions in the country, were referred to as 'British-type' schools (ESSARP, 1995). In 1926, an organisation known as 'The British Scholastic Association' was set up to provide a forum for British headteachers of English-medium schools in Argentina and Uruguay, to discuss topics of common interest. This later became 'The English-Speaking Scholastic Association of the River Plate' (1975), better known by the acronym ESSARP, which has been influential in the development of English Language Teaching and Bilingual Education programmes in the country, particularly in the Buenos Aires area.

With the political, educational and cultural distancing of Argentina and Britain after the South Atlantic Conflict, the 'British-type' schools came to be recognised rather as 'bicultural' schools. The use of this term in the Argentine context refers to schools which teach a full British curriculum as well as the standard Argentina curriculum (British Council, 1997b). Other implications of biculturalism, as discussed in Chapter 3, are not usually explicitly addressed, however, in these schools (Banfi, 1999, personal communication). These private schools attract children from affluent and influential families who aspire to greater social and professional advantage by being bilingual or multilingual in two or more world languages. More details of each type of school will be given below.

Bicultural or 'community' schools

The 'English-type' or bicultural schools referred to above, are part of a more general phenomenon which have their origins in 'community' schools, or in other words, institutions which were founded to cater for the educational needs of children from specific immigrant communities in Argentina. Today there are a wide variety of such schools, ranging from the *Goethe Schule* for German, *Cristofolo Colombo* for Italian, *Colegio Tarbut* for Hebrew, *Licée Français* for French, and St Alban's College for English, among many other examples of schools catering for specific language groups (Banfi, 1999, personal communication).

With regard to English–Spanish schools, there is a predominance of British-based establishments, where a British content-based curriculum is used as a means of developing English language skills. For North American residents, there are schools such as the Lincoln community school, a large and well respected institution which also serves the needs of the international community in Buenos Aires.

In Table 8.1, Banfi and Day (2001) show the development of these types of schools in Argentina during the nineteenth and twentieth centuries. As can be seen, the authors have divided this process into four phases: Pioneer, Early Traditional, Late Traditional, and Modern. Initially, many of the students were of English-speaking origin, then later in the Early Traditional period this changed to include French, Italian and German speakers. In the last two periods, Late Traditional and Modern, Spanish first language speakers were in the majority. Nowadays bilingual schools

Table 8.1 Four generations of schools

Generation	Dates	Schools
Pioneer	1820s to1890	Buenos Aires Foreign School Society – 1829 St Andrew's Scots School – 1838 (English)
Early Traditional	1890s to1920s	St George's College – 1898 (English) Goethe Schule – 1897 (German)
Late Traditional	1930s to early 1970s	St Paul's College – 1954 (English) Colegio Franco – Argentino – 1945 (French) Tomás Devoto – 1937 (Italian)
Modern	Late 1970s to 1990	Colegio Las Candelas – 1993 Instituto Koreano-Argentino – 1991

(Taken from Banfi & Day, 2001)

in the country cater overwhelming for Argentine children (95%) with a minority of children (5%) who come from an international itinerant elite community (Banfi & Day, 2001).

As may be expected, the schools have kept their original names. However, there is nowadays a different connotation associated with these, as explained by the Headmaster of St Andrew's Scots School, 'The word 'Scots' which the School proudly bears, no longer indicates ethnic exclusivity, but refers to the origin of its founders and the influence of this origin in the educational, ethical, and spiritual development of those who receive their education in this School' (Escuela Escocesa San Andrés, 1988: 10).[3]

The traditional system used at these schools is that of parallel curricula, where students either take all subjects in Spanish in the morning, thus complying with the official education requirements, and English in the afternoon or the opposite, i.e. English in the morning and Spanish in the afternoon, (Banfi, 1999, personal communication). This means that students follow two different and separate academic syllabi, one national and one foreign. Recently, however, there have been moves to integrate these two systems, in order to avoid excessive overlapping of content. There has also been a move to adopt international examinations in many of these schools

Case Sketch 8.2 shows in more detail how one particular long-established school of this type operates.

Case Sketch 8.2   St Andrew's Scots School, Buenos Aires (based on written information supplied by the school)

Name of School: St Andrew's Scots School, Buenos Aires.

Date of   1838.
Foundation:

History:	*Founded to cater for the needs of children of early Scottish settlers and closely associated with the Scottish Presbyterian Church. Originally all girls, in 1839 the first boys were admitted. In 1966, St Andrew's Scots School for Girls was opened, which in 1980 joined with the Boys' School to form a co-educational institution.*
Number of Students:	*1,900 students, from 3–18 years old.*
General School Aim:	*To provide an education that will contribute to the formation of healthy Argentine citizens in mind and spirit, without distinctions of race and creed, thus conforming to the country's basic culture and official programme.*
Language Aim:	*To produce students who are academically equal in both Spanish and English.*
Curriculum:	*In English the students follow a curriculum based on the British system of education which leads to the International General Certificate of Secondary Education (IGCSE) examinations. In Spanish, the students follow the Argentine National Curriculum. During the last two years 80–90% of students study for the International Baccalaureate Diploma.*

As can be seen, this school aims at producing balanced academic bilinguals, who are conscious of their Argentine background and culture and yet are able to function appropriately in an international academic context. At kindergarten level, ages 3–5 years old, emphasis is on a total immersion of the children in English, in order to prepare them for a bilingual education in primary and secondary school, where some subjects are taught in English and some in Spanish, depending on the time of day. There is thus evidence of a strong separation approach to language use, based on both subject area divisions and time of day.

The school prides itself on offering a wide range of sporting, dramatic and musical extra-curricular activities, some of which show a strong British cultural influence, such as Scottish Country Dancing, rugby and cricket. The school has also adopted the British-based House system, originating in the elite 'public' (expensive private) schools of Eton and Harrow, where initially pupils were housed in different buildings or 'houses' each with a separate name. Thus, all students when they enter the school are required to be members of one of a series of smaller groupings, traditionally known as 'Houses', which cut across grade level divisions. These are designed to 'develop a healthy competitive team spirit in academic, artistic and sporting matters' (Escuela Escocesa San Andrés, 1988: 125). Each house is named after a former teacher or school governor who contributed to the progress of the school over the years: William Brown, James Dodds, James Fleming, and John Monteith Drysdale.

In 1988, the school founded its own university consisting of a School of Economics, Business Administration, Political Science, International Relations and Accountancy at undergraduate level mostly conducted in Spanish and in 1996 a postgraduate Masters degree programme in Economics and Finance which includes occasional postgraduate courses in English.

English–Spanish bilingual schools

English–Spanish bilingual schools have been in great demand throughout Argentina in recent years, as increasing numbers of parents consider English an essential component of their children's education. In addition, there has been general concern expressed about standards in state schools (due to low budgets and low teachers' salaries). Thus private bilingual education is considered an attractive alternative by many parents (Banfi, 1999, personal communication). ESSARP brings together about 100 of such schools, around 80% of which are in the capital, Buenos Aires and the remaining 20% in the provinces.

In upper-middle-class neighbourhoods, there is a rapidly expanding industry in bilingual play schools which aim at preparing young children for entry to the more prestigious bilingual schools. Many of the teachers in these centres are recent graduates of bilingual schools and often do not have formal teaching qualifications or training (British Council, 1997b), though they do have inside knowledge on what the schools expect.

ESSARP has established a series of guidelines used to evaluate schools claiming to be bilingual. Among these criteria are: the number of hours of foreign language tuition (a minimum of 12 weekly periods is stipulated); the number of international examinations offered; and the number of years the school has been functioning. The main criterion generally is the aspiration to teach content through English, rather than just teach it as a subject within the curriculum (Banfi, 1999, personal communication).

However, as we have indicated above, the term has wide coverage, and may be used loosely to refer to many different types of institutions, which offer a range of possibilities in regard to such things as date of foundation, fees, staffing and future student expectations. Thus, some schools have a long-established reputation, dating from the middle of the nineteenth century or the beginning of the twentieth century, while others are only 10 years old. Some employ foreign contract teachers, while others have 100% Argentine staff. In some bilingual schools students go on to undergraduate study abroad, while others have more modest aims, preparing their graduates to reach an intermediate level (Cambridge First Proficiency) of English language proficiency. In fact, however, as in other South American countries, such as Colombia, there is a growing tendency nowadays for increasing numbers of students to study for their first degree at an Argentine university and then go abroad to an English-speaking country for postgraduate study.

The English–Spanish bilingual schools have adopted an overtly separation approach to language use according to time of day and officially do not approve of code-switching. Some schools adopt a points system and use these to discourage students from speaking Spanish during an English activity.

Traditionally, the emphasis in English–Spanish bilingual schools in Argentina has been on secondary school level, rather than primary, and on the teaching of English as a second or foreign language. So when Lorna Corley inaugurated the ESSARP Teachers' Centre in Buenos Aires in 1985, she decided to redress the balance by prioritising primary bilingual education and reducing what she considered 'the rigid concept of teaching English as a second language' then in vogue (ESSARP, 1995: 10). She, thus, stressed the need to provide books on education in the centre's library, rather than exclusively on the teaching of English as a second or foreign language.

She also turned her attention to the needs of the Spanish-speaking staff of bilingual schools saying, 'As an Argentine, I realised that the school is "one" and the children are exposed to different teachers who must share a common philosophy' (ESSARP, 1995: 11). This was an important recognition of the need for bilingual schools in Argentina to override the traditional divide between primary and secondary education, and also to reject an exclusive concern with the foreign language, at the expense of the first language resulting in negative consequences for the status and motivation of Spanish-speaking teachers. Furthermore, the founding director of the ESSARP Teaching Centre was foresighted enough to acknowledge the need, 'to develop research programmes in our bilingual schools, which are so different from comparable institutions abroad' (ESSARP, 1995: 11), a priority which is still in its infancy in Argentina, though there has been some recent interest expressed by ESSARP in carrying out research in this area (Banfi, 1999, personal communication). This call has been echoed by Armendáriz (1999: 13) in the wider scenario of Argentine ELT in her reflection that, 'The new Millennium finds us looking for a new paradigm that not only looks outside Latin America, but delineates a profile that requires a versatile local epistemological framework rooted in local educational demands'.

Private English language teaching provision

The situation in Argentina in the private ELT sector has much in common with developments in Brazil outlined in the previous section, so only a brief report will be included here.

US Binational centers

In Argentina, there are at present 17 binational centers which have the status of autonomous Argentine institutions promoting mutual understanding between Argentina and the United States by means of the provision of cultural, educational and information activities. The largest of these is the *Instituto Cultural Argentino Norte-Americano* in Buenos Aires, which has been in existence since 1927 and which channels all applications and international examinations for students who wish to study in the USA. Since 1995, a joint US–Argentine TESOL MA programme has been in existence, aimed at providing Argentine EFL teachers with an academic qualification in their area of work. The courses are taught by TESOL faculty from California State University, who travel to Argentina for intensive five-weekly periods (British Council, 1997b).

The *Culturas Inglesas*

There are a significant number of institutions belonging to the *Asociación Argentina de Cultura Inglesa*, the oldest such association in Latin America, with institutions dating from 1927. The *Culturas* have always had strong links with Britain, initially through the British Embassy and later through the British Council, although these were interrupted for 11 years, as a result of the South Atlantic Conflict in 1982. Since then, however, the British Council has worked with the *Culturas* on a number of joint ventures, such as a setting up of the National Resource Centre for Teachers of English and the creation of the British Arts Centre. At present though, unlike the situation in Brazil, there is no common code of practice among the Argentine *Culturas*, thus there is wide diversity in policy and practice between members (British Council, 1997b).

Present trends in ELT in Argentina seem to indicate two main directions for the future. The first is a growing internationalisation of the profession, with more teachers attending international conferences and using resources available through the internet. Thus, 'the strong feeling of isolation that used to exist in Argentina due to the distance away from the nerve centres of ELT in the UK and the United States' is no longer evident (Potter, 1999: 68). The second direction, almost paradoxically, concerns the growing awareness of the importance of encouraging local expertise, rather than relying on foreign support, as expressed by Cristina Banfi (1999: 6) when asked what she thought was the most significant present issue in the field of ELT. She said, 'The increasing awareness that solutions, answers or truths are not to be found elsewhere, but can and should be found by teachers themselves.'

Summary

The situation of bilingualism and bilingual education in Argentina clearly reflects different political and economic influences evident in the country at the present time, which appears to be at an important point of transition. On the one hand, there is evidence to suggest that the traditional allegiance of older Argentines to Britain has been somewhat eroded by political and economic effects of the South Atlantic Conflict. On the other hand, there are signs that researchers and teachers working in the fields of bilingual education and ELT are recognising the need to create local knowledge based on local or regional needs, rather than to depend on external expertise. As Armendáriz (1999: 12) notes, 'It is not a question of minimising the impact and contribution that experts overseas might make to our midst. It is imperative to start doing reflection and introspection to find possible solutions to our local problems, Argentine or otherwise, within South America.' The same author recommends 'constructing an agreed upon national/regional opinion rooted in local needs'.

This perception is in line with a growing realisation that bilingual speakers in Argentina may well need to communicate with non-native rather than with native speakers in contrast to what has traditionally been expected. Thus, students and teachers must be prepared to cope with variety in all forms, 'variety of Englishes, variety of "experts", variety of teachers, variety of students, variety of purposes, tasks and outcomes' (Banfi, 1999: 6). It remains to be seen whether these tendencies will be confirmed and whether the debate between the relative merits of British versus American English will, in fact, be resolved in favour of the less culturally marked 'English for International Communication' in line with this growing global orientation rooted in recognition of local realities.

On the other hand, the creation of Mercosur has provided an economic grouping within the subcontinent which is affecting not only economic and political policies of member countries but is also having a marked effect in the field of language and education, emphasising the importance of Portuguese as a potential rival to the traditional hegemony of English. While there is still enough support for English in the country for the British Council to declare in a recent publication, 'Despite the development of Mercosur, it is a knowledge of English that middle and upper class Argentines aspire to, rather than Portuguese' (British Council, 1997b: 28) this situation is rapidly changing, as can be seen by the bilateral agreement for Brazilian teachers of Portuguese to teach the language in Argentina in coming years. Thus, there may well be changes in the number of Provinces that choose English as their obligatory foreign language in the future.

COLOMBIA

General Perspectives

Colombia may be seen geographically as the gateway between South and Central America, with coastlines bordering two oceans, the Atlantic and the Pacific. It is the fourth largest country in South America and has an estimated population of over 36 million people, according to figures produced in 1995. Some of these are descendants of the European, mostly Spanish, colonisers who first arrived in the country in the sixteenth century, while others are of Amerindian or Black origin, The majority of the population, however, are of mixed blood as a result of intermarriage among these three groups.

From a sociolinguistic point of view, Colombia may be divided into two main sectors: majority language contexts which include the teaching and learning of English, French, German, Italian and Hebrew as foreign languages to first language speakers of Spanish, and minority situations, which involve the use of Spanish as a second language and minority community first languages, such as native Amerindian languages, English and Spanish based Creoles, and Colombian Sign Language.

In the case of majority language contexts, English is the foreign language which enjoys the highest status in the country, particularly in the domains of education, business and tourism (Zuluaga, 1996). North American English is generally the most favoured variety due to the 'overwhelming attraction of the USA by dint of historical connections, family and teacher connection, proximity and of sheer glamour image' (British Council 1989: 10). Except for its use in small expatriate communities, mainly found in the capital, Santafé de Bogotá, neither English, nor any of the other foreign languages referred to above, is generally used as a means of communication within the country. One notable exception are foreign films, either shown in cinemas or increasingly hired out from video shops, where the original commentary is kept and Spanish subtitles are added.

During the period of the Spanish colonisation of Colombia, particularly in the seventeenth and eighteenth centuries, most schools were private. School language teaching had its origin in the Catholic mission schools, where Latin, Greek and Spanish were taught. The sons and daughters of the wealthy were sent to study abroad, in France and England, and on their return, promoted the spread of these languages in the country, particularly French, which was considered the language of culture and society (Zuluaga, 1996).

Following Independence from Spain in 1810, the *Escuelas de Primeras Letras* (First Letters Schools) were set up, based on liberal principles derived from the French Revolution. These later became primary schools. Then, the *Escuelas Superiores de Artes Liberales* (Higher Schools for the Liberal Arts) were established at secondary level.

After the Second World War, English became the most important foreign language in Colombia, due to economic expansion, social, political and economic influence and the technological development of the United States. It was taught at secondary school level, alternating with the use of French. Thus, in 1979, after a visit by the Colombian president to France, a decree was issued, making English compulsory for Grades 6 and 7 and French mandatory for Grades 10 and 11, with a free choice of either English or French in Grades 8 and 9. As a report compiled by the British Council (1989) reveals,

> The Colombian Ministry of National Education has no firm foreign language policy for the secondary school curriculum . . . concerning the place of English and French, with decisions being made as a result of political pressures rather than educational considerations. (British Council, 1989: 7)

In practice, most schools chose to teach English for four years and French for two, with an intensity of three hours per week at all levels, except the final two years, when foreign languages were taught for two hours.

More recently, with the General Education Law (1994) foreign languages were introduced at primary school level, usually in 3rd Grade primary, and it was stated that at this level attention should be focused on: 'The acquisition of elements of conversation and reading in at least one foreign language' (Article 21, m). Although no particular foreign language is specified by law, most institutions have adopted English.

Elite Bilingual Education Provision

Typologies

Bilingual education in Colombia is associated principally with private bilingual schools set up to cater for the rich elite. These are found mainly in urban areas, particularly in the cities of Santafé de Bogotá, Medellin, Cali, Cartagena, and Barranquilla and have increased greatly in demand over the last decade. There are around 40–50 bilingual schools currently in existence in the country, most of them providing English–Spanish bilingualism. The longest established institutions were founded in the 1910s and 1920s in order to provide the sons and daughters of the representatives of multinational companies stationed in Colombia and members of the expatriate communities with access to suitable bilingual and bicultural programmes.

Since then, this type of educational provision has been extended to cater for Colombian nationals and today most of the students in bilingual schools come from monolingual Colombian families who wish to do postgraduate study abroad (de Mejía, 1996). According to preliminary results from a study in progress carried out in two well-established English–Spanish bilingual schools in Cali (de Mejía, in progress), the majority of parents surveyed wanted a bilingual education for their children to enable them to study abroad at university level and to have better job opportunities when they returned.

Although there is no legislation referring to the development of private bilingual education programmes in Colombia, present-day bilingual schools can be divided roughly into two groups. The first group consists of those schools which have a strong foreign connection, such as *The German School*, with branches in Bogotá, Medellin, Cali and Barranquilla, and the *Colombo Británico School* in Cali. This type of school has close contacts with foreign governments and often receives direct financial support, or the appointment of foreign teachers to work in the schools. The headteachers are usually foreign nationals and many of the materials and books used are imported. Students often have the opportunity to have direct contact with the foreign country through exchanges or supervised visits organised by the schools, and international exams like the German *Sprachdiplom* or the *International Baccalaureate* are offered as well as the Colombian High School Diploma.

The expressed aims of some of these institutions are 'to offer a . . . bilingual and bicultural education which will allow the best use of the Spanish and English language (and) which will strengthen the values and traditions of the students' own culture and respect for . . . other nations and cultures leading to better understanding' (Colombo Británico School, Cali, 1998); and 'to educate the student to be open to the world and (to work) for international understanding in the spirit of peace' (The German School, Medellin, 1995). These schools generally promote a high level of bilingual proficiency in the majority of their students, as witnessed by the high scores gained in international examinations, such as the Test of English as a Foreign Language (TOEFL), the International General Certificate of Secondary Education (IGCSE), and the International Baccalaureate (IB), but are often less successful in coping with identity crises and cultural confusion among their school graduates.

The second group of bilingual schools are private national institutions which aim at a high level of student proficiency in at least one foreign language, usually English, in addition to the first language, Spanish. Most of these establishments were founded by individuals or small groups of people, generally Colombians (Araújo & Corominas, 1996). Examples of such schools are *The Montessori School* in Medellin and *Los Nogales School* in Bogotá. Some of these schools may be classified as bilingual institutions, in the sense that they have a high degree of contact with the foreign language, foreign teachers and use two languages as media of instruction, yet they often do not class themselves openly as such, because they wish to emphasise their role as educators of Colombian citizens. The headteachers are generally Colombian and are conscious of the importance of social and ethical values in education to counterbalance what they see as a strong tendency towards social disintegration in the country.

These types of schools thus express their aims as, 'to educate in freedom' and 'to reach a high level of proficiency in the foreign language' (Colegio Montessori, Medellin, 1997); and 'to educate Colombians who seek personal excellence by means of service to others' and 'to prepare students for the realities of international communication and the changing demands on emerging professionals,'(Colegio Los Nogales, Bogotá, 1997). Many of the students in these schools reach a high level of proficiency in the foreign language, especially in reading and writing academic discourse, although there is usually no international examination requirement to demonstrate this.

In spite of the hegemony of English and French as foreign languages in Colombia, this section will, in fact, focus on the influence of another important foreign language within the country, German. The reason for this is to provide some variation from a predominately Anglo perspective established in this chapter and to correct the possible, though mistaken, implication that English-based bilingualism is the only area to show significant advances in the field.

The German schools

In Colombia, unlike Brazil, Argentina and Chile, there are no sizeable German-speaking colonies, such as Puerto Montt (Chile). According to Castañeda (1996: 7), 'in Colombia the presence of this (the German) colony is proportionally very reduced and . . . closed'. In contrast to the early historical development of English and French within Colombia, German influence was particularly strong during the late nineteenth century and in the twentieth century. Ceballos and Ceballos (1993) associate active German involvement with the arrival of three educational missions sent from Germany to Colombia, at the request of the Colombian government. The first arrived in 1872 and lasted until 1878; the second lasted from 1924 to 1935, with a break of one year; and the third spanned the period 1965 to 1978.

The importance of these three official missions stems from the fact that they not only participated actively in the development of education in Colombia in the state system but they also helped in the creation by the German colonies in Colombia of the four private German schools (*los Colegios Alemanes*) in Barranquilla, Cali, Medellín and Bogotá, particularly in the areas of the training and development of teaching staff, the implementation of new teaching methodologies, the teaching and learning of Science from primary school onwards, and the clarification of the role of the state in education.

The setting up of the German schools in Colombia was the direct result of 'the decided action of members of the German colonies in each of the four cities where parents, who wanted their children to be educated in the German language . . . backed by the pedagogical and cultural tradition of their homeland, founded a corporation' (Ceballos & Ceballos, 1993: 150). The first German school to be founded in the country was in Barranquilla in 1912. Then in 1922, there followed the school in the capital, Bogotá, and its counterpart in Cali in 1935. (The school in Medellín is much more recent, dating from 1968.) The three oldest German schools passed through a difficult time in the 1940s when they were forced to close, their German national staff were deported, and their property confiscated because of anti-German sentiment generated as a result of the Second World War.

Since the early 1950s, however, the German schools in Colombia have consolidated their position as centres of academic excellence and promotion of the German language and culture. They have received substantive economic support from the German government, which consists mainly in money for maintenance of buildings and physical installations; budget for teaching materials; and the funding of a number of German language teachers sent out to teach in these schools. Furthermore, the headteachers of all four schools are appointed in Germany and are subject to government rulings for German schools abroad. The continuing of this aid is dependent, to a large extent, on the maintenance of high academic and German language levels (Viteri, 1996).

The majority of the staff are Colombian, or German nationals resident in the country, while 90% of the students are Colombian and come from upper-middle-class or upper-class families. According to a recent survey carried out on bilingual schools in Colombia (de Mejía & Tejada, 2001), graduates of the German schools are expected to be 'citizens of the world, who are responsible for their actions, who respect national values and those of other countries, as well as having a high level of proficiency in three languages'. The three languages in question are German, English and Spanish and students are expected to take international examinations, such as the *Test of English as a Foreign Language (TOEFL)* and the German *Sprachdiplom*, which includes tests of the students' knowledge about Germany and German literature, as well as evidence of linguistic ability, to certify that their foreign language proficiency will enable them to study in prestigious universities in Colombia, the USA or in Europe.

Until the 1960s, as the number of German-speaking students in the schools was high, 50% of the curriculum was taught in German and large numbers of teachers were officially sent out from Germany. However, recently this has diminished and currently in three of the four schools in Colombia, foreign language teaching is considered primarily a subject area, rather than a medium of instruction, although there is some evidence of German-speaking teachers teaching areas such as Social Studies or Maths in German. In general, the students receive a weekly average of between four to six hours German language tuition throughout their school career. The methodological approach is basically communicative from preschool (4 years old) until the pupils reach 3rd Grade primary (9 years old), when they begin more formalised study of the foreign language until they leave school in Grade 11 (Viteri, 1996). The second foreign language, English, is introduced as a subject area in Grade 4 (10 years old).

The German school in Bogotá, *Colegio Andino*, in contrast, offers two types of foreign language programme, one subject-based, and the other using both Spanish and German as media of instruction. In this school the bilingual programme, called the *Selecta* programme, takes one year longer than the normal Colombian Baccalaureate (12 years instead of 11). Students can choose whether they wish to be part of this programme which will lead to the award of the German Baccalaureate. The school then selects suitable candidates according to their level of proficiency in German, and as to how far teachers feel that the students will be able to cope with subjects taught through the medium of German.

Case Sketch 8.3 gives more details about how the German School in Medellin functions.

Case Sketch 8.3   The German School in Medellin (based on material from a recent study by de Mejía & Tejada, 2001)

Name of School:	*Deutsche Schule (Colegio Alemán) Medellín.*
Date of Foundation:	*1968*
History:	*A group of German parents from the colony in Medellín decided to found a school to strengthen the German language and culture in their children.*
Number of Students:	*809 students, from 4 to 18 years old*
Number of Teachers:	*112, including 15 foreigners (8 of whom are officially sent out from Germany by the German government)*

General School Aim:	*To guide students in developing their own criteria and to encourage their personal, moral and social development.*
Language Aims:	*To teach and to enable students to experience the languages, values and culture of Colombia and of the German Republic. To prepare students for encounters with other nations and cultures, so that they will be open to the world in a spirit of international understanding.*
Curriculum:	*The school follows a Colombian curriculum. In order to help students to develop a good level of proficiency in both German and English which will allow them to study in good universities in Colombia, the United States and Europe, emphasis is placed on a good grounding first in the mother tongue (Spanish for the majority of the students) and then in the foreign language. German is taught generally by means of comparative grammatical analysis.*

The German schools are characterised by the emphasis they place on in-service teacher education and development programmes, particularly aimed at locally recruited teachers in the schools. The Pedagogical Centre in Bogotá, founded in 1979, co-ordinates this process by offering methodology seminars and workshops for teachers in the German schools in the Northern Andean region, Colombia, Ecuador, Peru, Venezuela and Bolivia.[4] Here the emphasis is on the teaching and learning of science, technology and foreign languages and all new teachers pass through a process of assessment and training during their first year at one of the schools. This is considered particularly important in the case of teachers who may have a good command of the German language but who may lack a sound pedagogical background (Viteri, 1996).

One area of potential difficulty for Colombian teachers is the use of standard textbooks and materials published in Germany by all German schools abroad. While this undoubtedly helps to centralise the supply and use of resources, it has also been criticised as leading to underestimating the value of 'the minimum socio-cultural conditions which define the particularities of learning and the development of these in individuals in a specific country' (Castañeda, 1996: 9).

As indicated above, in Colombia there is no immediate need for students to learn German, in the same way as there is for English, due to the geographical proximity of the United States. Many students in the German schools come from Colombian families where contact with German language and culture is practically zero. For this reason, the German schools make considerable efforts to introduce their students to aspects of German culture and traditions. As one former pupil of the German school in Cali remembers, 'There are the traditional feast days that I experienced during my first days at school . . . such as *Karnaval* (Carnival), *Laternenfest*

(Lantern Day), the arrival of St Niklaus, the *Osterhase* (The Easter Bunny)' (Viteri, 1996: 1).

Furthermore, one of the most important aspects of the curriculum in the German schools in the country is the cultural exchange scheme in Grade 9 or 10, which allows students to experience living and studying in Germany for a period of between four to six months. As the headteacher of the Cali German school remarks, 'the students . . . learn that the nation situated in the heart of Europe is kind'. This experience reinforces the intercultural character of these schools, reflected in their official designation as 'cultural corporations', which aims to strengthen the ties between Colombia and Germany through an understanding of language, music, theatre, dance and sporting events.

Higher and further education in German

In spite of a perception that 'German is culturally very distant' (de Mejía & Tejada, 2001) for the majority of Colombians, there is recent evidence that the position of the language is growing stronger within the country. The Goethe Institute, the official German cultural body which offers foreign language tuition and cultural activities to the general public, is becoming increasingly popular. The Institute also hosts seminars directed at teachers of German in universities and bilingual schools in Colombia. There are also certain Colombian universities, such as the Universidad Externado in Bogotá, which require students of Business Studies who demonstrate proficiency in English and French, to study German as a third foreign language.

In an important development in 1989, the first undergraduate foreign language programme in German in the whole of the Andean region was set up in the National University in Bogotá, the largest university in the country, whereby future teachers of German can study aspects of the German language, literature and civilisation and translation as part of a four-year degree programme. This initiative has been supported by the German Academic Exchange Service in an agreement signed in 1999 to facilitate exchanges between students and staff at the National University and the University of Mannheim in Germany.

In the area of technical bilingual education, in cities where a number of German firms have their headquarters, such as Bogotá and Medellín, former students of the German schools can study for qualifications in international commerce which are recognised jointly in Colombia and in Germany, thanks to inter-institutional agreements.

Summary

From the above it can be seen that the function of the German schools in promoting bilingualism and interculturalism has changed over the years. Initially, these catered for the desire of the expatriate German colonies in the main Colombian cities of Bogotá, Barranquilla and Cali to maintain their language and culture, with the official support of the German government. Nowadays, however, children who enter the schools are mainly monolingual Spanish speakers, who have to learn

German as a foreign language, in an overwhelmingly Spanish language environment. Their parents are attracted to the schools particularly because of their high academic standards and sense of discipline rather than the immediate desire for them to learn German. The German government, on the other hand, has specifically tied economic support to high levels of student proficiency in the German *Sprachdiplom*. Thus, the schools are faced with the dilemma of promoting a language which for many young Colombians does not have immediate relevance and which is perceived as 'difficult' (Castañeda, 1996: 10). For this reason, the schools make conscious efforts to raise the profile of German, projecting it as 'the international language of science' (Colegio Alemán, Medellín, 1994: 78), associated with Albert Einstein, Max Weber and Martin Heidegger.

Conclusion

In general, we can see from this brief survey of the state of elite bilingualism and bilingual education in these three South American nations that there has been a gradual change from the initial provision of bilingual, intercultural education for children of expatriate or immigrant communities to more recent developments involving mainly monolingual country nationals. In this sense, it may be said that elite bilingual education has moved from being a priority of minority groups to a national educational concern, particularly in Argentina and Colombia. As we have seen, in Brazil the situation is somewhat different in that foreign language provision is centred in institutes and language schools, rather than in the education system.

As noted elsewhere, there is considerable variety in the type of institutions that are classified as bilingual schools. Some have strong foreign connections, while others aim at providing high levels of foreign language proficiency at national level. Some institutions class themselves as intercultural or bicultural, while others are concerned rather to strengthen their students' sense of regional or national identities. Thus, it is difficult to categorise very precisely the characteristics of elite bilingual education provision in these countries. It is rather a question of identifying the different linguistic and cultural features of such programmes in relation to their institutional aims and philosophies.

In the choice of languages there is also evidence of considerable change. While English is undoubtedly the international language that is perceived as most valuable by parents and students in bilingual schools in Colombia, Brazil, and Argentina, there is evidence that other world languages, such as Portuguese and Spanish are altering the linguistic balance in the foreign language arena, due to recent political developments.

Thus, in general, it may be said that the situation of elite bilingual education in these three countries is in a state of flux, both in relation to the spread of different modalities of educational provision, and with respect to the languages in play. From the reports presented in this chapter it is clear that this presents interesting opportunities for further research, both at national and international levels.

Notes

1. Marina MacRae is a lecturer in Bilingualism and Bilingual Education at the Universidade de São Paulo, Brazil.
2. Cristina Banfi is a graduate of INES in Lenguas Vivas 'J.R. Fernandez' in Argentina as a Teacher of English. She also holds an M.Phil. in Linguistics from the University of Cambridge and a Ph.D in Linguistics from University College, London. She has taught at University level in the UK, the US and in Argentina and also at Teacher Training Colleges and schools at primary and secondary school level. She has organised and participated in international academic conferences, published articles, and edited a journal. Currently, she is Head of the Languages Department of the Universidad Católica Argentina, Academic Co-ordinator of the ESSARP, and President of the Association of Teachers of English of Buenos Aires.
3. Author's translation.
4. According to recent information (Ricardo Castañeda, 1999, personal communication) the Pedagogical Centre virtually ceased to exist in 1997. This was, in part, due to budget cutbacks by the German government for German programmes in South America, resulting from changing priorities in German cultural politics, with increasing attention being focused on Eastern Europe (Ingrid de Tala, 2000, personal communication). This has caused difficulties for schools teaching German in the North Andean region, particularly with regard to pre-service and in-service teacher training and the obtaining of textbooks and other teaching material. Ricardo Castañeda is a lecturer in German at Universidad Nacional in Botota; and Ingrid de Tala is a lecturer in the Department of Modern Languages at Universidad del Valle in Cali.

Chapter 9
Asia: 'Languages of the Head and Languages of the Heart'

Introduction

This chapter is devoted to considering issues of elite bilingualism in three Asian countries: Japan, Hong Kong and Brunei. Each of these nations shows a different pattern of historical, sociocultural and educational influences. Japan, which until relatively recently considered itself a largely monolingual nation, is currently experiencing an upsurge of interest in bilinguals and bilingualism, and a recognition of its reality as a multilingual society with regard to indigenous languages spoken in the country, such as the *Ryukyuan* and *Ainu* languages. Furthermore, the influence of a small but powerful sector of the population, the so-called 'returnees' (see Chapters 1 and 5) has had an important effect on changing perceptions of multilingualism and multiculturalism with respect to international languages such as English, in Japan. The spread of immersion programmes in the country also provides evidence of this new change in direction.

Hong Kong, in contrast, has had a long history of multilingual and multicultural influence, due to periods of Sino-British colonialism throughout the nineteenth and twentieth centuries. This has left a marked influence on the development of the current language streaming policy which divides the Hong Kong education system into a small number of English-medium Anglo-Chinese schools, and a majority of Chinese-speaking middle schools. The return of Hong Kong to China in 1997 has had an effect on the language balance, in that both Cantonese and *Putonghua* (Mandarin) are increasingly used in daily interaction, while English continues to be the language of international commerce.

The third country discussed in this chapter, Brunei Darussalem, is both multilingual and multiracial. Different varieties of the Malay language are used in different domains, as well as indigenous languages such as *Tutong, Belait* and *Penan*. The use of English among the ruling class dates from the time Brunei was a British Protectorate in the nineteenth century. Recently, Brunei has implemented an official

183

Dwibahasa (bilingual) education programme, which uses both Malay and English as media of instruction in the education system, in an attempt to facilitate higher levels of English language proficiency among the school population, without giving rise to language or cultural shift in this Moslem monarchy.

JAPAN

General Perspectives

Japan consists of four large islands, Hokkaido, Honshu, Shikoku and Kyushu and over a thousand other islands situated between the North Pacific Ocean and the Sea of Japan in East Asia. It has an estimated population of 125.5 million people (1995 figures). Japanese is the official language of the country, though other native and immigrant community languages are also spoken, such as the *Ryukyuan* languages, the *Ainu* language, Korean and Chinese.

In contrast to Hong Kong (see next section) which has long acknowledged its multilingual and multicultural reality, debate about linguistic pluralism has developed only relatively recently in Japan (Maher & Yashiro, 1995), in spite of the long-established presence in the country of various ethnic minority and immigrant groups such as the *Ainu*, the Korean and Chinese communities and the Okinawan *hafu* (half) or mixed race. Researchers have attributed this, in part, to the drive towards cultural and linguistic homogeneity characteristic of the Meiji government (1871–1912), which then continued until the end of the Second World War in 1945.

This conception of social uniformity involved the establishing of the idea of 'one people, one language, one culture' which was reflected in the official postwar campaign to promote *Nihonjinron*, or Japanese identity by focusing on its cultural and linguistic uniqueness. Thus, frequently the Japanese have shown low tolerance towards difference and diversity, seeing these as potential sources of confusion and disorder. This is reflected in the traditionally small percentage of international marriages in the country. In 1991 only 3.4% of all marriages registered involved a Japanese national and a non-Japanese partner (Yamamoto, 1995). Furthermore, the Okinawan *hafu*, people of Okinawan, Japanese and North-American heritage, have often been stigmatised, because of their mixed race and their multilingualism and multiculturalism, as not being truly Japanese.

However, there are now signs of change in this respect. According to a newspaper report from *The Daily Yomiuri* summarised in *Bilingual Japan* (1998), the number of international marriages is actually increasing, while the total level of marriages in Japan is on the decline. There is evidence to show that the percentage of Japanese adults who say that they have reservations about marrying a foreigner has declined from 67% in 1986 to 30% in 1992. Furthermore, Maher and Yashiro (1995) report that in the latter half of the 1980s books on bilingualism started to enter the Japanese mass media, and to date, there is increasing interest in all aspects of bilingualism and multiculturalism.

Various reasons have been given for this. One is the increasing mobility of many sections of Japanese society, who routinely travel abroad on business or due to academic commitments. There is also the growing impact of the 'returnees', Japanese nationals, both children and adults who return from a prolonged stay overseas, about whom more will be said later. In addition, since the 1980s many non-Japanese people, such as Indochinese refugees and foreign workers, have immigrated to the country. All these factors have helped towards the growing recognition among the population that, 'Japan is not a monolingual country. It is a multilingual country, whose national language is Japanese' (Yashiro, 1995: 151).

English in Japan is generally considered a foreign language, not used as a means of communication within the country, except in certain towns in the Okinawan area, as a result of a thirty year period of colonisation by the United States after the Second World War. Since 1947, English has had a high profile in the country as an international language associated with the economic success characteristic of the postwar period. In 1987, the Japanese Ministry of Education began bringing in young teachers from Western countries under the Japan Exchange and Teaching (JET) Program to help boost English teaching in the school system (Goebel Noguchi, 2001). In a recent study carried out to ascertain the attitudes of students in two Japanese universities towards bilingualism Yamamoto (2001: 40) reported that the subjects of the study considered the term 'bilingual' as referring to elite bilinguals who 'speak Japanese as a native language and have managed to achieve a high level of proficiency in English, which is considered important for success in education and professions in Japan'.

However, rather paradoxically, in spite of its prestige value, the actual level of English language proficiency attained by the Japanese as reflected in the Teaching of English to Speakers of Other Languages (TOEFL) scores, is not high. According to an international comparison carried out in 1990–1991, Japan ranked 48 out of a total number of 54 countries with an average score of 493 (cited in Honna, 1995). Perhaps for this reason, English–Japanese bilingual adults are accorded high status and are in great demand in the job market.

The widespread use of written English by scientists and medical practitioners in Japan poses an interesting challenge to the linguistic situation described above. It has been reported that although most doctors are not fluent speakers of English, they do, in fact, write medical notes and patients' records (*karute*) in English (John Maher,[1] 1998, personal communication). Furthermore, the Japanese medical profession is one of the largest English publishing groups in the world of medicine. According to Maher (1986), in 1980 Japan produced more medical articles in English than Canada, Australia and New Zealand combined. This author also found that older doctors valued English-language technical literature even more highly than younger colleagues, and suggests that the adoption of English among the medical profession 'as a new language for academic communication has been a powerful symbol for the future advance of Japanese science in the international community' (Maher, 1989: 313).

Recently, there have been moves to adopt English as Japan's second official language. In 2000, a Government Advisory Committee recommended this revolutionary idea saying that 'Japan should aim at having all citizens acquire a working knowledge of English', stressing that English was 'a tool in the international community'. The Committee also recommended revision of the country's immigration policy 'to encourage foreigners to live and work in Japan' (*Japan Times*, 20 January 2000). The report of this proposal sparked a lively debate in the country reflected in the media, with many people arguing that young Japanese do not speak their first language properly and that this should be attended to before considering the study of a foreign language (Stephen Ryan, 2000, personal communication).[2]

Within this general panorama of language use in Japan it is important to include a small, but very influential group of highly mobile middle-class students, commonly referred to as 'returnees'. The term 'returnees' is used in Japan to refer particularly to children and adolescents whose parents have been posted abroad on business or due to political reasons for an extended period of time (more than two years), who then return to their homeland to live. According to statistics issued by the Ministry of Foreign Affairs in 1998, 49,670 Japanese expatriate children lived outside Japan, most of whom would return back to be known as *kikokushijo* (returnees).

Although this phenomenon is true of other countries, and research in this area has been carried out since the 1970s (Sussman, 1986) the situation in Japan is different, in that returnees, until recently, were perceived as a group in urgent need of re-acculturation back into Japanese society. These children, from upper-middle-class backgrounds, were conceived of as a problem population because of their lack of proficiency in Japanese, their different patterns of behaviour, and even their inability to eat rice properly (Yashiro, 1995).

Since the late 1970s, however, things have changed in this respect. As the concept of Japanese monolingualism and monoculturalism began to change, the idea of education for international and intercultural understanding has become popular, as shown by a wealth of university courses offered on such subjects as 'International Exchange', and 'International Communication'. Furthermore, organisations such as 'The Japan Association of International Education' and 'The Society for Intercultural Education' have been set up to start implementing these ideas at school level. Thus, instead of being seen as a problem, the returnees have begun to be recognised as a valuable human resource and have been given the opportunity to share their experience with regular students in the schools (Yashiro, 1995). They are increasingly seen as agents of internationalisation, who can help to open up Japanese society to the reality of linguistic and cultural diversity, rather than as alien elements.

In 1992, approximately 31,000 children and adolescents returned to Japan from overseas and this number is increasing annually. Their parents have mobilised to ensure that they receive special consideration when applying to university. This campaign has resulted in the creation of quotas for returnees in schools and in many prestigious national and private universities. However, this development has also come under attack as evidence of preferential treatment for an emerging international elite class (Kanno, 2000).

In spite of this special treatment, however, many returnees still face problems in readapting back into Japanese society. Some have difficulty using Japanese, particularly in writing the *Kanji* script. Others have a good command of the language but do not know how to use it appropriately in social interaction. Many feel victimised or 'left out' by their classmates. In addition, although there is an established tradition of the Japanese government financing Japanese language classes for this population, returnees often find it difficult to maintain their knowledge of foreign languages acquired abroad, as there are no official programmes which cater for languages other than Japanese. There are, however, some private organisations, such as the 'Japan Air Lines Coordination Service' which are now beginning to offer maintenance language courses, but even bearing this in mind, returnees' bilingual development and bicultural perceptions often suffer in the face of the overwhelming impact of a society which emphasises the merits of conformity to accepted social and cultural norms.

In a study examining the experiences of four returnees, both while they were abroad and later on their return, Kanno (2000: 13) came to the conclusion that these students were the focus of conflicting desires. On the one hand they wanted to be included in what they perceived as mainstream society, both abroad and back in Japan. On the other, they felt the need to 'assert their uniqueness' with regard to everyone else, especially through demonstration of their foreign language proficiency. The researcher suggests that 'the kind of identity into which bilingual students are cast as the speakers of a language has a tremendous impact on their relationship with that language and its development', and concludes that if bilingual returnee students are appreciated for their bilingual and bicultural resources they will be able to attain their maximum potential and function successfully as cultural mediators.

Elite Bilingual Education Provision

Immersion programmes

Although English is taught as a foreign language in virtually every school in Japan in a programme that started in 1947, bilingual education as such is in its infancy. There are reports of the recent creation of preschool and primary immersion programmes, such as a Kindergarten in Miyazaki, a small city of approximately 300,000 people, and Katoh Gakuen in Namazu, Shizuoka, two hours distant from Tokyo,. While reports on these initiatives are necessarily fragmentary, I will give some details of these two programmes in order to give an idea of how bilingual education provision is beginning to be implemented in Japan (see Case Sketch 9.1).

Case Sketch 9.1 **Miyazaki Immersion Programme** (based on Thomas, 1996)

Name of School: *Miyazaki Kindergarten*

Date of Foundation: *1992*

Age Range: *Children from 2½–5 years old.*

General School Aim: *To prepare students from a young age to compete favourably in educational pursuits.*

Language Aim: *To promote additive bilingualism.*

Language Use: *Language domains are established within the institution. The Japanese-speaking staff talk only Japanese outside the classroom, while the Australian-English-speaking staff use only English within the classroom.*

Curriculum: *The programme begins with an almost total immersion in the foreign language (90%) for 2½–3 years olds. The following two years show an increase in the use of the first language, 75% English; 25% Japanese for the 3–4 year olds, followed by 65% English, 35% Japanese for the 4–5 year olds. The curriculum is activity centred, using a hands-on approach. This involves associating actions such as cutting, colouring and gluing paper shapes with instructions given by the teacher and repeated by the children in the foreign language. There is also a daily English language lesson. In the first language classes, the children are introduced to the Hiragana writing system, computers and music.*

    Although there has been no formal research carried out of the programme, there are reports of positive parental responses, as evidenced in high enrolment figures. Furthermore, teachers testify to the success of the programme in reaching institutional goals. However, as there are no immersion programmes available in the area at primary level, children cannot continue their studies in a bilingual setting. This situation has led to calls for programmes which will continue bilingual development at primary and high school level in the area (see Case Sketch 9.2).

Case Sketch 9.2 **Katoh Gakuen Immersion Programme** (based on report presented by Bostwick, 1999, and reviewed by Smith, 1999; Bostwick, 2001)

Name of School: *Katoh Gakuen*

Date of Foundation: *1992*

Teachers:	*Ten native speaking English teachers – four from the USA, three Canadians, two Australians, and one Briton. Four Japanese teachers were teamed with the immersion staff to help with such things as communication with the parents in Japanese.*
Students:	*350 students, 98% Japanese, from preschool to Grade 6. The majority come from middle or upper-middle class families, but few parents speak or understand English.*
Language Aim:	*To develop additive bilingualism and biliteracy skills, without negative consequences for children's academic, linguistic, or intellectual development.*
Cultural Orientation:	*Japanese as well as English language and culture are valued and many of the traditional Japanese festivals are part of the school programme.*
Curriculum:	*Partial immersion in English and Japanese. 50–65% of programme is presented in English. Japanese Language Arts, Music and Art are taught in Japanese. Students follow the standard Japanese Ministry of Education curriculum with the same text and test content. Key concept terminology in subjects such as Science and Maths are taught in the Japanese Language Arts class, after they have been introduced in English. An integrated, thematic approach has been adopted. Initial literacy is given in Japanese and assessment of students' academic achievement is carried out in both languages.*

Parents are free to choose whether their children will join the immersion programme in English and Japanese or a parallel programme, conducted in Japanese, with three hours per week of English language classes. The North American Bilingual Education Director of the programme, Mike Bostwick, reports that there is no difference in socio-economic status or IQ scores between children entering the two programmes. He also notes that there is a positive relationship between developing levels of proficiency in the students' two languages, 'Typically, the children's second language development mirrors first language development – students with strong Japanese skills tend to have better English skills. It's not a perfect correlation, but it is fairly high' (Kamada, 1998a: 9).

In 1998, the first class graduated from the immersion programme in Katoh Gakuen. They averaged slightly better scores than students in the monolingual (Japanese-only) classes in the school on the Japanese National Achievement Tests in Mathematics and Japanese. Their English language proficiency was measured by the Iowa test of Basic Skills and placed them only a year and a half behind students in English-only courses in United States primary schools.

These two immersion programmes show that it is possible to replicate the successful language development associated with Canadian immersion in a Japanese context. The influence of key Canadian immersion researchers, such as Jim Cummins and Fred Genessee, especially in connection with Katoh Gakuen, has been important in establishing the credibility of Japanese immersion within the country and abroad.

One of the innovations in the Katoh Gakuen programme in comparison with the Canadian programmes has been the recruitment of foreign native-speaking English teachers from Canada, Australia, the US and Britain who are not bilingual in English and Japanese. This does not appear to have affected the success of the programme. Furthermore, the English textbooks used in the different subject areas are, in fact, translations of standard Japanese textbooks, rather than texts designed for first language speakers of English. Another key aspect of the second programme is the close relationship maintained with the parents. Surveys of parents' views are regularly taken, which has allowed the school to know how parents feel about the decisions taken.

International Schools

Japan has a long history of International Schools in the largest cities, such as Tokyo, Yokohama and Kobe which dates back to the foundation in 1872 of the Saint Maur International School in the port city of Yokohama by the Sisters of the Institute of the Infant Jesus Order. The aim of this school was to provide a Christian, Western education for children of foreign residents. Thus, Saint Maur forms part of a group of International Schools in Japan, such as St Mary's International School, Tokyo, and Seisen International School, which provide a specifically Christian orientation in their programmes, although most accept students from all religious denominations. They are generally single-sex schools.

Another group of schools, such as the Aoba Japan International School, Tokyo, and the Yokohama International School, are non-denominational, coeducational schools which cater for a wide range of nationalities and creeds and seek to promote understanding and respect towards different cultures and beliefs. Although the majority of the families who send their children to International Schools in Japan are diplomats, business or professional members of the international community residing in Japan, there are also returnee pupils of Japanese origin who have lived abroad and who wish to continue their education in a bilingual and multicultural environment.

In most of these schools English is the primary medium of instruction, but the study of Japanese is also included as an integral part of most curricula, catering for students with zero up to native proficiency levels. Other languages offered are Spanish, French and Latin. There are, however, a number of elite schools, particularly in the Tokyo area, which cater for children of German. French, Korean and Chinese extraction.

Most schools base their teaching on pedagogic models which derive from the US or UK which allows for easy transition to schools throughout the world. Some provision is also made for students to familiarise themselves with Japanese cultural activities, such as calligraphy, origami and aikido, as well as taking part in the celebration of Japanese festivals. Many offer courses leading to the US High School Diploma and the International Baccalaureate and students usually continue their education after graduation in universities in the USA, Europe and Japan.

In the late 1990s, in spite of their elite prestige, many of these schools experienced severe economic difficulties as a result of the South East Asian currency collapse of 1997. The Japanese companies who customarily paid the school fees for their employees' sons and daughters cut their budgets. Some institutions were forced to close. Others had to cut back drastically on student numbers, thus clearly demonstrating the link between elite bilingual provision and economic considerations (Sachiyo Fujita Round, 1998, personal communication).[3]

Higher education

Japan has an impressive number of institutions which offer Higher Education degrees. To date, there are 95 national universities, 36 public universities and 337 private universities which offer four year undergraduate degree courses. In addition, there are 38 national, 52 public and 459 junior colleges which offer two-year courses, which sometimes include specialist training (John Maher, 1998, personal communication). Thus, it is considered 'normal' for a Japanese child to go to university or college. Furthermore, there is an enormous emphasis on academic achievement as measured by the name of the particular college or university entered. As noted by Bostwick (2001: 276) 'Entrance to a top university is seen as a sure "ticket" to the best opportunities after graduation'.

Considering the status of English within the country, there is growing pressure to create another level of English language college education. In the 1980s, many North American universities set up branches in Japan to teach college courses in English. However, these were not entirely successful, as Japanese parents preferred to continue sending their children to Japanese universities, combined with visits to Europe or North America for language training (John Maher, 1998, personal communication). There are, however, some exceptions to this trend. One of these is the 'International Christian University' of Tokyo, set up 50 years ago, immediately after the Second World War. It is the only bilingual university in the country and caters for a wealthy population, using both Japanese and English as media of instruction.

According to its President, the creation of the university was based on the premise that 'knowledge of languages and other cultures would speed the processes of democratization and internationalization of Japan' (ICU Prospectus, 1998). Based on information given for that year, the total number of student enrolments was 2,857, of which 95% were Japanese and 5% non-Japanese students representing 28 countries. The bilingual nature of the institution is emphasised in the information sent to prospective students in the following fashion, 'At ICU, … both Japanese and English are used in classes'.

Summary

As can be seen from the above discussion, Japan is beginning to acknowledge its reality as a multilingual and multicultural society in spite of a long tradition of cultural and linguistic isolation. Part of this acknowledgement is manifested in a marked upsurge of interest in bilingualism and multiculturalism in both the elite circles of returnee families and partners in international marriages, as well as in the minority languages situations of guest workers and immigrant communities. Both these sectors are conscious of the need to revive and/or maintain the different languages they speak, and there have been calls to actively foster the growth of bilingualism in Japan on a more structured basis (Oka, no date). This recommendation is particularly apposite, bearing in mind the *ad hoc* nature of much of the reaction towards returnee students and the creation of new bilingual schools which are sometimes unable to provide continuity of contact with foreign languages at different educational levels.

HONG KONG

General Perspectives

Hong Kong is situated at the south-eastern tip of China and consists of a total area of only 1070 square kilometres. Most of the territory is made up of islands, which include Hong Kong Island and Kowloon, as well as 235 outlying islands (Baker & Prys Jones, 1998).

The present sociolinguistic reality of Hong Kong society reflects the dual nature of its colonial past as a strategic prize which has belonged to both China and Great Britain at different times during the nineteenth and twentieth centuries. About 98% of the population is ethnic Chinese, with Cantonese as their mother tongue. This language serves as a powerful cohesive factor, together with a traditionally strong family ethos to make for a strongly tight-knit society (British Council, 1995). Many of the population of Hong Kong have family links within mainland China, particularly in the southern Guangdong province, yet few speak the official language of the People's Republic, Mandarin, also known as *Putonghua*. English is the language of the dominant elite and the language of administration and the law. It is used by many people in their work situation and hence is considered the language of power and educational and socio-economic advancement in the area.

According to Lin (1996), Hong Kong government policy has contributed in four main ways to the current status of English in an area which, on 1 July 1997 was finally handed back by Britain to the Chinese after a 99-year lease agreement had expired, to become a Special Administrative Region of the People's Republic of China. First of all, English has been the official legal and government language since Hong Kong became a British colony in 1842 and it was only in 1974, as a result of pressure from the Chinese Language Movement, that Chinese gained official status in the country. Secondly, there is a history of English-medium higher education in the country which dates from the foundation in 1911 of the University of Hong

Kong. Thirdly, the British-based accreditation system of professional qualifications in force for areas such as accountancy, medicine and engineering means that all Hong Kong professionals need to have a good level of proficiency in English. Finally, English is the most important selection criterion for official posts of high rank in the civil service and government administration.

The differential relationship between English and Chinese reflects the changing relationship between China and Hong Kong during the nineteenth and twentieth century. The nineteenth century saw the growth of a class of 'linguistic middle-men' or translators of English and Chinese for purposes of trade between China and Britain. These bilinguals were the product of their education in missionary schools in Hong Kong and they gradually 'gained status as a new elite class to which others, noting the link between English language and improved status, aspired' (Pennington, 1998a: 26). Thus, right from the beginning, there was a powerful connection established between perceptions of wealth and prosperity, and proficiency in English in the country.

In spite of Hong Kong's status as a British Crown Colony, China continued to exert great cultural, economic and political influence on Hong Kong, up until 1949. Many Chinese-medium schools were created at this time and Hong Kong students were able to study at prestigious Chinese universities on the mainland. However, after the Chinese communist revolution in 1949, there was a change in position. As a result of being embargoed by the United States for its role in the Korean War, and isolated by the West and the Soviet Union in the 1950s and 1960s during the Cultural Revolution, China adopted an isolationist stance in world affairs, and a position of cultural and economic separation from Hong Kong.

Initially, in the second half of the twentieth century, therefore, Hong Kong had no direct access to alternative Chinese educational and sociocultural influences. However, in the 1960s and 1970s there was a great upsurge in the country's economic status, when it changed from being a small fishing port to become an industrialised city, specialising in textile manufacturing. Trade with China increased during the 'open-door' policy of the 1980s and 1990s and Hong Kong developed into one of the most important business and financial centres in the world, largely concerned with the re-export of products processed in China (Ho, 1994, cited in Lin, 1996).

Somewhat paradoxically, however, this economic nexus with China did not lead immediately to an increase in status in Chinese in Hong Kong, but rather to an increased emphasis on the need for a mastery of English by the workforce as a result of its importance as a world language of international trade and communication. As noted by Poon (1999: 134) 'with Hong Kong's growth as an international centre of trade and finance, accompanied by an escalating literacy rate, English has become much more widely used in the territory'. Hong Kong's perceived position as a 'solid logistical platform' from which to initiate business dealings with China (*The Economist*, 1998) meant that Western companies sought out partners in Hong Kong who understood business dealings in both cultures to act as international linguistic and cultural brokers.

Nevertheless, proficiency in English is not spread evenly across the population. It tends to be restricted to a relatively small sector of the Hong Kong Chinese population, which includes university lecturers, secondary school English teachers, some media presenters, and other professionals 'associated with international concerns' (Pennington, 1998b: 9), all of whom need to use the language in their work environments.

There have also been some indications of a change in attitude with regard to the relative importance of English and Chinese in the country. At the beginning of the 1980s it was reported that Hong Kong adolescents showed some preference for English, coupled with a fear of losing their Chinese cultural identity (Pierson *et al.*, 1980). Later studies (Bickley, 1990; Pennington & Yue, 1994; Pennington, 1998b) have argued, however, that pro-Chinese sentiment is gathering momentum in the country, especially in relation to *Putonghua*, which in its written form is known as 'Modern Standard Chinese'. This is a standard variety of Chinese which has been used as a lingua franca within China since the 1930s and which is now the official language of the People's Republic of China. However, only a relatively small number of the population of Hong Kong use *Putonghua* in their daily lives; about 1% of the population speak this variety as a first language and about 17% as a second language, according to Baker and Prys Jones (1998).

Putonghua has been commonly taught as a school subject in Hong Kong since 1990 and has been considered by some researchers (Bauer, 1984; Cheung, 1985) as equal to English in its prestige value. In contrast, Cantonese, the first language of the great majority of the population, is seen by many as the language used principally for communication in informal or casual domains.

The official termination of British rule in 1997 seems to have accelerated changes in the linguistic balance of these three languages in what is now officially a Special Administrative Region of the People's Republic of China. According to Pennington (1998b) there is evidence of a shift towards the use of both Cantonese and *Putonghua* and away from English in the region. However, according to Lin (2001), English still plays a powerful role in certain key sectors such as international trade and finance, and it remains the medium of instruction in the majority of universities and professional training programmes. In addition, it appears that many Hong Kong Chinese who left the territory and raised their children in English-speaking countries, such as Canada, USA, England and Australia, are now returning to the region. Consequently, the number of English-speaking bilinguals is on the increase.

Thus, English has conserved its status as 'a socioeconomically dominant language in Hong Kong society' (Lin, 2001: 143), even though both Cantonese and *Putonghua* are increasingly used in daily life. There is also evidence of the rise of a 'vernacular' form of Cantonese which incorporates 'elements of English language and culture which have been transformed or *retranslated* in relation to local language and culture' and which serves as 'a vibrant and creative resource for developing new identities and new discourses to meet the communicative and psychological needs of the Hong Kong people' (Pennington, 1998b: 12).

Elite Bilingual Education Provision

Anglo-Chinese schools

This complex multilingual situation detailed above is reflected in the educational sphere, which is characterised by parallel Chinese and English provision. The government has been widely criticised for the lack of a coherent language in education policy and many educational developments have been the result of a *laissez-faire* approach on the part of the authorities (British Council, 1995). Recently, however, there have been steps to remedy this situation in that the Hong Kong Standing Committee on Language Education and Research (SCOLAR) commissioned a research report to appear in 1999 with the express purpose of, 'informing language education planning in post-1997 Hong Kong' (Lin & Man, 1998, personal communication).

At present, most children in the country (around 90%) go to Chinese-medium primary schools. However, there are also a number of exclusive English-medium kindergartens and primary schools which cater for a small group of wealthy families and which cultivate a Westernised English-speaking elite among the local Chinese population. These constitute 'feeder schools' for the prestigious, high-quality English-medium secondary schools in the country. Such institutions form part of what are generally referred to as 'Anglo-Chinese' schools, where the official medium of instruction is English in all subject areas except Chinese History, Chinese Language and Literature. These schools have a long history in that they date from the beginning of British colonial rule in 1842 and were originally in the hands of missionary bodies. The other form of secondary education provision is the Chinese middle school, where the curriculum is taught completely in Chinese, normally Cantonese, though this has never been officially defined, with the exception of English taught as a subject area.

Although these two modalities are generally presented as representatives of a 'dual' education system, there is evidence to demonstrate that in reality there exists an educational continuum, as some Chinese schools use English texts because appropriate Chinese texts are unavailable and some Anglo-Chinese schools use Chinese texts for certain subject areas, to enable students to understand the content being taught (Johnson, 1994).

Anglo-Chinese schools have become increasingly popular in Hong Kong during the last 30 years. They have risen from 57.9% of all secondary schools in 1960 to 91.7% in 1990 (Lee, 1993) and since the late 1970s have increased their range of intake to include pupils from non-wealthy backgrounds. According to So (1984), this expansion of English-medium education was determined by a period of rapid economic development in the region which opened up new employment opportunities for those with high levels of English. Thus, parents see Anglo-Chinese schools as the key to English language proficiency, which they believe will allow their children access to higher education and socio-economic advancement.

However, there are a number of studies (Yu & Atkinson, 1988; Lin, 1990, 1996; Lee, 1993; Pennington, 1995) which document an educational and linguistic reality of life in Hong Kong Anglo-Chinese schools which is at variance with these beliefs. They show that for many children the radical break from Chinese as medium of instruction in primary schools to English in secondary schools constitutes a major barrier to learning, and leads to widespread code-switching by both teachers and students in an attempt to come to terms with this problem. Since the English-medium policy of Anglo-Chinese schools does not officially allow code-switching and decrees that all written work and assessment must be done in English, all use of Cantonese in the classroom has to be surreptitious and restricted to the oral domain. Thus, teachers are placed in a dilemma. As Lin (1990) reports, teachers accept that ideally they should use English alone in the classroom, but in order to help their students to understand what is going on they have to resort to a range of communicative resources, such as intonation, demonstration, gesture and code-switching.

There is also some evidence (Cheung, forthcoming) to suggest that code-switching helps teachers to cope with the multiple and often conflicting social roles that teachers in Anglo-Chinese schools have to assume in their work, such as being counsellors, class administrators, liaising with parents and maintaining classroom control, as well as being concerned with the teaching and learning process. In spite of calls by researchers, such as Johnson (1983), Lin (1990, 1996) and Cheung (forthcoming) to consider classroom code-switching in a positive light, the educational authorities have traditionally dismissed 'mixed-code' teaching and learning as educationally unsound.

In 1994 the Hong Kong government attempted to eliminate code-switching in the school system by adopting a linguistic streaming policy, which divided schools into three groups: Chinese-medium, English-medium and dual medium. They considered that 30% of students would benefit from an English-medium education, while the remaining 70% should go to either Chinese-medium or dual medium schools.[4]

This policy aroused widespread controversy and was rejected by many parents and school authorities who considered that it created unjust divisions within the school population as it denied the possibility of economic and social advancement to most students by refusing them access to English-medium education. Parental pressure also meant that most schools opted for English-medium rather than Chinese-medium status (British Council, 1995).

In 1997 the Education Department issued two documents which established guidelines regarding the issue of language in education. Dual medium schools were abolished, and it was stated that most secondary schools in Hong Kong should adopt Chinese as the language of teaching and learning in all academic subject areas. English-medium education was to be restricted to schools which could demonstrate to the Education Department that their teachers and students were able to teach and learn effectively in English. This meant, in effect, a policy of streaming students according to how far they were able to study effectively in English or Chinese. It was later announced that out of 414 secondary schools, 300 would be Chinese-medium, while 114 would be allowed to continue to use English from September 1998 onwards.

This measure was proclaimed by some as more realistic, in that it forced schools to come to terms with the reality of their classroom language practices (Pennington, 1998a). However, it has also resulted in reinforcement of the public perception of the superiority of the English-medium schools over Chinese-medium education and led to great protests among parents of students in those schools which were forced to change to Chinese. In effect this policy has reversed the trend apparent in the 1970s of widening the intake range of Anglo-Chinese schools to include pupils from lower income groups. English-medium schools in post-colonial Hong Kong have thus gone back to being the privilege of an elite group of students who have the opportunity of acquiring high levels of proficiency in English in optimum conditions.

Bearing in mind the above, we may now consider how far Anglo-Chinese schools have achieved their goals in producing students who are bilingual in Chinese and English and whether students in these schools are in fact able to use their languages in their academic activities. In relation to the first concern about students' bilingual proficiency, Chan in consultation with Johnson and Hoare (1996, cited in Lin, 1996) found in a study of 59 secondary schools in Hong Kong that most of them operated in a bilingual oral mode and that the amount of English used varied according both to the academic ability level of the students and to the nature of the subject being taught. Thus, English was used more with higher ability students and also more in English language classes than in the content areas of Maths and Science. The students, perhaps naturally enough, also had a strong preference for talking to each other in Chinese. Another important finding was that the correlation between the amount of English reported to be used in the classroom and the students' progress in English language proficiency was not high. (For an in-depth illustration of language alternation practices in one Anglo-Chinese secondary school see Chapter 4.)

In relation to the question about the ability of students to use both languages in their academic activities, in a study carried out by Yu and Atkinson (1998) with Form 4 pupils in two schools (one government aided and the other private), it was found that most students were much more proficient in Chinese than in English. The explanation given for this finding was that most of the subjects lived in predominantly Chinese-speaking environments, where they had little contact with English outside the classroom. Thus, English was considered basically a school language. Furthermore, as many of the students surveyed regarded their mother tongue (Chinese) as being inferior to English, it was concluded that they suffered from a conflict of identity which prevented them both from learning English effectively and also from being fluent in Chinese. In other words, the bilingualism of many students in Anglo-Chinese schools in Hong Kong may be considered subtractive rather than additive.

Hong Kong International Schools

In addition to the Anglo-Chinese schools described above, there is also another type of elite bilingual provision in Hong Kong – the International Schools. The schools generally cater both for students from Hong Kong itself and for international students from many different nationalities. In one such school, the Li Po Chun United World College of Hong Kong, 40% of the students come from Hong Kong while the remaining 60% come from over 50 countries, ranging from Argentina to Mozambique and India. The schools aim at fostering international understanding and mutual tolerance, using cultural diversity as a means of enriching the curriculum.

They are generally English-medium institutions but offer their clientele courses in Chinese language, Chinese history and Chinese studies as well as tuition in French and German in some cases. Many of the schools explicitly highlight key references to Chinese history and culture in their curriculum description, encouraging both Asian and non-Asian students to develop a greater understanding of China and Hong Kong, in the general context of the economic, social and cultural development of South Eastern and Eastern Asia. One school has divisions based on dynasties, rather than the traditional British concept of school houses, which is an example of an attempt to incorporate local traditions into the international school arena.

Thus, on the one hand, most of the schools have curricula based on US or UK models and offer students a variety of international examinations including The International Baccalaureate, The International General Certificate of Secondary Education (IGCSE) and the United States Scholastic Assessment Test (SAT), so that graduates have access to international higher education opportunities in USA and Europe. On the other hand, many of them try to provide their students with an understanding of local and regional issues which takes advantage of Hong Kong's geographical, economic and political situation as the 'Gateway to Mainland China'.

This understanding comes through the scheduled academic courses on Chinese Art, Literature, History, Geography, Philosophy and Economy and also through extra curricular activities, such as student community service visits to ethnic minority groups in Mainland China, courses in Chinese calligraphy and Chinese cookery and also participation in Chinese Music and Dance groups. In this way, the International Schools in Hong Kong try to reconcile their status as institutions which are preparing students for life and work in a global forum, with their aims in promoting and developing local and regional interests.

Higher education

As noted above, Hong Kong has had a long tradition of English-medium higher education. The oldest and most prestigious is the University of Hong Kong (1911), which was originally the 'College of Medicine for the Chinese', established in 1877. Together with the more recent Hong Kong University of Science and Technology (1991), this institution has steadfastly upheld a policy of using English as the medium of instruction. The only Chinese medium university in the area is the Chinese University of Hong Kong, founded in 1963 in response to popular pressure (Lin, 1996).

In addition, around 66% of all teaching staff at Hong Kong tertiary institutions are expatriates, many of them from Britain, who are attracted by the high salaries offered and by the 'sheltered' cultural environment, which at least until 1997 often meant that foreign lecturers were not involved in many cross-cultural encounters with other Hong Kong residents (British Council, 1995).

The main argument for justifying English as the medium of instruction in most tertiary institutions in Hong Kong is that English is the language of science and technology and international scholarship. However, this also means that much higher education has only been available to students who are proficient in English, thus restricting foreign knowledge and expertise to a small elite, who often emigrate from Hong Kong to Western countries after graduation, thus depriving the area of much native talent. Moreover, many students from Hong Kong often choose to do their university studies abroad, particularly in the US (around 5000 students per year); Britain (around 3500 per year); and Canada and Australia (around 3000 each per year) In 1995 there were at least 21 exchange agreements in force between higher and further educational institutions in Britain and Hong Kong (British Council, 1995).

Summary

As has been mentioned above, Hong Kong is an example of a country whose colonial past has deeply influenced both present language use and attitudes to the three languages in the current language arena – Cantonese, *Putonghua* and English. Political and economic developments have highlighted the use of English as a prized symbolic resource in Hong Kong society. Thus, access to English, both through the Anglo-Chinese school system and through International Schools is considered of paramount importance by parents, who have reacted strongly against government attempts to deny their children access to English-medium education by means of an official streaming policy.

However, the political, commercial and linguistic situation of Hong Kong is changing rapidly, particularly since the end of British colonisation in 1997, and it remains to be seen whether Hong Kong will continue to be recognised as an important bridgehead to the rest of southern China, as well an important business centre within the whole of the East Asia region. It also remains to be seen whether the growing importance of *Putonghua*, the official language of all of China, will alter the linguistic balance in the educational sector, now that Hong Kong is a Special Administrative Region of the People's Republic of China.

One possible scenario is that *Putonghua* may take over some of the functions currently fulfilled by English in Hong Kong, including its current role in the educational system. While this may be seen as a threat to the power of English in the area, it may also be seen in a positive light as clarifying the role of English as an international language of business, while freeing it from negative connotations of colonial dominance (British Council, 1995).

In the educational domain, a change to *Putonghua* as the official language of education would have major implications for curriculum development, teacher-training and publishing and materials production. It is also uncertain how far elite English-medium education will be allowed to continue in its current form with its international orientation, bearing in mind the political and social stance of the authorities of Mainland China.

It is within this scenario that Poon (1999: 142) has called for a revision of the current educational and linguistic streaming policy in favour of a 'true' bilingual curriculum which aims to promote bilingual education, i.e. the use of both English and Chinese as media of instruction for all students in Hong Kong, what the author calls '"streaming by subject" rather than "streaming by class"'.

BRUNEI DARUSSALAM

General Perspectives

While the first two situations described in this chapter, Japan and Hong Kong, have a fairly high international profile, the third example to be considered here, that of Brunei Darussalam, or Brunei, is less well-known. It is included, as it presents an interesting example of a country which has officially attempted to come to terms with an existing multilingual situation by establishing an elite bilingual education policy which associates two prestige languages, English and Malay with different roles in society. English is related to the demands of trade, industry and commerce, 'a language of the head' (Abdul Aziz, 1991, cited in Jones, 1997: 211), while Malay is considered as the language of national unity, culture and religion 'a language of the heart' (Abdul Aziz, 1991, cited in Jones, 1997: 211). This *Dwibahasa*, or two language educational system, will be examined in more detail in the following section. First, some indications of the current sociolinguistic situation in the country will be discussed.

Brunei is a small multilingual and multiracial state on the north-west coast of the Island of Borneo. The estimated population in 1995 was around 292,000, out of which 68.8% are ethnic Malay, 18.3% Chinese, 5% from different indigenous groups and a further 7.9% come from other groups. The official language of the country is *Behasa Melayu*, a variety of Malay which was the common lingua franca in the South Eastern archipelago from the sixteenth century onwards. *Behasa Melayu*, which is also known as *Behasa Indonesia* and *Behasa Malaysia* in these national environments, is the standard form of the Malay language which is used only for formal situations in Brunei. It is also officially taught and used as the medium of teaching and learning in the Bruneian school system. On some official occasions it is also used to frame discourse essentially mediated through the local variety known as *Behasa Brunei*. The latter is a less formal variety of Malay which functions as the language of trade, travel, and interethnic communication. Thus, it is *Behasa Brunei* that may be considered the real 'language of the heart'. This variety is most often used in the classroom to mediate or to bring knowledge into being (Andrew Cath,[5] 2000, personal communication).

Other varieties of Malay used in the country are: Royal Malay, *Kedayan*, *Kampong Ayer* and *Pasar Malay*. In addition, the majority of Bruneians, being Moslem, learn Arabic at school. The Chinese population uses a number of language varieties, including Mandarin at school, while there are also a variety of indigeneous language such as *Tutong*, *Belait*, *Dusun Bisaya* and *Murat* (which are Austronesian languages) as well as *Iban* and *Penan* (which are North Sarawak languages) (Jones *et al.*, 1993).

The British influence in the area began in the nineteenth century and from 1888 until 1983 Brunei was a British Protectorate, though never a colony as in the case of Hong Kong. Thus, although the royal court of Brunei functioned in Malay, English was the language of the administration and the leading families either provided their sons with private English language tuition or sent them to study in English-medium schools in Malaya (Jones *et al.*, 1993). A knowledge of English therefore rapidly became a marker of elite status within the country.

After the discovery of oil in the 1920s, English became increasingly used in the private industrial sector as well as in the area of finance and for multilingual meetings. This led to the establishment of English-medium education in selected schools to cater for the demand for bilingual clerks to act as brokers to deal with English-speaking oil and gas company representatives on the one hand, and with members of the public who only spoke Brunei Malay, on the other. The first Brunei Town Government English School was opened in 1951, with its first secondary class in 1953. By 1959 there were three English-medium schools (including one for girls) compared with 52 Malay primary schools (Andrew Cath, 2000, personal communication). The other official domain for English in Brunei, which has resulted from its former status as a British Protectorate, is the legal system, where English is used as the language of the written statutes and of the courts.

A language survey carried out in 1989–1990 (Jones *et al.*, 1993) showed that English is used on a daily basis by a large number of young Bruneians mainly from middle and upper-middle-class families under the age of 35 who have grown up during the oil boom in the country. As in Hong Kong, parents see fluency in English as a key to their children's future success, but they also fear the influence of an alien culture on the traditional elements of Bruneian society, formalised recently as the Malay Islamic Monarchy ethos, which is now officially promoted as the ideological basis for contemporary Brunei society and its development. This has led to official attempts by the sultan and the ruling elite to promote the Malay language and culture and the Islamic religion as key elements of the 'national cultural identity' in contrast to their private preference for using English and for promoting the Anglo-Bruneian connection (Braighlinn, 1992: 20).

Thus, it can be seen that the three languages spoken by most Bruneians – Brunei Malay, English and Arabic – are used in different domains within the country. Brunei Malay is used for social interaction, English for business, the law, and recreational purposes, and Arabic for religious concerns (Baetens Beardsmore, 1999).

Elite Bilingual Education Provision

The *Dwibahasa* policy

After full independence in 1984, a new bilingual education system was designed in order to ensure the use of both Malay and English as languages of instruction within the school system to replace the previous system of separate English and Malay medium schools. This *Dwibahasa* policy[6] was aimed at ensuring 'the sovereignty of the Malay language, while at the same time recognising the importance of the English language' (Government of Brunei, 1992, cited in Martin, 1996: 131). In fact, however, most students in the programme will probably speak three languages, as Brunei Malay is very different from standard Malay or *Behasa Melayu*. According to Baetens Beardsmore (1999) one of the main concerns of the Brunei government is to provide higher levels of English proficiency without this leading to language and cultural shift.

The official distribution of the two languages in the bilingual policy is as follows: Standard Malay is the language of instruction in the first three years of primary school for all subjects except English language. Then from Primary 4 onwards there is a division of languages according to subject area. Thus, the 'technological' areas: English, Maths, Science and Geography are taught in English, while the subjects concerned with traditional values: Malay, Islamic Studies, Physical Education, Art, Civics and, more recently History, are taught in Malay (Gunn, 1997). This arrangement may be characterised as a sequential bilingual model, which in a similar manner to Hong Kong, involves a change of language medium between the initial primary school years and secondary and university education. At tertiary level there is some evidence of a translingual education system among staff who are Malay speakers, where written material in English is used together with oral explanations in Malay (Gunn, 1997). However, as there are many expatriate university staff who do not speak Malay, this practice is not common.

As most Bruneians are Moslem, the majority of pupils at primary school go to Coranic schools in the afternoon, after they have finished their regular classes in the morning. Here they have intensive tuition in Arabic and learn Arabic script, which is also used in Malay. They thus have to come to terms with three official languages, Malay, English and Arabic, and two scripts in primary school: ' the western alphabet for Malay and English, and the Arabic script for Malay and Arabic' (Baetens Beardsmore, 1999: 2).

In the late 1980s and early 1990s, the Brunei Ministry of Education set up a well-financed curriculum development unit in order to produce Bruneian textbooks for the areas of English Language, Geography and History written in English which were appropriate culturally and politically for use in this Moslem monarchy. The first secondary Science textbook for Form 1 was published in 1998, followed by Science books for Form 2 in 1999. They have been evaluated as being of high quality in regard to language and production, and teachers are actively encouraged to use these in their teaching (Simon Colledge, 1999, personal communication).[7]

In this respect, Cath (in progress) aptly observes:

> Perhaps one of the most conspicuous effects that the process of Islamicization has brought to bear on the science taught in Bruneian classrooms is in the adoption of a Qu'anic citation to precede each unit of the newly published second year textbook. Unit 10, for example, is 'Electricity and its application at home' that among other topics tackles current, power, circuits, fuses and sockets. Under a photograph of spectacular multi-forked lightning appears an epigraph in (the) Malay, followed by the English gloss: And (He created) the sun, the moon, the stars subjected to His Command. Surely His is the Creation and the Commandment. Blessed is Allah, the Lord of the 'Alamin' (mankind and all that exists) [Surah Al-A'raf; Verse 54].

Thus, as can be seen, there is no separation of science from Islamic religious values.

The aim of the bilingual policy in Brunei is to produce school graduates who are competent in both Malay and English, and longitudinal studies have been set up by the Brunei Ministry of Education to evaluate the success of the school programmes. Changes resulting from this process of evaluation have included the teaching of History in Malay instead of in English at primary level, to emphasise the cultural links with the language (see below). There is also more emphasis now on initial literacy in both Malay and English to facilitate the process of the transference of literacy skills from one language to the other (Baetens Beardsmore, 1999).

There has been some critical academic reaction to the policy in relation to the development of the Malay language as a medium of literary expression and analytical thought. Braighlinn (1992: 21) sees this development as being 'thwarted' by the *Dwibahasa* policy which, in his view, 'has given priority to English as the medium of instruction throughout the education system'. He also maintains that because English cannot be understood by many school students, they receive 'virtually no education at all' but their parents are reassured by 'the illusion of equality' provided by the bilingual policy.

In a similar fashion to the situation in Hong Kong, teachers and students come to terms with the linguistic reality of the classroom by extensive use of code-switching. Peter Martin (1996) in his study of code-switching in primary classrooms in Brunei, notes that neither of the two languages officially used in the bilingual programme is the first language of many of the pupils and the transition from Malay to English in Primary 4 as the language of instruction for cognitively difficult subjects is often traumatic. In his analysis he observed that heaviest code-switching was used in Science and History lessons by teachers attempting to clarify concepts and lexical items, such as 'ivory' and 'tortoise-shell' taken from textbooks written in English. Martin (1996: 141) explains this in the following way, 'Not only is the content matter of History taught in the upper primary school very closely linked to local culture, but . . . the level of English vocabulary required is outside the students' capability.'

At secondary level Cath and McClellan (forthcoming) have observed a similar use of code-switching into Bruneian Malay to provide explanations or glosses of unknown lexical items in teacher-dominated bilingual classrooms. However, in their analysis of a simulation or role-play exercise, where students had much more control over the talk, they noted that instances of code-switching often co-occurred with requests for clarification at points of pressure where the interaction was threatening to break down. The use of this bilingual strategy in this way indicates a much more active student involvement in the learning process than in transmission-oriented pedagogy.

One major problem that has been noted in the *Dwibahasa* system is that most of the teachers who are teaching in the bilingual education programme have not themselves been educated within this system. Therefore, it is understandable that 'linguistic and pedagogic insecurity may prevail among teachers who are trying hard to apply the *dwibahasa* programme without much preparatory training' (Baetens Beardsmore, 1999: 10). The same author notes that the pedagogic strategies used tend to lead to the development of reactive, rather than active language learning on the part of students, and a concern with the production of slot-filling, one-word responses used for purposes of labelling, which gives the illusion that the pupils are acquiring English. However, once graduates of the system, who may also be future parents, come to dominate, then this should lead to greater understanding of what the bilingual policy is designed to achieve and how best to reach the academic and linguistic goals which have been proposed.

International Schools

Although many of the elite families still send their children abroad for primary and secondary education, there are also a number of International Schools in Brunei, such as 'The International School', 'The Jerudong International School', 'The Panaga School for Shell Employees' and 'The Berakas International School'. They cater for a wide range of nationalities and offer their students English-medium education based largely on the British National Curriculum with 'some adaptation to suit local conditions' (ECIS Handbook, 1997/8). Malay is generally taught as a subject within the curriculum. In spite of the high fees charged, these schools are heavily subscribed by expatriate families and by Brunei Malays (Gunn, 1997) and often have long waiting lists.

There is a difference in intake policy seen in different International Schools. Jerudong International School, for example, has always had local Bruneian pupils as well as international students, whereas the Berakas International School has only recently reopened its doors to the children of local residents. The reason given for not accepting enrolments previously was that the school did not offer locally required course on religion, language and civics (Gary Jones,[8] 2000, personal communication). Now, however, following changes in the school constitution, there is greater local involvement in the running of the institute, and higher numbers of students from economically privileged and socially ambitious Bruneian families.

Higher education

Brunei's bilingual education policy has implications at university level. The Universiti Brunei Darussalam (UBD), founded in 1985, conducts most of its teaching in English, rather than in Malay, although the model of university adopted is similar to that of a Malaysian university (Gunn, 1997). The staff are generally recruited from foreign Moslem countries or are British expatriates, although recently there have been moves to appoint Bruneians to key positions at departmental, faculty and administrative levels. In fact, however, the majority of the educationally mobile students in the country still choose to go abroad, preferably to the UK for higher education particularly in the fields of medicine and engineering.

In this respect, it has been reported that 'The Centre for British Teachers Education Service', the major recruitment agency for foreign primary and secondary school teachers who want to work in Brunei, has offered a number of 'Queen Elizabeth II Education Scholarships for university study in Britain at both undergraduate and postgraduate level. These are aimed at Bruneian students or professionals, 'who can demonstrate both academic excellence and the potential to become leaders, decision makers and opinion formers in the field of Bruneian education and training' (Andrew Cath, 1999, personal communication).

Case Sketch 9.3 offers The Universiti Brunei Darussalam as one example of a bilingual university.

Case Sketch 9.3 The Universiti Brunei Darussalam (based on information kindly supplied by Andrew Cath and Gary Jones)

Name of Institution:	*The Universiti Brunei Darussalam*
Date of Foundation:	*1985*
Number of Students:	*around 1,500*
History:	*The University was originally situated in a Teachers' College before moving to its present site in 1995. It was founded in order to decrease reliance on overseas tertiary education courses. Recent developments include the upgrading of the Faculty of Islamic Studies to the status of an institute (1999), and the inauguration of the Academy of Brunei Studies.*

Present Situation: The University is in the process of trying to localise. Thus, while initially virtually all academic staff were expatriates, mainly from Britain, Malaysia and Australia, nowadays the ratio of foreign to local staff is 70: 30. Most foreign staff now come from the Indian sub-continent. The present Vice Chancellor, who is an expert in Islamic law, was the first Bruneian to be appointed professor. In the area of administration, most of the staff are local and speak Brunei Malay, whereas before they were multinational. Notices, which formerly used to be solely in English, are now written in Malay, English or in both languages. One difference in this trend is the change in the number of foreign students. Initially there were very few, but now approximately 10% of the student body is from overseas, particularly from Benin, Seychelles, Thailand, Malaysia and Afghanistan. There are also a number of scholarships available to be awarded to international students

General Aims: According to the present Vice Chancellor, the main aim of the institution is to become 'the centre of excellence' and to 'fulfil its role as a resource centre, a think tank for Negara Brunei Darussalem'. The programmes offered are aimed at reflecting an Islamic orientation and research is oriented towards 'national needs and aspirations, rather than . . . personal interest'.

Language Aims: The University aims at preserving and promoting the Malay language, exploiting the potential of English for its academic and practical value, and sustaining the teaching of Arabic for its formal religious significance in relation to the cultural perception of the state.

Curriculum: Curriculum emphasis is on providing courses leading to teaching qualifications at degree, diploma and certificate levels in ESL, Malay language and literature, different branches of Islam, geography, history, economics, maths and science. There are also degree courses in management and public policy.

Language Policy and Use: Three languages, Malay, English and Arabic are used in the institution. Originally there was an almost equal number of Malay and English-medium undergraduate courses. Now, however, most courses are given in English, except Malay language, literature and history and courses on culture. There are also Arabic-medium courses in the area of Arabic Language and Islamic Studies, and Chinese is used often in student discussion in Science classes, where there are proportionally more Chinese than Bruneian Malay speakers. In general, the

Language Policy and Use (cont):	*students' level of listening and reading skills in English is well developed. However, they often find difficulty in following instruction in unfamiliar subjects. Thus, Malay remains the practical instrument for mediation of knowledge. Discussion with students may be cued in English but it is often resolved in Malay.*

Summary

As has been discussed above, elite bilingual education in Brunei has been officially institutionalised in the government's *Dwibahasa* policy which recognises English and Standard Malay as the two prestige languages to be used in the education system in an attempt to cultivate an English-speaking, educated sector of the population while retaining allegiance to traditional Islamic values. Thus, academic knowledge is compartmentalised in the curriculum and associated with different language varieties. Holistic or Islamic knowledge (Gunn, 1997) is mediated through Malay, and the natural and social sciences are taught in English.

Furthermore, the cosmopolitan status of English in the country among the ruling elite confers social rewards on anglophones and, unlike the situation in many former colonial nations, does not carry negative connotations. This situation is supported by the existence of a large expatriate community, including British military presence in the country. This all ensures that politically Brunei is distanced from neighbouring radical, nationalist pan-Indonesian policies, which are seen by the authorities as a threat to the country, and yet helped to consolidate a sense of national identity as a Malay Islamic monarchy, while maintaining friendly ties with Britain and the West.

Conclusion

In this chapter we have examined the situation of elite bilingualism and bilingual education in three very different Asian countries. Two of these nations, Hong Kong and Brunei, have been strongly marked by the multilingual consequences of colonial type relationships with Britain during the nineteenth and twentieth centuries. The third country, Japan, has been characterised by a traditional emphasis on cultural and linguistic homogeneity which has only recently shown signs of change towards a revaluing of multilingualism and cultural pluralism.

In all three countries private bilingual education has had a long tradition. In the latter part of the twentieth century there have been moves to extend this type of provision. In Hong Kong, traditional Anglo-Chinese schools opened their doors to a wider public during the 1970s and 1980s. In Brunei, in the 1980s a new bilingual education system, *Dwibahasa*, replaced separate English-medium and Malay-medium schools, while more recently in Japan there have been initiatives to establish immersion type schools, especially at primary school level. In all three cases, being bilingual in English has been associated with high status and prosperity and for these reasons parents have been favourably disposed towards these developments. Nevertheless, political and religious considerations have been influential in ensuring that the status of the national language, be it *Putonghua*, Japanese, or *Behasa Melayu* is officially recognised and supported. It remains to be seen how far these bilingual policies will be extended or revised in the future.

Notes

1. Dr John Maher is Professor of Linguistics at the International Christian University in Tokyo,. He has written extensively on the development of English as an international language of Medicine, as well as on the linguistic minorities in Japan. He is currently Review Editor of *International Journal of Bilingual Education and Bilingualism.*
2. Stephen Ryan is Publications Director of *Bilingual Japan* and a member of the Editorial Board of *The Bilingual Family Newsletter.*
3. Sachiyo Fugita Round has MAs from Lancaster University, UK and Hitotsubashi University, Japan. She teaches English part time at Shiraume Junior College and Daitobunka University, and Japanese at Hitotsubashi University. She has written articles on language acquisition in bilingual children.
4. Dual medium schools have been categorised as schools which run both Chinese-medium and English-medium classes at the same level.
5. Andrew Cath has an MA in Language Studies from Lancaster University (UK). He is currently a lecturer at the University Brunei Darussalam. Formerly he taught English at two of the country's secondary schools.
6. See Chapter 12 for an analysis of a policy document relating to the *Dwibahasa Policy.*
7. Simon Colledge has been involved in English Language Teaching in Europe, the Far East and South America since 1984. From 1995 to 1996 he worked as a Teacher of English in a bilingual secondary school in Negara Brunei Darussalam.
8. Dr Gary Jones is Deputy Director of the Language Centre at the University Brunei Darussalam. He is a founder member of the institution, and has published widely on language use in Brunei in international journals.

Chapter 10
Europe: Prestige Languages and International Communication

Introduction

Mainland Europe is a continent where the need for foreign language learning has been traditionally promoted in the light of the geographical proximity of many nation-states speaking different language varieties. In this chapter we will discuss the situation of elite bilingualism and bilingual education programmes in four Western European nations: Finland and Sweden in the north, Belgium in the centre, and Catalonia (Spain) in the west.

In the past, Finland and Sweden have had close historical connections which are reflected today in the number of bilingual speakers of Finnish and Swedish in both nations. International Languages, such as English and German, are high priority in Scandinavia as they provide speakers with linguistic access to the rest of Europe. We will begin by discussing the development of Finnish–Swedish immersion programmes in Finland from their beginnings during the late 1980s, particularly in the coastal bilingual areas around Vaasa/Vasa, under the guidance of staff from the Department of Nordic Languages of the University of Vaasa. In the case of Sweden, we will examine in detail one particular International School *Kungsholmen's Gymnasium* in Stockholm, in relation to the changing linguistic scene.

The third country discussed in this chapter, Belgium, is officially designated as trilingual in French, Flemish and German. Brussels, the capital, is home to many international organisations and a large number of International Schools, as well as three European Schools. We will focus on one of these (Brussels I) to see how multilingual language proficiency is fostered among students.

Finally, we will discuss the recent development of Catalan–Castillian immersion programmes in Catalonia, an autonomous region within the Spanish state. These programmes form part of a political and linguistic strategy adopted by the Catalan authorities aimed at raising the status and use of Catalan within the area, which has contributed considerably to the high profile of the Catalan language in the region today.

FINLAND

General Perspectives

Finland is a Northern European country bordering the Baltic Sea, which serves geographically as a buffer state between the Scandinavian nations of Norway and Sweden on one hand and Russia on the other. It has a total estimated population of 5 million people (1995), of which 93.5% speak Finnish as a first language (Baker & Prys Jones, 1998). For centuries the country was part of the Swedish Empire until 1809 when it was conquered by Russia. After independence from Russia in 1917, Finland was declared a bilingual nation with two official languages, Finnish (used by approximately 92% of the population) and Swedish (used by approximately 6% of the population).

Swedish is spoken by around 300,000 people who mainly live in the coastal areas and near the capital, Helsinki. Although they form a minority numerically, legally they constitute one of the two linguistic groups that make up the Finnish nation. The Finnish Language Law of 1922 established that language use in the Administration and in the Law Courts depended on the linguistic characteristics of the administrative district concerned. Thus, if there are more than 3000 people who speak a language other than Finnish the district is considered bilingual (European Office for Minority Languages, 1996).

According to a study carried out by Strömman (1993) there is evidence of a diminishing use of Swedish in certain Finnish business companies and in the number of bilingual speakers, and an increase in the number of monolingual Finnish speakers. This situation reflects changes in the increased use of Finnish throughout the society, and the fact that since 1950 there has been a high level of emigration to Sweden by Swedish-speaking Finns, due to better economic prospects, though recently this trend has shown signs of stabilisation.

There are also other languages used within the country, such as Sámi, which is a minority language spoken by the Sámi nomads who live in the north of Finland, near the Arctic Circle, as well as in the north of Norway, Sweden and Russia. Russian is also spoken by around 14,000 people who are mainly engaged in trade and commerce.

Although Finland is often considered a Scandinavian country, in fact Finnish is not related to the other Scandinavian languages of Norwegian, Swedish and Danish, which are mutually understandable. This is one of the reasons that Swedish is generally considered a high status language within the country, as it allows Finnish speakers to gain access to communication and economic and cultural co-operation networks within the whole Nordic area (Artigal & Laurén, 1990) and is a necessary prerequisite for those who wish to enter a profession in Finland (Björklund, 1997). English is taught as a foreign language within the school system and is also considered a prestige language leading to wider international communication. As Laurén (1991: 68) remarks, 'We devote a lot of time in the schools of the Scandinavian countries to teaching languages . . . Our economy as well as our culture demand that most of us master several languages at a high level'. As Björklund and Suni (2000) have recognised, the influence of the European Community has been an important driving force in this respect.

Prestige[1] Bilingual Education Provision

It was within this general panorama that the first Swedish-Finnish immersion programme began in 1987. According to accounts by Laurén (1991, 1992) Vesterbacka (1991) and Björklund (1997), the immersion school movement in Finland has its origin in the Vaasa University bilingual education project led by Professor Crister Laurén, Head of the Department of Nordic Languages.

In similar fashion to developments in Australia (see next chapter on Oceania), the Canadian immersion programme was seen as a suitable model for this experimental bilingual project in the Finnish context. As Laurén (1992: 13) explained,

> One advantage of following this model was that we did not experiment. The model is tested, we converted it for use in Finland, studied how our particular pair of languages, Finnish/Swedish, operates for immersion schools, and considered how the additional language taken in the programme should be treated.[2]

However, this time it was not parental pressure (as in Canada) or government policy (as in Australia) that primarily prompted the initiative, but the influence of a group of politically active women in Vaasa, in consultation with members of the Department of Nordic Languages of the University of Vaasa that led to the first Swedish immersion programme in Vaasa. Members of the Department of Nordic Languages provided the idea, in the sense that they gave information about the immersion model and explained why they thought that immersion would be a suitable bilingual programme for Finland. They also formed part of the follow-up committee on immersion in Vaasa (Siv Björklund, 2001, personal communication).[3] Thus from the beginning the Finnish–Swedish immersion programme enjoyed both political and academic credibility.

Furthermore, as in Canada and Australia, external circumstances were favourable to the project, in that both Finnish and Swedish are considered prestige languages within Finland and attitudes towards the learning of Swedish are generally positive, particularly within the bilingual areas of the country. In addition, it was emphasised to the families of potential participants that Swedish immersion was a good preparation for the future learning of other foreign languages. Furthermore, the advantages and disadvantages of immersion education were publicly debated in the media at both local and national level (Björkland, 1997) ensuring a high profile for the venture.

In line with Canadian developments, the immersion modality adopted in the Vaasa project was early total immersion. Thus, 25 kindergarten children aged six, from monolingual Finnish-speaking homes, were admitted to the first experimental immersion group in 1987 where bilingual teachers and their assistants used Swedish consistently for the four hours per day that the children spent at preschool, though the children were allowed to reply in their first language if they wished. The group went on to primary school after one year, where they continued with their immersion in Swedish for nine years with a third language being started in Grade 5. The pupils' first language, Finnish, was gradually introduced into the curriculum (around 10% of teaching being carried out in Finnish during First Grade Primary) until there was an approximate language balance of 50% Swedish, 5% in a third language and 45% Finnish) (Gustavsson & Mård, 1992).

The third language used in the Finnish immersion programmes in Vaasa is English, but may be another language in different places, for instance German is the third language in the south of Finland. English is taught as a subject area, rather than a medium of instruction as is the case of Swedish. As a result of initial programme evaluations, the third language is now introduced much earlier in the programme, usually in Grades 1 and 2 in order to promote functional multilingualism in the students. A fourth language is also offered in many current programmes. Moreover, immersion principles have been recently applied to the teaching and learning of these languages in that L3 teachers would only use this language with their students and L4 teachers likewise (Björklund & Suni, 2000).

Although the results of the earlier introduction of the third and fourth language are still being evaluated, Björklund and Suni (2000) report that a small-scale study carried out among students in Vaasa/Vasa Swedish immersion programme in 1997–8 has shown that according to their perception of their classroom language use students consider that they are active speakers of all four languages taught in the programme.

Thus, it may be seen that the immersion programmes in Finland, as in Australia, have introduced important modifications into the original model, in the sense of providing a multilingual rather than a bilingual orientation, in line with the need for Finns to be able to use various languages in their daily lives and work.

The enthusiastic reception given to the experimental project in Vaasa led to the creation of other immersion programmes in Espoo, Helsinki and in Kokkola, catering for different age ranges. In Espoo, for instance, a language immersion playgroup for children 0–6 years old was set up. This playgroup still exists today, but has been restricted to children 3–6 years old, due to the definition of immersion as a successive bilingual education programme (Siv Björklund, 2001, personal communication). By the end of the 1998–9 school year there were approximately 2000 pupils involved in Swedish immersion programmes in Finland, and 2500 in English immersion. Immersion programmes in French, German, Russian and Finnish were also reported. Figure 10.1 details the spread of Swedish immersion programmes in Finland from 1988 to 1999.

Number of schools in Finland offering Swedish immersion 1988/1989 - 1998/1999

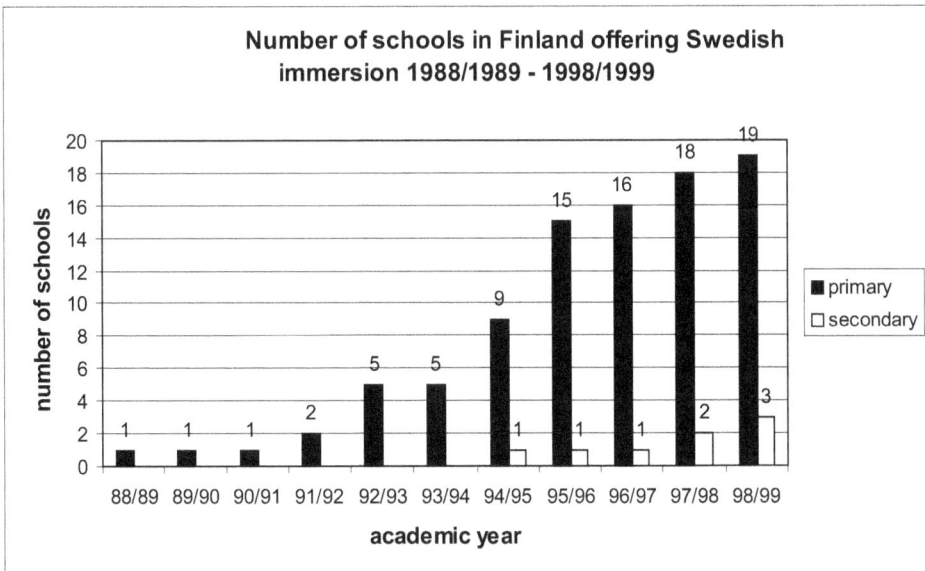

Figure 10.1 Number of schools in Finland offering Swedish immersion 1988/9–1998/9

(Taken from Buss & Mård, 2001)

Parents were closely involved in developments, as can be seen from the list of recommendations (in Text Box 10.1) taken from a leaflet explaining the general tenets of language immersion education in Vaasa/Vasa.

Text Box 10.1 Advice for parents with children enrolled on an immersion programme in Vaasa/Vasa

- *Do not tell your child that s/he is to start 'immersion' in August; after a big build-up some children are surprised to arrive at an ordinary school.*
- *Do not formally teach your child to read or write Finnish, as these skills are first learnt in Swedish.*
- *Do not ask your child to translate. For a child the language of immersion is a method rather than an aim.*
- *Do not attempt to correct your child if you are uncertain of the exact pronunciation or expression.*
- *Volunteer to help at school when possible, e.g. by joining a group of parents supporting the immersion programme.*
- *Do not give into the temptation to boast about what your child has achieved. If your child is eager to speak Swedish, encourage it, but do not make it a chore.*

- *Do not compare your child's progress with that of the neighbour's child. In immersion both the learning order and the learning rate vary.*
- *Read stories to your child in Finnish.*
- *Encourage your child to watch Swedish language television programmes.*
- *Take your child to Swedish cultural events, e.g. to the theatre, cinema, concerts.*
- *Let your child know that you are pleased with her/his progress.*
- *Speak positively about the immersion programme, the teacher, and the school.*
- *Express any questions or concerns you might have to the teacher, not to your child.*

As can be seen from Text Box 10.1, these recommendations for parents are based on a mixture of motivational, educational, and linguistic principles. The advice about learning to read first in the second language is in line with practices established in the Canadian immersion programmes (Swain & Lapkin, 1982). The emphasis on non-translation is also representative of the principal of language separation which has traditionally been part of immersion orthodoxy. However, the recommendations relating to participation in Swedish cultural events is reminiscent of the Australian immersion connections with the German communities, rather than of the largely classroom-based emphasis of the Canadian experience.

In Case Sketch 10.1, we present a description of one Finnish school which has implemented a Swedish immersion programme, in order to show how some of the ideas referred to above have been put into practice.

Case Sketch 10.1   The Keskuskoulu Immersion Programme (based on information kindly provided by Martina Buss, University of Vaasa/Vasa, 2000)

Name of School:	*Keskuskoulu Primary School, Vaasa/Vasa.*
Number of Students:	*500, all from Finnish-speaking homes, aged 7–12 years old.*
Number of Teachers:	*24, 50% of whom are Finnish speakers and work in the mainstream – monolingual Finnish – programme and in the immersion programme, and 50% are Finnish–Swedish bilinguals, working in the Swedish immersion programme. Teachers work in teams according to grade level, not language (Grades 1–6).*
General School Aim:	*To work eagerly and energetically in a challenging environment for this moment and for the future.*

Language Aims	*For the students to learn to use the immersion Language (Immersion Programme) both orally and in writing as an instrument of communication and to become acquainted with its structure. For the students to become interested in Swedish literature. For the students to be able to look for information from different sources.For the students to be able to write stories.*
Curriculum:	*The curriculum for the immersion programme is the same as for the mainstream programme, except for classes in Swedish (the immersion language). It is developed by all the teaching staff together and is revised every year.*
Methodology:	*Integrated teaching which means that teaching materials are drawn from different subject areas, and self instructional tasks are used both in the immersion programme and in the mainstream.*

Research on Methodological Issues in Immersion Programmes in Finland

Research carried out on the Canadian immersion programmes, particularly in the 1970s and 1980s, focused almost exclusively on programme evaluation in relation to the impact of immersion education on the linguistic, intellectual and attitudinal development of the children involved in the study in relation to the development of children in other types of Core French programmes (Lambert & Tucker, 1972). In Finland, however, researchers at the University of Vaasa were particularly interested in examining some of the methodological assumptions in this type of educational provision, claiming that the adoption of immersion principles facilitate 'a pedagogic-didactic renewal' (Laurén, 1992: 21).[4]

In 1991, Christer Laurén proposed what he called, 'a two-phase-didactics for school' in which he argued that an ideal programme for second language learning at school would involve a sequence of two phases:

Phase A

(a) very early; at kindergarten and primary school;
(b) using language almost exclusively as an instrument;
(c) goals: especially for reaching native-like pronunciation, automatised basic syntax, efficient communicative strategies and positive attitudes towards language learning.

Phase B

(a) following Phase A;

(b) using language mainly as an instrument;
(c) language teaching emphasised;
(d) goals: especially for developing lexicon and syntax according to cognitive level.

(Laurén, 1991: 71)

The advantage of this two-phase model according to the researcher, is that it creates a basic level of linguistic fluency at an early stage of language learning when prerequisites are optimal, which can later be expanded on and extended.

This shows clearly that Laurén is espousing a view of language learning primarily as a communicative activity which depends greatly for its success on the motivation of the participants involved. As preschool and primary school teachers will testify, this level of motivation is far more easily obtained during early childhood, rather than during the more rebellious years of adolescence. Furthermore, the initial emphasis on content-based instruction through the medium of a second or foreign language, rather than an emphasis on the learning of language as a linguistic system is in accordance with immersion principles. However, the emphasis on attaining native-like pronunciation in the second or foreign language is something which has not been greatly emphasised in the Canadian model.

Another important area to do with bilingual education methodology and the process of language acquisition in young children has been discussed by Vesterbacka (1991) in relation to the development of meaningful, ritualised routines in context-bound situations in the Vaasa immersion programme. The researcher noted the favourable comments of observers of the kindergarten class as to the children's 'fluent and correct Swedish' (Vesterbacka, 1991: 39) during their first year of immersion education. She accounted for these perceptions by examining the children's language use in Swedish in relation to what she termed 'routines' and 'patterns'. The former she characterised as 'unanalysed utterances with no changes within them', and the latter as 'utterances where one or two elements can be changed' (Vesterbacka, 1991: 39).

When using routines, such as *städa undan* (clean up) or *vi ses imorron* (see you tomorrow) the children used the expressions appropriately in social interaction, even though they had not separated the meaning of each individual word. Thus these expressions seemed initially to constitute 'chunks' of language for the children. The researcher hypothesised that the gradual building up of a number of context-bound situations on a daily basis ensures that the linguistic messages inherent in these situations gradually become part of the context and easily accessible to the young learners. In other words, the message itself becomes ritualised.

One of the important advantages of promoting these ritualised routines is that they help to give the children confidence to express themselves at an early stage in their process of bilingual development. For this reason, Vesterbacka maintains that they should be recognised as an important teaching and learning strategy for this stage in immersion programmes.

At a later stage, children can be helped to enlarge these resources by adding, 'new linguistic elements within the same context or by gradually introducing new contexts which are closely connected with the old context' (Vesterbacka, 1991: 41). Gradually the children's use of the unvarying expressions or routines shows some kind of change, such as the addition of another lexical item, or the combination of different routines into one utterance. These patterns show evidence of creative language use where the children are able to use the language routines to serve their own developing awareness of the potential power of their linguistic resources in two languages to communicate with others in meaningful contexts in an effort to fulfil their basic needs as efficiently as possible.

Summary

The Swedish immersion programmes in Finland are an interesting development both in relation to the ever-increasing literature written on international immersion education, and also as part of a distinctly Finnish phenomenon. As evidence of this, we note that much of the bibliography referred to in recent articles on this subject (Laurén, 1992; Björklund, 1997) is written in Finnish or in Finnish–Swedish and is therefore only accessible to a very restricted national audience.

Furthermore, Finnish immersion shows signs of a typically European slant in that international languages other than the immersion languages (Finnish and Swedish) form an integral part of these programmes. This is explained by Björklund (1997: 99) in that although both these languages are high prestige within the country, they are, in fact, 'internationally minor languages' within a wider European context and therefore students also need access to major international languages such as English or French in order to study and work effectively in Europe. This multilingual perspective has also given rise to research initiatives which are of interest to other European nations' concerns with school multilingualism, and has provided a solid basis from which to examine a reality which is 'more chaotic, multifaceted and complicated today than in the past' (Björklund & Suni, 2000: 219).

The emphasis on methodological and didactic considerations in Finnish immersion research is a welcome complement to the concern with programme evaluation which typifies many Canadian immersion studies and also reflects the educational interests of the Vaasa University researchers. Since 1991, the Continuing Education Centre of the University of Vaasa has provided courses in distance mode on aspects of bilingual theory, research and methodology specifically aimed at the needs of immersion teachers. Currently, a course offering 10 credit units for teachers and researchers is advertised on the university web page which stresses in-depth study opportunities in the areas of language immersion teaching strategies and language acquisition research.

SWEDEN

General Perspectives

Sweden is a Northern European country bordering Finland on the east and Norway on the west. The total population is around 8.8 million people, according to 1995 figures. Around 93% of the population are classed as native Swedish speakers (1986 figures) and the two most important minority languages are Finnish, spoken by 300,000 people, and Sámi (approx. 10,000 speakers) (Baker & Prys Jones, 1998). Other minority groups in Sweden include Danes, Germans, Norwegians, Latvians, Serbo-Croats, and Turks.

Sweden and Finland were united as one nation for 650 years and thus historically Finnish is the country's second language. At the beginning of the eighteenth century Finns made up 4% of the population of Sweden, and today they are found in the centre of the country and in the main urban areas (European Office for Minority Languages, 1996).

In the late 1980s, Sweden experienced a period of strong economic growth and Swedish industry expanded abroad. In 1989, Europe and internationalisation became key words in political discussions due to Sweden's proposed entry into the European Community. It was at this time that the Soviet Union collapsed and Eastern European countries were suddenly recognised as new and promising markets for Swedish companies. Upper and middle-class Swedes saw a wider, promising new world opening up both for themselves and for their children.

Elite Bilingual Education Provision[5]

The demand for higher education in French and German expanded after Sweden's entry into the European Community in 1995 and the universities started new programmes for European Community interpreters and translators. They also offered an increasing number of programmes in English. Schools and universities joined European Community teacher and student exchange programmes and a number of Swedes were transferred to other European cities, such as Brussels, Strasbourg and Luxembourg.

This interest in mobility and language learning coincided in the early 1990s with the opening of so-called 'free schools' in the country within a policy of state descentralisation. They were financed by public funds, but governed by private initiatives. These semi-private schools expanded rapidly, especially in the large cities, and provided free tuition with an emphasis on computer studies and bilingual education particularly with reference to English.

These Swedish–English bilingual schools have much in common with the Canadian immersion programmes: parental demand, the positive attitude of the local authorities, the acceptance of both teachers and students involved in the bilingual programme, and the high status of the immersion language. In order to qualify for entry to these bilingual schools students need high grades from primary school and they often need to pass a language test. Because of these requirements most immigrant children are excluded from these programmes in favour of those from middle-class backgrounds.

Throughout the 1990s these bilingual programmes grew in popularity. However, there were also criticisms voiced by certain sectors. In 1995, the Swedish Academy and the Swedish Language Council expressed concern about the need for students in bilingual programmes at secondary school level to master their first language at an academic level. They also stressed the importance of teachers coming to terms with the technical terminology of their subjects in English.

Bearing this in mind, in 1998, at the request of the Swedish government the Swedish Language Council drew up an 'Action Programme for the Promotion of the Swedish Language' where certain measures for the preservation of Swedish were drawn up. These included: the language normally used in compulsory and upper secondary school education and a final passing grade in Swedish should signify that the students have a good command of both the spoken and written language; and the requirement that if schools wished to introduce bilingual education they must be able to guarantee the ability of their students to use Swedish in academic discourse.

We will now examine, in more detail, the international section of one particular International Secondary School in the capital, Stockholm, as an illustration of a form of elite bilingual provision in Sweden.

Case Sketch 10.2   Kungsholmen's Gymnasium Stockholm (based on information kindly supplied by Kerstin Ekeland)

Kungsholmen's Gymnasium has a long history. It was founded in 1905 and over the years has become one of the most well-known and prestigious schools in Stockholm. It caters for students from 16 to 19 and has an average number of 1000 students: 600 girls and 400 boys. Half of these students belong to the International Section of the school which follows the Swedish national curriculum but which uses English for most subject teaching and learning. The school also hosts an International Baccalaureate (IB) programme.

Students and teachers

Half of the students in the International Section are Swedish and come from Swedish primary schools. Most of them have chosen to study there because of future career opportunities. Some come from international bilingual families and others from highly educated immigrant families; 50% of these speak only Swedish at home. Others come from Swedish families who have lived abroad for some time or who have attended English-speaking primary schools in Stockholm. The IB programme includes Swedish students of Swedish backgrounds, Swedish students of foreign backgrounds, and foreign students with international backgrounds.

The teachers who work in the International Section of the school come from various backgrounds; some from the USA, some from England, Ireland, South Africa, Zambia and Canada, as well as some teachers from Sweden. They quickly learn the social codes characteristic of each language in the school. These include the custom to address English-speaking teachers by their surnames, Mr So and So, while Swedish-speaking teachers are addressed by their first names. This leads to the curious practice of addressing a teacher by his or her surname in the corridor and by his or her first name in the classroom if he or she is teaching Swedish.

School language use

In the International Section of the school every subject is taught in English, except Swedish. As 50% of the students are of Swedish nationality, this is the language that is predominantly heard at breaktime and in the school café and in the school yard. However, foreign students who speak little Swedish complained about this practice and now teachers have been asked to reinforce the use of English at all times.

All students, however, have to study Swedish. Those whose first language is Swedish study Nordic language and literature in Swedish, while foreign students study Swedish as a foreign language. In this sense, the host country language is given a high profile in the school curriculum.

The teachers are all bilingual with a good level of proficiency in both English and Swedish. Staff meetings and parents' meetings are held in English and in Swedish, depending on the section. The school nurse, the careers adviser, the office staff, the caretakers and even the cleaning staff are all bilingual. Code-switching is officially forbidden among students, but is reported to be frequent among teachers.

Summary

In this section we have examined a second Nordic country, Sweden, and have seen how recent social and political developments have led to an increase in the demand for bilingual education programmes, particularly with regard to English. Parallel with this demand has come concern for the development of the Swedish language.

We have also looked in some detail at *Kungsholmen's Gymnasium* where there has been an on-going debate among teachers at the school as to whether the school itself is monolingual or bilingual. Officially, the International Section is described as monolingual, i.e. English-medium, to differentiate practices from other bilingual schools in the country which use different languages for different subject areas. There are, however, strong arguments for seeing the school as bilingual, in the sense that two languages, English and Swedish, are used as media of teaching and learning at different times. The curriculum is Swedish, and the school programme helps students to gain access to Swedish universities. Thus, we can say that the school has maintenance and enrichment of the two school languages as its pedagogic aim.

BELGIUM

General Perspectives

Belgium is situated in the heart of Western Europe, bordering The Netherlands in the north, Germany and Luxembourg in the east, and France in the south. It has an estimated population of 10 million (1995 figures) and has three official languages: French, Flemish and German. German is very much a minority language within Belgium, spoken only by about 1 per cent of the population in the extreme south-east of the country (Baker & Prys Jones, 1998). The two languages most used are Flemish, in the northern half of the country, and French or Walloon, in the south, spoken by about 33% of the total population. Other languages used mainly by immigrant communities in the larger cites are Moroccan Arabic, Turkish, Italian and Spanish.

Although traditionally French has been seen as the language of power and prestige, favoured by the social elite within the country and enjoying 'the benefits of standardisation and international currency' (Baetens Beardsmore, 1990: 2), since the end of the Second World War in 1945, Flemish, the majority language, has shown an increasing revaluation, due in part to the economic and political ascendancy of the Flemish area in the postwar period (Rebuffot, 1993). Nowadays, in a reversal of former practices, French-speaking upper-middle-class families in Brussels are sending their children to Flemish-speaking primary schools to be 'submersed' in the second language. This has also been referred to as 'wild immersion' (*immersion sauvage*, Braun, 1991, cited in Rubuffot, 1993: 41) and has led to certain negative effects in the development of the children's first language, French.

The capital, Brussels, home of the European Union, is an officially bilingual city situated within the Flemish region of the country, though the majority of the population of Brussels, in fact, speak French. Multilingualism, primarily in French and Flemish (Dutch[6]) is the norm in the Brussels employment market, and is encouraged by easy access to official TV programmes from Spain, Italy, Britain, Germany, France and The Netherlands (Leman, 1993).

By law, all school children in the capital must be taught the second language (either French or Flemish as the case may be) as a subject from the age of 7 onwards, though this is not a requirement in the rest of the country. According to Baetens Beardsmore (1990), children attending Flemish-medium schools generally reach a high level of proficiency in French, mainly because of the predominant use of this language in the outside school environment. Children who go to French-medium schools generally fail to reach high levels of proficiency in Flemish due to the lack of opportunities to practise the language outside school.

The fact that Flemish-speakers are geographically and socially dispersed throughout the population of Brussels means that they often operate as bilingual individuals, rather than as members of Flemish language groups, and there is evidence (Louckx, 1987, cited in Baetens Beardsmore, 1990) to show that the higher their social level, the more likely Flemish-speakers in Brussels are to use French as their daily language of communication.

Elite Bilingual Education Provision

As befits a cosmopolitan city, Brussels is home to a range of International Schools which cater for the children of the multilingual population who live and work in the city. Many of these are employees of the multinational and European organisations which have their headquarters there. Thus, we have institutions such as, the International School of Brussels, the Scandinavian School of Brussels, and The European Montessori School, among others. While the Scandinavian School and the Montessori School are advertised as teaching a variety of languages, such as Swedish, Norwegian, Finnish and English in the first case, and English and French in the second, the British and US international schools generally offer only English-medium instruction. As Coreen Sears, a former ESL teacher and Co-ordinator at the International School of Brussels, remarks, 'The students at ISB are being taught through the medium of English, and the bilingualism or dual language nature of their experience is entirely dependent on whether their parents choose to set up classes/send their children to the Japanese/Korean, etc. schools for Saturday morning classes . . . The students whose first language is not English however, are certainly potentially in an elite bilingual situation' (Sears, 1999, personal communication).

There are, however, a group of European schools in Brussels which are highly multilingual as part of their philosophy. Originally founded in 1958, the school known as Brussels I (Uccle) is one of the earliest of the network of European schools established to cater for the education of the children of European civil servants working in Brussels. In 1976, a second school (Brussels II) was founded in Woluwe, and in 1997 a third school (Brussels III) was opened. The following account of aspects of school life in Brussels I, depicted in Case Sketch 10.3, is based on research on educational and language matters carried out by Hugo Baetens Beardsmore (1990); Baetens Beardsmore and Anselmi, 1991). (For general considerations about the philosophy and educational policies of the European School model see Chapter 1.)

Case Sketch 10.3   Brussels European School I (Uccle)

The first European School in Brussels (Brussels I) is the largest of the schools, catering for around 3400 students (1994 figures) from kindergarten to age 18. According to a study carried out in 1994 (cited in Swan, 1996), at this time there were students from 40 nationalities enrolled at the school, speaking around 36 different languages, thus providing a wide range of different linguistic and cultural backgrounds.

While children of European Union (EU) staff are guaranteed automatic admission to the school, priority is also given to other children of nationals of EU member states, and children from countries outside the EU may also be admitted under certain circumstances. However, not all European Union staff in fact choose to send their children to this type of school. According to a study carried out in 1982 (cited in Swan, 1996: 112), the percentage of parents employed by a European Union-related institution who chose a European School for their child at that time was as shown in the following table:

Percentage enrolment at European School (Brussels) 1982

Nationality	%
Belgian	9
British	57
Danish	73
Dutch	57
French	43
German	56
Greek	54
Irish	74
Italian	56
Luxembourg	67

Thus, it can be seen that relatively few Belgian EU staff chose to send their children to the Brussels school at this time. A later study carried out in 1983 (cited in Swan, 1996) found that some of the reasons that parents gave for choosing a different type of education for their children were: distance between home and school; unacceptability of the school's bilingual policy; a perception that the school was too narrowly academic in outlook; complaints that no alternative to the European Baccalaureate was available as a means of evaluation.

Brussels I contains eight linguistic subsections which cover all the official languages of the member states of the EU except Portuguese. Thus, Danish, Dutch, English, French, German, Greek, Italian and Spanish are all used as teaching–learning media within the school. Each child is assigned to one of the eight subsections, depending on their language profile, and the subsection language constitutes the basic language of instruction (Baetens Beardsmore, 1991). These groupings are designed primarily to help towards the development of the student's first language and cultural identity. The subsections vary in size. In the 1986/1987 school year there were 738 students registered in the French subsection at secondary level, but only 270 in the Danish subsection (Baetens Beardsmore, 1990).

However, the students also start learning a second language in the primary school, either English, French or German. In Brussels I, French is the most popular second language. In the second year of secondary education a third language is introduced into the curriculum. Many students, in addition, become proficient in a fourth or even a fifth language as a result of a language mixing policy aimed at social engineering (Baetens Beardsmore, 1991). This is an interesting development and one to be borne in mind within any discussion of how to promote foreign language proficiency. Echoing an earlier statement by Fishman (1977: 102) that 'School use of language is just not enough', Housen and Baetens Beardsmore (1987) came to the conclusion that high levels of foreign language proficiency could not be explained solely by curricular design, but that extra curricular factors played a key role in determining how far students made use of opportunities outside the classroom to generate output in their weaker languages.

Language use within the school

Although the lingua franca of the school is generally French and pedagogical interaction between teachers and students tends to be monolingual in the relevant language of instruction within the classroom, the intensely multilingual nature of Brussels I leads to a high level of complexity in code-switching by students in self-initiated inter-student contact outside the classroom. In 1991, Baetens Beardsmore and Anselmi carried out a revealing study of student code-switching in out-of-class interaction among secondary school students between the ages of 14 and 18 in the Italian subsection of the school.

They observed that Italian pupils in Brussels were characterised by 'their exuberance, liveliness and extroversion' (Baetens Beardsmore & Anselmi, 1991: 408) and that they tended to express themselves frequently in Italian, regardless of their interlocutor's competence in the language. The researchers also observed that code-switching was not regarded negatively when used with non-Italian speaking students and that there were few rigid social constraints on which language to use at what time within the micro-community of the school.

Their conclusions about the role of code-switching in creating meaning in multilingual interaction lend support to Swain's (1985) output hypothesis, in which she argues that output fulfils a vital role in the process of language acquisition in that it 'pushes' the acquirer to use his/her linguistic resources as precisely, coherently and appropriately as possible in a process of negotiation of meaning. The emphasis on experimentation with target language structures in the production of comprehensible output and the willingness to take linguistic 'risks' noted in this multilingual population may be seen as a learning strategy, as shown in the following exchange between a Danish boy and his Italian interlocutor:

Example 1

{Italian utterances given in normal font; Spanish code-switch in bold; and English translation in italics}

A: Mia sorella é tornata tutta **bronceada** !
    My sister came back all sunburnt !
B: Abbronzata ?
    Sunburnt ?   (Baetens Beardsmore & Anselmi, 1991: 415)

Here, the Italian speaker (Speaker B) implicitly questions the appropriateness of the Danish speaker's use of a lexical item in Spanish rather than in Italian, yet obviously understands the meaning that this speaker wants to communicate and helps in this process by supplying the Italian equivalent 'Abbronzata'.

The researchers also noted a high number of multilingual blends in the data they collected, usually involving adapting the phonology of one language to apply to the morphology of another, leading to the creation of a type of 'in group' jargon used with comic effect, as in the examples below:

Example 2

French	Italian blend
je me casse	*io mi casso*
I clear off	

les flics arrivent	*arrivano i flicchi*
the cops are coming	

Italian	English blend
imbranato	*imbranation*
clumsy	

esaltato	*esaltation*
excited	

Italian	English/French/Spanish blend
Ho cannato tutto	*I have canné todo*
I have failed the lot	

(Baetens Beardsmore & Anselmi, 1991: 416)

These examples show a sophisticated awareness among multilingual pupils at the Brussels I European School of how to maximise the 'ludic potential' (Sharwood Smith, 1989, cited in Baetens Beardsmore & Anselmi, 1991) of their proficiency in different languages in a creative and amusing fashion. This playing with language reinforces a multilingual in-group identity based on a realisation of their ability to combine language-specific items into meaningful communication.

Summary

Belgium is an interesting example of a country which is officially bilingual and yet has been the scene of a long-standing linguistic conflict between the Flemish and French-speaking communities, which at times has threatened the maintenance of the Belgian state in its present form. In Brussels, it is generally only the older population (from 60 onwards) who identify with both French and Flemish and who code-switch frequently between these two languages (Treffers-Daller, 1992). The younger population of the city tend to use either one language or the other and the researcher suggests that the relatively low number of code-switches found among the young inhabitants of Brussels in her study may be explained in part by 'the fact that Brusselers no longer consider the mixed code to be an appropriate expression of their identity (Treffers-Daller, 1992: 244).

However, the presence of many multinational and European organisations in the city has led to the foundation of a large number of bilingual and multilingual schools which, to a greater or lesser extent, promote multilingualism and multiculturalism. One of the foremost of these establishments in this field is the first Brussels European school, which, as we have seen, actively fosters high levels of multilingual proficiency in its students. However, as we have also noted, this is a result of both the European School curriculum and also the opportunities for negotiated output in their various languages that the students enjoy in the immediate school community and in the wider Belgian national scene. This underlines yet again the need to consider bilingual or multilingual schools as part of a wider community context in the light of their success in the development of highly proficient bilingual or multilingual individuals.

The question of students' developing identities is something which has been far less studied, in spite of the fact that one of the original ideals of the founders of the European schools movement was the cultivation of a 'European identity' expressed in the Protocol to the Statute of the European Schools in the following terms, 'Without ceasing to look at their own lands with love and pride, they will become in mind Europeans . . .' (Swan, 1996: 27). According to the same author, there is some evidence to suggest that students and former students of European Schools like Brussels I are less susceptible to national myths and stereotypes and have been able to develop 'a concept of national differences that is far more mature than that of their fellow Europeans at home' (Swan, 1996: 35) and in this way, the European Schools movement can be said to have gone some way in the pursuit of the creation of a European identity in those it educates.

CATALONIA

General Perspectives

In contrast to all the other areas discussed in this chapter, Catalonia is not an independent nation-state. Situated in the north-eastern part of the Iberian peninsula, Catalonia forms part of Spain. However, that being said, Catalonia is also an autonomous community, referred to as 'a country' (*país*) with its own laws, parliament, government and administration, having been granted self-governing status under the Statute of Self-Government implemented in 1978. For this reason, we are considering it here as a self-contained area, with certain historical, linguistic and cultural characteristics which distinguish it from the rest of the Spanish state.

The population of Catalonia is around 6 million, in relation to a total population of 39 million for the whole of Spain (1986 figures), and it is one of the most developed and industrialised regions. For more than 700 years, Catalan was the official language of Catalonia and the only language spoken in this territory (Artigal, 1997). However, after the War of Spanish Succession in 1714, Catalan gradually became restricted to domestic use and Spanish (*Castellano*) became widespread. This process of language shift was accelerated after the Spanish Civil War (1936–39), when General Franco became ruler of the country and embarked on a policy of 'cultural and linguistic homogenisation' (Artigal, 1997: 134) which forbade any manifestation of Catalan language, culture and identity. The media was also decreed to be exclusively Spanish-speaking.

After the death of Franco in 1975, the new Spanish Constitution made Spanish the official state language and all other languages of Spain also official in their respective autonomous communities. Thus, the Catalan Statute of Self-Government of 1978 granted Catalan co-official status with Spanish within Catalonia and proclaimed it to be the heritage language of the area, '*la llengua propia de Catalunya*' (Catalonia's own language) (Article 3). In 1983, the Law of Linguistic Normalisation 'was passed by which Catalan was guaranteed its status as an official language in the public service and in education.

Today, the official bilingual status of the region and an active political, linguistic and cultural campaign on the part of the Catalan authorities and support groups has led to a significant revival and revaluation of the prestige and status of Catalan, particularly in the capital of Catalonia, Barcelona, even though Spanish continues to be the dominant language, particularly in such domains as the media, the law courts and commerce. In a recent study on language use among young people in Barcelona, Boix (1990: 210) notes that native Catalans, who are generally located, 'in the intermediate and upper social levels in Catalan society' generally choose to speak Catalan, whereas the Castillian group, who are mainly immigrants from other regions of Spain and who come paradoxically either from the lowest or the highest social positions, generally choose to speak Spanish. However, in a study on language choice in everyday interaction among a mixed group of young Catalan and Castillian speakers, the researcher noted that, 'all participants . . . irrespective of their ethnolinguistic group, chose either Catalan or Spanish indiscriminately, to a greater or lesser degree' (Boix, 1990: 221). He concluded from this that combination of different language choices could be considered as an emphasis of the speakers on questions of solidarity rather than power, where they wished to foreground, 'a neutral position in a particular interethnic encounter and gain access to a wider range of roles within the community' (Boix, 1990: 222).

One of the key areas in which the Catalan government has concentrated its efforts on raising the profile of Catalan is in the domain of education. Artigal (1997) charts three stages in this process:

(1) 1978–83, the emphasis on Catalan as a subject within the school curriculum.

(2) 1983–93, the establishment of three types of school according to the main language of instruction (i.e. Catalan-medium instruction, Spanish-medium instruction, and bilingual instruction in which an initial emphasis on Spanish is replaced progressively by the use of Catalan as a medium of instruction).

(3) After 1993, a single model using Catalan as the official medium of instruction throughout the school system, with minimum input of Spanish.

It is against this background that we will now discuss the development of Catalan immersion which is an interesting example of a prestigious bilingual education programme which does not, in fact, cater for students of high socio-economic status.

Prestigious Bilingual Education Provision

Catalonia is one of the most recent examples of a political and cultural context in which immersion programmes are being set up. The autonomous Catalan government has political as well as educational goals in mind and aims to encourage all its citizens to participate in public life. In contrast to the situation in Canada, where parental pressure was largely responsible for initiating the process of developing appropriate bilingual programmes, the official re-establishment in 1983 of Catalan as well as Castillian as, 'languages proper to education', in Catalonia was seen specifically by the regional government authorities as a means both to integrate the large non-Catalan speaking immigrant population into Catalan life and to upgrade the status of Catalan and thus, 'to create favourable attitudes to its use and the need to learn it' (Mar-Molinero, 1989: 310).

As previous surveys in 1982 had revealed an unsatisfactory level of proficiency in Catalan attained by pupils studying the language as a school subject, an experimental total immersion programme was set up in 1983 in Santa Coloma de Gramat. This was an area where few people spoke Catalan and an immersion programme was considered the most efficient means to achieve the autonomous government's aim of equal student proficiency in both Catalan and Castillian by the end of the compulsory education cycle (EGB) at age 14 (Arenas, 1986: 107). Thus, the goal was an additive form of bilingualism.

The programmes were designed to include groups of children in a classroom situation where more than 70% were non-Catalan speakers. The Spanish-speaking immigrant communities are primarily working class, but aspire to learn Catalan because Catalan is seen within Catalonia as a high-prestige minority language associated with social mobility (Mar-Molinero, 1989: 309).

When it was first introduced, the Catalan immersion programme was based on four principles:

(1) The total duration was four school years between the ages of 4 and 8 (although more recently the programme has been extended up to the age of 14).

(2)   The programme focused on the early school years.
(3)   Parents' consent for their children's participation in the programme was obligatory, bearing in mind their right to be able to choose the language in which
their children should be educated, according to the Law of Linguistic Normalisation.
(4)   The children's education was initiated in Catalan, which is the first school language in Catalonia

(Arenas, 1992: 24–5)

Although there has been relatively little research carried out to date to evaluate
the linguistic and academic results of immersion programmes in Catalonia, the
general conclusion arrived at by Artigal (1997: 145) based on the existing evidence is
that, 'the Catalan immersion program can be considered to be a pedagogical model
that, within its own specific situation, achieves the goal of students acquiring
competence in two languages without any significant cognitive and academic loss'.
Furthermore, according to on-going partial evaluations carried out by teachers and
pupils involved in the immersion programme, the overall assessment has been,
'extremely positive . . . with regard to efficiency and operation in general' (Arenas,
1992: 29).

It must be remembered, however, that the Catalan immersion programme, as is
the case with any other form of bilingual education provision, cannot be judged
solely in educational terms. In this situation, in particular, the underlying political
agenda has led to strong divisions between Catalanists and supporters of the rights
of the Spanish language, centred mainly in the capital, Madrid. There has been
concern voiced in the Spanish press (*La Vanguardia*, 1993) that Spanish speakers in
Catalonia have been pressurised to place their children in Catalan immersion
programmes against their wishes as there is often no alternative educational provision in Spanish in local areas. Supporters of the Catalan government have argued
that this is part of a campaign orchestrated outside Catalonia for political motives.
They maintain that, 'the schools enjoy the autonomy to develop their educational
project' and 'linguistic immersion is always applied when there is the agreement of
the parents; the Government never conjugates the verb "impose"' (*La Vanguardia*
Newspaper, 25–9–93).

These differences were resolved to a great extent by a ruling from the Spanish
Constitutional Court in Madrid in 1994, which declared that the implementation of
a single educational model giving priority to Catalan was, in fact, constitutional,
due to the general presence of Spanish in the social milieu and that therefore this did
not infringe the rights of the Spanish-speaking population, individually or collec-
tively (Artigal, 1997).

Case Sketch 10.4 will exemplify how one particular school in Terrassa, Catalonia
has implemented an immersion programme for Spanish-speaking children living
in the area.

Case Sketch 10.4   Joan Marqués Casals School, Terrassa, Catalonia

This case study is based on an article written in 1992 by Margarita Garrigo Fullola and Carmiña Airas Barreal, two teachers working at the Joan Marqués Casals school in the city of Terrassa. It focuses on how the teachers organise their bilingual language programme with children from 8 to 9 years old, and the types of classroom activities and materials they use in their teaching.

The school is situated in a suburb of Terrassa, an industrial city 30 km from Barcelona. Its main industry is textiles. The school caters for the children of workers in the textile factories who emigrated to Terrassa from different areas of Spain during the 1950s and 1960s. The general socio-economic level is low and their first language is Spanish. The total number of students is 1000, from 4 to 14 years old. The language aim of the programme is to develop fluency in oral and written skills in both Catalan and Spanish and provide students with a basic knowledge of English.

The curriculum is Early Total Immersion organised according to five two-year cycles as seen in the following diagram:

The Distribution of the Primary Courses in the Terrassa Total Immersion Programme

	Kindergarten	**Catalan Immersion Programme**
Compulsory	*Two groups, 4–5 years old.*	*Oral introduction*
Primary	*Two groups, 5–6 years old*	
School	**Initial Cycle**	*Written introduction*
	Two groups, 6–7 years old. First level.	
	Two groups, 7–8 years old. Second level.	
	Middle Cycle	*Catalan first language*
	Two groups, 8–9 years old. Third level.	
	Two groups, 9–10 years old. Fourth level.	*Spanish second language Introduction*
	Bridge Cycle	*English third language*
	Two groups, 10–11 years old. Fifth level.	
	Two groups, 11–12 years old. Sixth level.	
	Upper Cycle	
	Two groups, 12–13 years old. Seventh level.	
	Two groups, 13–14 years old. Eighth level.	

(Taken from Garrigo & Airas, 1992: 131)

The whole programme is supervised by the Head of Studies and the Co-ordinators of the five cycles. Each of the cycles shown in the diagram above, functions relatively independently of the others in the programme and is served by four tutors. Normally each group of new students entering a cycle spends two years with the same tutor.

In the third cycle of the programme the children are already fluent in oral Catalan and have a basic knowledge of Catalan lexis. They can read and write short texts and are familiar with simple orthographic norms. They also have experience of working in small groups and are able to work independently, without supervision.

Learning Centres

In the Middle Cycle, there are 12 hours of Catalan every two weeks, which is divided into three group sessions and nine hours working in learning centres in small groups. The group session is seen as an introduction to the later work in the learning centres and may involve the reading and discussion of a text, such as a story, after which the teacher explains the work in the learning centres over the following two weeks.

There are a total of eight learning centres, the contents of which are changed every two weeks. These are: the language learning centre, the spelling learning centre, images learning centre, the reading learning centre, the dictionary learning centre, the 'we write' learning centre, the calligraphy learning centre and the dictation learning centre. Each of these centres provides a series of tasks and activities that the children work through. Four of these are compulsory: language, spelling, reading and writing, and four are optional. Thus, the children have a certain independence in deciding which activities they choose. They note these down in a notebook and these are then checked and commented on together with the teacher. Towards the end of the two-week period, there is a group session in which the pupils discuss which Learning Centre they prefer and what difficulties they have experienced.

In this Middle Cycle Spanish is also introduced into the curriculum for the first time for four hours a week. No textbooks are used; instead wide access is provided to videos, cassettes, TV and radio programmes in Spanish. There are also two hours of workshops where Spanish is the language of interaction.

The two teachers consider that the introduction of oral and written Spanish into the Catalan immersion programme has not been problematic because of the following factors:

- the teaching techniques are very different from those used in teaching Catalan;
- the context and situations of learning are different;
- the children are Spanish speakers outside school in their home environment.

(Garrigo & Airas, 1992)

Teacher Training Provision

The Catalan authorities (unlike their counterparts in Canada) were faced with a vast teacher training problem. Many of the teachers working in the area were non-Catalan speakers and of those that were, few were qualified to teach the language (Siguan, 1984, cited in Petherbridge-Hernandez, 1990: 219). In 1992, the University of Barcelona published a survey on the use of Catalan among students in the School of Teacher Training (*La Escuela de Maestros*) in the University, which showed that only 30.2% were first language speakers of Catalan, in contrast to 59.6%, whose mother tongue was Spanish.

After experiments with various forms of short-term inservice training schemes (*Reciclatge*[7] instituted in 1978 and FOPIs[8] introduced in 1983), the Catalan government decided in September 1989 to initiate 30-day immersion teacher training cycles for primary school teachers working in immersion programmes. These courses were designed both to improve teachers' language fluency as well as to provide them with first-hand experience of exposure to immersion programmes.

A series of thematic areas was studied. Each of these was treated from four angles: communicative actions, morpho-syntax, vocabulary and phonetics. Emphasis was placed on communicative dialogue and pupil activities. Participant evaluation of the courses was highly positive, especially concerning improvement of oral skills (Bel: 1990). Another indication of the success of these programmes was the observation that the 'teachers not only spoke Catalan when they were spoken to by the instructor but also among themselves' (Arenas, 1992: 17).

However, in spite of these initiatives, this problem has not been completely solved, as is evidenced by a statement by Miquel Siguán, the former director of the Education Sciences Institute of the University of Barcelona, observing that the greatest difficulty for the progressive 'Catalanisation' of teaching, 'was the teachers' own (first) language' (*El Periódico* Newspaper, 17–11–93).

One recent response to this situation has been provided by the staff of the School of Teacher Training at the University of Barcelona. They have offered all first-year students the possibility of a diagnosis of their linguistic position in relation to their knowledge and use of Catalan, before beginning their studies in this language. Another strategy used in the university is the provision of a Self-Access Centre, where students can reinforce and extend their knowledge of Catalan through the use of computerised programmes, videos and cassettes, with the aid of a Catalan specialist.

These measures demonstrate the interest and determination of the authorities in Catalonia to implement Catalan immersion programmes as a means of increasing the use of Catalan as well as Spanish in daily interaction in the region.

Summary

It can be seen from the above that the Catalan–Spanish immersion programme constitutes an important strategy in the Catalan government's policy of raising the status and use of the Catalan language in the area. Thus, this initiative has a high

profile within Catalonia and may be seen as an example of prestige bilingual education, which does not involve a high socio-economic status group.

As part of a policy of 'Catalanisation' centred in education, Artigal (1997)
considers that immersion has contributed greatly towards the present situation in
which the Catalan language has changed from being completely absent in the
Catalan education system in 1975, to becoming 20 years later, 'the main vehicle of
instruction and interaction in kindergarten and primary school' (Artigal, 1997: 147).
While relatively little research has been carried out to date on this initiative, there
have been a large number of articles written by Catalan researchers and Catalan
government supporters which focus on the merits of this immersion programme
(see Artigal, 1990, 1991, 1997; Arenas 1986, 1988, 1989; Vila, 1985, 1996; Arnau &
Boada, 1986; Arnau *et al.*, 1992). However, as mentioned above, there have also been
some problems in that recent legislation upholding the right of the Catalan government to implement a single educational model which gives priority to Catalan over
Spanish has meant the reduction of the possibility of individual choice on the part of
parents. Another difficulty has been raising of the Spanish-speaking immersion
teachers' proficiency in Catalan, aimed at providing high quality pedagogical interaction in both Catalan and Spanish, in order to ensure optimum development of
these two languages in their students.

Conclusion

In this chapter we have looked at the elite or prestigious bilingual education
provision in four Western European countries: Finland, Sweden, Belgium and
Catalonia. In each case, different language pairs have been discussed: in Finland,
Swedish and Finnish; in Sweden, Swedish and English; in Belgium, Flemish and
French; in Catalonia, Spanish and Catalan. We have also examined different modalities of elite or prestigious bilingual education: immersion programmes in Finland
and Catalonia; International Schools in Sweden; and European Schools in Belgium.

We have seen how different historical and political circumstances have led to the
creation of these programmes. In Finland it is significant that the immersion movement started in one of the bilingual areas of the country under the guidance of
academics from the Department of Nordic Languages of the University of Vaasa,
whereas in Catalonia immersion in associated with the political initiative of the
Catalan government to raise the status of Catalan within the area after a long period
of linguistic repression and centralisation under General Franco. In Sweden, the
upsurge in the learning of foreign languages which accompanied Sweden's entry
into the European Community led to increasing demands for bilingual programmes at secondary school level. In Belgium the officially bilingual city of
Brussels is host to a number of international Bilingual Schools as well as to three
European Schools, which foster a high level of multilingualism among its students.

It is also interesting to note that while teachers and researchers who are associated with these different types of bilingual provision – Immersion, European
Schools and International Schools – organise events and conferences related to their

particular concerns (cf. the ECIS annual conferences and the European Immersion Conferences), there is, as yet, no international forum for debate on issues across these areas.

Notes

1. In this section we have referred to 'prestigious' rather than 'elite' bilingualism due to fact that Swedish is considered a high-status language in Finland. The term 'elite', initially used, was questioned by Siv Björklund in the following terms, 'I . . . use the word "elite" but use it when talking about bilingual programs where students are selected on the basis of IQ or language skills and where students have to pay a lot to enrol. In fact, we contrast immersion to other elite programs and argue that immersion is a "normal" bilingual program since there is no other criteria than monolingualism at the outset of the program' (Siv Björklund, 2001, personal communication).
2. Translation from Finnish–Swedish by Philip Clover.
3. Siv Björklund is Acting Professor in School Language Acquisition, Swedish Immersion, in the Department of Nordic Languages at Vaasa University.
4. Translation from Finnish–Swedish by Philip Clover.
5. The author is greatly indebted to Kerstin Ekelund for permission to use much of the information in this section. Kerstin Ekelund is a language teacher, having taught Swedish as a first language and as a second language, French and Italian for 20 years. She has worked in a number of secondary schools in Stockholm. For the last 10 years she has been working as a language teacher at an International Secondary School in the capital.
6. Flemish is also known as Dutch, which is the official language of The Netherlands (Baker & Prys Jones, 1998).
7. *Reciclatge* courses were designed for practising teachers and were held after school hours.
8. *FOPIs (Formacion Profesional Institucional)* were courses of eight hours per week for practising teachers. They involved exposure both to the Catalan language and to aspects of Catalan culture during the academic term.

Chapter 11
Oceania: Immersion in Languages Other than English

Introduction

The continent of Oceania is made up of a vast number of island groups located in the Pacific Ocean. Lotherington (1998) makes reference to three ethno-geographic regions: Melanesia, in the south-west Pacific, a highly multilingual area; Polynesia, which includes New Zealand, is located both in the North and South Pacific, where several regionally-distributed languages are used; and Micronesia, situated in the central and western parts of the North Pacific, which is very linguistically homogeneous. Australia constitutes the largest landmass in the whole of the region. Although in the first half of this century, Australia was associated with a 'White Australia Policy', after the 1970s this became increasingly untenable due, in part, to increased in-migration from the Middle East and Asia (Bodi, 1994). Thus, during the 1980s and 1990s, Australia has been shifting towards increased acknowledgement of its multilingual and multicultural status.

AUSTRALIA

General Perspectives

Australia is the sixth largest country in the world in area, with an estimated population of 17 million people (1991 figures), 90% of whom are of European descent, mainly British, who migrated to Australia *en masse* after the Second World War in the 1940s and 1950s. The other 10% include immigrants from Asia, and the indigenous Aboriginal peoples who make up around 1.5% of the total population of the country (Baker & Prys Jones, 1998).

The official language is English, spoken as a first language by about 82.6% of all Australians, which holds a position of unquestioned social and economic power within the country. However, there are also other widely used community languages, such as Italian, German, Greek, Polish, Spanish, Chinese, Filipino and Vietnamese.

At the same time, widespread language shift towards the majority language is evident, encouraged by an official language policy during the 1960s and 1970s which focused on the importance of providing teaching programmes in English as a second language for immigrants, rather than any overt concern for the maintenance of their minority community languages (Baker & Prys Jones, 1998). This was in line with a self-image of Australia at the time as 'a British outpost in the Pacific pursuing a rigid assimilationist policy on its large migrant population' (Clyne, 1991: 55). Thus, for example, members of the Dutch community in Australia, numbering 95,000 people in 1986, have been considered 'quick to discard their language and culture and adapt to the dominant group' (de Bot & Clyne, 1994: 18, cited in Baker & Prys Jones, 1998: 158). Language shift from Dutch to English from first to second generation immigrants in this community has been greater than in any other language group in the country.

In the 1980s, however, there was a radical change in federal government policy which largely reversed this monolingual vision. This was exemplified in the formulation of the *National Policy on Languages* (1987) under the leadership of Joe Lo Bianco. This policy document had four main aims: English for all, support for Aboriginal and Torres Strait Island languages; provision of a language other than English for all Australians; and equitable and widespread language services (Lo Bianco, 1987, cited in Moore, 1996). In this pluralist vision, multiplicity of languages was seen as an important resource for the development of a dynamic society. Thus, '[a]lthough English is indisputably the language of public life, it is one among many as a resource' (Moore, 1996: 475).

As a result of these developments there was a greater recognition of the multilingual and multicultural nature of the country by many Australians and, 'a widespread official and societal acceptance of bilingualism as something legitimate, desirable and advantageous to the Australian nation as well as to individuals' (Clyne, 1991: 55).

In 1991, however, the effect of these ideas in relation to national languages in the country was somewhat diminished, due to a change in official policy, reflected in the *Australian Language and Literacy Policy* promulgated by the Department of Employment, Education and Training of the Federal Government. While the main goals of this policy sought to develop and maintain effective literacy for all Australians in English, as well as to expand and improve the learning of languages other than English, these were seen rather in terms of foreign languages 'to enhance Australia's role as a trading nation' (Moore, 1996: 479), rather than Aboriginal or Torres Strait Islander languages. In 1994, a report by the Council of Australian Governments prioritised the learning of the languages of Australia's principal Asian trading partners: Mandarin, Indonesian, and Korean (Moore, 1996).

Nevertheless, there is now far greater official support at state government level for community language provision at primary and secondary school level than there was in the 1970s. As evidence of this, we can refer to the publication in 1984, in the influential southern state of Victoria, of a key language educational policy document which recommended that, '[E]ach school council should ensure that its program enable students progressively to acquire proficiency in another language used in the Australian community' (Ministry of Education and Ministerial Advisory Committee on Multicultural and Migrant Education, 1984: 17, cited in Fernandez, 1996: 73). This effectively legitimised the mainstreaming of languages other than English (LOTE) within the school curriculum in the whole of the state and was followed in 1995 by a further policy statement which featured bilingual education for all children as one of three models recommended for Victoria schools (Clyne, 1991). Today in Australian schools there are more than 60 languages other than English studied.

Elite Bilingual Education Provision

Bilingual schools

Rather paradoxically in view of the monolingual/monocultural tradition outlined in the previous section, bilingual education in Australia can trace its roots back to the nineteenth century, when Lutheran church schools taught subject areas of the curriculum in German as well as in English. In fact, before the outbreak of the Second World War in 1914, there were a total of 59 bilingual German–English schools in South Australia, 10 of which were in the state of Victoria.

However, these early developments were not followed up until the 1970s, partly because of a climate of xenophobia generated as a result of two world wars, which led to a fear of foreign influence and foreign languages and cultures, allied with a perception that the teaching of foreign languages would involve a process of, 'enculturation of cultural elites' which should be avoided (Baker & Prys Jones, 1998: 502).

In the 1970s though, there was evidence of a change in perspective in educational circles. On the one hand, there was growing interest at government and at institutional level in the Canadian French immersion programmes established in the mid-1960s and, on the other, there was an evident determination on the part of the Australian Federal Government to offer all children a second language at primary school level, 'in order to reach out to the world' (de Courcy, 2002: 3).

Consequently, the last three decades have seen the establishment of a number of immersion type programmes, based on the Canadian model, in some of the major Australian cities. The most frequent foreign languages chosen were either French or German, but there is also evidence of initiatives involving Chinese, Japanese and Indonesian (de Courcy, 2002). Most of the immersion programmes started in Australia were of the partial immersion type, either early or late, rather than total immersion characteristic of many Canadian initiatives. Late partial French immersion programmes were started in 1985 in Benowa State High School, Queensland (de Courcy, 1997) and in Mansfield High School, Queensland in 1991 (Stevens, 1995); a late partial immersion programme in Hebrew was initiated at

Mount Scopus College in Melbourne in 1990 (Lorch *et al.*, 1992); and early partial immersion education in German was offered to primary school children at St Peter's Junior School, Queensland (Tisdell, 1995), and at Bayswater South Primary School in Victoria (Fernandez, 1996), among many other similar projects.

Most of these initiatives were led by teachers or parents who were dissatisfied by the foreign language provision available at the time. In the case of the Bayswater South Primary School situated in a suburb of Melbourne, a group of language professionals who were in close contact with the Association of German-speaking Communities decided to try to re-establish German language education programmes at four primary schools in Victoria which had a relatively high number of German speakers, and which included Bayswater South (Fernandez, 1996). In 1996, Sue Fernandez wrote a detailed account of this experience, which has developed into a flagship bilingual education programme in Australia. In the following section I will give a brief description of the genesis and development of this German–English partial immersion model, foregrounding particularly the socio-historical roots and the pedagogical evolution of this pioneering programme.

Case Sketch 11.1   Bayswater South Primary School

In 1981, funding was obtained from the Victorian Advisory Committee on Multicultural and Migrant Education to finance one German-speaking teacher shared between two schools which were interested in establishing some form of German language provision within their institutions. One of these schools, Bayswater South, which catered for mainly middle-class English-speaking children from 5 to 11 years old, decided to set up a partial immersion programme, based on the Canadian model, while the other school chose 'a more traditional second language programme' (Fernandez, 1996: 58).

The decision to offer German, rather than French or Spanish, was a natural one for these schools in that this suburb of Melbourne was settled in 1941 by members of the Temple Society, a South German Protestant group which had established itself in Palestine and was interned in Australia during the Second World War. This community established a German language nursing home, a community hall, a church, and a German Saturday school in the area. Later, delicatessens, butchers and cakeshops where German was spoken were also set up. During the 1980s, approximately 4% of children in the Bayswater South school came from German-speaking families.

These links established with the German-speaking community in the area differentiate this venture from the Canadian situation where each immersion programme normally constitutes an educational French-speaking island within a largely non-French-speaking community context. In Melbourne, however, institutional rela-

tions with German speakers outside the school provide a valuable resource for the students, allowing them opportunities to extend the school language experience to the community as well as involving parents and other interested community members. Thus, the Bayswater South German programme is designed to support the language maintenance and enrichment of students from German-speaking families, as well as to provide for the language acquisition of those who have had no previous contact with German and who wish to learn 'a major trading and specialist language' (Fernandez, 1996: 58).

Curriculum design and language use

Another key difference between this Australian immersion programme and the Canadian model relates to the amount of time devoted to instruction in the second language. In the Bayswater South programme up to 20% of the curriculum is given in German, while in partial immersion programmes in Canada the norm is around 50%. Initially the programme was offered as an elective to two classes, Grades 1 and 3 where German was used to teach science, art and physical education for five hours per week.

The reasons given for choosing these subjects as German-medium areas are interesting. They were seen as 'doing subjects' involving a strong non-verbal component which, it was thought, would help the children participate successfully in learning activities in what was an initially unfamiliar language for the majority of them. Science was considered a 'discovery' subject which encouraged active hands-on involvement in learning and thus helped to establish links between linguistic and cognitive development. Art allowed for the introduction of basic concepts, such as colour, size and texture, and also allowed for a lot of individual teacher–student interaction. Physical education was felt to be good at encouraging listening skills and relating to actual physical experience of actions such as running, catching, throwing, etc.

Social Studies and Music were divided according to subject matter into units which were taught in English and units taught in German in order to strengthen the relationship of language and specific cultural elements, based on practices introduced in the pre-1916 Australian bilingual German programmes, referred to above. Maths, on the other hand, was only taught in English, due mainly to parents' fears that basic mathematical concepts would suffer from being taught though the medium of a second language.

Thus, it can be seen that the programme organisers gave careful thought, not only to quantitative considerations, related to differential amounts of first language versus second language contact and use, but also took into account educational concerns regarding different types of methodological practices and their relevance to the immersion process, as well as cultural content orientation. This demonstrates the importance of going beyond purely taxitative, quantitative aspects of second or foreign language provision in immersion programmes, to a consideration of pedagogical factors which may enhance students' acquisition.

Policy and practice: A mutual symbiosis

As noted in Chapter 1, the genesis of the Canadian immersion programmes was closely tied up with political considerations reflected in the Canadian government's decision to implement 'the youth option' represented by immersion education as its bilingual policy. A similar development may be noted in the Australian situation, as described by Sue Fernandez (1996). In her historical account of the setting up of the Bayswater South German immersion programme in the 1980s and 1990s, she traces the constant intertwining of pedagogical and linguistic concerns with government policy initiatives. For instance, in 1982 she charts the evident success of the programme in terms of the enthusiasm and interest generated in the teachers and students involved, and its acceptance amongst the immediate community, against the background of gradual change in federal government decisions on language policy issues, reflected in the establishment of a committee of six Senators to inquire into questions of the use, maintenance and teaching of languages other than English.

Their report, published in 1984, highlighted the superior results of the immersion programme in comparison with the second language programme adopted by the other school and so projected the influence of the bilingual programme far beyond the narrow school community. This higher profile facilitated increased funding and the possibility of widening the scope of the project to other classes within the school. However, rather surprisingly in view of these findings, the report concluded that it was unlikely that 'programs of this kind will become a wide-spread model for second language learning in Australia, at least for some time to come' (A National Language Policy, 1984: 138, cited in Fernandez, 1996: 74).

Nevertheless, in spite of this prediction, interest in immersion programmes continued to grow in Australia, as is shown by Lo Bianco's (1989: 16, cited in Fernandez, 1996: 84) report for the Victoria State government which states, 'School programs immersing English mother tongue children in another language are the best possible sorts of second language programs and can yield very high levels of mastery over both languages'.

A key political development came in 1992 when Languages Other Than English (LOTE) were included as one of the eight main learning areas adopted by the Australian Education Council. This, in turn, led to renewed interest on the part of politicians, administrators and teaching staff in the approach and methodology used in the Bayswater South bilingual programme.

In 1994, the Victorian Ministry Advisory Council on Languages Other than English published a report which provided strong support for immersion type programmes in the following terms, 'That content-based/immersion programs be promoted as the best models for achieving high levels of communicative competence in the LOTE' (Directorate of School Education, 1994: 28, cited in Fernandez, 1996: 90).

Thus, it can be seen that the undoubted success of the Bayswater South bilingual programme in terms of pedagogical innovation in the Australian context was *enhanced and consolidated by policy developments at state and federal level. This clearly demonstrates the mutual benefits afforded by a close relationship between policy and classroom practice, where practice informs policy and policy supports practice in the implementation of viable educational alternatives in the field of bilingual education.*

A developing vision of bilingual practice

As mentioned above, the German–English bilingual programme differed in certain fundamental ways from the Canadian model in terms of amount of contact time in the second language and relationships with the German-speaking Temple community. Fernandez's (1996) account also provides an interesting on-going account of the adjustments made to the programme over the years, which helps to explain why certain changes in the initial formulation were seen to be necessary in the light of changing demands and the influence of specific contextual factors.

She notes that the initial enthusiasm generated by the novelty of the immersion experience in teachers, pupils and parents gradually changed after two years to a sense of boredom and frustration on the part of many of the children about what they saw as their stagnating level of progress, as well as a lack of challenge in the classroom activities they engaged in. The response to this 'plateau' period (already observed in the Canadian programmes) was to reduce some of the subject areas originally given in German, such as Art and Physical Education, as these were felt to offer few opportunities for promoting speaking and writing skills as the children's level of German proficiency increased. Instead, a reading programme was introduced as an attempt to give variety to the lessons and to add a greater sense of challenge, and new subjects, such as Health and Drama were introduced in German. These changes had the effect of revitalising, to some extent, the children's motivation.

Another source of difficulty which led to a re-evaluation of the relationships between German-medium (bilingual) teachers and classroom teachers, was the growing disquiet among the latter about the timetabling constraints and the disruption to classes caused by the extension of the programme in 1984. A lack of consultation and inadequate provision of information for school staff about the bilingual programme, and a certain amount of rivalry between the two groups of children (bilinguals and non-bilinguals), also led to difficulties. However, these problems were overcome by introducing a system of inservicing and consultation with staff on a regular basis, as well as recommending that classroom teachers should learn basic greetings and formulaic expressions in German to demonstrate their interest in the bilingual programme.

A further problem area noted around this time was the problem of fragmentation and lack of continuity experienced in the divisions between different subject areas, with extended lapses of time between follow-up sessions. This was solved by introducing a thematic approach for the middle school, integrating Social Studies, Art and Music for three of the five German-medium classes (see similar development in the

Casablanca American School, Morocco section). Teachers reported favourably on this development, observing, 'The thematic approach has proved to be more integrated and meaningful. Lessons have been able to be 'followed up' at the same time giving (the German medium teachers) and the classroom teachers flexibility with the timetable' (Fernandez, 1996: 79).

Another important step which marked the consolidation of the programme at institutional level was the phasing out of its elective status from 1987 onwards, thus ensuring that the bilingual programme would involve all children entering the preschool level and constitute an integral part of the life of the school.

The documenting of the changing nature of this experience of bilingual education provision bears witness to the importance of Baetens Beardsmore's (1995: 140) warning about not importing, 'any single model, no matter how well-tried, without the necessary modifications to specific local circumstances . . . merely because the research background has proved their effectiveness in the context for which they were developed'.

As we have seen above, the constant process of monitoring seen in the Bayswater South bilingual programme has taken account of some fundamental constraints inherent in the local situation, and has led to important modifications to the programme which distinguish it from the original Canadian model and help to explain its success in the Australian context.

Higher education

Although I have not been able to find any reference to German being used as a language of teaching and learning in a bilingual programme at tertiary level in Australia, there are reports of interesting ventures based on immersion principles with university undergraduates in French in the University of Newcastle, New South Wales (Caldwell, 1995), in Japanese in Central Queensland University (Cross, 1995; Chapman, 1995) and in Chinese in Queensland (de Courcy, 2002). In these programmes the emphasis has been on providing foreign or second language partial immersion programmes in teacher training courses at tertiary level with the aim of creating a pool of suitably qualified teachers in French and Japanese. The French immersion programme started in 1995 with an intensity of four hours per week, while the Japanese programme, set up in 1993, aimed at providing between 50 and 80% of the total course content in Japanese and incorporating an in-country component where the students had to spend three to five months in Japan. The Chinese immersion programme, which began in 1991 and terminated at the end of 1993, was important in proving to the Queensland authorities that an immersion programme in a character-based language was feasible (de Courcy, 2002).

The French Immersion project ran into some initial resistance on the part of other area staff teaching in the Primary Bachelor of Education (BEd) programme who were afraid that the innovation might encroach on their territory (Caldwell, 1995). The Japanese programme, however, incorporated within the Languages and Cultures Initial Teacher Education Program (LACITEP), does not seem to have encountered such problems, and graduated its first cohort in 1995.

In an interesting paper, Chapman (1995) describes in detail how one subject area in the Japanese programme, Health and Physical Education, was able, 'to provide a diverse, rich environment that can help to address some of the issues emerging in immersion education and to address its inadequacies . . . one practical example of how appropriate language and culture contexts can be introduced into an immersion program' (Caldwell, 1995: 112). The author shows how criticisms of immersion programmes as being sociolinguistically impoverished and leading to the development of artificial language use in immersion students (Harley & Swain, 1984) may be addressed by focusing on particular speech registers in Japanese, appropriate for particular situations. Students are required to plan, peer teach and report on (in Japanese) an area of the subject curriculum they have selected with a partner. They are thus required to use the appropriate politeness forms (*masu* and *desu*) when speaking to the whole group, and the 'plain' forms (*-ku, -su, -ru*) when speaking among themselves (Chapman, 1995). In this respect, the author notes that Japanese onomatopoeic expressions, such as *koro koro, kura kura*, commonly used in daily conversation, can be particularly well reinforced through this type of programme.

Furthermore, the emphasis on the cultural component in this programme involves the inclusion of particular Japanese games and sports where students interact in Japanese, where there is also native speaker interaction as well as, 'videos and realia from Japan, demonstrations, discussions, student / lecturer explanations and comparisons with Australia . . . adding an extra dimension to cultural awareness activities' (Chapman, 1995: 111–12).

A recent qualitative study into the experiences of immersion learning of a group of second year students in a late Chinese immersion programme at a university in Queensland carried out by Michèle de Courcy in 2002 provides interesting insights into how learners view the ongoing process of learning another language, in particular a language very different from their first language (English). Basing her findings on diary and interview data, as well as classroom observation, the author discusses two important aspects of the process: how students made sense of the classroom, and how the students went about the task of producing the immersion language.

De Courcy (2002) found that the group of immersion students seemed to pass through four distinct phases in trying to make sense of classroom interaction: the first stage involved a heavy reliance on translation as a receptive strategy; during the second stage, the 'key words' stage, learners used their understanding of key lexical items to help them guess the meaning of the rest of the utterance; in the third stage the students were able to relax and concentrate on 'getting the gist', or the main idea; while by the fourth stage the learners did not seem to be conscious that they were communicating in another language.

As the author notes, the use of translation as a receptive strategy in an immersion programme seems to be at odds with official immersion policy of a separation approach to language use based on Swain's (1983) principle of 'bilingualism through monolingualism'. Nevertheless, according to the empirical data analysed, this seemed to be a common initial strategy used by members of the Queensland Chinese immersion programme in order to try to make sense of classroom interaction in Chinese. Later, when they reached the third stage where they were able to relax, the learners began to understand how far the stress produced by their previous efforts of trying to understand every word, had been counterproductive. The final stage involved the reward of realising that 'all of a sudden, things make sense' (de Courcy, 2002: 79).

In relation to the question of productive use of Chinese by the students, the author observes that the learners complained that they received scarcely any feedback on their pronunciation. They felt strongly that 'gentle but persistent attention to pronunciation would have improved their acquisition of Chinese' (de Courcy, 2002: 82). Similarly, the group felt that it was important to pay attention to formal aspects of the language 'in relation to student needs and within the context of meaning, not just in isolated "grammar" lessons' (de Courcy, 2002: 85). They thus indicated their intuitive need for an effective integration of both analytic and experiential focuses in which attention to both form and function are closely and appropriately linked (Harley et al., 1990).

Conclusion

Recent developments in the area of bilingualism and multilingualism in Australia point to the increasing impact of languages other than English in the national arena. A growing recognition and valuing of the multilingual and multi-cultural nature of the country, coupled with an anti-isolationist economic and foreign policy have provided a fertile climate for the creation of innovations in second and foreign language pedagogy. These projects have resulted in the development of immersion-type programmes at all levels of the educational system, aimed at producing high levels of student proficiency in international languages which are seen to be important for Australia's future development.

Currently, immersion teaching and learning has a high profile as seen by the rapid expansion of programmes throughout Australia, particularly in the states of Queensland, New South Wales, Victoria, South Australia and Western Australia. In 1993, the Australian Association of Language Immersion Teachers (AALIT) was formed to cater for the interests of administrators, teachers and students from all sectors of education (primary, secondary and university) and represents languages as diverse as English, French, German, Indonesian, Italian and Modern Standard Chinese. The Association publishes the *AALIT Journal*, as well as a number of books on the Australian immersion experience. It has also collaborated in the setting up of a distance education Immersion Language Teaching Unit at the University of Queensland to help prepare teachers (both preservice and inservice) for work in the expanding immersion programmes.

Chapter 12

The Discourse of Elite Bilingual Education: A Critical Analysis

Introduction

In the previous five chapters, which have focused on the development of elite bilingual education programmes in specific contexts of implementation, we have included a number of case sketches which provide details of how specific institutions have come to terms with the need to provide bilingual programmes for middle-class students who wish to learn prestigious international languages. The data for these portraits come mainly from information sent out by the institutions concerned.

The discourse of elite bilingual education, as reflected in this type of school brochure, or prospectus is designed, in the first place, to attract future clients to the educational establishment in question. It has, therefore, a basically persuasive purpose, similar, to some extent, to commercial advertising. As most of the schools and colleges which offer bilingual education programmes for upwardly mobile and internationally active students are private, their very existence depends on attracting families who are prepared to pay, sometimes very large amounts of money, for the type of educational provision they offer.

Elite or prestigious bilingual education programmes are often initiated as individual institutional responses to the needs of particular groups or individuals, who for one reason or another, seek an alternative to state or public sector education provision. At times, however, such programmes form part of national or regional language policy, as in the case of the *Dwibahasa* bilingual education policy in Brunei, and the Catalan immersion programmes in Catalonia. In these latter cases, there is official government support for and advocacy of the need for these types of bilingual programmes, which are often justified and legitimised in official documents.

In this chapter we will discuss both discourse genres referred to above. First of all, we will examine the type of discourse associated with the advertising of certain individual elite bilingual education programmes with regard to ways in which relationships are constructed in the discourse between the schools and potential parents, as well as the image created of the services offered by these institutions. In the second part of the chapter we will go on to discuss the opening address given by the Brunei Minister of Education in the context of an International Conference on Bilingualism and National Development held at the Universiti Brunei Darussalam in 1991, which constitutes an example of a policy statement on the development of bilingual education in the country. We will focus on how the Minister's speech reflects ways in which social forces dynamically structure and shape the discourse practices revealed in the analysis.[1]

In the discussion of both these discourse genres, the documentation produced by individual bilingual schools and the Brunei Minister's speech, we will adopt a perspective associated with critical discourse analysis as developed by Fairclough (1989, 1992). A 'critical' approach, according to Fairclough (1989: 5) may be defined as an approach which aims 'to show up connections which may be hidden from people – such as . . . connections between language, power and ideology'. The reason for adopting this type of approach is that it allows us to situate discussion of linguistic and textual features within a wider perspective of language as social practice, an approach which has characterised the stance adopted in this book.

Fairclough (1989, 1992) maintains that linguistic or textual analysis cannot be considered as an end in itself but has to be seen within a three-dimensional relationship between processes of text analysis, processes of discourse analysis, and analysis of the social context or the social conditions of production and interpretation. In his view, text analysis refers to 'language analysis of texts', whereas discourse analysis is concerned with 'the nature of the processes of text production and interpretation, for example, which types of discourse . . . are drawn upon and how they are combined'. Analysis of the social context, on the other hand, involves issues such as 'the institutional and organizational circumstances of the discursive event' (Fairclough, 1992: 4). These relationships are set out in Figure 12.1.

What is important to recognise is that this type of analysis involves 'interpretations of complex and invisible relationships' (Fairclough, 1989: 27) and that these depend on what the analyst sees as important in a particular text. Thus, each analyst will select and interpret key textual features in line with his or her knowledge of the socio-political and cultural conditions which can be seen to have had an incidence in the processes of production of individual texts, both written and oral.

An Analysis of Selected Extracts Taken from the Advertising of Elite Bilingual Educational Programmes

We will begin with an examination of the discourse characteristic of International Schools which offer bilingual education programmes to upwardly mobile, higher economic status, majority-language-speaking individuals. We will focus on the following three main aspects: (1) the relationship constructed between the advertiser (the educational establishments) and the consumer (the parents of poten-

```
┌─────────────────────────────────────────────────┐
│           Social conditions of production        │
│    ┌───────────────────────────────────────┐     │
│    │         Process of production          │     │
│    │        ┌─────────────────┐             │     │
│    │        │      Text        │             │     │
│    │        └─────────────────┘             │     │
│    │        Process of interpretation       │     │
│    │  Interaction                           │     │
│    └───────────────────────────────────────┘     │
│            Process of interpretation             │
│   Context                                        │
└─────────────────────────────────────────────────┘
```

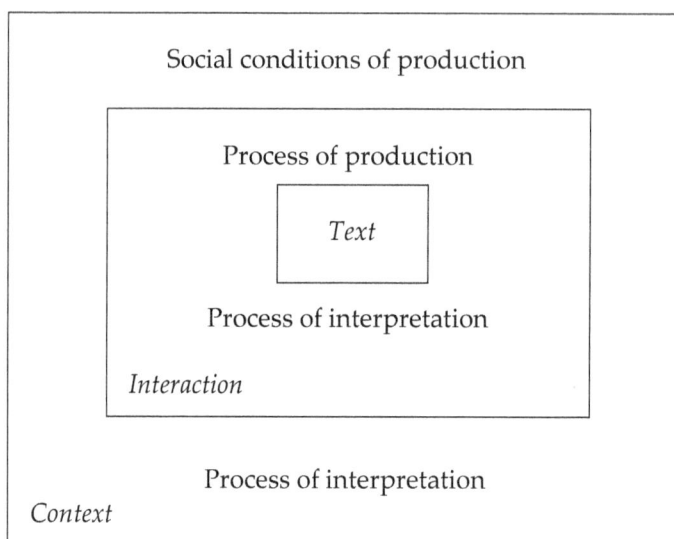

Figure 12.1 Discourse as text, interaction and context (taken from Fairclough, 1989: 25)

tial new students); (2) the image created; and (3) the construction of subject positions for clients (Fairclough, 1989).

The prospectuses, brochures and other information sent to prospective parents of new International School students have certain features in common with commercial advertisements in that their basic purpose is to convince parents to send their children to the schools in question. However, the audience targeted by these institutions is much more restricted in numbers and has more precise characteristics than the audience appealed to in general commercial advertising. In order to try to categorize this particular audience in more detail we will now examine the perceptions of two International School principals who contributed to the editorial section of *The John Catt Guide to International Schools* (1998), in which principals of five International Schools expressed their view of the benefits of education from an international perspective.

Paul Mclean, Principal of the American International School in Salzburg (Bingham, 1998: vi), writes, 'International schools are forced . . . to consider the needs of students and parents in the sense that they are world citizens . . . in a world of growing interconnectedness'. Schools therefore need to direct student interest towards 'the responsibilities required of a concept (of) world citizenship which stresses the interdependencies of communities and individuals'.

According to M.J. Cooper, Principal of the British School of The Netherlands (Bingham, 1998: vii), the increasing integration of Europe and the wide range of the global economy will lead to the creation of new and exciting employment opportunities for young people in the twenty-first century. In order to ensure 'success in the global market place' a purely academic education is not sufficient, as 'Tomorrow's entrepreneurs will need exceptional interpersonal skills to relate to others and to work successfully within a mobile and multicultural society'. Thus, they will need to be able to 'work professionally in more than one language and will be trained to understand cultural differences, having studied alongside friends from many different countries'. The same author considers that a priority for an internationally mobile family is to be able 'to transfer smoothly to a new location, maintaining an uninterrupted education as well as to pass examinations which qualify them for entrance in to university in the country of their choice'.

Thus, it can be seen that these two principals feel that what International Schools should be offering prospective parents and students at group level are: ways of constructing international relationships; a high level of interpersonal skills; bilingual or multilingual proficiency; appreciation of cultural difference. At an individual level, emphasis is on responsibility, adequate responses to new challenges and opportunities, and entrepreneurship. At an academic level students need the possibility of both educational continuity as well as the necessary preparation to be able to achieve good standards in order to enter prestigious international universities.

We will now examine a number of brochures and prospectuses sent out by International Schools in the USA, Europe, Asia, Africa and South America to prospective parents and students in the light of the above statements and taking into account the three categories proposed by Fairclough (1989). The brochures were selected according to geographical location (to get a spread over different continents) and bearing in mind the extent to which they exhibited the features discussed in Fairclough's (1989) study. This analysis does not make claims to reflect the type of discourse used by all International Schools but aims to provide an indication of how some schools construct relationships and images for potential parents and students. It also does not pretend to categorize any one institution as better or worse than others.

The relationship constructed between the educational establishments and the parents of potential new students

The brochures of eight establishments were initially selected for analysis, according to the criteria described above. These were: Canadian Academy, Kobe, Japan; Graz International Bilingual School, Graz, Austria; International School of the Peninsula, California, USA; Northlands, Buenos Aires, Argentina; The British Council School of Madrid, Madrid, Spain; The International School of Tanganyika, Dar es Salaam, Tanzania; Tohoku International School, Sendai, Japan; and West Island School, Hong Kong, China.

In reply to my request for information from the schools, indicating a possible interest in sending my children to the establishments in question, I received information in a variety of linguistic modes. Three of the eight institutions sent back monolingual publications in English; four brochures were bilingual (English–Spanish (2), English–Japanese, English–German); and one brochure was trilingual

(English–French and Chinese), thus acknowledging the possibility of non-English speaking parents needing access to school information.

Most of the brochures exhibited a mixture of features characteristic of two discourse types: the discourse of educational information and the discourse of advertising, to a greater or lesser extent. A typical example is provided by the International School of the Peninsula which begins by stating:

Extract 1

> The International School of the Peninsula provides a superior immersion-based bilingual and multicultural education to students from pre-kindergarten through middle school. Our programs challenge children to realize their full potential, while they learn to work together toward common goals.

The first sentence adopts an impersonal style characteristic of the discourse of educational (public) information. In the second sentence, however, there is a change towards a more personalised style, characteristic of certain styles of advertising, through the introduction of the corporate 'our' to identify the addresser as spokesperson for the school community.

A similar tendency of a move from the impersonal to the personal can be seen in another of the selected brochures, that of the Graz International Bilingual School (GIBS) which claims:

Extract 2

> GIBS has a number of goals. Our primary objective is that our pupils learn a second language (German or English) and eventually achieve a near-native command of it.

These can be seen as examples of what Fairclough (1989: 62) refers to as 'synthetic personalization' a strategy which gives 'the impression of treating each of the people "handled" *en masse* as an individual'. A sense is created of an individualised 'caring' addresser is who is directing a personal message to the prospective parents reading the brochures, while retaining the initial impression of 'seriousness' and 'objectivity' associated with an impersonal style of presentation of the institution.

Some brochures, however, reverse the process. They begin with a direct personalized appeal, as in the case of the Canadian Academy in Kobe, and follow this up with more 'objective' information.

Extract 3

> Japan. An exciting place to be. An adventure for you and your family. An experience you will treasure for the rest of your life.

> Kobe. Only 40 minutes from bustling Osaka, 60 minutes from historic Kyoto and, traditionally the city of choice for the expatriate community. Kobe is also the obvious place for Canadian Academy to be.

This brochure addresses a prime concern of your life in Japan – the education of your children. At Canadian Academy, we are structured to provide your child with a challenging educational experience. We are also eminently qualified to help you as parents understand your child's development.

Canadian Academy was founded in 1913 upon Christian concepts and evolved to serve an international community in Japan.

Here expatriate parents, who are also referred to as members of 'an international community' are the explicit addressees ('you as parents'). An appeal is made both to them as individuals attracted by the excitement, adventure and valuable experiences that Japan offers, and as parents concerned about the quality of their children's education. In the latter respect, the corporate addresser reassures them that the school has the necessary expertise to help them in this important undertaking. This personalized appeal is then followed up by a description of the foundation of the school and its current status, written in an impersonal 'informative' style.

The image created

We will now examine the same three extracts analysed above from the point of view of the image they establish for the type of educational provision being promoted.

In Extract 1, the school is one of the few which explicitly refers to its programmes as 'bilingual and multicultural education' and is consequent with this position in that it provides a trilingual prospectus and includes a description of the nature of bilingualism for prospective parents in the following terms:

Extract 4

Our school is a bilingual school whether you choose the French-American or the Chinese-American program. Pursuing bilingualism will represent a real commitment for the entire family. It will be necessary to show a positive attitude and offer as much support from home as possible. The motivation of the parents is essential.

Other establishments refer rather to the learning of second or other languages, as in the case of Extract 2, or to the use of 'one common language (English) for communication and friendship' among its multilingual population (Tohoku International School).

The type of modifiers used in the three extracts exemplify excellence. In Extract 1, the programme is categorised as 'superior'; in Extract 2, students are expected to achieve a 'near-native' command of their second language; while in Extract 3, the education offered is described as a 'challenging' experience under the guidance of 'eminently qualified' personnel.

Other terms used to characterise the high level of the educational provision offered by the eight selected International Schools include: *the best practice, academic excellence, excellent qualifications, qualifications to gain access to the most prestigious universities in the world, an outstanding educational experience, a fully bilingual education . . . to the highest international standard.*

From the above it is apparent that the image being created for the readers is that of a level of academic excellence which will enable school graduates to pursue their ambitions of tertiary education in any part of the world.

However, academic excellence is not the only image that is created. As can be seen in Extract 5 (below) there is also emphasis on the development of social and interpersonal skills alongside individual talents.

Extract 5

> Tohoku International School (TIS) . . . exists to meet the academic needs of the Tohoku region's expatriate community and Japanese students who wish to graduate from English speaking high schools and colleges. The multiplicity of cultures represented by our students and faculty provides a uniquely enriching environment which teaches appreciation of diversity in others. Within this community of cultures, students are provided (with) experiences which develop a strong sense of their individual potentials, as well as an understanding of the responsibilities of their global citizenship.

Here, the parents of two different groups of students are being explicitly addressed: those who form part of the local expatriate community and home nation students from Japan. The fact of being educated in a multicultural community is portrayed as providing students with the experience necessary to learn tolerance and understanding of difference at a social level as a preparation for their future role as citizens of the world. Within this social vision there is also an emphasis on the importance of developing individual capabilities and responsibilities.

A similar message is provided in Extract 6 which comes from the brochure of an International School in a very different part of the world – Tanzania.

Extract 6

> The International School of Tanganyika Ltd . . . IST is committed to the development of students who are confident, compassionate, responsible citizens of an increasingly global society with a passion for knowledge and self development.

Here, what is offered is again preparation for global citizenship, with particular emphasis on the individual characteristics of confidence, responsibility, and self-development. The new element included in this extract is compassion.

In information about West Island School, Hong Kong, this aspect is developed in more detail, as can be seen in Extract 7.

Extract 7

> Our students are privileged to be educated in West Island School – but privilege brings responsibility and we expect them to go on to be leaders in the communities in which they find themselves and to be carers with the courage to stand up

for right and equality. We teach our students to be life-long learners and we develop in them the skills to access knowledge and to be self disciplined and independent. All students are highly valued in West Island School and we try by every means to help them achieve their potential what that may be. Value added is our aim.

In the above extract the privileged status of the students is linked with their social responsibilities as leaders concerned for basic human rights. The individual qualities emphasised are self-discipline and independence. The term 'value added', normally associated with financial operations, is used perhaps in a double sense to suggest not only 'value for money' but also to suggest the individual valoration given to each student in the school.

Similar aspects are also referred to in the information sent out by others of the selected schools in the following manner: *a positive environment, education for life, wide variety, a wide range of opportunities and challenges, social responsibility, social aspect of team work, open-mindedness, social maturity, fostering independent thinking and creativity, equipping for the challenges of the twenty-first century.*

From this brief survey about the image created in these brochures and prospectuses we can conclude that the overall impression given is that of superiority. Reference is made to excellence at all levels: academic provision, bilingual or multilingual proficiency, future opportunities to gain valued qualifications, and consequent access to a privileged lifestyle. Graduates of these programmes are portrayed as outstanding human beings, possessing, on the one hand, unusual leadership qualities and capacities to deal with problems and challenges and, on the other, the maturity to appreciate diversity, to be tolerant and understanding, and to be a defender of those who are less fortunate. The image thus created is that of a 'superclass' of individuals ready to take on their role on the world stage in the new millennium and prepared for success throughout life thanks to their International School education. This is very much in line with the perceptions of the two International School principals examined earlier in this chapter.

These ideas of success based on individual merit and the development of all one's talents and potential are closely associated with the values linked with contemporary capitalist society and, according to Fairclough's (1989: 206) vision, may be seen as an ideological frame which 'packages together social subjects in particular sorts of relationship, activities, settings, values, and so on, in a powerful prescription for how one should live, or at least what one should acknowledge to be the best way to live, in the modern world, together with the myth that this lifestyle is open to everyone'.

The construction of subject positions

The term 'subject positions' is used by Fairclough (1989) to refer to the notion of the social roles in which people participate in discourse. In a school situation, typical subject positions would be: principal, teacher, student or parent. The ideal subject position set up for the readers of these brochures is that of parents 'whose needs and values and tastes are those embedded in this frame' (Fairclough, 1989: 207).

According to the image created in the brochures analysed, these parents will either be members of what is at times referred to as 'the international community' or 'the expatriate community', or they will be part of the host country society. In both cases, they are portrayed as being academically and socially ambitious for their children's future, which is seen in terms of a global, international vision, in which international languages, such as English, are a necessity.

They will most probably belong to a community of high economic status who are accustomed to enjoying the advantages of a modern lifestyle and therefore look for schools that provide appropriate settings in terms of spacious facilities, pleasant environments, appropriate infrastructure and a low student–teacher ratio. Visual images of school buildings and facilities in the form of photographs are provided in the majority of the brochures. These picture modern constructions; teachers working with individuals or groups of five or six students; children from different races working happily together; students using computers and carrying out experiments in well-equipped laboratories; performing in school shows and engaged in such sports as canoeing, yachting, baseball or athletics in spacious school grounds.

Thus, these International Schools construct subject positions for potential parents as people of good taste, accustomed to the best for themselves and their families, and therefore demanding of high standards for their children's education. Presumably parents who are considering the advantages of an International School education for their sons and daughters will identify with the image created both verbally and visually and accept the positioning set up in the brochures. In this way, they will be encouraged to pay the fees necessary for their children to be able to benefit from this type of educational provision.

Implications for School Policy and Practice

We will now consider the implications of this type of analysis for school policy and practice. One of the primary contributions that critical discourse analysis can make to linguistics or education is that of consciousness-raising, or in Fairclough's (1989) view, it can enable people to appreciate connections which are normally hidden. In other words, becoming aware of how and why particular types of educational provision have developed in the way they have can help researchers, teachers and students understand the reasons for their success or failure, and the reasons for their continuing influence. As Heller (1997: 269) claims with respect to any bilingual education programme and research agenda, 'results can best be understood in the context of the interests it represents and the characteristics of the population it serves'.

The question that may now be asked is, what is the value of these insights provided by critical discourse analysis and critical language awareness to teachers who work in elite bilingual programmes? What is the relationship of this type of vision to classroom practice and school policy? In this respect, Fairclough (1989) suggests a four-part pedagogical strategy which involves the following stages: students' reflecting on experience; systematising the results of these reflections; providing social explanations; and developing practice.

Bearing this in mind, one suggestion might be for teachers and their students to examine policy documents such as school brochures, syllabuses, statements of school philosophy, type of bilingual programme offered, which refer to the aims and mission of the institutions they work for, and to discuss how far these are reflected in everyday classroom practice. Then, reasons for possible discrepancies between policy statements and practice might be analysed and commented on, and recommendations for future developments drawn up.

Another possibility, as suggested by Freeman and McElhinny (1996: 268) in relation to language and gender, might be to get students to conduct an ethnography of communication study in their bilingual schools and classrooms, and also in the wider community, where they 'learn to look, how to ask questions, and how to listen in order to account for when, where, by whom, to whom, in what manner, and in what particular circumstances particular speech acts are used' particularly with regard to differential power relations and the use of more than one language. The classroom can then provide a forum for students and teachers to discuss their findings and the implications of these, as well as suggesting 'creative alternatives' (Freeman & McElhinny, 1996: 268).

An Analysis of the Inaugural Address by The Bruneian Minister of Education to the 'Bilingualism and National Development Conference', Brunei, 1991

Having examined in some detail the discourse associated with the advertising of certain elite bilingual programmes, we will now turn to an analysis of the speech given by the Bruneian Minister of Education on the occasion of the inauguration of the 'Bilingualism and National Development Conference' in 1991 which constitutes a rationale for the official *Dwibahasa* bilingual policy.

As discussed in Chapter 9, the *Dwibahasa* bilingual education system was initially implemented in Brunei in 1985 as official government policy, sanctioned by the Sultan. Its aim was to replace the established tradition of separate English and Malay-medium schools by ensuring the use of both languages within different spheres in the official school system. The 'Bilingualism and National Development Conference' in 1991 was an attempt to evaluate six years of *Dwibahasa* in the light of the relationships between language, society and education in the bilingual context (Cath, 1994). The participants were officials, academics and teachers, both Bruneian and foreign. The speech which forms the basis of the analysis in this section was given by the Bruneian Minister of Education at the opening ceremony of the Conference. It fulfils, according to Cath (1994: 1) not only a symbolic function, but also constitutes 'a working statement of Brunei's language policy which in itself contributes to the maintenance and reproduction of the country's social and economic structures'.

The analysis will first look at discourse practices, then textual aspects will be examined, and finally, these analyses will be situated within the wider perspective of social practice. The full text of the speech itself is provided below, as without this it is very difficult to make sense of the analysis and the interpretation of its discourse and social significance.

YB Pehin Orang Kaya Laila Wijaya Dato Seri Setia Haji Awang Abdul Aziz bin Begawan Pehin Udana Khatib Dato Seri Paduka Awang Haji Umar

Assalamu – Alaikum – Warahmatullahi-Wabarakatuh.

5   *Vice-Chancellor Dato Haji Abu Bakar, Chairman of the Bilingualism and*
     National Development Organising Committee, Deputy Minister, Distinguished Guests,
     Excellencies, Ladies and Gentlemen,
     I feel both pleased and honoured to officially open this conference on 'Bilingualism and
     National Development: Current Perspectives and Future
10   *Trends'. The subject is an important one for everyone in Brunei Darussalem*
     and all of us here, whether government officials, language planners, linguists,
     educationalists or teachers have something to learn from the conference. As a
     government minister I am immediately aware that in discussing language matters we are
     dealing with something that is at the very root of a person's and
15   *therefore a nation's being. The languages that we use are a reflection of ourselves, they*
     make a statement about us, they are a measure. This is the emotive side of language
     planning, but there is also the instrumental side. Language can perform the function of a
     tool: it can be used for opening doors and providing access to wider horizons. In Brunei
     Darussalam we are
20   *constantly witness to this process; in fact, we were so, even before the arrival of European*
     languages.
     This is a multilingual country. As Bruneians, many of us were exposed to two or more
     languages even before starting our school careers. This progressive acquisition of
     languages brings with it progressively wider horizons, greater
25   *awareness and understanding of other people and the way they live and thus serves to*
     increase our knowledge and wisdom. The introduction of European languages,
     particularly the English language, took this process a step further and opened Brunei and
     its neighbours to global perspectives and global markets. In the process, we have also
     been exposed to cultures and influences
30   *from the rest of the world. As a result, we have become aware that, in addition to its role*
     as medium for information, language can also be a channel for cultural transfer. We
     need to be selective in what we choose to adopt in Brunei but, while we are aware of the
     potential dangers, we also realise that no country can exist in a cultural or economic
     vacuum.
35   *Brunei Darussalam is today well placed to take advantage of its rich linguistic heritage.*
     The majority of people in this country are Malay, and the Malay language, God willing,

will always remain our national language. It is, if you like, the language of our soul, a part of what identifies us as Bruneians and as such is something that we should never want to lose and have no intention of

40 *losing. Our cultural heritage and understanding of the Malay Islamic Monarchy concept should ensure this, as will an understanding of the factors that caused language loss in other countries. Brunei Darussalam today finds itself in a position where the future role of its own language is assured while at the same time, because of historical links, it is also in a position to acquire as a second*

45 *language what is now the planet's first truly global language, English.*
English is today a language that transcends national borders. It is no longer the preserve of the British or American people but has been transformed into a multi-ethnic means of world communication. With the spread of the new varieties of English across the world in recent years, English is no longer an

50 *elitist colonial language but instead has become the key for access to full involvement in the world's affairs. Brunei was of course never a colony and we have no colonial ghost to exorcise. We are also fortunate in having been given the opportunity to witness and learn from how other countries in this region have fared in their own language planning programmes.*

55 *Brunei does not face language cultural loss as a result of using English as the country's second language; this is not a country in which bilingualism is a negative feature but one in which it is additive. Ours is a country in which the role of the first language is assured and where the second language has an instrumental but not an emotive role to play; the sort of country that linguistic*

60 *researchers have identified as having the most to gain from pursuing bilingual education policies. At the risk of repeating myself, but this is a very important point and one that perhaps should be repeated, Malay will always remain the national language. Its place in our society will not be usurped by English, but we can use English as a tool for the good of national development.*

65 *Linguists, teachers and educationalists present at this conference, as well as parents who have no immediate or professional interest in the field of bilingualism, should all find much of interest and value in the papers presented and in the discussion that will ensue. Bilingualism, by definition, relates to language acquisition and thus to the theory and practice of first and second*

70 *language acquisition. These in turn must take into account recent developments in socio and psycholinguistics, in contrastive analysis and in how languages relate to the societies in which they are used. It is a subject that must surely encompass all our various interests. Any research into bilingualism, bilingual education and national development must, in addition, take into account the*

75 *attitude, prejudices and expectations of pupils, parents and teachers. This is not an esoteric subject that is of little interest to anyone outside a university, but rather a subject of immediate relevance to all of us involved in education and government and one that can only be tried and tested in practical work and research in many levels of the educational hierarchy.*

80 *My ministry and the Universiti Brunei Darussalam are keenly aware of the need to*

participate in and support research analysing the implementation of our own bilingual
education programme as well as other areas relating to bilingualism and language
change. To a very great extent, the staging of this conference is testimony to this interest
and I should hope that many important links can be

85 *forged over the next four days that will herald an era of greater liaison between the UBD*
and interested bodies overseas. We believe that Brunei already has something to offer in
the field of bilingual research. Members of the university's academic staff are at the
forefront of work being done on language use in Borneo and this has been particularly
appreciated and welcomed by the Borneo

90 *Research Council. In addition, long-term research into the adoption of a bilingual*
education system within the country has been instigated, and I am quite sure that those
lecturers involved in any of the language related research projects will be pleased to
discuss their work at this gathering. The opportunity for informal but informed discussion
is, after all, one of the less obvious but

95 *surely one of the most important reasons for attending a conference such as this.*
A greater understanding of what it is to be bilingual, to adopt bilingual education
policies, to raise our children bilingually and to live in a bilingual or multilingual society
will continue to concern us for the foreseeable future. This conference will address these
issues and should thus generate interest which will

100 *reach beyond this campus and beyond the borders of Brunei Darussalam. The issues to*
be discussed have far-reaching implications and it seems likely that this conference will
play a significant role in pointing the way forward for bilingual studies worldwide in the
1990s.
Finally, may I extend a very warm welcome to all foreign colleagues. I hope

105 *you will all have some time to see a little of our country and that your stay*
will be a pleasant one. I must also thank all members of the Universiti Brunei
Darussalam, especially Mr Graeme Cane and Dayand Rosnah Haji Ramly, for
all their efforts in bringing about this conference.
Ladies and gentlemen, Bismillahirrahmanirrahim, I take great pleasure in

110 *declaring the Bilingualism and National Development Conference open.*

Discourse analysis

The rhetorical frame for this speech is typical of Malay public discourse, which is characterised by its formality and the inclusion of religious formulae to give authority to the content expressed. Thus, the speech begins by citing the full form of the Minister's name used in the programmme (*YB Pehin Orang Kaya Laila Wijaya Dato Seri Setia Haji Awang Abdul Aziz bin Begawan Pehin Udana Khatib Dato Seri Paduka Awang Haji Umar*). Then follows the full traditional Arabic salutation: *Assalamu – Alaikum – Warahmatullahi-Wabarakatuh*, which means 'Peace be upon you and the Mercy of God and His Blessings'. This constitutes part of the Islamic Profession of Faith, but has its origins in pre-Islamic civilisation and is conventionally used in Brunei, even in the presence of non-Moslems. The use of the *Basmalah* formulaic expression ('In the Name of God the infinitely Good, the ever Merciful') at the beginning of the final paragraph reinforces the religious framing of the speech, legitimising the temporal order of affairs with reference to religious authority, thereby encouraging 'the listener's acceptance of the message' (Cath, 1994: 3).

The concepts of culture and religion are explicitly linked and highlighted in the reference to the Malay Islamic Monarchy (line 40). In many contexts, such as school assemblies and media reports, this concept is regularly invoked as a type of verbal emblem, authorising an unspecified action. In this particular case, the authorisation concerns the importance of recognising bilingualism in Malay and English as a national priority, while discounting the acceptance of biculturalism in favour of 'our cultural heritage' (line 40).

The national language (Malay) is strongly defended as 'the language of our soul, a part of what identifies us as Bruneians' (lines 38–39), thus clearly stressing the link between language and national identity, again with a religious reference. English is seen from a historical perspective as one of 'the European languages . . . (which) opened Brunei and its neighbours to global perspectives and global markets' (lines 26–29). Moreover, the instrumentality of English as a world lingua franca 'that transcends national borders' (line 46) is explicitly flagged. English is portrayed as an international language, not as a dominant colonial language associated with either Britain or the United States. It is positioned as non-elitist in character and facilitating access 'to full involvement in the world's affairs' (lines 50–51).

In rather paradoxical fashion, the Minister also recognises Brunei as a bilingual and multilingual country (lines 22 and 56) and refers to this as 'additive' (line 57) rather than subtractive. This makes indirect reference to other indigenous languages spoken in the country. However, this reference is not pursued, as the speaker returns again and again to one of the central tenets of his discourse: that 'the role of the first language (Malay) is assured . . . It's place in our society will not be usurped by English' (lines 57 and 63). As Cath (1994) recognises, the discourse of political orthodoxy exemplified in this speech is similar to what Fairclough (1989: 22) calls 'the rhetoric of standardization', where evidence of linguistic diversity is minimised in favour of focusing on the positive effects of standardisation and unification of the national language, in order to sustain existing power structures.

If we now consider the multiple audiences that the Minister is directing his speech towards, we note how he takes pains to position himself as an 'insider' in relation to the academic community concerned with research in the field of bilingualism and bilingual education. He is speaking primarily to an international audience of linguists and educationalists and he must convince these representatives of the academic community of his credibility in the 'educational hierarchy' (line 79). He thus refers to such themes as the attitudinal aspects of language learning (lines 14 and 75); cultural pluralism (lines 29–34); language and ethnicity (lines 15–16); English as a culturally neutral language (lines 46–51); the essential primacy of Malay (lines 36–40); and the growth and range of bilingual studies (lines 70–75).

There are, however, other 'audiences' present, in addition to academics which the Minister needs to address. He represents the Sultan and is speaking to a

Bruneian public of 'pupils, parents and teachers' (line 75). He is also speaking to an administrative audience of 'government officials (and) language planners' (line 11). He thus uses traditional Malay forms of framing, salutation and formality of register which for Bruneians 'would act as a measure of the authority of the speech' (Cath, 1994: 6). The main content of the speech, however, is directed rather to the international and national conference participants.

Text analysis

According to Baker (1993: 153), 'Sociocultural, political and economic issues are ever present in the debate over the provision of bilingual education'. This is evident in the Bruneian Minister's speech. The academic topics, bilingualism, bilingual education, language planning, etc. are combined with references to the Minister's political role, as government official (line 13), and his designation of 'My ministry' (line 80) as a partner of the university in the creation and evaluation of the national bilingual education programme. The voice of the Minister here is clearly that of a politician, rather than an academic, as can be seen in his frequent use of strong categorical statements, unmodified by the explicit markers of modality, such as 'might', 'could', 'likely', etc., which are characteristic of academic discourse.

An extended example of this can be seen in lines 55–64. In the first part of the paragraph, the Minister uses strong categorical statements which are presented in an 'objective' fashion. In other words, he universalises their origin as established 'facts', 'Brunei does not face language cultural loss', 'this is not a country in which bilingualism is a negative feature'. 'Ours is a country in which the role of the first language is assured'. When he does introduce modality (in line 62), it is significant that he chooses the modal verb 'will' in the expression 'Malay will always remain the national language' to indicate predictive insistence, thereby strengthening the force of his preceding remarks.

Another textual characteristic of the Minister's speech is the foregrounding of references to Brunei or 'we', referring to Bruneians or the government of Brunei as agent in the thematic position of the clause, as can be seen in the following examples: 'Brunei was of course never a colony' (line 51); 'we have no colonial ghost to exorcise' (lines 51–52); 'we are also fortunate in having been given the opportunity to witness . . .' (lines 52–53); 'Brunei does not face language cultural loss' (lines 55); 'Ours is a country' (line 57); and 'we can use English as a tool' (line 64). In addition to the foregrounding of Brunei as agent in the clause, we can also note the extended use of the active voice in these statements.

The combined effect of the use of categorical statements and the references to Brunei as clausal agent, together with the use of the active voice throughout the speech is that of certainty, rather than possibility. Brunei is positioned as being in control of its own historical and cultural destiny and not subject to outside influences. The fact that references to the country and government are presented as 'given' or known information in the 'theme' of the clause, rather than as 'new' information (Halliday & Hasan, 1976) reinforces the *status quo* and suggests 'that the listeners are being recruited to a specifically Bruneian bilingual agenda' (Cath, 1994: 10).

Social practice

In order to situate appropriately the discourse and textual analysis provided in the previous sections we must now interpret the discussion in relation to a wider vision of language as social practice, or, in other words, in terms of the social context or social conditions which determine the processes of the production and interpretation of the discourse (Fairclough, 1989). In the case of Brunei, this involves an explanation which takes into account the relations of power concentrated in the figure of the Monarch, the Sultan, his family and the privileged class of aristocrats known as *Pengiran*.

According to Cath (1994), the power structure in Brunei has changed little since the early nineteenth century. There was an attempt to introduce democratic principles of government in 1962, but this was short-lived, the election was annulled and a subsequent rebellion was put down with the help of British troops. The State of Emergency, decreed to deal with the uprising, has been renewed every two years since then and the Sultan enjoys a position of considerable power and influence, enhanced by the revenues deriving from the country's oil industry.

The sense of certainty and strength noted in the Minister of Education's speech fits in well with the hegemonic model of government adopted in Brunei, which is characterised by both religious and cultural orthodoxy and according to Cath, 'manages to reproduce existing social inequalities while appearing to offer equality of opportunity' (Cath, 1994: 12–13) by means of the proclamation of the *Dwibahasa* bilingual education system as an element of government policy for all schools. Malay–English bilinguals form an educational and social elite and generally occupy well-paid and responsible positions in the country. The majority of government jobs advertised in the official bulletin require candidates to speak, read or write English well. Although the Minister does mention 'the attitude, prejudices and expectations of pupils, parents and teachers' (line 75), he seems to take little real account of the differing aptitudes, needs and sensibilities of bilingual individuals in their daily lives. Thus, bilingualism in Malay and English is seen very much as a personal possession rather than a social right, with those bilinguals who form part of the linguistic elite maintaining their traditional social advantage at the expense of other less-well educated individuals and speakers belonging to minority language groups in Brunei.

We may, therefore, conclude that although the Minister's speech refers to the benefits of bilingualism and bilingual education in general, and there is no direct reference to the *Dwibahasa* (Malay–English) bilingual education policy, the benefits of being bilingual in terms of the construction of national identity and the provision of access to wider horizons are implicitly limited to those who are bilingual in the languages which have been legitimised as appropriate for education in Brunei, Malay and English. As we have discussed above, Malay is explicitly referred to as 'our national language' (line 37), and English is recognised as an important means of global communication and economic and political advancement at international level. Other languages spoken in the country are not specifically designated as important, prestigious or useful 'for the good of national development' (line 64) and thus bilingualism or multilingualism in these cases is not included as part of national educational policy.

Thus, it can be seen in the case of bilingualism in Brunei Darussalam that 'education is a crucial site for the reproduction of . . . symbolic dominance and of the relations of power it stands for' (Martin-Jones & Heller, 1996: 9). The national *Dwibahasa* bilingual education policy ensures that the interests of the ruling class in the country are safeguarded. The control thus exercised over both the highly valued linguistic resources of the Malay and English languages, and over the educational institutions that distribute these resources allows the authorities to regulate access to other prized resources, such as employment in official government agencies and promotion to key positions in the country.

Conclusion

In this chapter we have examined, in some depth, features of the discourse of elite bilingual education as exemplified in two discourse genres, International School brochures, and language policy statements. By means of a critical analysis which situates discussion of linguistic and textual features within a vision of language as social practice we have attempted to show how selected educational documents have been constructed, and how they indirectly reproduce and legitimise existing power relations.

The importance of analysing the covert meanings and ideologies underlying public discourse is related to the fact that, as Fairclough (1989: 42) recognises, 'people are not generally aware of determinations and effects at these levels and Critical Language Study is therefore a matter of helping people to become conscious of opaque causes and consequences'. Awareness-raising, as the same author acknowledges, is a necessary first step in the process of emancipation. For this reason, it is important that teachers recognise that this type of analysis is not just an intellectual exercise carried out by academics far away from the realities of classroom practice, but that it can help both them and their students to recognise how they and the programmes they represent have been positioned in official institutional discourses and suggest ways in which they may contest positionings that may be seen as inappropriate or unacceptable.

It must be acknowledged, in addition, that the interpretations provided in this chapter are necessarily subjective in that they foreground certain textual and discoursal elements and explain these in terms of particular aspects of the social context that the analyst sees as important. However, as the evidence for these interpretations is available, the reader has the opportunity of deciding for him or herself how far they are convincing and how far they help in the understanding of the impact of certain official pronouncements in relation to elite bilingual education provision.

Note

1. The author is greatly indebted to Andrew Cath (1994) for permission to use extracts of the analysis reproduced here.

Chapter 13

Common Problem Areas in the Practice of Bilingual Pedagogy in Elite Educational Contexts

Introduction

In Chapter 4 we examined some key issues involved in the processes of teaching and learning in different elite bilingual contexts in relation to classroom language use, the relationship between content and language, and cultural considerations. In this chapter we will look more closely at issues of bilingual pedagogy *per se*, particularly from the point of view of practitioners who are involved in teaching bilingual students on a daily basis in immersion programmes, European Schools and in International Schools. We will present a series of concerns expressed by teachers from elite bilingual schools in different parts of the world as part of a survey designed to tap teachers' perceptions on how they deal with problem areas in their teaching. In this way, we hope to be able to give voice to individual teachers and how they see key aspects of their classroom practice. These concerns will then be discussed in the light of wider pedagogical issues.

Teacher Perceptions on Bilingual Classroom Practice

In order to find out how teachers currently working in elite bilingual contexts in different parts of the world saw their classroom practice, a questionnaire relating to common problem areas encountered in bilingual pedagogy was designed and sent out via the readership of *The Bilingual Family Newsletter* in November 1999.[1] In addition, copies of the questionnaire were circulated through personal contacts to practitioners working in bilingual schools in Colombia, Hong Kong and Finland. The first section of the questionnaire aimed at establishing the general sociolinguistic and educational context of the institution, while the second section focused on the identification of two specific problem areas encountered by teachers in their day-to-day classroom practice.

Table 13.1 Main topics discussed in teacher survey

Main problem areas noted in survey	Topics discussed
Motivation and opportunities to use foreign or other languages	Real need to use foreign language. Finding productive time with the individual child. Children's preference for interaction in dominant language. Challenges leading to opportunities for communication in foreign language. Student motivation and everyday language use. Lack of challenge to improve level of foreign language skill.
Student language proficiency level	Failure to become bilingual. Length of time in ESL programme. Low level of student understanding. Foreign language translation. Active use of second language. Grammar mistakes and success in international exams. National examinations presented in first language.
Development of biliteracy	Initial biliteracy. Motivation in learning to read. Reading comprehension. High oral but low written foreign language proficiency.
Language and content	Understanding concepts in content areas. Evaluation of conceptual development in the foreign language. Pacing of bilingual education programmes.
Language and culture	Cultural norms. Cultural elements and textbooks. Children's foreign language and culture preference.
Child and adolescent development	Use of foreign language and problems of classroom control. Noisy classes. Concentration. Self consciousness in using the foreign language. Student desire not to be different.
Parental involvement	Family involvement and parent interest. Premature removal from ESL programme.
Material and human resources	Teacher-produced materials. Materials in specialised content areas. Lack of textbooks and Ministry of Education guidelines. Bilingual training courses for content area teachers. Change over of teaching staff. Lack of teacher knowledge about immersion.

The teachers were also asked to reflect on the probable reasons for the problems they identified, how they had tried to solve them, and with what degree of success.

In total, 70 teachers completed the questionnaire. Replies were received from the following countries: Australia, Austria, Belgium, Britain, Canada, China (Hong Kong), Colombia, Finland, France, Germany, Japan, Spain, Switzerland, Thailand, United States. For purposes of discussion, we have grouped the replies into eight main areas of analysis, as can be seen in Table 13.1. Alongside each main area we have indicated some of the specific concerns raised by individual respondents. Rather than conducting a quantitative analysis, we will focus on some of the key points raised by the respondents and discuss these in the light of current bilingual pedagogical thinking.

Motivation and Opportunities to use Foreign or Other Languages

This was one of the major areas of concern noted among the respondents to the survey ranging across different grade levels. Thus, teachers at preschool level replied, expressing their worries about such topics as creating the need to use the foreign language among young children, finding sufficient productive time with individual children, and children's obvious preference for interacting in the dominant society language. Primary school teachers focused on problems such as the low status or valoration of the first language, and the need to incorporate challenging activities in the classroom to stimulate higher level of production in the foreign language. At high school level, teachers noted difficulties arising from heterogeneous levels of foreign language proficiency, problems of teaching large classes and the difficulty of instituting student-centred approaches, and a diminishing level of contact with the foreign language in the curriculum at this level.

We will now look at some of these concerns in more detail. First we examine three cases reported in the survey, one from Colombia, one from Finland, and one from Australia where pre-school teachers comment on aspects of motivation and opportunities for use of the foreign language among their young pupils.

Case 13.1   Real need to use foreign language

The foreign-language co-ordinator at pre-school level of an English–Spanish bilingual programme in Cali (Colombia) reported that one of the main problems she had found in her teaching was that the children did not have a real need to use English, as although the language of instruction was English in the school, the pupils communicated in Spanish in their everyday lives at home and among each other at school. Thus, they did not have a real motivation to interact in the foreign language. The ways she had tried to cope with this were to create artificial needs within the school, such as organising presentations of the children singing and reciting rhymes and poems in English for the parents, song festivals and cultural events. She also thought it was important for the school to recruit foreign, native-speaking teachers at primary and secondary school level. She said that in her experience it was more difficult to 'create needs' for learning English at secondary school level because the students were involved in passing Colombian exams (in Spanish) and saw English as less important to their immediate needs. At preschool level this worked better because of integrated approaches to curriculum organisation.

Case 13.2 Finding productive time with the individual child

A problem area identified by a teacher in an English–Finnish immersion preschool programme in Vaasa (Finland), where Finnish is the first language of the majority of the children, referred to the fact that it was often difficult to find productive time with all children, as 'the more demanding children were getting the most attention, thus the most language exposure'. Ways of dealing with this difficulty that had been tried in her school were: to divide the children into smaller groups so that there was more possibility of individualized attention, to employ more native English speakers among the staff, and to create learning centres based on different themes, such as transportation, dressing-up, clay, library, computers. She also observed that it was important to limit the number of children in each centre by the use of different coloured tickets. The teachers were present with the children in the centres so that language input was on-going, even though the children were involved in free-play activities. She reported that these strategies had led to very satisfactory results especially when the teachers managed to maintain a high level of motivation. In sum, she felt that 'immersion teaching requires very dedicated language teachers'.

Case 13.3 Children's preference for interaction in dominant language

One reply to the questionnaire came from a Brazilian teacher working in a Portuguese language playgroup in Sydney, Australia, which caters for young children 0–5 years old, designed 'to foster the use of the Portuguese language and Brazilian culture among mixed Australian–Brazilian-born children'. She reported that one of the main difficulties that she had experienced was that children tended to reply to teachers in the dominant language (English) and that they often spoke to each other in this language too. She explained this by saying that these children were used to speaking to their non-Brazilian friends in English, and that 'their "share of thought" in Portuguese is minimal compared with English'. The ways that the teachers tried to solve this problem were to ensure constant Portuguese language input and to try to attract children who did not go to daycare and who were therefore used to using Portuguese as their language of communication with their immediate family and outside.

Some teachers who replied to the survey felt that the basic unreality of using a foreign language in school in situations where both teachers and pupils can all speak the dominant society language (such as Spanish in Colombia or English in Australia) might be counteracted by employing more native speakers of the foreign languages in question. Others felt that pedagogical solutions such as trying to extend 'the routines and the play school language by creating new environments', such as a trip to a farm or a trip to the airport, might create the necessary dynamism to encourage young children to use a foreign language.

The situation reported in these three cases, about young children's reluctance to use the language they are in the process of acquiring, is common. As Wode (2000: 6) says, 'children tend not to make much use of their new language even after three years . . . most of the time there simply is no need to do so'. Young children quickly realise who are the adults that can use the dominant language and therefore react accordingly. They also know that most of their companions speak the same first language, 'so that from their point of view, there is no vital reason at all to take the trouble of resorting to an unknown language' (Wode, 2000: 4).

Understanding, though, is different. Both Baker (1995) and Wode (2000) agree that comprehension precedes production by quite a margin. In this context it is very important to reinforce the use of 'formulas and formulaic expressions that denote frequently recurring rituals, such as greetings, farewells, commands to quiet down, to clear up, to brush one's teeth . . . etc.' (Wode, 2000: 5). Although, as Vesterbacka (1991) and others have established, young children generally do not fully understand the structure of these type of expressions they quickly attach meanings associated with the context of situation to these phrases, and soon learn to use them appropriately.

Acquisition of frequently recurring lexical items is usually rapid, though there is often the danger that children do not fully understand what they are referring to when they use these vocabulary items. In this respect, Wode (2000) following Weber and Tardif (1991) recommends the use of hand puppets which encourage the children to join in acting out certain familiar roles from their everyday experience. In the role of 'interpreter', the child can be asked to interpret for two puppets, one which is a newcomer to the school and does not understand the foreign language, English, and the other who speaks English. The translation provided by the child into the first language (German in this case) helps to ascertain how far s/he has understood the English used by the newcomer puppet.

Similar observations about the need for challenges and new opportunities for foreign language use were made at the primary school level in relation to the 'plateau' effect (referred to in the description of immersion programmes in Chapter 1), as can be seen in Case 13.4, reported from Switzerland.

Case 13.4   Challenges leading to opportunities for communication in foreign language

A teacher-trainer in Valais, a bilingual canton in the French part of Switzerland, working with German–French immersion programmes at primary level observed that after two years of being involved in these programmes, students often stated experiencing a 'plateau effect', i.e. they did not feel they were making any further progress in the immersion language (German). She also noted that some students said that they were tired of 'playing a role' and wanted to go back to being themselves and using their first language. The solution she proposed was to 'modify the rhythm and way of teaching by adding another challenge, like a visit, an exchange, an Internet project with another class'. She felt that the key to further developments in this area was appropriate teacher training which could yield a 'pool of teaching practices'.

At secondary or high school level a feeling of self-satisfaction with the level of foreign language proficiency reached, as well as the perception of lack of relevance for the foreign language in their everyday life sometimes led to lack of student motivation as can be seen in Case 13.5, from Hong Kong (China), and Case 13.6, from Karlsruhe (Germany).

Case 13.5 *Student motivation and everyday language use*

In Hong Kong, a Canadian teacher working in an English-medium school at high school level, where English was used as medium of instruction for half of the school subjects taken by the students and Cantonese for the other half, observed that many students were not very motivated to learn English, especially in the upper forms, because 'using English for everyday purposes was a distant reality for most ESL learners' and that they had little need or urgency to use spoken English in their lives. The teacher had tried to motivate students by setting up after-school, extra-curricular activities which involved the students using English. He reported that the students seemed to enjoy the activities but complained that there were too many students and too little time.

Case 13.6 *Lack of challenge to improve level of foreign language skills*

A British teacher in the European School in Karlsruhe (Germany) noted that many bilingual students did not see the need to make an effort to improve the level of their foreign language skills, because they felt confident about their knowledge of language and could carry out the tasks set by the teacher easily. The teacher had tried to extend their range and get the students to write 'in a more mature style' by setting challenging and motivating tasks, such as group work on 'difficult' texts involving a wide range of vocabulary and the use of different registers. She noted in this respect that bilingual students had more limited vocabulary in comparison to their monolingual counterparts, but that they were not aware of this.

These types of problems refer to more general aspects involved in the teaching–learning process, i.e. how to keep students well-motivated towards learning throughout the curriculum. It is here that the teacher's knowledge of his or her pupils and his or her professionalism comes into play in devising activities and practices which may help learners over these difficult moments. In terms of a language plateau, the experience of being able to use the foreign language in an actual context of use, as a result of an educational visit or exchange, often helps students to realise the importance of what they are learning as being part of 'real' communication with people who speak other languages.

Similar problems to those raised in the survey have also been noted in Canadian French immersion, where programmes have been set up in areas where French is not used by the local community on a daily basis. This is the case in the cities of Toronto and Vancouver, where French immersion students are mainly anglophones from the majority language group who are learning French as a minority language. In the United States a similar situation occurs in the Mid-West where 'there are so few sources of reinforcement that occur naturally for learners of French . . . that (Glenwood) School and its teachers are really going it alone,' (Hickman, 1992: 95). In these areas the foreign language relates to 'a distant world . . . that will perhaps never be encountered' (Hickman, 1992: 96). Thus, immersion teachers are the principal promoters and arbiters of the language the children are learning in the programme, and on them falls the responsibility of providing meaningful contexts of language use within the school and classroom.

This explains the observation (Hickman, 1992) that students in these types of immersion programmes often do not have sufficient opportunities to engage in functional, personally meaningful uses of language but instead will adopt teacher-sanctioned goals in classroom communication, rather than attempt to satisfy personal communicative needs. Furthermore, most of their communication is teacher-directed, with the whole class acting as audience. There is little evidence of peer interaction in the immersion language, especially in the early years. This style of teaching and learning is understandable, given that 'for all practical purposes the only "proficient user" (of French) talking regularly to a child . . . (is) his or her classroom teacher' (Hickman, 1992: 94).

Student Language Proficiency Level

Various primary and secondary teachers commented on the proficiency levels of their students. One teacher in an International School in Bangkok, Thailand, felt that it was very difficult for students to become bilingual as they lived in a Thai-speaking atmosphere. Another teacher in an International School in Vienna, Austria noted that many students spent a long time in the school's ESL programme. Teachers in Hong Kong and Canada complained about difficulties their students had in understanding the foreign or second language, and a teacher in Vaasa, Finland, was concerned to get her students to use the second language in a more active fashion. These cases are reported in more detail below.

Case 13.7 Failure to become bilingual

A primary school teacher at an International (English-medium) School in Bangkok (Thailand) observed that in her experience 'many children study English for years at the school yet fail to become bilingual, especially Thais'. The reasons the teacher gave for this were that the students were living in a Thai environment and spoke Thai outside school and inside school at playtime. The teacher said that she had stressed that students when learning had to use the target language (English) and were not allowed to resort to their first language. Although the situation was improving, the fact that there was a high percentage of Thai students in the school so 'when grouping it is hard to pair Thais with non-Thai speakers', and 'Thais, of course, will naturally converse in their L1'. The teacher noted that this affected their written production as they were thinking first in Thai and then writing in English.

Case 13.8 Length of time in ESL programme

A teacher at an English-medium International School in Vienna (Austria), which aimed at educating children of the international community in the city, reported that many Viennese, German mother-tongue students at the school from Grades 2 to 3 onwards were having to spend a long time in the ESL programme, because of their low level of English proficiency. She also noted that 'their German often remains simple and their English doesn't develop'. Some of the reasons she gave to explain this situation were: lack of language aptitude; the fact that many of the children were neglected, in the sense that not enough attention was paid to their educational and linguistic needs; there were too many German-speaking students in the institution; some pupils suffered from academic overloading; and teachers used inappropriate teaching methods. Ways of solving this problem included 'discussing the matter with colleagues and parents in order to find individual ways to solve it'. The teacher reported that this process was on-going and there was some indication of success in raising the students' level of proficiency in both languages in order that they might be able to cope with schooling carried out almost completely through the medium of English.

Case 13.9 Low level of student understanding

A teacher in an English-medium school in Hong Kong (China) reported that 'when I speak in English, many students (in Grades 3–6) don't understand', even though the language aim of the school was the use of English as the medium of instruction. In order to cope with their low level of understanding of the language of classroom interaction the teacher said he had tried to speak slowly. However, he had found that this strategy was not always possible, 'as we need to catch up the teaching schedule'.

Case 13.10   Foreign language translation

A Canadian teacher working in a late French immersion programme in Chatham, Ontario (Canada), where half the courses were taught in French and half in English, said that he had found that many high school students were not able to understand instructions given in French for more complex tasks, such as projects, because they had become accustomed to waiting for the teacher to translate into English. He said that he had implemented a novel strategy to cope with this in that he only offered English translations during the lunch hour or after school. He evaluated the results as being highly successful as 'students had to make an effort to "get it" rather than be embarrassed by coming in for "extra help"'. Thus, 'This problem went away, even in Grade 9, as my reputation of what standard of French I expected got around'.

Case 13.11   Active use of second language

This case documents the observations of a primary school teacher working in a Swedish–Finnish immersion programme in Vaasa (Finland). She said that one of the main difficulties she had experienced in her teaching was how to get the children to use Swedish (the second language) more actively. As she explained, 'how can you get them to use the second language more and more?' especially as the pupils knew that both teachers and classmates could communicate better in Finnish. To encourage this, she had tried to create the habit in the children of using Swedish, and to help them by providing key content vocabulary before beginning new topic areas. These key words were written up on the blackboard so that the children's attention was drawn to them and were used as stimuli to encourage student production in Swedish. Furthermore, certain weeks in the school year were set aside to concentrate on the Swedish language, and pupils were told in a friendly fashion that 'Immersion teachers don't understand Finnish now'. The teacher felt that the situation was improving in that some students were using a lot of Swedish. However, there were others who were still not using Swedish at all. She felt that the teacher needed to work consciously in trying to get all the class to use the immersion language and that if children saw their classmates using Swedish they would think, 'we are immersion students, we use Swedish'.

Two of these cases (Cases 13.7 and 13.11) are similar to a certain extent to the first problem area reported above, motivation and opportunities to use L2, in that teachers and students see it as 'more natural' to use their first language in classroom interaction, as they share a common L1. For this reason, their foreign or second language often does not develop to an appropriate level of proficiency. In this respect Myriam Met (2000) maintains that it is important that teachers in bilingual education programmes focus on how students' language skills can be 'stretched, refined, and expanded beyond their present level of attainment'. As strategies to achieve this, she provides the following suggestions. Giving students open-ended tasks which require extended output helps to promote language growth much more than activities which only require short answers or 'fill in the blank' responses. Requirements to 'think aloud' and explain how students arrived at their answers help them to become conscious of the process they have gone through and necessarily involves extended oral production in answers. Another strategy recommended by Met (2000) is to scaffold tasks to support language output. This involves the teacher supporting the students in their output (both oral and written) by such means as graphic organisers (e.g. drawing up tables on the board with such headings as: What I think I know, what I want to know, etc.)' or by means of tasks that involve learners matching pictures to written descriptions as a preliminary step to describing experiments or procedures carried out in class.

Met (2000) also suggests reversing the traditional sequence of language learning (listening, speaking, reading and writing) in favour of beginning with writing (or drawing in the case of younger children) so that pupils have time to think about how to formulate their ideas in words before expressing them orally. In this way, the author claims, 'writing can be a scaffold for speaking'. She also recommends a focus on reading as a vital means of improving language performance, particularly the following types of reading activities at primary school level: reading aloud; shared reading between teacher and pupils where teachers and pupils talk about the text as they go along; guided reading and independent reading both of which help students to go beyond their present level of language proficiency.

In addition to levels of linguistic proficiency related to programme demands there are also external measures represented in national and international examinations In Case 13.12 and Case 13.13, teachers in Colombia express their concern about students' ability to be successful in both types of exams. In Case 13.12, students' lack of knowledge of grammatical structures is seen as placing them at a disadvantage in international exams. In Case 13.13, the teacher is concerned that students have sufficient contact with academic content areas in both languages because of their need to present national as well as international examinations.

Case 13.12   Grammar mistakes and success in international exams

Two teachers in English–Spanish bilingual schools in Cali (Colombia) referred to the students' lack of adequate knowledge of grammatical structures, particularly in written work which prevented them from doing well in international exams. They put the blame for this on the structure of the English syllabus in the schools which emphasised a communicative, rather than a grammatical approach to foreign language learning. They felt that while it was necessary to recognise that contextualisation was important, it was also necessary to pay explicit attention to grammatical aspects in the programme.

Case 13.13   National examinations presented in first language

A teacher in Cali (Colombia) commented on the need to include both languages in the content areas and not associate different subjects with different languages, as often happens in Colombia. This is particularly necessary as students have to present final examinations at national level in their first language. The teacher was worried that students who have consistently studied Science, for example, in English throughout their schooling might not be in a position to do well in examinations set in Spanish. As a solution, the teacher suggested using a Preview–Review type of methodology, so that the students had contact with the subject area in their two languages.

The first of these cases relates to a difficulty frequently noted in immersion programmes in Canada and the US: the development of a 'distinct interlanguage' on the part of immersion students in their communication in the immersion language (Lyster, 1987, cited in Kowal & Swain, 1997: 285). Initial concentration on experiential teaching and learning in the early programmes in meaning-oriented classrooms meant that students were able to understand messages without necessarily being called upon to undertake analysis of the relation between form and function (Swain, 1988). This, while leading to a high degree of language comprehension, put students in the position of having to communicate new and often complex ideas in a language in which they were not fluent. They were therefore forced to make use of gesture, common knowledge, and paralinguistic strategies to supplement their lack of grammatical competence in French in expressing their ideas. Thus, while 'immersion students may be fluent and demonstrate native-like understanding of spoken and written language . . . their production falls far short of native-like . . . in terms of grammar, syntax, and native-like phraseology' (Met, 2000).

This observation has been explained by the hypothesis that students, when they achieve a certain level of strategic competence in their use of the immersion language, i.e. when they are able to communicate what they want to say or write, often do not see the need to further refine their level of language proficiency. In the survey this was clearly noted by two foreign teacher respondents in Colombia (one from the US and one from New Zealand) at high school level, when they commented that in their experience students in bilingual schools had no yardstick to compare themselves with and consequently came 'to the mistaken conclusion that they were good speakers of English'.

This situation is not helped by the fact that immersion teachers often provide learners with inconsistent and sometimes random feedback concerning their use of the immersion language, added to which the input available to students in the classroom may be functionally restricted (Swain, 1988). Kowal and Swain (1997: 286) recognise that as yet there has been little research carried out to help students 'move beyond their current interlanguage . . . (and) to encourage the development of autonomous learners who can function independently and yet accurately'. However, nowadays much more attention is being paid to the interrelationships between analytic or form-focused and experiential or communicative-focused activities at classroom level, to ensure that students may develop both communicative fluency and linguistic accuracy (cf. Harley *et al.*, 1990; Rebuffot & Lyster, 1996).

The second case shows how bilingual programmes should reflect the type of language demands represented by the exams students need to take. These will necessarily have an effect on the curriculum. The so-called 'washback' effect of international examinations, such as the International Baccalaureate or the Test of English as a Foreign Language Exam (TOEFL) on school curricula needs to be taken into account when considering their suitability for the institution in question. When selecting an examination of this type, it is useful to consider how far the present school curriculum develops the skills required for the examination adopted, and how far additional skill areas need to be incorporated within the existing bilingual programme. The value of international examinations, apart from providing wider validity for results obtained in national systems of evaluation, lies in the modifications introduced in the content and orientation of school programmes to make them more in line with international requirements and therefore more appropriate for a global vision.

In many countries, students also need to take national exams and therefore need to be able to formally display their knowledge in all content areas in both their languages in order to graduate successfully. Once again, this has repercussion on the nature of the bilingual programme offered by particular institutions.

Development of Biliteracy

The development of biliteracy, or communication around written text in two languages (Hornberger, 1990), is an aspect which may have been overlooked in many bilingual school programmes, in part, perhaps, due to the legacy of an initial enthusiasm with the Communicative Approach to language teaching and learning in the late 1980s and early 1990s where emphasis was on oral rather than on written communication. In the cases described below, teachers at preschool, primary and secondary school level report different problems relating to the processes involved in written comprehension and production. The first two cases reflect the dilemma faced by many teachers in bilingual schools, whether it is better to start the reading and writing process in the child's L1 or the school language. The third case refers to the importance of pupils developing reading comprehension strategies as well as the more mechanical decoding skills. In Case 13.17, a teacher at a European School in Germany notes a discrepancy between the good oral proficiency of her high school students in contrast to the deficiency of their written production.

Case 13.14 *Initial biliteracy*

This case was sent in by a mother, who is also a part-time tutor of English and Spanish. She reported that her 2-year-old son was attending a bilingual nursery school in London (England) which aimed at helping children speak and understand fluent Spanish. For this reason, in the morning only Spanish was used and in the afternoon only English. The problem this mother was struggling with concerned learning to read. She knew that at 5 years old her son would enter an English private school where he would be expected to know how to read in English. On the other hand, the mother felt strongly that she really wanted her son to begin this process in Spanish. The strategy she had adopted to resolve these contradictory demands was to read a story to him in Spanish with alphabet exercises, followed by another story and alphabet exercises in English.

Case 13.15 *Motivation in learning to read*

A teacher in Cali (Colombia) reported that she had noticed some Spanish-speaking children at preschool level were not very motivated to start the reading process in English. She noted, 'I read stories in English. They say, most of the time, 'Please, in Spanish'. She said that as the school policy was to teach reading in English, the only way round this was to recommend to the parents to teach their children to read in Spanish, before starting school. As she observes, 'When the parents co-operate in this process the results are excellent, because children acquire reading in L2 easily'.

Case 13.16 *Reading comprehension*

A teacher involved in Swedish–Finnish in Vaasa (Finland) noted that it was difficult for young children to understand what they were reading in Swedish (their second language). They were happy to decode the text mechanically, 'they are happy with mechanical reading', but often could not talk about what they had understood from their reading. In order to help the children deepen their understanding of the text, the teacher tried to get them to contextualise their answers and to get them to explain in their own words what they understood. The teacher did not agree with beginning the reading process in the first language (Finnish) as she felt that this would be confusing for the children. As she says, ' It would be upside down, two different things, because Swedish is the tool for looking for information'. She also mentioned that an early attempt to teach reading in Finnish and Swedish simultaneously was not successful. In order to ensure a good level of comprehension, the teacher felt it was important that the reading texts used should be at an appropriate level and be interesting and meaningful for young learners.

Case 13.17   High oral but low written foreign language proficiency

In the European School in Karlsruhe (Germany) a British teacher noted that while many of her secondary level students had a good level of oral foreign language proficiency, accuracy in their written work was much lower. The teacher thought that this was because 'emphasis on communication in the early years means students are confident and do not recognise the problem'. She suggested using written work to make the students aware of the problem, and underlined the importance of reading, and the explicit teaching of grammatical aspects of the language to improve writing proficiency. She also suggested the use of the spell check in word processors as 'helpful in enabling students to produce final correct versions'.

According to researchers in the field of bilingualism (Hornberger, 1989, 1990; Hornberger & Skilton-Sylvester, 2000) it is important to include an explicit focus on biliteracy as well as bilingualism in bilingual education programmes. In this way, students may be enabled to develop appropriate literacy skills in both their languages and learn how to use the different rhetorical patterning characteristic of different discourse types in different languages.

Baker (1995) maintains that while it is more common to start the process of becoming literate in the learner's stronger language, in some cases, such as the total immersion programmes in Canada, children learn to read and write first in their second or foreign language. Both processes usually result in fully biliterate children in majority language situations, as development of reading and writing in one language transfers to the process of becoming literate in another.

In order to help children refine and extend their biliteracy skills, Sarah Hudelson (1994) suggests that teachers make use of the following strategies: creation of a print-rich environment by the provision of books, charts, written information, a reading corner, etc.; the encouragement of a collaborative classroom environment where children see other learners as resources and where they can work together on common literacy tasks; the opportunity for learners to use dialogic writing, where they can interact in writing with a more proficient user of English; and reading aloud to children on a daily basis. These types of strategies help to make learners active participants in their own learning and provide them with opportunities to use both oral and written language for a variety of communicative purposes.

Language and Content

Difficulties involving the relationship between language and content areas in the curriculum was a topic which particularly concerned teachers at preschool and primary level in bilingual schools in Cali, Colombia. Several teachers expressed their worries as to whether the children they taught really understood the concepts they were learning in the school language (English). A related concern was whether to evaluate linguistic development at the same time as conceptual matters. Another problem reported was the question of pacing in bilingual education programmes and whether this should be similar to that used in monolingual programmes or whether bilingual programmes needed a different rhythm. These concerns will be described in more detail below.

Case 13.18   *Understanding concepts in content areas*

In two teacher replies from English–Spanish bilingual schools in Cali (Colombia) the problem area identified is the teaching of subject areas (or content) through the foreign language, in this case English. The question worrying the teachers was whether the children really understood the concepts. They felt that the pupils' level of proficiency in the foreign language made it difficult for them to fully grasp the concepts presented, and did not allow them to express their feelings in this language. The teachers had attempted to solve the problem by designing classroom language policies indicating when it would be considered appropriate for teachers and students to use their two languages. This drawing up of policy guidelines by the teachers themselves has proved successful, in that the teachers said that they felt relaxed about using both languages in the classroom at different times, without losing the idea of using the foreign language as a medium of instruction.

Case 13.19   *Evaluation of conceptual development in the foreign language*

One of the main problems encountered in the teaching of content areas in the foreign language (English) by a teacher in an English–Spanish bilingual school in Cali (Colombia) at primary level was that while students could understand and handle concepts in their first language, they had difficulty doing this in the foreign language. The teacher added that 'it is still not clear in our school the extent to which we can either integrate or separate content and L2 when we evaluate how much the students have assimilated knowledge. We sometimes feel we should evaluate the concepts more than the language but we don't know how to do it without "endangering" the bilingual curriculum'. The teacher said that she had tried to lower the language level a little so that the children could grasp meanings and follow instructions more easily. She had also given the students the chance to show orally in their first language (Spanish) what they had understood. However, this was a little difficult as the institution expected the students to function totally in English in these content areas and was not very happy about the teacher allowing the students to use Spanish in these classes.

The teacher said that because of the strategies she had used she noted that some of the students seemed more motivated and that their self-esteem rose. However, her own doubts about the relationship between language and content persisted, particularly because she had found no guidance in this area in school policy documents.

Case 13.20 Pacing of bilingual education programmes

A problem of pacing in bilingual education programmes was reported by a teacher in an English-Spanish bilingual school in Cali. In his view 'bilingual education needs a special scope and sequence, but people in charge of handling these matters usually don't have any background in bilingualism and just transfer the pacing of monolingual programs into bilingual programs and expect the same pacing'. This teacher had tried to make others aware of this problem at subject level meetings, where he recommended varying the pacing of the programmes taking into account the different learning processes of bilingual learners to the teaching of content areas. He felt strongly that those responsible for curriculum planning in the school should be well-qualified in the theory and practice of bilingual education so that the decisions they made would be informed by bilingual principles and not 'what they supposed it should be, based on common sense'.

The relationship between language and content is a key issue in bilingual education programmes, such as immersion. The concerns expressed above by primary school teachers reveal that this is an area of great uncertainty for many practitioners. We may recall here the situation of the teacher in Hong Kong (Case 13.9) who was worried about 'catching up' with schedule demands. In this respect, Met (1994: 164) recommends activities which are 'experiential, hands-on, cognitively engaging, and collaborative/cooperative'. Experiential, hands-on activities, supplemented by concrete materials (both visuals and realia) help to make input comprehensible by matching experience with language and making abstract concepts concrete.

Met (1994) considers that the teacher plays a vital role in helping children whose foreign language proficiency is very limited. S/he helps them in the process of negotiating meaning by using context-embedded tasks (Cummins, 1981), in other words, activities that use many supports for meaning to help make language understandable. S/he also assists them by interpreting pupil responses as an indicator of the effectiveness of the communication. Relating new knowledge to knowledge that the pupils already possess is another useful strategy in helping children towards understanding of concepts presented in the foreign language. Moreover, teachers make efforts to make their classroom talk comprehensible by modifying their speech in significant ways, such as by speaking more slowly, by emphasising key words or phrases, by using vocabulary that is more familiar to the pupils and by simplifying syntactic structures. They also attempt to use a wide range of paralinguistic devices, such as body language, gestures and facial expression to help the children associate language and meaning (Met, 1994).

Another way of trying to reduce some of the difficulties experienced by pupils learning through the medium of a second or foreign language is through careful planning and sequencing of activities. As Met (1994: 161) affirms, 'All good teachers must be good planners', but teachers who teach through a language which is not the student's first language need to carry out additional planning activities, such as sequencing content objectives according to the complexity of language skills required by the student; planning content lessons that contain language objectives, reminding teachers working in bilingual programmes that they cannot disclaim responsibility for their students' language learning as well as their conceptual development; planning instructional activities which move from being context-embedded and cognitively undemanding, to activities which are more cognitively demanding and rely on fewer external supports for meaning (context reduced) (Cummins, 1981).

Philip Hoare (2000) working in the context of immersion programmes in Hong Kong has observed the types of strategies teachers use at Junior High School level (12 years old) to help their students cope with learning Science through English. In dealing with new (mainly technical) vocabulary the two teachers in the study used translation of terms into Cantonese. They also checked student learning by requiring students to provide Cantonese equivalents for English terms or to provide a definition of key concepts. Another strategy used was the keeping of a science vocabulary notebook where students wrote down a synonym for the term, a definition and some additional language information.

In use of questioning, Hoare (2000) noted that one of the teachers he observed engaged in an 'ongoing dialogue with the class' characterised by a large number of teacher questions which helped to focus students' attention on the content under discussion. The teacher also modified questions by rephrasing them to help students understand and also to help students construct appropriate responses. In addition, he created a rich language environment in his classes by providing examples and analogies which helped to widen the students' thinking and add to the quality of the explanations.

Hoare (2000) concludes that it is important not to simplify language use to such an extent that the concepts are diminished. He maintains that it is also important to enrich classroom interaction in content teaching and learning so that students may be provided with a variety of means for their learning. He points out, however, that this rich language use also needs to be accompanied by 'explicit support for students' understanding and for their own use of the target language'.

The question of evaluation raised in Case 13.19 has been discussed in some depth by Brinton et al. (1989). They see what they term 'content based instruction' as leading to dual goals: the learning of another language and the mastery of content knowledge. Thus, teachers need to be continually aware of 'the interface between language and content in evaluation' (Brinton et al., 1989: 183). A Science teacher cannot only restrict him or herself to testing how far the students have acquired scientific concepts but must also be involved, at least to a certain extent, in evaluating language development. In this sense, evaluation in bilingual education programmes differs greatly from evaluation for first language speakers where language learning is not at stake in the same way.

Met (1994) suggests that problems of how to assess pupil conceptual mastery when they lack the linguistic means of demonstrating their knowledge my be overcome by such non-verbal strategies as acting out their knowledge, multiple choice test involving visual prompts, as well as by on-going classroom observation by the teacher. Brinton *et al.* (1989: 184) recommend using 'more frequent, briefer, and less demanding assignments' than those required of first language speakers.

The question of pacing in bilingual education programmes has not often been explicitly addressed, though Dodson and Thomas (1988) noted the temporary retardation of concept development of L2 beginners in total immersion programmes in Wales in relation to monolingual learners; this has also been observed in the Canadian immersion programmes as well (Baker, 1996). This thus implies that the pacing of bilingual programmes should reflect these differences, particularly during the initial stages of bilingual development.

Language and Culture

The interrelationships between language and culture is an area which also particularly concerned teacher-respondents in bilingual schools in Colombia. One teacher remarked on what she saw as a Latin tendency to talk all the time and not to listen to what others had to say. Another referred to problems using textbooks designed for first language speakers in particular cultural settings, such as the United States or Britain. A third teacher remarked on how parental values affected children's perceptions of foreign languages and cultures. We will now look at these ideas in more detail.

Case 13.21   Cultural norms

One of the foreign (British) teachers in a Colombian English–Spanish bilingual programme noted that children constantly used their first language (Spanish) in her classes, in spite of all her efforts to get them to speak to her in English. She attributed this to a lack of concentration on their part and a desire to talk all the time. In her opinion, this was a cultural problem. She explains, 'I don't believe that they (the children) feel English is an important part of the curriculum. They like to talk and concentration is a big problem for many children. It is a cultural thing to talk all the time and not to listen carefully to others and respect what they have to say.' The teacher said that she had tried to encourage the children to speak only English in her classes, but had had very little success.

Case 13.22   Cultural elements and textbooks

A primary school teacher in an English–Spanish bilingual programme in Cali (Colombia) said that she found it difficult to handle cultural elements from both the children's native cultural background and from the foreign culture in teaching content areas, such as Social Science. The textbooks used in the school came from the USA or the UK and were aimed at ESL rather than EFL learners. Thus there were

*many 'cultural capsules' which foreign language students found difficult to inter-
pret, as many of the students had not had any direct contact with the foreign culture.
As she saw it, 'Our students are learning EFL and that makes a difference. Some of
them haven't had any direct contact with the second culture, therefore those
"capsules" can cause more confusion than clarity'. The strategy the teacher used to
try to help her pupils make sense of these aspects was to get them to make contrast
with similar cultural aspects in Colombia, so that the students could make a connection with something they were familiar with. She said that her task was made easier
if a native-speaker from an English-speaking cultural group was present in the classroom.*

Case 13.23   Children's foreign language and culture preference

*A teacher in Cali (Colombia) reported that some children had a definite preference for
anything to do with the foreign language (English), rather than the first language
(Spanish). She attributed this to the fact that many families give US culture high
priority and see it as superior to Colombian customs and ways of behaving. The
teacher felt it was important that the school should give weight to the home culture of
the students as well as the foreign culture, and demonstrate the advantages of
knowing the similarities and differences of both cultural systems.*

An important factor to take into consideration in bilingual programmes which
necessarily involve some degree of contact with other cultures is how far the teacher
is culturally attuned to the students, especially in the initial stages of schooling. This
awareness will involve taking into account the values commonly associated with
foreign cultures by parents and relatives. The advantages of employing native
speakers of the foreign or second language in terms of models for language acquisition, particularly in the area of pronunciation, must be weighed up against their
ability to relate to the children in their care, both linguistically and culturally. In this
respect, the Canadian early immersion programmes have always insisted on the
need for teachers of the initial grades to be bilingual in both French and English, so
that they can understand and help children in difficulty. What has not often been
stressed is the need for intercultural understanding.

Many teachers dealing with cultural aspects in their everyday practice are often
not very aware of the implications of such aspects for their learners. They may be
native speakers of the foreign or second language and yet not be 'intercultural
speakers' (Byram, 1998: 113). Thus, the first step is to raise their awareness of these
issues. Byram (1998) suggests various ways that intercultural consciousness can be
developed in bilingual classrooms, such as comparative analysis in pedagogically
appropriate ways of how different languages express different cultures; understanding by the teacher of ways in which the explicit introduction of cultural

elements from other cultures relativises and challenges what is taken for granted in the national or state curriculum; and that teachers should have developed 'intercultural speaker intuitions' (Byram, 1998: 113).

Furthermore, methodological implications of adopting an intercultural, comparative perspective involve such questions as: whether it is better to juxtapose conflicting views of different cultural practices or whether it is more appropriate to complement accepted cultural views with other, different versions and how to incorporate this within the available materials.

Child and Adolescent Development

Up to now, we have been concentrating on pedagogical issues related mainly to linguistic and conceptual development in bilingual education settings. In this section we will examine questions relating to problems of classroom control, initial experiences of bilingual schooling, and the reluctance of many adolescents to use the foreign or second language. Each of these areas will be exemplified by specific cases reported by teacher respondents. The first two refer to primary school situations in Spain and Switzerland; the third case comes from a pre school teacher in Colombia and the last two refer to secondary or high school experiences in Finland and Colombia.

Case 13.24   *Use of foreign language and problems of classroom control*

The problem reported in this case was that of a primary school teacher in an English–Spanish immersion programme in Cadiz (Spain). She said that foreign language teachers at primary school level often had problems of class control because they were required to use the foreign language at all times. To combat this, she suggests, 'Engage support from Spanish (first language) teachers'. However, the respondent also said that if both languages were used in the classroom for purposes of classroom control, she felt that the children would refuse to use the foreign language for communication.

Case 13.25   *Noisy classes*

A teacher-trainer in Valais, a bilingual canton in the French part of Switzerland, working with German–French immersion programmes at primary level said, 'Teachers report that immersion classes are noisier than others because the "average difficulty" aimed at by the teachers provokes a lack of concentration of the "good" and the "bad" pupils (by under- and over-challenge)'. If the students did not get the message at once in the foreign language, instead of listening and participating they engaged in side-discussions, disturbing behaviour, etc. She reported that another related difficulty stemmed from the fact that the French teachers often did not under-

> stand the Swiss-German variety used by the students, so they complained that some
> pupils laughed at them in Swiss-German behind their back. This also led to distur-
> bance in the class.
>   The ways teachers had tried to cope with this was by establishing 'didactic
> contracts'. In other words, 'teachers and pupils set common rules for the whole class'.
> Furthermore, during in-service teacher training they were shown strategies indi-
> cating how to capture the attention of the pupils (working in smaller groups,
> interesting themes) to avoid difficulties of class control. All non-German teachers
> were advised to learn German, but since the variety taught was standard German,
> not the local Swiss-German used in everyday communication, this continued to be
> problematic for many staff.

As any teacher knows, problems of classroom control are not restricted to bilingual education programmes. They are part of the teaching and learning process,
particularly at primary and secondary school level. Strategies, such as group work,
or dividing learners into different areas depending on their linguistic level and
assigning differing tasks accordingly, can help to reduce the frustration often
engendered in heterogeneous classes, where the more able students feel 'held back'
by those whose language level is lower.

> **Case 13.26   Concentration**
>
> Various teachers in English–Spanish bilingual schools at pre school level in Cali
> (Colombia) reported that children at this level had difficulty in concentrating during
> activities conducted in the foreign language. As one teacher explained, 'I think chil-
> dren switch off after a certain time of hearing a foreign language'. Some teachers felt
> that this might be due to problems the children had in adapting to being at school for
> the first time, or because it was the first time that they had come into contact with the
> foreign language on a regular basis. The teachers recommended motivating the chil-
> dren to continue using the foreign language by means of such pleasurable activities
> as games and songs, and also by teachers carefully planning and sequencing activi-
> ties to provide variety. Another idea proposed was for the teacher to work with small
> groups 'so that there is more control over the children to give quality time rather
> than quantity, and organise the lessons to be more varied'. Thus, the children would
> have an intense, but short time of instruction, followed by a lot of reinforcement.

Wode (2000) observes that teachers in bilingual programmes at the level of
preschool need to contextualise the use of the new language as much as possible.
The reason for this is that children need situational and contextual cues to be able to
acquire the language input they are exposed to. The researcher notes that this
contextualisation involves the same kind of techniques which are familiar from

good preschool teaching, emphasising the fact that bilingual teachers at this level need to be first and foremost trained to teach preschool children, with knowledge of how to cope with the short attention spans and the restlessness characteristic of pupils at this age.

In the two cases reported below, teachers in Colombia and Finland describe the particular problems experienced by adolescents in bilingual education programmes. At this stage, students sometimes refuse to use the school language or express a wish to be like the majority of students who are not in a bilingual situation.

Case 13.27   Self consciousness in using the foreign language

Three teachers in English–Spanish bilingual schools in Cali (Colombia) referred to the fact that teenagers were often reluctant to speak English in front of their classmates. The reasons given for this were self-consciousness, peer pressure not to use the foreign language, low self-esteem, poor foreign language skills, and feelings of intimidation and embarrassment. The teachers had tried to help the students overcome these feelings in various ways, such as creating a comfortable environment within the classroom and giving the students the confidence to face their mistakes; by providing constant incentives and motivation to raise self-esteem; and by creating an English-speaking atmosphere in the classroom. They felt that they had been fairly successful in this endeavour, but pointed out that the students were very conscious of the fact that it was much easier to communicate in their first language and so had to be constantly encouraged to use the foreign language. Some teachers also said that the proficiency level of the English teachers themselves was not high and that they refrained from talking in English to the students 'to avoid being laughed at by them'.

Case 13.28   Student desire not to be different

In the Swedish–Finnish immersion programme in Vaasa (Finland) three secondary teachers reported that some students, especially in Grade 7, refused to use Swedish during the lessons. They explained this by saying that these adolescents were rejecting their parents' choice for them of Swedish immersion and were manifesting a desire to be like the other students in the mainstream Finnish programme in the school. The teachers had tried to combat this tendency by asking them to reformulate what they said originally in Finnish in Swedish, by such strategies as: 'How do you say it in Swedish?', 'What did you say?', 'I didn't hear you'. In these ways they accepted the students' contribution to the classroom interaction but indicated that these were given in the 'wrong' language. They reported moderate success with these endeavours, saying that they as teachers were very persistent and that as the students were in the immersion programme they had to become proficient in the immersion language. As one of the teachers said, 'They are in immersion, they must learn the language, we don't give up'.

One of the ways that adolescents sometimes assert their difference with the status quo is by refusing to speak the foreign or second language that they have developed during their primary school years (Nussbaum, 1991). To a certain extent, this may be related not only to the rebelliousness typical of adolescence but also from the fear of being different from their monolingual peers. This tendency is also often combined with a lowering of the amount of contact with the foreign or second language in bilingual programmes at high school level. As a developing sense of identity and difference is characteristic of this stage, it would seem appropriate to extend discussion on the social construction of identities and cultural practices, in an attempt to place the learning of foreign languages and cultures in a different, wider perspective. Furthermore, direct contact with people from other cultures by means of visits or exchanges would help to give students a more realistic appreciation of their language proficiency level.

Parental Involvement

Parental involvement and interest in their children's progress is important at all stages of schooling, but particularly at preschool and primary level when children are making the transition from home to school. However, some parents seem to feel that once they have placed their sons and daughters in a bilingual school, their responsibility is ended. This constitutes problems for the teachers, as can be seen in Case 13.29. Another difficulty related to parents refers to the opposite situation: parents who are over-anxious about their children's language development and who pressure to have them removed prematurely from the ESL programme, as reported by a teacher in an International School in Brussels.

Case 13.29   Family involvement and parent interest

Two teachers working in English–Spanish bilingual schools in Cali (Colombia), where Spanish is the first language of the majority of the students, reported that the families of some of the young children in bilingual education programmes were not involved in the process, either because of lack of interest or lack of time. In fact, sometimes after enrolling their children in the bilingual programme their parents did not show any further interest in their foreign language learning process. The way the teachers attempted to solve the problem was to try to improve communication between home and school and to develop parents' consciousness of the need for close contacts with their children's teachers. They also encouraged the children to use phrases, words and songs in the foreign language and thus to create a school–home motivation to use the foreign language in a spontaneous fashion.

Case 13.30   Premature removal from ESL programme

This case was described by a teacher working in the International School of Brussels (Belgium), where English is the first language of the majority of the students in the school, although the languages of the host country are French and Flemish. The school aims at providing a supportive learning environment, where students will acquire a level of social and academic English which will allow them to achieve success in all areas of school life.

The teacher reported that due to a belief among parents that young children can absorb languages very easily and also because of a lack of understanding about the possible down-side of exposure to a variety of languages before literacy is established in one, some parents pressurised teachers to remove their children from the ESL programme into the mainstream programme too soon. As she says, 'There is pressure from parents to move children out of the ESL programme and into French before their language skills are sufficiently solid.' The way the school has responded to this issue has been to organise presentations on the matter for parents, and to stimulate discussion at parent-teacher conferences. The teacher reported that the situation was improving, but that it was difficult to convince some parents that their children needed sufficient time in the ESL programme before moving to French. She recognised the need for a solid body of research on multilingualism on young children, as much of the current understanding of these matters by teachers in the school was based on observation and experience, but was not backed up by research findings.

In a recent paper, Wode (2000) states that, 'Although bilingual preschools are not infrequent, they are rarely, if ever, studied scientifically in the way required for . . . this paper'. This lack of research evidence, also referred to by the teacher in the International School of Brussels, means that often parents' expectations are set unrealistically high in relation to how fast their children can acquire another language. As Wode (2000: 3) warns, 'Although it is customarily believed that young children can learn additional languages fast and at native-like levels of competence, this does not mean that it may take only a year or two for their pronunciation to become native-like'.

As well as the need to educate parents about the realities of young children's rate and level of second or foreign language acquisition it is also important to recognise that bilingual preschool programmes involve the same considerations as monolingual ones, with the only difference being the use of another language. Thus, the support of parents in helping their children maintain contact with and enthusiasm for the new language is vital, just as their support is vital in helping young children adapt to the new experience of being at school.

Material and Human Resources

The first part of this section will focus on what several teachers see as a real problem in elite bilingual programmes, the lack of suitable materials both from the point of view of language level and from the point of view of content. In some cases, teachers have been forced to make their own material to supplement the deficiencies of printed sources, as teachers in the Swedish immersion programme in Finland report. In Canada, too, a teacher working in French immersion complains of a lack of suitable textbook material.

Case 13.31 Teacher-produced materials

One of the difficulties encountered by a teacher in a Swedish–Finnish immersion school at primary level was to find suitable materials for use in the programme. Teachers had found that it was necessary to develop their own materials, as the commercially produced materials were directed at first language speakers of Swedish in Sweden and were not suitable either in content or language for second language Finnish learners. Although teacher-made materials often led to good results, developing them was very time-consuming and made inroads into the teachers' free time as 'planning and material-making are done outside of teaching time in Finland'.

The teacher felt that a key to solving this difficulty was the new immersion centre, due to be set up at the Centre for Continuing Education at the University of Vaasa (Finland). The Centre had received government financing for a specialist teacher to produce and develop materials specifically for the immersion programme and to make these available to those teachers who requested help in this area.

Case 13.32 Materials in specialised content areas

In the Swedish–Finnish immersion programme in Vaasa (Finland) some of the secondary school teachers complained of the lack of appropriate material in Swedish as a second language, as they had found that commercial textbooks designed for first language speakers of the language were too difficult for their students. Furthermore, the content of textbooks in some areas, such as Social Studies, had to be different from texts used in Sweden, due to difference of historical and geographical concerns. The way that the teachers had come to terms with the situation was to design their own material taken from magazines, newspapers, etc. They thought that, in general, this material had led to good results in student learning and had stimulated the students to carry out research in groups on different topics. They noted 'the students are familiar with working in groups and like researching information'.

Case 13.33   Lack of textbooks and Ministry of Education guidelines

The problem of suitable textbooks and Ministry of Education guidelines for immersion programmes in Canada was raised by a high school teacher in a French late immersion programme. He said the reason for this was that immersion was still relatively new and therefore there was only a small demand for textbooks for the immersion market. Furthermore, there was 'not much training in writing curriculum for French immersion'. The teacher had tried to solve this problem by 'blending English First Language and French First Language ministry guidelines as well as texts to create courses of study'. The results have been evaluated as only moderately successful, as much of what was created was still too demanding for the level of the immersion students.

The question of the availability of appropriate teaching material is a vital issue in any type of teaching and learning situation. In bilingual education programmes there are additional complications as recognised by Willets and Christian (1990: 233) who note that in the US context, 'The hardest task for any program, it seems, is to find integrated language and content materials . . . that coincide with locally adopted texts and district requirements'.

Met (1994: 165) agrees with the observation of Case Study 13.32, that commercially produced materials are usually not appropriate 'for students learning content in a language new to them'. There is usually a mismatch between the linguistic levels and levels of cognitive maturity assumed by the commercial material writers, as well as the potential complications of unfamiliar cultural settings. The basic decision to be made is whether teachers should adapt existing materials to their own situations or whether they should develop their own. There are advantages and disadvantages in both positions. While commercially produced materials are less appropriate for particular contexts, they are often more visually sophisticated and appealing than teacher-produced materials and vice versa.

It should also be noted that producing material requires time and dedication on the part of the teachers concerned and that this needs to be recognised at an institutional level. As Brinton *et al.* (1989: 22) point out, one of the key implications of adopting a content-based approach in bilingual programmes is that there is release time set aside for the development of curriculum and materials or that there is 'support and remuneration for extensive coordination and for materials and curriculum design'.

In the second part of this section we will concentrate on problems related to teacher training and development, especially in the area of content teaching and immersion methodology, as reported by teachers in Colombia and Finland.

Case 13.34   Bilingual training courses for content area teachers

Two primary school teachers in Cali (Colombia) commented on the problem schools have in finding bilingual teachers who have been trained to teach subject areas through the medium of a foreign language. One teacher felt that this training in specialised areas had to be done outside Colombia, while the other saw it mainly as a financial problem for schools which could not afford to hire bilingual subject teachers, who could request higher salaries due to demand for their services. The schools had tried to solve this problem by, on one hand, hiring people with degrees in related areas, such as bilingual engineers with teaching experience to teach Maths. Another solution, especially at primary level, was to hire foreign language specialists and then send them on in-service courses to increase their grasp of content area requirements. However, one of the teachers observed that 'the lack of formal training causes problems for both the students and the empirical teacher'.

Case 13.35   Change over of teaching staff

A teacher working in an English–Spanish bilingual school in Cali (Colombia) observed that because the foreign (non-Colombian) staff came from teaching monolingual first language speakers of English they usually did not have much understanding of the nature of bilingual education programmes in Colombia. In addition, they were hired on short two-year contracts and often found it difficult to accept cultural differences in the school community. Because of the temporary nature of their appointment the foreign staff tended to be more aware of the problems of the institution, rather than the improvements that had taken place over the years. The way the school had tried to come to terms with this was to create policy documents relating to the teaching of the foreign language, 'to try to develop consistency in approaches and so that teachers are aware of the strategies used'.

Case 13.36   Lack of teacher knowledge about immersion

A preschool teacher working in the Swedish immersion programme in Vaasa (Finland) observed, 'Not all teachers in immersion really know what immersion is'. She considered that many such teachers tended to treat the pupils as first rather than second language learners and considered that 'they need to understand that these children are not Swedish. Many teachers teach very fast and therefore limit the children's output'. She considered that more information and practical workshops about how to teach in immersion programmes were necessary and complained that 'teachers want to have "recipes" so they don't have to think for themselves'.

Lack of suitably qualified and experienced teachers is an area of difficulty which is not unique to bilingual schools, but is sometimes accentuated by the need to hire trained subject specialist teachers who are bilingual. Often, there are relatively few practitioners with this profile who are available to teach. Thus, institutions need to consider other alternatives to help overcome these staffing difficulties.

One way of supplementing the supply of trained bilingual subject specialists is to institute a team-teaching approach involving bilingual language teachers and monolingual subject specialists. However, the success of this modality depends on close consultation and joint planning between the two teachers involved so that the resulting programme is coherent and pays sufficient attention to the development of aspects relating to both language and content areas.

In order that practitioners' intuitions may be directed along appropriate paths and to encourage classroom initiatives informed by current theory in the area of bilingual education, on-going teacher development is being increasing seen as vital to the success of bilingual education programmes.

Although these concerns are not new, particularly in immersion research (see Harley *et al.*, 1990; Johnson & Swain, 1997) there has been little published research in the area. In 1992, Bernhardt and Schrier discussed the development of immersion teachers in relation to a prototype training model developed in the US which consisted of interweaving university-based experiences in second language research, classroom management, curriculum and public policy with field-based experiences in these same four areas. In this way, it was felt that theory would walk hand in hand with practice.

In 2000, Philip Hoare and Stella Kong in Hong Kong carried out a study into language-related attributes (i.e. language-related knowledge, skills and attitudes) for English immersion teachers in Hong Kong and how these have been used to inform a specialised in-service teacher education course set up at the Hong Kong Institute of Education. These authors used two main sources for their construction of a general framework of language-related attributes for immersion teachers: theories of second language learning which explain how immersion education can help students develop high levels of bilingualism, and experiences of implementation in different immersion contexts which focus on the constraints inherent in specific situations.

As a result of their analysis, the two researchers postulate six basic attributes required by immersion teachers in general: bilingual proficiency; immersion teaching strategies aimed at integrating language and content across the curriculum; knowledge of the target language system; understanding of the theories of second language learning and immersion education; commitment to immersion education; and knowledge of the target culture (Hoare & Kong, 2000).

The in-service teacher education course at the Hong Kong Institute of Education caters mainly for Mathematics or Science specialists. It integrates development of the six attributes referred to above within two main strands: a curriculum strand and a language development strand and focuses on such issues as: the principles underlying 'the judicious use of Cantonese as a resource in English immersion content subject classes to support the use and learning of English' (Hoare & Kong, 2000: 10), the provision of language support in teaching, an understanding of language in education policies in Hong Kong, and the rationale behind immersion education and its application in the specific context of Hong Kong.

These two initiatives point to the need for teacher education and development provision which are specifically directed towards the needs of teachers who are working in elite bilingual programmes in particular contexts, helping them to see general theoretical principles of language learning in relation to specific contextual issues and in developing critical insights towards their own pedagogical practices.

Conclusion

In this chapter we have examined issues related to bilingual pedagogy and practice as reported by teachers working in elite bilingual education contexts in different parts of the world. By adopting an approach which highlights specific cases in particular situations we have initially situated the discussion in terms of the particularities of individual teachers and their learners in specific classrooms. In other words, we have been at pains to convey the voices of teachers sharing from their experience of the day-to-day reality of their work in bilingual classrooms, rather than the observations of researchers. The comments at the end of each section have been aimed at widening the focus of the cases presented to cover aspects of bilingual practice which have been seen as common to different contexts of implementation.

In the literature on elite bilingual programmes there is little documentation of how teachers in different international contexts see their classroom practice and what problems they face in their teaching. In this chapter what has emerged clearly from the cases sent in, is that while institutional bilingualism can lead to high levels of student proficiency in the use of two or more languages, there are many cases which document a different scenario. The basic unreality of simulating an 'immersion', either total or partial, in a language other than the student's first language, combined with teachers' frequent insistence that they do not speak the students' mother tongue, when there is clear evidence to the contrary, points to the difficulty in maintaining the fiction of a specially created foreign language environment within schools and other educational institutions. The question of motivation in these circumstances becomes all-important.

While parents who send their children to what are often expensive bilingual education programmes are usually highly motivated and concerned about their off-springs' future success, students at secondary or high school level often experience the frustration of a 'plateau' period where they do not appear to be advancing in their language learning process. The other, opposite scenario, documented in some of the cases in this chapter, is that students may have an over-optimistic view of their language proficiency level and feel that they do not have to make any further efforts to improve. In both cases, it falls to teachers to help students come to terms with a realistic view of their skills and abilities in two or more languages, as well as encouraging them in difficult moments during the process. An international forum where teachers working in different types of elite or prestigious bilingual programmes could air their views and learn from the experience of other colleagues, would seem to be a useful development.

It is also important to recognise, as we did in Chapter 1, that while local contextual factors directly affect and 'constrain' aspects of bilingual pedagogy, there are certain common threads running through the individual cases which may profitably be discussed in relation to wider pedagogical issues such as, how to ensure appropriate parental involvement in the transition from home to school; how to get teachers from different backgrounds and different areas of specialisation to work together; how to manage classroom control; and how to deal with a lack of suitable teaching material. This helps us to remember that bilingual pedagogy is a sub-branch of general pedagogy and that teachers in bilingual programmes are first and foremost educators, and secondly bilingual language specialists.

Note

1. *The Bilingual Family Newsletter* is pubished four times a year by Multilingual Matters, Frankfurt Lodge, Clevedon Hall, Victoria Road, Clevedon, England BS21 7HH (http: / / www.multilingual-matters.com).

Chapter 14

Conclusions and Future Perspectives on Practice and Research in Elite Bilingual Education

Introduction

In this final chapter of the book, I will integrate and foreground some of the main strands which have been interwoven throughout the previous discussions. In weaving, it is said that while the weaver is in the process of combining colours and threads, and concentrating on individual details, it is impossible to get a perspective on the total effect of design and colour and how the individual aspects blend together and contribute to the whole. This is the purpose of the final chapter – to step back and view the tapestry as a whole. In addition, I will indicate further perspectives and lines of enquiry that may profitably be pursued in the future. I will also make recommendations for effective policy and practice in the area of elite bilingual education which follow from the general discussion,

Dominant Themes and Issues

My brief in this book, as expressed in the original proposal formulated by the series editors, Nancy Hornberger and Colin Baker in 1997, has been to 'write comprehensively about the 'state of elite bilingual education' in a . . . global sense'. One of the dangers in trying to write comprehensively is the possibility of providing only superficial coverage of the issues involved. I have tried to avoid this by dividing the book into two main sections, Part 1 (Chapters 1–6) where I have concentrated on general perspectives and issues which may be of interest to teachers, students, and researchers in the area of elite bilingualism, and Part 2

(Chapters 7–13) where I have focused on aspects of elite bilingual education provision in specific contexts of implementation. In Part 1, some of the themes which have been developed are: the different educational responses that have arisen to cater for the requirements of highly mobile, higher socio-economic status students who need to be fluent in more than one international language; a classification of different types of elite bilingual education provision; a definition of terms used in the book; characteristics of bilingual classroom interaction; the development of intercultural and cross-cultural understandings; multiple identities and their relationships with nationality; intercultural education and the development of intercultural competence; cross-cultural understandings and perceptions in international business communication; as well as a consideration of the different roles and relationships developed by students, teachers, parents and administrators in different types of bilingual education programmes.

Chapter 6 was positioned as a transitional chapter, which on one hand traces the development of research in the field of elite or prestigious bilingualism, and on the other, describes a collaborative research project aimed at the construction of a bilingual curriculum in an elite context, within a climate of empowerment among the participants. It thus combines a focus on general perspectives on research issues with an emphasis on one particular research experience in the field.

In the following chapters in the book, Chapters 7–11, the emphasis has been on developments in elite bilingualism and bilingual education in specific contexts of implementation. Thus, the socio-historical and educational circumstances which have led to the creation of different types of educational provision in selected countries in the five continents have been analysed. This leads on to a consideration of the contribution of a critical discourse analysis approach to policy and practice in elite bilingual settings in Chapter 12, followed by an examination of issues relating to bilingual pedagogy and practice, as reported by teachers working in elite bilingual education programmes in different parts of the world in Chapter 13. The grounded nature of the discussion in this second section of the book has been reinforced by a selection of case sketches which exemplify specific examples of how different participants and institutions have responded to the challenges posed by the need and/or the desire to become bilingual or multilingual.

Globalisation and localisation

As can be seen in this brief review of themes and issues, there has been a conscious attempt to deal with the tension generated between globalising, internationalising forces, promoting increasing mobility and enhanced communications and the need to become bilingual or multilingual in an ever-shrinking global marketplace, and the influence of local contextual factors in constraining and shaping the type of opportunities available to achieve these aims in the light of national, regional or institutional policies and philosophies.

It is, nevertheless, important to take into account that the notion of 'tension' in relationships between globalisation and localisation is not an absolute. Robertson (1995: 40) maintains that, 'globalization – in the broadest sense, the compression of the world – has involved and increasingly involves the creation and the incorporation of locality, processes which themselves largely shape, in turn, the compression of the world as a whole'. Thus, in this view, the forces of globalisation and the forces of localisation can been seen not only as opposing tendencies, but as 'complementary and interpenetrative; even though they certainly can and do collide in concrete situations' (Robertson, 1995: 40).

A consideration of the mutual interrelationships between 'global' and 'local' helps to situate the reader within a vision which goes beyond the immediate context of implementation and yet remains anchored in the situational realities of how parents in different parts of the world strive to provide their children with access to valued linguistic and cultural resources which they believe will enable their sons and daughters to be successful in the future.

In this connection, it is important to recognise the need to avoid the trivialisation and the reduction of subtle understandings and insights to generalisations and stereotypes, as noted by Fishman (1977, cited in García, 1991) and Byram (1997). Direct application of general linguistic and educational principles to decisions involving classroom language use without considering key aspects of the sociocultural, economic and political context of implementation, as reflected in specific classroom ecologies and language use outside the classroom, may be insufficient to ensure appropriate bilingual or multilingual development in these situations.

Language, power and processes of empowerment

Another of the interwoven strands evident throughout the book has been the relationships between language, power and processes of empowerment in elite bilingualism and bilingual education. As Bourdieu (1982, 1991), Fairclough (1989, 1992), Cummins (2000) and others have recognised, there are various modalities in which power can be exercised. As well as physical force or coercion, power may be exercised 'through the manufacture of consent to, or at least acquiescence towards it' (Fairclough, 1989: 4). Furthermore, power may also be characterised in terms of the possibility of developing critical consciousness about the influence of the relationships of domination and the ability to position oneself differently in daily social relationships (Gieve & Magalhaes, 1994).

In different sections of this book (Chapters 2, 6, and 12, in particular) we have been concerned to focus on issues of power in relation to the conceptualisation of language as a symbolic resource which can receive different values depending on the marketplace of social interaction. Equally, we have considered the role played by education in providing selective access to prized symbolic resources, such as bilingualism and multilingualism in prestigious world languages.

Just as these values are not absolute, it is also possible to modify established hierarchical educational practices through collaborative research processes, where the focus is on a redistribution of the unequal power relations, expert–non-expert, traditionally accepted as normal in research projects involving teachers and university professors in the field of elite bilingual education. In this type of project, according to guidelines established by Cameron *et al*. (1992), the emphasis has been on the active participation of all participants in the research process and a recognition of their capacity to assume a greater role and responsibility for decision making, not only during the project itself, but also in subsequent processes of change and modification. In other words, we have tried to demonstrate how it is possible to facilitate the process of participant empowerment by questioning the vertical nature of the roles established between researcher and researched and opening up the possibility of wider action.

In addition, we have been concerned to incorporate a critical discourse analytical perspective into a discussion of different discourse types associated with elite bilingual education, in an attempt to raise consciousness about ways in which selected educational documents have been constructed and how they reproduce and legitimise, either directly or indirectly, existing power relations designed to support the established *status quo*. We have also discussed how these types of insights may be related to the pragmatics of policy making and school practice.

Interdisciplinary approaches to elite bilingualism and bilingual education

Another key strand developed in this book has been the importance of seeing elite bilingualism and bilingual education as an interdisciplinary field where political, linguistic, sociolinguistic, psycholinguistic and educational concerns meet, and where individual researchers have pursued their academic interests in the interrelations between individual disciplines. The changing, developmental nature of these concerns has also been addressed, as exemplified in the case of the Canadian immersion researchers. Writing in 1990, Tosi characterised the main thrust of immersion research in Canada as operating 'within the psychometric tradition which attempted to demonstrate the educational value of bilingualism' relating to 'pedagogically oriented theory that would immediately influence curricula and classroom instruction' (Tosi, 1990: 109–10). He saw these concerns in contrast to sociolinguistic-oriented work on bilingualism as exemplifed in the work of Martin-Jones and Romaine (1986) which 'sought to create a humanistic impact on people's attitudes and on language status' (Tosi, 1990: 110). As we have seen in Chapter 6, recently there has been evidence of changing perspectives within immersion research which have focused more on qualitative, process-oriented projects. In this respect, it is also important to bear in mind the notion of continua (Hornberger, 1989; Hornberger & Skilton-Sylvester, 2000), introduced in Chapter 2 to demonstrate the interrelatedness and complexity of the phenomena of bilingualism and bilingual education rather than focusing on discrete, individual aspects.

Further Lines of Enquiry

In this section we will discuss the issues and areas of research which would seem to be indicated by the developments charted in this book in relation to elite bilingualism and bilingual education. We will particularly focus on issues to do with International School and European School education, but will also draw links between research into these manifestations of elite bilingual provision and research into aspects of bilingual pedagogy, classroom discourse and language use in bilingual education in general.

International Schools as bilingual education

As noted in Chapter 6, while research into immersion programmes is widespread and well-recognised, there has, as yet, been little research carried out into specific issues relating to International Schools. In part, this may be due to the perception noted in Chapter 2 that researchers may be studying a pampered minority (Harding & Riley, 1986) and that they would do better to involve themselves with 'more deserving' aspects of community bilingualism.

Recently, however, there is evidence to show that these perceptions are changing. In the University of Bath (UK) there currently exists a Centre for the Study of Education in an International Context, where researchers focus specifically on developments within international education, a category which includes both monolingual and bilingual International Schools, and offer students opportunities to undertake collaborative research projects in this area leading to MPhil, PhD and EdD degrees. The Centre also provides in-service workshops and seminars for teachers and administrators and offers opportunities for staff development through participation in modular M.A. degree schemes in Summer Schools and through distance learning.

Furthermore, the Third International Symposium on Bilingualism, organised by the University of the West of England in Bristol (UK) in April 2001, included the category of 'Elite Bilingualism' among one of the areas recognised as being of interest to researchers on bilingualism. Thus, it may be seen that the process of legitimating elite bilingualism and bilingual education as a worthy and appropriate object of study and enquiry within the field of bilingual studies has begun and it is hoped that future developments may lead to a consolidation of this area of research at international level.

Ethnographic research on elite bilingual education

Another line of enquiry, not restricted to studies in elite bilingualism but of interest to researchers in the area, relates to the importance of carrying out ethnographic research on aspects of elite bilingual education programmes within their sociocultural context. The importance of this type of research in relation to classroom language practices was recognised in the early 1980s by Zentella (1981: 130) when she observed, 'Until . . . an ethnographic approach is undertaken, it seems premature to ban codeswitching from the classroom when we do not know what we are banning along with it.' As result of this type of study in elite bilingual educational contexts, it is hoped that teachers may become more deeply aware of their classroom language and pedagogical practices, 'of how they and their pupils actually use the L1 and L2 in their teaching and learning, rather than how they think they *ought* to act' (de Mejía, 1994: 409). This process of informed consciousness-raising may well lead to the development of a classroom language policy, which could provide flexible guidelines for classroom language use and pedagogical practices, reflecting particular institutional needs (cf. Recommendations below).

Elite bilingual education programme types and contexts

Other key areas of further research indicated as a result of the discussion in this book involve issues of differential language use in different bilingual education programme types. Thus, for example, it would be interesting to examine in more depth how certain European Schools and some International Schools manage to promote high levels of multilingualism among their students, while the Canadian immersion programmes have been criticised by some researchers (Lyster, 1987; Met, 2000) as propitiating the development of artificial language use, 'a distinct interlanguage' (Lyster, 1987, cited in Kowal & Swain, 1998: 285), in their students. In this respect, the issue of student language use outside the school seems fundamental to the discussion (cf. the report on the European School Brussels I, Chapter 10). In addition, it would be valuable to carry out research on the so-called 'bilingual' International Schools and their 'monolingual' counterparts (Murphy, 1990), to establish how far bilingualism is actively promoted in individual school programmes, and how far schools consider it important to provide enrichment models of bilingual or multilingual education in order to help their students maintain, develop, and extend all their languages (Hornberger, 1991).

Throughout this book we have maintained that it is essential to consider the development of specific modalities of elite bilingual education in relation to their sociolinguistic and cultural context of implementation, also taking into account a historical perspective, as we have tried to do in the country profiles included in Chapters 7–11. In two handbooks for teachers in International Schools published recently (Murphy, 1990; Sears, 1998) the emphasis has been on providing 'the theoretical findings and practical applications that are relevant to mainstream teachers in International Schools' (Sears, 1998: 2) on a general level. Thus, the commonalties of highly diverse situations have been foregrounded. While this is a necessary strategy in order to provide material which is of interest to International School teachers in general, we would strongly argue for the need for studies to focus on specific forces which have led to the creation of particular types of elite bilingual education provision in different countries. As Coreen Sears (1998: 7) aptly remarks, 'International Schools develop in response to the needs of the expatriate communities that exist in a particular location. They vary in size, facilities, methods of funding, model of administration, type of programme and in the make up of their student body'. This essential variability helps to ensure their relevance to the community they serve and is also of interest to researchers in the field who are concerned with discussing their development.

Elite bilingualism, power and empowerment

A final important line of enquiry which has been discussed at various points throughout this book is that of the relationships between elite bilingualism, power and empowerment. This is an area which has not been greatly developed in relation to elite bilingualism. Rather, recent studies that have been carried out in the field of bilingualism (Heller, 1994; Martin-Jones & Heller, 1996; Freeman, 1998; Cummins, 2000; Heller & Martin Jones, 2001) have focused their discussion on language minority contexts. We would maintain that a focus on the relationships between bilingualism and power relations in majority language contexts would be an interesting contribution to the debate, in line with Pennycook's (1994, 1995) analyses of the cultural politics of English as a world language.

Recommendations for Effective Policy and Practice

In this section we will formulate a series of recommendations which follow from the discussions on policy and practice that have been sustained throughout this book. Some of these recommendations refer to national or international concerns, such as the drawing up of national policy guidelines with regard to institutional and classroom language use, the development of biliteracy and the position of cultural apects, and the need for an international forum to debate issues of interest to those who work in the field of elite bilingual education. Other recommendations are directed more at individual educational establishment in the hope that they will examine how far their institutional policies and practices facilitate the development of all their students' languages.

Formulate explicit bilingual policy statements based on empirical studies

We have examined a policy document (see the Brunei Minister of Education's address to the Bilingualism and National Development Conference, 1991, in Chapter 12) where national guidelines for the *Dwibahasa* (Malay–English) bilingual education policy were outlined. This is one of the few instances where an elite bilingual programme has been the subject of policy guidelines (another example in relation to prestigious bilingual education provision is the Catalan–Castillian bilingual programme, see Chapter 10). One of the recommendations we would make, therefore, is that bodies in charge of issues related to education and language planning in each country, after carrying out appropriate studies, should draw up national policy guidelines to inform those schools who wish to implement elite bilingual education programmes. This would have the advantage of ensuring a certain amount of homogeneity in a field characterised for its heterogeneous nature and would help educational establishments avoid some of the more common pitfalls involved in issues such as classroom language use, institutional language use, and the treatment of cultural elements. These policy documents would reflect current thinking on bilingual education at national and international level and would be liable to on-going modification according to contextual factors inherent in individual situations. Thus, they would act as flexible guidelines rather than rigid dictates.

Question monolingual classroom language practices in bilingual contexts

Another recommendation that would seem to be appropriate in the light of the discussions in this book is what may be seen as a 'common sense' approach to classroom language use based on monolingual criteria but used in potentially bilingual situations, i.e. when students have different first languages, should be re-examined in the light of what is known about bilingual and multilingual programmes for upwardly mobile students. In this way, traditional 'English medium' schools might consider the advantages of providing institutional support for their students' first languages, as well as their foreign or second languages. International exams, such as the International Baccalaureate, should also be examined, as recommended by Tosi (1989) to see how far they are actively promoting bilingualism or multi-lingualism, rather than monolingualism in an international language.

Situate classroom language use in wider local and global contexts of language use

A further recommendation, in line with Heller's (1990) call to see classroom language use in a wider context, is that classroom or institutional language use should not be considered in isolation, but within the context of wider community use, both nationally or in International School terms, from the point of view of the host nation and also in the context of the wider international or global community of which elite bilingual schools form a part. As has been seen in the European Schools' context and in the German immersion schools in Melbourne, Australia, if there are opportunities for interaction in all the students' languages outside the classroom, this can lead to a consolidation and an enrichment of institutional language in other domains, so that student language use is not restricted to exposure to academic discourse alone.

Furthermore, as we have noted in Chapter 4, elite bilingual schools are not islands which exist independently of local and international community contexts. As recognised by Heller and Martin-Jones (2001: 420) in relation to minority bilingual education provision, 'it is necessary to link the interactional and institutional order of schools and other educational institutions to the social order of communities and therefore to link the consequences of practices in educational settings to other social categories and processes'.

Increase the scope and reach of bilingual education teacher development

In Chapter 13 we noted in different parts of the world, in Hong Kong and Colombia, for example, the need for preservice and inservice teacher development programmes which specifically focus on questions related to bilingual education, such as the type of styles and strategies which help bilingual learners learn effectively in their particular situations. This is in line with a growing tendency to see bilingual provision not only in linguistic terms in relation to issues such as the relative ratios of language contact or the place of code-switching in elite bilingual programmes, but also in educational terms, where the role of the teacher as educator rather than linguist is foregrounded. As we have seen in the case of European Schools, teachers who are trained to work in national monolingual school systems have often not been trained to deal with the type of issues arising in bilingual or multilingual settings and therefore are in need of the support provided by teacher development programmes to help them become more effective in their work as bilingual educators.

Provide international opportunities to discuss issues related to elite bilingual education

Although there have been various initiatives within the elite bilingual education sector to provide opportunities for debate and discussion of common problems and issues (see for example, the European Council of International Schools (ECIS) annual conferences, and the European Conferences on Immersion Programmes), these tend to focus particularly on issues to do with one particular type of elite bilingual educational provision. There is also need for an international forum to discuss common concerns of research, policy and practice in elite bilingual education and to promote joint initiatives. Such developments would counteract long traditions of secrecy and isolation maintained by many schools, partly due to competitive reasons, but also because many have historically functioned as individual units and have not seen the need to participate in joint ventures. In this way, research on elite bilingual education would have the possibility of an open debate and this would help in the process of legitimisation of the field, referred to above.

Final Comments

In this book we have referred mainly, but not exclusively, to developments within elite bilingualism and bilingual education in relation to English, in situations where this language is either a second or foreign language. At times, we have also looked at native English speakers and their attempts to become bilingual or multilingual, as in the case of the French immersion programmes in Canada, and the German immersion programmes in Australia. Occasionally, we have considered the position of other languages, such as German in Colombia, French in Morocco, Swedish in Finland, and Catalan in Catalonia. A question that has not been addressed in any depth is the relationship of English to other majority languages in the context of elite bilingual education. We need to ask which are the languages associated with this type of educational provision and whether in the future the language balance is likely to remain the same.

Another important consideration is the question of the value of elite bilingualism and bilingual education in relation to the field of bilingualism studies as a whole. In this respect it is interesting to note that Joshua Fishman, well known for his work on endangered minority languages and community bilingualism, has also carried out research into the enrichment context of international elite bilingual schools within a vision of cultural pluralism. It can thus be argued that the study of elite bilingualism and bilingual education as discussed in this book is not just the concern of a tiny group, but makes an important contribution to the field of bilingual studies in general, because it enlarges the debate to include not only minority but also majority language speakers. In the words of Fishman (1977, cited in Garcia, 1991:

281), 'Enrichment bilingual education . . . gives an additional window on the world . . . Enrichment bilingual education has in mind the expansion of intellect and personality'. This expansion of intellect and personality is equally desirable for bilinguals from minority communities as it is for bilinguals from upwardly mobile, middle-class backgrounds.

References

Abdulaziz-Mkilifi, M.H. (1972) Triglossia and Swahili–English bilingualism in Tanzania. *Language in Society* 1 (1), 197–213.

Absalom, D. (1996) Immersion English in China. *AALIT Journal* 4, 6–10.

Adiv, E. (1984) An example of double immersion. In H.H. Stern (ed.) *The Immersion Phenomenon. Special Issue No. 12 of Language and Society*. Ottawa: Commissioner of Official Languages, 30–32.

Anderssohn, A. (1996) Question on pronunciation. *Bilingual Family Newsletter* 13 (4), 7.

Anderssohn, A. (1998) When intercultural families are also inter-faith families. *Bilingual Family Newsletter* 15 (2), 3.

Araújo, M.C.and Corominas, Y. (1996) Procesos de adquisición del Inglés como segunda lengua en niños de 5–6 años, de colegios bilingues de la ciudad de Cali. Cali: Universiad del Valle. Unpublished MA thesis.

Arenas i Sampera, J. (1986) *La Immersio Linguistica Escrits de Divulgacio*. Barcelona: La Llar del Llibre.

Arenas i Sampera, J. (1988) *La Llengua a L'ensenyament Primari als Països Catalans*. Barcelona: La Llar del Llibre.

Arenas i Samper, J. (1989) *Absencia i Recuperación de la Llengua Catalana a L'Ensenyament a Catalunya (1979–1983)*. Barcelona: La Llar del Llibre.

Arenas i Samper, J. (1992) *Language and Education in Catalonia Today*. Barcelona: Generalitat de Catalunya, Departament d'Ensenyament.

Armendáriz, A. (1999) On 'luminaries', reaching consensus and the quest for a local view. *ELT News and Views* 6.2, 12–13.

Arnau, J. and Boada, H. (1986) Languages and school in Catalonia. *Journal of Multilingual and Multicultural Development* 7 (2&3), 107–122.

Arnau, J., Comet, C., Serra, J.M. and Vila, I. (1992) *La Educación Bilingüe*. Barcelona: ICE/Horsori.

Arthur, J. (1994) Talking like teachers: Teacher and pupil discourse in Botswana classrooms. *Language, Culture and Curriculum* 7 (1), 29–40.

Artigal, J.M. (1990) El context compartit com a base de l' 'ús/adquisició'de la nova llengua. In *Primeres Jornades d'Ensenyament de la Llengua*. Barcelona: Universitat Autónoma de Barcelona.

Artigal, J.M. (1991) The Catalan immersion program: The joint creation of shared indexical territory. *Journal of Multilingual and Multicultural Development* 12 (1&2), 21–33.

Artigal, J.M. (1997) The Catalan immersion program. In R.K. Johnson and M. Swain (eds) *Immersion Education: International Perspectives*. Cambridge: Cambridge University Press.

Artigal, J.M. and Laurén, C. (1990) Immersion programmes in Catalonia and Finland. A comparative analysis of the motives for the establishment. In C. Laurén and S. Vesterbacka (eds) *Language Immersion School of Vaasa/Vasa*, Vaasa: University of Vaasa, School of Modern Languages.

Auerbach, E. (1995) The politics of the ESL classroom: Issues of power in pedagogical choices. In J. Tollefson (ed.) *Power and Equality in Language Education*. Cambridge: Cambridge University Press.

Baetens Beardsmore, H. (1979) Bilingual education for highly mobile children. *Language Problems and Language Planning* 3 (9), 138–55.

Baetens Beardsmore, H. (1986) *Bilingualism: Basic Principles*. Clevedon: Multilingual Matters.

Baetens Beardsmore, H. (1990) *Bilingualism in Education: Theory and Practice*. Brussels Preprints in Linguistics. Brussels: Vrije Universiteit Brussel & Université Libre de Bruxelles.

Baetens Beardsmore, H. (1991) Bilingual education. In J. Lynch, C. Modgil and S. Modgil (eds) *Cultural Diversity and the Schools: Consensus and Controversy*. Basingstoke: Falmer Press.

Baetens Beardsmore, H. (ed.) (1993a) *European Models of Bilingual Education*. Clevedon: Multilingual Matters.

Baetens Beardsmore, H. (1993b) European models of bilingual education: Practice, theory and development. In G. Jones and A.C. Ozóg (eds) *Bilingualism and National Development*. Clevedon: Multilingual Matters.

Baetens Beardsmore, H. (1993c) An overview of European models of bilingual education. *Language, Culture and Curriculum* 6 (3), 197–208.

Baetens Beardsmore, H. (1995) European models of bilingual education. In O. García and C. Baker (eds) *Policy and Practice in Bilingual Education. Extending the Foundations*. Clevedon: Multilingual Matters.

Baetens Beardsmore, H. (1999) Language policy and bilingual education in Brunei Darussalam. Paper presented at the session of the Royal Academy for Overseas Sciences, Class for Political and Moral Sciences, Palace of the Academies, Brussels, 14 December, 1999.

Baetens Beardsmore, H. and Swain, M. (1985) Designing bilingual education: Aspects of immersion and 'European School' models. *Journal of Multilingual and Multicultural Development* 6 (1), 1–15.

Baetens Beardsmore, H. and Anselmi, G. (1991) Code-switching in a heterogeneous, unstable, multilingual speech community. In European Scientific Network on Code-switching and Language Contact, *Papers for the Symposium on Code-switching in Bilingual Studies: Theory, Significance and Perspectives* 11. European Science Foundation.

Baker, C. (1988) *Key Issues in Bilingualism and Bilingual Education*. Clevedon: Multilingual Matters.

Baker, C. (1993) *Foundations of Bilingual Education and Bilingualism*. Clevedon: Multilingual Matters.

Baker, C. (1995) *A Parents' and Teachers' Guide to Bilingualism*. Clevedon: Multilingual Matters.

Baker, C. (1996) *Foundations of Bilingual Education and Bilingualism* (2nd edn). Clevedon: Multilingual Matters.

Baker, C. (2001) *Foundations of Bilingual Education and Bilingualism* (3rd edn). Clevedon: Multilingual Matters.

Baker, C and Prys Jones, S. (1998) *Encyclopaedia of Bilingualism and Bilingual Education*. Clevedon: Multilingual Matters.

Banfi, C. (1999) English teaching in the Cono Sur. *ELT News and Views* 6 (2), 6.

Banfi, C. and Day, R.A. 2001 'The Argentine chicken and the English egg': Bilingual schools and the itinerant elite. Paper presented at the 'Third International Symposium on Bilingualism', University of the West of England, Bristol, 18–20 April.

Barbour, S. (1996) Language and national identity in Europe: Theoretical and practical problems. In C. Hoffmann (ed.) *Language, Culture and Communication in Contemporary Europe*. Clevedon: Multilingual Matters.

Barrett, J. (1994) Why is English still the medium of education in Tanzanian secondary schools? *Language, Culture and Curriculum* 7 (1), 3–16.

Bauer, R.S. (1984) The Hong Kong Cantonese speech community. *Language Learning and Communication* 3 (3), 243–414.

Bel, A. (1990) Immersion programmes for teachers. In *Noticies del S.E.D.E.C.* Barcelona: Generalitát de Catalunya.

Bernhardt, E. (ed.) (1992) *Life in Language Immersion Classrooms*. Clevedon: Multilingual Matters.

Bernhardt, E. and Schrier, L. (1992) The development of immersion teachers. In E. Bernhardt (ed.) *Life in Language Immersion Classrooms.* Clevedon: Multilingual Matters.

Bickley, G. (1990) Attitudes towards English language learning in Hong Kong – Frederick Stewart's evidence. *World Englishes* 9, 289–300.

Bilger, C. (1997) Bilingual children's foreign language learning in school. *The Bilingual Family Newsletter* 14 (2), 5.

Bilingual Japan (1998) Focus on international marriage 7 (4), 8.

Bingham, D. (ed.) (1998) *The John Catt Guide to International Schools.* John Catt Educational Ltd.

Björkland, S. (1997) Immersion in the 1990s: A state of development and expansion. In R.K. Johnson and M. Swain (eds) *Immersion Education: International Perspectives.* Cambridge: Cambridge University Press.

Björklund, S. and Suni, I. (2000) The role of English as L3 in a Swedish immersion programme in Finland: Impacts on language teaching and language relations. In J. Cenoz and U. Jessner (eds) *English in Europe. The Acquisition of a Third Language.* Clevedon: Multilingual Matters.

Blanton, L.L. (1998) *Varied Voices on Language and Literacy Learning.* Boston: Heinle & Heinle.

Bodi, M. (1994) The changing role of minority languages in Australia: The European and the Asia-Pacific nexus. *Journal of Multilingual and Multicultural Development* 15 (2&3), 219–28.

Boix, E. (1990) Language choice and language switching among young people in Barcelona: Concepts, methods and data. In European Scientific Network on Code-switching and Language Contact *Papers for the Workshop on Concepts, Methodology and Data.* European Science Foundation.

Bostwick, R.M. (2001) Bilingual education of children in Japan: Year Four of a partial immersion programme. In M.G. Noguchi and S. Fotos (eds) *Studies in Japanese Bilingualism.* Clevedon: Multilingual Matters.

Bourdieu, P. (1977) The economics of linguistic exchange. *Social Science Information* 16 (6), 645–68.

Bourdieu, P. (1982) *Ce Que Parler Veut Dire.* Paris: Fayard.

Bourdieu, P. (1991) *Language and Symbolic Power.* Cambridge: Polity.

Bourjade, N. (2001) Bilingualism and mathematics. *Bilingual Family Newsletter* 18 (2), 6.

Braighlinn, G. (1992) *Ideological Innovation under Monarchy. Aspects of Legitimation Activity in Contemporary Brunei.* Amsterdam: VU University Press.

BRAZ-TESOL (1998) *Newsletter* June 1998.

Brinton, D.M., Snow, M.A. and Wesche, M.B. (1989) *Content-Based Second Language Instruction.* London: HarperCollins, Newbury House.

British Council (1989) *A Survey of English Language Teaching and Learning in Colombia: A Guide to the Market.* London: English Language Promotion Unit.

British Council (1995) *A Landmark Review of the Use, Teaching and Learning of English in the People's Republic of China.* London: The British Council.

British Council (1997a) *Landmark Review of ELT in Brazil 1997.* London: British Council.

British Council (1997b) *Landmark Review of ELT in Argentina 1997.* London: British Council.

Buitrago, H. (1997) La cultura en un programa de inmersión en la sección primaria de un colegio de Cali: Políticas y prácticas pedagógicas. Unpublished monograph study. Cali: Universidad del Valle.

Buss, M. and Mård, K. (2001) Swedish immersion in Finland – facts and figures. In S. Björkland (ed.) *Language as a Tool. Immersion Research and Practices.* Vaasa: University of Vaasa.

Byram, M. (1997) *Teaching and Assessing Intercultural Communicative Competence.* Clevedon: Multilingual Matters.

Byram, M. (1998) Cultural identities in multilingual classrooms. In J. Cenoz and F. Genesee (eds) *Beyond Bilingualism: Multilingualism and Multilingual Education.* Clevedon: Multilingual Matters.

Caldwell, J. (1995) The French immersion programme – Newcastle Faculty of Education, the

University of Newcastle. In *Conference Proceedings Second Biennial Conference, Australian Association of Language Immersion Teachers (AALIT)*.

Cambra Giné, M. (1991) Les changements de langue en classe de langue étrangère, re-évaluation d'une certaine organisation du discours. In *Papers for the Symposium on Code-switching in Bilingual Studies: Theory, Significance and Perspectives*. Strasbourg: E.S.F. Science Foundation.

Cameron, D., Frazer, E., Harvey, P., Rampton, M.B.H. and Richardson, K. (1992) *Researching Language. Issues of Power and Method*. London: Routledge.

Camillieri, C. (1985) *Antropología Cultural y Educación*. Paris: Unesco.

Carder, M. (1991) The role and development of ESL programmes in International Schools. In *The World Yearbook of Education*. Kogan Page.

Castañeda, R. (1996) El aprendizaje de una lengua extranjera: Un asunto de inter-culturalidad? Unpublished manuscript.

Cath, A (1994) Opening doors, wider horizons? A critical account of the inaugural address to BAND91. Unpublished manuscript.

Cath, A. (in progress) The language of Lower Secondary Science interaction. Research Project, Universiti Brunei Darussalam.

Cath, A. and McClellan, J. (forthcoming) 'Right. Let's do some ah, mm, speaking': Patterns of classroom interaction in Brunei Darussalam.

Cavalcanti, M. (1996) Collusion, resistance and reflexivity: Indigeneous teacher education in Brazil. *Linguistics and Education* 8, 175–88.

Ceballos, D. and Ceballos, I. (1993) La participación de los alemanes en el desarrollo de la educación en Colombia. In Mayr and Cabal (eds) *Presencia Alemana en Colombia*. Bogotá : Editorial Nomas S.A.

Centroa Colombiano de Eestudios en Lenguas Aborígenes (1989) *Memorias: Lingüística y Educación*. Bogotá: Universidad de los Andes.

Chapman, D. (1995) Acquisition through activity. In *Conference Proceedings Second Biennial Conference*. Australian Association of Language Immersion Teachers (AALIT).

Cheung, C. M. (forthcoming) 'Jing jyu jaa jiu, gwong dung waa jaa jiu': Code-switching practices in two bilingual classrooms in Hong Kong.

Cheung, Y. (1985) Power, solidarity and luxury in Hong Kong: A sociolinguistic study. *Anthropological Linguistics* 27, 190–203.

Clark, R., Fairclough, N.L., Ivanic, R. and Martin-Jones, M. (1987) Critical language awareness. *C.L.S.L. Working Papers*. Centre for Language in Social Life, Lancaster University.

Clark, R., Fairclough, N.L., Ivanic, R. and Martin-Jones, M. (1990) Critical language awareness Part I: A critical review of three approaches to language awareness. *Language and Education* 4 (4), 249–60.

Clark, R., Fairclough, N.L., Ivanic, R. and Martin-Jones, M. (1991) Critical language awareness Part II: Towards critical alternatives. *Language and Education* 5 (1), 41–54.

Clyne, M. (1991) Immersion principles in second language programs – research and policy in multicultural Australia. *Journal of Multilingual and Multicultural Development* 12 (1&2), 55–65.

Cochran-Smith, M. and Lytle, S.L. (1993) *Inside/Outside: Teacher Research and Knowledge*. New York: Teachers College, Columbia University.

Coffman, R. (1992) Immersion: A principal's perspective. In E. Bernhardt (ed.) *Life in Language Immersion Classrooms*. Clevedon: Multilingual Matters.

Colegio Alemán, Medellín (1994) *Anuario 1993–1994*. Medellín: Servigraficas.

Condon, D.L. (1993) Culture shock. *The Bilingual Family Newletter* 10 (2), 7.

Coulmas, F. (1992) *Language and Economy*. Oxford: Blackwell.

Criper, C. and Dodd, W.A. (1984) *Report on the Teaching of English Language and its Use as a Medium in Education in Tanzania*. Dar es Salaam: British Council.

Cross, R. (1995) From the other side of the desk: A student's perspective on a tertiary language and culture immersion program. In *Conference Proceedings Second Biennial Conference*. Australian Association of Language Immersion Teachers (AALIT).

Cumming, A. (ed.) (1994) Alternatives in TESOL research: Descriptive, interpretive and ideological orientations. *TESOL Quarterly* 28 (4), 673–703.

Cummins, J. (1980) The entry and exit fallacy in bilingual education. *NABE Journal* 4 (3), 25–59.

Cummins, J. (1981) The role of primary language development in promoting educational success for language minority students. In California State Department of Education (ed.) *Schooling and Language Minority Students. A Theoretical Framework*. Los Angeles: California State Department of Education.

Cummins, J. (1986) Empowering minority students: A framework for intervention. *Harvard Educational Review* 56 (1), 18–36.

Cummins, J. (1989) *Empowering Minority Students*. Sacramento, CA: California Association for Bilingual Education.

Cummins, J. (1991a) The politics of paranoia: Reflections on the bilingual education debate. In O. García (ed.) *Bilingual Education: Focusschrift in Honor of Joshua A. Fishman* (Volume 1). Amsterdam/Philadelphia: John Benjamins.

Cummins, J. (1991b) Forked tongue: The politics of bilingual education: A critique. *The Canadian Modern Language Review* 47 (4), 786–93.

Cummins, J. (1994) Knowledge, power and identity in teaching English as a second language. In F. Genesee (ed.) *Educating Second Language Children: The Whole Child, The Whole Curriculum, The Whole Community*. Cambridge: Cambridge University Press.

Cummins, J. (2000) *Language, Power and Pedagogy: Bilingual Children in the Crossfire*. Clevedon: Multilingual Matters.

de Courcy, M. (1997) Benowa High: A decade of French immersion in Australia. In R.K. Johnson and M. Swain (eds) *Immersion Education: International Perspectives*. Cambridge: Cambridge University Press.

de Courcy, M. (2002) *Experiences of Immersion Learning. Case Studies of Learners in French and Chinese Late Immersion Programs*. Clevedon: Multilingual Matters.

Delgado-Gaitan, C. (1990) *Literacy for Empowerment: The Role of Parents in Children's Education*. New York: Falmer.

de Moraes Menti, M. (1999) Brazil report. *E.L.T. News and Views* June 1999b Year 6 (2), 84.

Dodson, C.J. and Thomas, S.E. (1988) The effect of total L2 immersion education on concept development. *Journal of Multilingual and Multicultural Development* 9 (6), 467–85.

ECIS (1997/1998) *The International Schools Directory*. Suffolk: John Catt Educational Ltd.

Eckert, P. (1980) Diglossia: Separate and unequal. *Linguistics* 18, 1053–64.

Engel, D. (1997) *Passport USA*. California: World Trade Press.

Engel, D. and Murakami, K. (1996) *Passport Japan*. California: World Trade Press.

Escuela Escocesa San Andrés (1988) *Un Siglo y Medio Despues*. Argentina: Asociación Civil Escuela Escocesa San Andrés.

ESSARP (1995) *The Scholastic Association of the River Plate 1985–1995*. Buenos Aires: ESSARP.

Fabbro, F. (1999) *The Neurolinguistics of Bilingualism: An Introduction*. Hove, East Sussex: Psychology Press.

Faltis, C.J. (1989) Code-switching and bilingual schooling: An examination of Jacobson's 'New Concurrent Approach'. *Journal of Multilingual and Multicultural Development* 10, 117–27.

Fairclough, N. (1989) *Language and Power*. London: Longman.

Fairclough, N. (1992) *Discourse and Social Change*. London: Polity Press.

Fasold, R. (1984) *The Sociolinguistics of Society*. Oxford: Basil Blackwell.

Ferguson, C.A. (1959) Diglossia. In A. Dil (ed.) 1972 *Language Structure and Language Use: Essays by C.A. Ferguson*. Stanford University Press.

Fernandez, S. (1996) *Room for Two. A Study of Bilingual Education at Bayswater South Primary School*. The National Languages and Literacy Institute of Australia.

Fishman, J.A. (1967) Bilingualism with and without diglossia: Diglossia with and without bilingualism. *Journal of Social Issues* 23 (2), 29–38.

Fishman, J.A. (1972) *The Sociology of Language*. Rowley, MA: Newbury House.

Fishman, J.A. (1976) *Bilingual Education: An International Sociological Perspective*. Rowley, MA: Newbury House.

Fishman, J. A. (1977) The sociology of bilingual education. In B. Spolsky and R. Cooper (eds) *Frontiers of Bilingual Education*. Rowley: Newbury House.

Fishman, J. (1978) Positive bilingualism: Some overlooked rationales and forefathers. In J. Atlatis (ed.) *Georgetown Roundtable on Languages and Linguistics*.

Fishman, J.A. (1980) Bilingualism and biculturalism as individual and as societal phenomena. *Journal of Multilingual and Multicultural Development* 1, 3–15.

Fishman, J.A. (1982) Sociolinguistic foundations of bilingual education. *Bilingual Review/La Revista Bilingüe* 9, 1–35.

Fishman, J.A. (1991) *Reversing Language Shift*. Clevedon: Multilingual Matters.

Forbes, O. (1997) La enculturación y la aculturación enlos procesos de construcción del saber en el desarrrollo bilingüe: Una propuesta para la discusión. *Voces* 2, 41–53.

Foucault, M. (1980) *Power/Knowledge*. New York: Harvester Wheatsheaf.

Freeman, R.D. and McElhinny, B. (1996) Language and gender. In S.L. McKay and N.H. Hornberger (eds) *Sociolinguistics and Language Teaching*. Cambridge: Cambridge University Press.

Freeman, R.D. (1998) *Bilingual Education and Social Change*. Clevedon: Multilingual Matters.

Freire, P. (1972) *Pedagogy of the Oppressed*. Harmondsworth: Penguin.

García, O. (1991) *Bilingual Education: Focusshrift in Honor of Joshua A. Fishman on the Occasion of his 65th Birthday*. Amersterdam / Philadelphia: John Benjamins.

García, O. (1993) Understanding the societal role of the teacher in transitional bilingual classrooms: Lessons from the sociology of language. In K. Zontag (ed.) *Bilingual Education in Friesland. Facts and Prospects*. Leeuwarden / Ljouwert GCO / MSU.

García, O. (1995) Spanish language loss as a determinant of income among Latinos in the United States: Implications for a language policy in schools. In J.W. Tollefson (ed.) *Power and Inequality in Language Education*. Cambridge: Cambridge University Press.

García, O. and Baker, C. (eds) (1995) *Policy and Practice in Bilingual Education. A Reader Extending the Foundations*. Clevedon: Multilingual Matters.

Garner, D. (1990) The international school ESL challenge. In E. Murphy (ed.) *ESL: A Handbook for Teachers and Administrators in International Schools*. Clevedon: Multilingual Matters.

Garrigo, F.M. and Airas, B.C. (1992) Working methods in a Catalan immersion programme – the view of two teachers. In C. Laurén (ed.) *Language Acquisition at Kindergarten and School. Immersion Didactics in Canada, Catalonia and Finland*. Vaasa: University of Vaasa.

Gee, R. (1998) A hotel as a bilingual resource. *Bilingual Japan* 7 (5), 10–11.

Geertz, C. (1973) *The Interpretation of Cultures*. New York: Basic Books.

Geertz, C. (1983) *Local Knowledge*. New York: Basic Books.

Gibson, J. (1984) For my kids, it's French without tears. In H.H. Stern (ed.) *The Immersion Phenomenon. Special Issue No. 12 of Language and Society*. Ottawa: Commissioner of Official Languages, 8–10.

Gieve, S. and Magahaes, I. (eds) (1994) On empowerment. In *Centre for Research in Language Education, Occasional Report 6: Power, Ethics and Validity*. Lancaster: Lancaster University.

Goodman, R. (1993) *Japan's International Youth*. Oxford: Clarendon Press.

Gray, P. (1999) What's in a name ? Naming adopted children. In *Bilingual Japan* 8 (2), 4–5.

Grosjean, F. (1982) *Life with Two Languages: An Introduction to Bilingualism*. Cambridge, MA: Harvard University Press.

Grosjean, F. (1985) The bilingual as a competent but specific speaker-hearer. *Journal of Multilingual and Multicultural Development* 6 (6), 467–77.

Grosjean, F. (1993) *Bilinguisme et Biculturisme: Théories et Practiques Professionelles*. Switzerland: Université de Neuchátel.

Grover, T. (1997) The trials and tribulations of a bilingual teenager. *The Bilingual Family Newletter* 14 (2), 4 and 6.

Gunn, G. (1997) *Language, Power and Ideology in Brunei Darussalam.* Ohio University Center for International Studies. Southeast Asia Series No. 99. Athens, Ohio.

Gustavsson, R. and Mård, K. (1992) Language immersion in Finland. In *Code-switching Summer School*, European Science Foundation Network on Code-switching and Language Contact. European Science Foundation.

Hakuta, K. (1986) *Mirror of Language. The Debate on Bilingualism.* New York: Basic Books.

Halliday, M.A.K. and Hasan, R. (1976) *Cohesion in English.* London: Longman.

Handscombe, J. (1990) The complementary roles of researchers and practitioners in second language education. In B. Harley, P. Allen, J. Cummins and M. Swain (eds) *The Development of Second Language Proficiency.* Cambridge: Cambridge University Press.

Hardcastle, P. (1999) On WWW at www.alakhawayn.ma/~P.Hardcastle/research.htm.

Harding, E. and Riley, P. (1986) *The Bilingual Family: A Handbook for Parents.* Cambridge: Cambridge University Press.

Harley, B. (1991) Directions in immersion research. In *The Journal of Multilingual and Multicultural Development* 12 (1–2), 9–19.

Harley, B. and Swain, M. (1978) An analysis of the verb system used by young learners of French. *Interlanguage Studies Bulletin* 3 (1), 35–79.

Harley, B. and Swain, M. (1984)The interlanguage of immersion students and its implications for second language teaching. In A. Davies, C. Criper and A.P.R. Howatt (eds) *Interlanguage.* Edinburgh University Press.

Harley, B., Allen, P., Cummins, J. and Swain, M. (eds) (1990) *The Development of Second Language Proficiency.* Cambridge: Cambridge University Press.

Hayden, M. and Thompson, J. (1998) Changing times: The evolution of the international school. In D. Bingham (ed.) *The John Catt Guide to International Schools.* John Catt Educational Ltd.

Haywood, T. (2000) Language education in International Schools. *The Bilingual Family Newsletter* 17 (3), 1–2.

Heller, M. (1990) French immersion in Canada : A model for Switzerland? *Multilingua* 9 (1), 67–85.

Heller, M. (1994) *Crosswords. Language, Education and Ethnicity in French Ontario.* Berlin: Mouton de Gruyter.

Heller, M. (1997) Review of C. Baker, 'Foundations of Bilingual Education and Bilingualism'. *Multilingua* 16 (2/3), 267–69.

Heller, M. (1999) *Linguistic Minorities and Modernity: A Sociolinguistic Ethnography.* New York: Longman.

Heller, M. and Martin-Jones, M. (eds) (2001) *Voices of Authority. Education and Linguistic Difference.* Westport, CT: Ablex Publishing.

Hickman, J. (1992) Whole language and literature in a French immersion elementary school. In E. Berhardt (ed.) *Life in Language Immersion Classrooms.* Clevedon: Multilingual Matters.

Hoare, P. (2000) A comparison of the effectiveness of a 'language aware' and a 'non-language aware' late immersion teacher. Paper presented at the 5th European Conference on Immersion Programmes, University of Vaasa, Finland, 17–19 August, 2000.

Hoare, P. and Kong, S. (2000) A framework of attributes for English immersion teachers in Hong Kong and implications for immersion teacher education. Paper presented at the 5th European Conference on Immersion Programmes, University of Vaasa, Finland, 17–19 August, 2000.

Honna, N. (1995) English in Japanese society: Language within language. *Journal of Multilingual and Multicultural Development* 16 (1&2), 45–62.

Hornberger, N.H. (1988) *Bilingual Education and Language Maintenance: A Southern Peruvian Quechua Case.* Dordrecht, Holland: Foris.

Hornberger, N.H. (1989) Continua of biliteracy. *Review of Educational Research* 59 (3), 271–96.

Hornberger, N.H. (1990) Teacher Quechua use in bilingual and non-bilingual classrooms of Puno, Peru. In R. Jacobson and C. Faltis (eds) *Language Distribution Issues in Bilingual Schooling*. Clevedon: Multilingual Matters.

Hornberger, N.H. (1991) Extending enrichment bilingual education: Revisiting typologies and redirecting policy. In O. García (ed.) *Bilingual Education: Focusschrift in Honor of Joshua A. Fishman* (Volume 1). Amsterdam/Philadelphia: John Benjamins.

Hornberger, N. H. (1992) Biliteracy contexts, continua, and contrasts. Policy and curriculum for Cambodian and Puerto Rican students in Philadelphia. *Education and Urban Society* 24 (2), 196–211.

Hornberger, N. (ed.) (1997) *Indigenous Literacies in the Americas. Language Planning From the Bottom Up*. Berlin: Mouton de Gruyter.

Hornberger, N.H. and Skilton-Sylvester, E. (2000) Revising the continua of biliteracy: International and critical perspectives. *Language and Education* 14 (2), 96–122.

Housen, A. (forthcoming) Processes and outcomes in the European School model of multilingual education. *Bilingual Research Journal*.

Housen, A. and Baetens Beardsmore, H. (1987) Curricular and extra-curricular factors in multilingual education. *Studies in Second Language* 9 (1), 83–102.

Hudelson, S. (1994) Literacy development in second language children. In F. Genesee (ed.) *Educating Second Language Children: The Whole Child, The Whole Curriculum, The Whole Community*. Cambridge: Cambridge University Press.

International Baccalaureate Office (1986) *General Guide* (5th edn). Geneva.

Ivanic, R. (1994) Collaborative research: Enriching the contribution or contaminating the data? In *Centre for Research in Language Education, Occasional Report 6: Power, Ethics and Validity*. Lancaster: Lancaster University.

Johnson, R.K. (1994) Language policy and planning in Hong Kong. *Annual Review of Applied Linguistics* 14, 177–99.

Johnson, R.K. and Swain, M. (eds) (1997) *Immersion Education: International Perspectives*. Cambridge: Cambridge University Press.

Jones, G.M., Martin, P.W. and Ozog, A.C.K. (1993) Multilingualism and bilingual education in Brunei Daruassalam. *Journal of Multilingual and Multicultural Development* 14 (1&2), 39–58.

Jones, G.M. (1997) The evolution of a language plan: Brunei Darussalam in focus. *Language Problems and Language Planning* 21 (3), 197–215.

Kamada, L. (1998a) Pioneering Japanese family: English at home and English immersion school (Part 2). *Bilingual Japan* 7 (5), 8–9.

Kamada, L. (1998b) A misunderstood mildly-retarded bilingual child in a Japanese public school. (Part 1) Background. *Bilingual Japan* 7 (6),11–12.

Kamada, L. (1999) A misunderstood mildly-retarded bilingual child in a Japanese public school. (Part 2) Randy in a conformist society. *Bilingual Japan* 8 (1), 15–16.

Kanno, Y. (2000) Bilingualism and identity: The stories of Japanese returnees. *International Journal of Bilingual Education and Bilingualism* 3 (1), 1–18.

Kowal, M. and Swain, M. (1997) From semantic to syntactic processing: How can we promote it in the immersion classroom? In R.K. Johnson and M. Swain (eds) *Immersion Education: International Perspectives*. Cambridge: Cambridge University Press.

Kramsch, C. (1991) Culture in language learning: A view from the United States. In K. de Boot, R. Ginsberg and C. Kramsch (eds) *Foreign Language Research In Cross Cultural Perspective*. Utrecht: Benjamin.

Kramsch, C., Cain, A. and Murphy-Lejeune, E. (1996) Why should language teachers teach culture? *Language Culture and Curriculum* 9 (1), 99–107.

Krashen, S. (1999) *Condemned without a Trial. Bogus Arguments against Bilingual Education*. Portsmouth, NH: Heinemann.

Krashen, S. and Terrell, T. (1983) *The Natural Approach: Language Acquisition in the Classroom*. Oxford: Pergamon.

Küpelikilinç, N. (1998) Multilingualism and identity. *The Bilingual Family Newsletter* 15 (2), 1–2 and 8.

Lambert, W.E. (1974) Culture and language as factors in learning and education. In F.E. Aboud and R.D. Meade (eds) *Cultural Factors in Learning and Education.* Bellingham, WA: 5th Western Washington Symposium on Learning.

Lambert, W.E. and Tucker, G.R. (1972) *Bilingual Education of Children: The St. Lambert Experiment.* Rowley, MA: Newbury House.

Lapkin, S. and Swain, M. (1984) Research update. In H.H. Stern (ed) *The Immersion Phenomenon. Special Issue No. 12 of Language and Society.* Ottawa: Commissioner of Official Languages, 48–54.

Laurén, C. (1991) A two-phase-didactics for school. *Journal of Multilingual and Multicultural Development* 12 (1&2), 6772.

Laurén, C. (ed.) (1992) Introduktion. In *Language Acquisition at Kindergarten and School. Immersion Didactics in Canada, Catalonia and Finland.* Vaasa: University of Vaasa.

Lee, W.O. (1993) Social reaction towards education proposals: Opting against the mother tongue as the medium of instruction in Hong Kong. *Journal of Multilingual and Multicultural Development* 14 (3), 203–16.

Leman, J. (1993) The bicultural programmes in the Dutch language school system in Brussels. In H. Baetens Beardsmore (ed.) *European Models of Bilingual Education.* Clevedon: Multilingual Matters.

Lewis, E.G. (1977) Bilingualism and bilingual education: The ancient world of the Renaissance. In B. Spolsky and R.L. Cooper (eds.) *Frontiers of Bilingual Education.* Rowley, MA: Newbury House.

Lewis E.B. (1981) *Bilingualism and Bilingual Education.* Oxford: Pergamon.

Lin, A.M.Y. (1990) *Teaching in Two Tongues: Language Alternation in Foreign Language Classrooms.* (Research Report No. 3.) Hong Kong: City Polytechnic of Hong Kong, Department of English.

Lon, A.M.Y. (1996) Bilingualism or linguistic segregation? Symbolic domination, resistance and code-switching in Hong Kong schools. *Linguistics and Education* 8, 49–84.

Lin, A.M.Y. (2001) Symbolic domination and bilingual classroom practices in Hong Kong. In M. Heller and M. Martin-Jones (eds) *Voices of Authority. Education and Linguistic Difference.* Westport Connecticut: Ablex Publishing.

Lindholm, K.J. (1990) Bilingual immersion education: Criteria for program development. In A.M. Padilla, H.H. Fairchild and C.M. Valadez (eds) *Bilingual Education: Issues and Strategies.* London, Newbury Park: Sage Publications.

Lorch, S.C., McNamara, T.F. and Eisikovits, E. (1992) Late Hebrew immersion at Mount Scopus College, Melbourne: Towards complete Hebrew fluency for Jewish day school students. *Language and Language Education* 2 (1), 1–29.

Lotherington, H. (1998) Trends and tensions in post-colonial language education in the South Pacific. *International Journal of Bilingual Education and Bilingualism* 1 (1), 65–75.

Lowenstein, A. (1995) Playing football in Esperanto. *The Bilingual Family Newsletter* 12 (2), 1–2.

MacRae, M. (1997) Language shift in the Anglo-Brazilian community in São Paulo: Language, culture and symbolic domination. Paper presented at the International Symposium on Bilingualism, University of Newcastle upon Tyne, 9–12 April.

McKay, S.L. and Wong, S.-L.C. (1996) Multiple discourses, multiple identities: Investment and agency in second language learning among Chinese adolescent immigrant students. *Harvard Educational Review* 66 (3), 577–608.

Maher, J. (1986) The development of English as an international language of medicine. *Applied Linguistics* 7 (2), 206–219.

Maher, J. (1989) Language use and preference in Japanese medical communication. In H. Coleman (ed.) *Working with Language.* Berlin: Mouton de Gruyter.

Maher, J. and Yashiro, K. (1995) Multilingual Japan: An introduction. *Journal of Multilingual and Multicultural Development* 16 (1&2), 1–17.

Mar-Molinero, C. (1989) The teaching of Catalan in Catalonia. *Journal of Multilingual and Multicultural Development* 10 (4), 307–26.

Martin, P. W. (1996) Code-switching in the primary classroom: One response to the planned and unplanned language environment in Brunei. *Journal of Multilingual and Multicultural Development* 17 (2–4), 128–44.

Martin-Jones, M. (1989) Language education in the context of linguistic diversity: Differing orientations in educational policy-making in Britain. In J. Esling (ed.) *Multicultural Education and Policy: ESL in the 1990s.* Toronto: OISE Press.

Martin-Jones, M. (1995) Code-switching in the classroom: Two decades of research. In L. Milroy and P. Muysken (eds) *One Speaker, Two Languages: Cross-disciplinary Perspectives on Code-switching.* Cambridge: Cambridge University Press.

Martin-Jones, M. (2000) Bilingual classroom interaction: A review of recent research. *Language Teaching* 33, 1–9.

Martin-Jones, M. and Romaine, S. (1986) Semilingualism: A half-baked theory of communicative competence. *Applied Linguistics* 7 (1), 26–38.

Martin-Jones M. and Heller, M. (1996) Introduction to the special issue on education in multilingual settings: Discourse, identities and power. *Linguistics and Education* 8, 3–16.

Marulanda, G.J. (1995) El método preview-review en la enseñanza-aprendizaje de las matemáticas en un contexto bilingüe. Unpublished monograph study. Cali: Universidad del Valle.

Matthews, M. (1989) The uniqueness of international education. Part 11. *International Schools Journal* (Spring), 24–33.

Mbise, A. (1994) Teaching English language reading in Tanzanian secondary schools. In C.M. Rubagumya (ed.) *Teaching and Researching Language in African Classrooms.*

McTigue, J. (1998) Help for a teenager in a foreign country. *The Bilingual Family Newsletter* 15 (1), 6.

Mejía, A.M. de (1994) Bilingual teaching-learning events in early immersion classes: A case study in Cali, Colombia. Unpublished PhD thesis. Lancaster: Lancaster University.

Mejía, A.M. de (1996) Educación bilingüe en Colombia: Consideraciones para programas bilingües en Colombia. *El Bilinguismo de los Sordos* 1 (2),1–25.

Mejía, A.M. de (1998) Bilingual storytelling: Codeswitching, discourse control, and learning opportunities. *TESOL Journal*, 7 (6), 4–10.

Mejía, A.M. de (1999) Selección linguistica y cambio de código en programs bilingües de inmersión en Cali. In A.M. de Mejía and L.A.Tovar (eds) *Perspectivas Recientes del Bilingüismo y de la Educación Bilingüe en Colombia.* Cali: Universidad del Valle.

Mejía, A.M. (in progress) Actitudes de los padres de familia hacia la educación bilingüe: Un sondeo. Research project, Universidad del Valle.

Mejía, A.M. de and Tejada, H. (2001) La construcción de una propuesta curricular bilingüe para colegios monolingues en Cali. Unpublished research report. Cali: Universidad del Valle.

Met, M. (1994) Teaching content through a second language. In F. Genesee (ed.) *Educating Second Language Children: The Whole Child, The Whole Curriculum, The Whole Community.* Cambridge: Cambridge University Press.

Met, M. (2000) Encouraging language use in immersion classrooms. Paper presented at the 5th European Conference on Immersion Programmes, University of Vaasa, Finland, 17–19 August.

Met, M. and Lorenz, E.B. (1997) Lessons from US immersion programs: Two decades of experience. In R.K. Johnson and M. Swain (eds) *Immersion Education: International Perspectives.* Cambridge: Cambridge University Press.

Milroy, L and Muysken, P. (1995) *One Speaker, Two Languages. Cross Disciplinary Perspectives on Code-switching.* Cambridge: Cambridge University Press.

Mitchell, S. (1999) The view of a second language specialist working for an education support service. In A. Yamada-Yamamoto and B.J. Richards (eds) *Japanese Children Abroad*. Clevedon: Multilingual Matters.

Mockus, A. (1995) El pasado está al frente, el futuro está atrás, Interview published in *Vivencias Universitarias* 14, 2–8.

Moll, L.C. (1992) Bilingual classroom studies and community analysis. *Educational Researcher* 21 (2), 20–4.

Moore, H. (1996) Language policies as virtual reality: Two Australian examples. *TESOL Quarterly* 30 (3), 473–97.

Muñoz, A. (1995) La educación intercultural hoy. *Didáctica*, 7, 217–40.

Murphy, E. (ed.) (1990) *ESL: A Handbook for Teachers and Administrators in International Schools*. Clevedon: Multilingual Matters.

Ndayipfukamiye, L. (1994) Code-switching in Burundi primary classrooms. In C.M. Rubagumya (ed.) *Teaching and Researching Language in African Classrooms*. Clevedon: Multilingual Matters.

Ndayipfukamiye, L. (1996) The contradiction of teaching bilingually in post-colonial Burundi: From *Nyakatsi* to *Maisons en Etage*. *Linguistics and Education* 8 (1), 35–47.

Noguchi, M.G. (2001) The crumbling of a myth. In M.G. Noguchi and S. Fotos (eds) *Studies in Japanese Bilingualism*. Clevedon: Multilingual Matters.

Noguchi, M. G. and Fotos, S. (eds) (2001) *Studies in Japanese Bilingualism*. Clevedon: Multilingual Matters.

Nussbaun, L. (1991) La lengua materna en clase de lengua extranjera: Entre la ayuda y el obstáculo. *Signos* 4, 36–47.

Ogbu, J.U. (1982) Cultural discontinuities and schooling. *American Education Quarterly* 14 (4) (Winter), 290–307.

Orejuela, M.C. (1997) Actitudes de los padres de familia de los alumnos del curso CMI del Liceo Paul Valery hacia la educación bilingüe. Unpublished monograph. Cali: Universidad del Valle.

Oka, H. (no date) Studies on bilingualism and their implication in Japan. Unpublished address given at the Opening of the Symposium on Bilingualism.

Olsen, P. and Burns, G. (1983) Politics, class and happenstance: French immersion in a Canadian context. *Interchange* 14 (1), 1–16.

Ovando, C.J. and Collier, V.P. (1987) *Bilingual and ESL Classrooms: Teaching in Multicultural Contexts*. Boston: McGraw-Hill.

Paradis, M. (2000) The neurolinguistics of bilingualism in the next decades. *Brain and Language* 71, 178–80.

Paulston, C. B. (1980) *Bilingual Education: Theories and Issues*. Rowley, MA: Newbury House.

Paulston, C.B. (1992) *Sociolinguistic Perspectives on Bilingual Education*. Clevedon: Multilingual Matters.

Peirce, B.N. (1995) Social identity, investment and learning. *TESOL Quarterly* 29 (1), 9–29.

Pennycook, A. (1994) *The Cultural Politics of English as an International Language*. London: Longman.

Pennycook, A. (1995) English in the world/the world in English. In J. Tollefson (ed.) *Power and Inequality in Language Education*. Cambridge: Cambridge University Press.

Pennington, M. (1995) Pattern and variation in use of two languages in the Hong Kong secondary English class. *RELC Journal* 26 (2), 80–105.

Pennington, M. (1998a) The folly of language planning; Or, a brief history of the English language in Hong Kong. *English Today* 54, 14 (2), 25–30.

Pennington, M. (1998b) Colonialism's aftermath in Asia: A snapshot view of bilingualism in Hong Kong. *HKJAL* 3 (1), 1–16.

Pennington, M. and Yue, F. (1994) English and Chinese in Hong Kong: Pre-1997 language attitudes. *World Englishes* 13 (1), 1–20.

Petherbridge-Hernandez, P. (1990) Teacher preparation in a bilingual setting: In-service training for teachers in Catalonia. *Journal of Multilingual and Multicultural Development* 11 (3), 215–26.

Phillipson, R. (1992) *Linguistic Imperialism*. Oxford: Oxford University Press.

Pierson, H.D., Fu, G.S. and Lee, S.Y. (1980) An analysis of the relationship between language attitudes and English attainment of secondary school students in Hong Kong. *Language Learning* 30, 289–316.

Pond, M. (1999) Strategies adopted in a school with a large number of Japanese pupils. In A. Yamada-Yamamoto and B.J. Richards (eds) *Japanese Children Abroad*. Clevedon: Multilingual Matters.

Poon, A.Y.K. (1999) Chinese medium instruction policy and its impact on English learning in post-1997 Hong Kong. *International Journal of Bilingual Education and Bilingualism* 2 (2), 131–46.

Poplack, S. (1980) Sometimes I'll start a sentence in Spanish y termino en español: Towards a typology of code-switching. *Linguistics* 18, 581–618.

Potter, M. 1999 A post pottered biography. *E.L.T. News and Views* Marsh 1999a Year 6 (2).

Qorro, M.P. (1989) Introduction. *Journal of Linguistics and Language in Education* 4 (2), 3–11.

Rajabu, R. and Ngonyani, D. (1994) Language policy in Tanzania and the hidden agenda. In C.M. Rubagumya (ed.) *Teaching and Researching Language in African Classrooms*. Clevedon: Multilingual Matters.

Rebuffot, J. (1993) *Le Point Sur . . . l'Immersion au Canada*. Quebec: Centre Educatif et Culturel.

Rebuffot, J. (2000) L'immersion au Canada: Politique, pedagogie et perspectives. Paper presented at the 5th European Conference on Immersion Programmes, University of Vaasa/Vasa, Finland, 17–19th August, 2000.

Rebuffot, J. and Lyster, R. (1996) L'immersion en français au Canada: contexts, effets et pédagogie. In J. Erfurt (ed.) *De la Polyphonie à la Symphonie. Métodes, Theories et Faits de la Recherché Pluridisiplinaire sur le Fait Français au Canada*. Leipzig: Leipsiger Universitätsverlag.

Redouane, R. (1997) From duality to complementarity: The case of Moroccan bilingualism. Paper given at the *International Symposium on Bilingualism, University of Newcastle upon Tyne, UK, 9–12 April*.

Ricento, T. and Hornberger, N. (1996) Unpeeling the onion: Language planning and policy and the ELT professional. *TESOL Quarterly* 30 (3), 401–27.

Roberts, C. (1987) Political conflict over bilingual initiatives: A case study. *Journal of Multilingual and Multicultural Development* 8 (4), 311–22.

Robertson, R. (1995) Glocalization: Time-space and homogeneity-heterogeneity. In M. Featherstone, S. Lash and R. Robertson (eds) *Global Modernities*. London: Sage Publications.

Robinson, G.L. (1985) *Crosscultural Understanding. Processes and Approaches for Foreign Language, English as a Second Language and Bilingual Educators*. Oxford: Pergamon Press.

Romaine, S. (1988) *Pidgin and Creole Languages*. London: Longman.

Romaine, S. (1989) *Bilingualism*. Oxford: Blackwell.

Romaine, S. (1992) *Language, Education, and Development: Urban and Rural Tok Pisin in Papua New Guinea*. Oxford: Oxford University Press.

Rubagumya, C.M. (1986) *Language Attitudes and their Influence on Language Policy. Proceedings: Conference on English in East Africa*. Nairobi: The British Council.

Rubagumya, C.M. (ed.) (1990) *Language in Education in Africa*. Clevedon: Multilingual Matters.

Rubagumya, C.M. (1991a) Language, social values and inequality in Tanzania: Reinterpreting Triglossia. *Working Paper 26, Centre for Language in Social Life*. Lancaster: Lancaster University.

Rubagumya, C.M. (1991b) Language promotion for educational purposes. *Working Paper, Centre for Language in Social Life*. Lancaster: Lancaster University.

Rubagumya, C.M. (ed.) (1994a) *Teaching and Researching Language in African Classrooms: A Tanzanian Perspective*. Clevedon: Multilingual Matters.

Rubagumya, C.M. (ed.) (1994b) Language values and bilingual classroom discourse in Tanzanian secondary schools. *Language, Culture and Curriculum* 7 (1), 41–54.

Salamone, A. (1992) Immersion teachers pedagogical beliefs and practices: Results of a descriptive analysis. In E. Bernhardt (ed.) *Life in Language Immersion Classrooms*. Clevedon: Multilingual Matters.

Samoff, J. (1990) The politics of privatization in Tanzania. *International Journal of Educational Development* 10 (1), 1–15.

Sears, C. (1990) Some common difficulties and how they can be avoided. In E. Murphy. (ed.) *ESL: A Handbook for Teachers and Administrators in International Schools*. Clevedon: Multilingual Matters.

Sears, C. (1998) *Second Language Students in Mainstream Classrooms: A Handbook for Teachers in International Schools*. Clevedon: Multilingual Matters.

Sharwood Smith, M. (1989) Cross-linguistic influences in language loss. In K. Hyltenstam and L. Obler (eds) *Bilingualism Across the Lifespan: Aspects of Acquisition, Maturity and Loss*. Cambridge: Cambridge University Press.

Sheffner, M. (1998) The notion of nation. *Bilingual Japan* 7 (4), 5–7.

Shibata, Y. (1998) Initial experiences at a British school: A mother's account. In A. Yamada-Yamamoto and B.J. Richards (eds) *Japanese Children Abroad*. Clevedon: Multilingual Matters.

Siguán, M. and Mackey, W.F. (1987) *Education and Bilingualism*. London: Kogan Page.

Skutnabb-Kangas, T. (1977) Language in the process of cultural assimilation and structural incorporation of linguistic minorities. In C.C. Elert *et al.* (eds) *Dialectology and Sociolinguistics*. UMEA: UMEA Studies in the Humanities.

Skutnabb-Kangas, T. (1981) *Bilingualism or Not. The Education of Minorities*. Clevedon: Multilingual Matters.

Skutnabb-Kangas, T. (1987) The education of the Finnish minority in Sweden. *Working Papers*. Roskilde University Centre, Denmark.

Sloan Management Review (1998) Hong Kong, un año después. *Summa* 133, 23–34.

Smith, C. (1999) The graduates of Japan's first immersion program. *Bilingual Japan* 8 (1), 10–12.

So, D.W.C. (1984) The social selection of an English-dominant bilingual education system in Hong Kong: An ecolinguistic analysis. Unpublished doctoral dissertation, University of Hawaii.

Stern, H.H. (1983) *Fundamental Concepts of Language Teaching*. Oxford: Oxford University Press.

Stern, H. (ed.) (1984) *The Immersion Phenomenon. Special Issue No. 12 of Language and Society*. Ottawa: Commissioner of Official Languages, 4–7.

Stern, H. (1990) Analysis and experience as variables in second language pedagogy. In B. Harley, P. Allen, J. Cummins and M. Swain (eds) *The Development of Second Language Proficiency*. Cambridge: Cambridge University Press.

Stevens, E. (1995) Parental support for the Mansfield High School French immersion programme. In *Conference Proceedings Second Biennial Conference, Australian Association of Language Immersion Teachers (AALIT)*.

Strömman, S. (1993) Time passes: Internal bilingualism in an enterprise in 1981. Paper presented at the Fifth International Conference on Minority Languages, Cardiff, Wales, 5–9 July.

Sussman, N. (1986) Re-entry research and raining. *International Journal of Intercultural Relations* 10, 235–54.

Swain, M. (1972) Bilingualism as a first language. Unpublished PhD dissertation, University of California, Irvine.

Swain, M. (1982) Immersion education: Applicability for non-vernacular teaching to vernacular speakers. In B. Hartford, A. Valdman and C. Foster (eds) *Issues in International Bilingual Education: The Role of the Vernacular*. New York: Plenum Press.

Swain, M. (1983) Bilingualism without tears. In M. Clarke and J. Handscombe (eds) *On TESOL '82: Pacific Perspectives on Language Learning and Teaching*. Washington, DC: Teachers of English to Speakers of Other Languages.

Swain, M. (1985) Communicative competence: Some roles of comprehensible input and comprehensible output in its development. In S. Gass and C. Madden (eds) *Input in Second Language Acquisition*. Rowley, MA: Newbury House.

Swain, M. (1988) Manipulating and complementing content teaching to maximize second language learning. *TESL Canada Journal 6*, 68–83.

Swain, M. and Lapkin, S. (1982) *Evaluating Bilingual Education: A Canadian Case Study*. Clevedon: Multilingual Matters.

Swain, M. and Lapkin, S. (1986) Immersion French in secondary schools: The 'goods' and the 'bads'. *Contact* 5 (3), 103–21.

Swain, M. and Johnson, R.K. (1997) Immersion education: A category within bilingual education. In R.K. Johnson and M. Swain (eds) *Immersion Education: International Perspectives*, Cambridge: Cambridge University Press.

Swan, D. (1996) *A Singular Pluralism. The European Schools 1984–1994*. Dublin: Institute of Public Administration.

Tardif, C. and Weber, S. (1987) French immersion research: A call for new perspectives. *Canadian Modern Language Review* 44 (1), 67–77.

TESOL (1992/1993) TESOL Statement on the role of bilingual education in the education of children in the United States. *TESOL Matters* 2 (6) 1–5.

Thomas, D. (1996) Early English immersion in Japan. *AALIT Journal* 4, 14–17.

Tisdell, M. (1995) The German partial immersion programme at St Peter's Junior School. In *Conference Proceedings Second Biennial Conference*. Australian Association of Language Immersion Teachers (AALIT).

Tollefson, J. (1991) *Planning Language, Planning Inequality: Language Policy in the Community*. London: Longman.

Tollefson, J.W. (1995) *Power and Inequality in Language Education*. Cambridge: Cambridge University Press.

Tosi, A. (1986) The evaluation of language competence in international education. Unpublished report. International Baccalaureate Office, Geneva.

Tosi, A. (1989) Bilingualism and language testing project. Unpublished report. University of London.

Tosi, A. (1990) Bilingual education. *Annual Review of Applied Linguistics* 10, 103–21.

Trappes-Lomax, H.R. (1990) Can a foreign language be a national medium. In C.M. Rubagumya (ed.) *Language in Education in Africa*. Clevedon: Multilingual Matters.

Treffers-Daller, J. (1992) A comparative perspective on language mixing. In European Science Foundation *Code-switching Summer School*. European Science Foundation Network on Code-switching and Language Contact.

United States Department of State Report (1998) *Morocco Country Report on Human Rights Practices for 1998*.

Valdés, G. and Figueroa, R.A. (1994) *Bilingualism and Testing: A Special Case of Bias*. Norwood, NJ: Ablex.

Vesterbacka, S. (1991) Ritualised routines and L2 acquisition: Acquisition strategies in an immersion program. *Journal of Multilingual and Multicultural Development* 12 (1&2), 35–43.

Vila, I. (1985) *Reflexionx sobre l'Educació Bilingüe: Llengua de la Llar i Llengua d'Instrucció*. Barcelona: Departament d'Ensenyament.

Vila, I. (1996) Educación bilingüe, motivación y actitudes. In M. Sigúan (ed.) *La Enseñanza Precoz de una Segunda Lengua en la Escuela*. Barcelona ICE/Horsori.

Viteri, A. (1996) Caracterización de la enseñanza de segunda lengua en un colegio de Cali. Unpublished manuscript.

Vraid, J. (2001) Bilingualism. In V.S. Ramachandran (ed.) *Encyclopaedia of the Human Brain.* San Diego: Academic Press.

Weber, S. and Tardif, C. (1991) Assessing L2 competency in early immersion classrooms. *Canadian Modern Language Review* 47, 916–32.

Willets, K. and Christian, D. (1990) Materials needed for bilingual immersion programs. In A.M. Padilla, H.H. Fairchild and C.M. Valadez (eds) *Bilingual Education: Issues and Strategies.* Newbury Park, London: Sage Publications.

Wode, H. (2000) Multilingual education in Europe: What can preschools contribute? Paper presented at the 5th European Conference on Immersion Programmes, University of Vaasa, Finland, 17–19 August.

Wolfson, N. (1982) *CHP, The Conversational Historical Present in American English Narrative.* Cinnarminson, NJ: Foris Publications.

Yahya-Othman, S. (1990) When international languages clash: The possible detrimental effects on development of the conflict between English and Kiswahili in Tanzania. In C.M. Rubagumya (ed.) *Language in Education in Africa: A Tanzanian Perspective.* Clevedon: Multilingual Matters.

Yamada-Yamamoto, A. (1997) Where East meets West. Language development of Japanese children in Britain. *The Bilingual Family Newsletter* 14 (3), 1–5.

Yamada-Yamamoto, A. and Richards, B.J. (eds) (1999) *Japanese Children Abroad.* Clevedon: Multilingual Matters.

Yamamoto, M. (1995) Bilingualism in international families. *Journal of Multilingual and Multicultural Development* 16 (1&2), 63–85.

Yamamoto, M. (2001) Japanese attitudes towards bilingualism: A survey and its implications. In M. Goebel Noguchi and S. Fotos (eds) *Studies in Japanese Bilingualism.* Clevedon: Multilingual Matters.

Yashiro, K. (1995) Japan's returnees. *Multilingual Japan, Special Issue of the Journal of Multilingual and Multicultural Development* 16 (1–2), 139–64.

Young, R. (1996) *Intercultural Communication.* Clevedon: Multilingual Matters.

Yu V.W.S. and Atkinson, P.A. (1998) An investigation of the language difficulties experience by Hong Kong secondary school students in English-medium schools: Some causal factors. *Journal of Multilingual and Multicultural Development* 9 (4), 307–22.

Zentella, A.C. (1981) *Ta bien,* you could answer me *en cualquier idioma:* Puerto Rican codeswitching in bilingual classrooms. In R. Duran (ed.) *Latino Language and Communicative Behavior.* Norwood, NJ: Ablex Publishing Corporation.

Zuluaga, O. (1996) *La Enseñanza de Lenguas Extranjeras en Colombia en 500 Años.* Popayan: Taller Editorial, Unicauca.

Index

Authors

Abdulaziz-Mkilifi, M.H. 39, 151
Acton, W. 52
Adiv, E. 29
Airas Barreal, C. 230, 231
Allen, P. 29, 127, 244, 275, 291
Anderssohn, A. 63, 103
Anselmi, G. 125, 222, 224, 225
Araújo, M.C. 105, 113, 176
Arenas, J. 228, 229, 232, 233
Armendáriz, A. 171, 172
Arnau, J. 233
Arthur, J. 154
Artigal, J.M. 210, 227, 229, 233
Atkinson, P.A. 195, 197
Auerbach, E. 136

Baetens Beardsmore, H. 5, 22, 23, 24, 25, 33,
    106, 125, 201, 202, 203, 204, 221, 222, 223,
    224, 225, 242
Baker, C. 1, 14, 23, 32, 33, 40, 41, 42, 44, 45,
    46, 48, 49, 66, 73, 83, 103, 104, 141, 142,
    151, 152, 165, 192, 194, 210, 218, 221, 235,
    236, 237, 260, 268, 277, 281, 294
Banfi, C. 125, 167, 168, 172, 173
Banks, J.A. 66
Barbour, S. 62
Barrett, J. 152, 153, 154, 156
Batibo, H.M. 151, 152
Bauer, R.S. 194
Bel, A. 232
Bernhardt, E. 127, 291
Bickley, G. 194
Bilger, C. 121
Bingham, D. 5, 248
Björklund, S. 211, 212, 217
Blanton, L.L. 141, 142, 144, 146, 147, 148, 149

Boada, H. 233
Bodi, M. 235
Boix, E. 227
Bostwick, R.M. 188, 191
Bourdieu, P. 36, 39, 48, 49, 154, 296
Bourjade, N. 81
Braighlinn, G. 201, 203
Braun, A. 110, 221
Brinton, D.M. 80, 82, 280, 281, 289
British Council 159, 162, 164, 166, 167, 170,
    172, 173, 174, 192, 195, 196, 199
Buitrago, H. 84
Burns, G. 28
Buss, M. 213, 214
Byram, M. 66, 67, 68, 74, 282, 283, 296

Cain, A. 66, 67
Caldwell, J. 242, 243
Cambra Giné, M. 77
Cameron, D. x, 128, 131, 132, 135, 296
Camillieri, C. 66
Carder, M. xi, 14, 15, 17, 18
Castañeda, R. 55, 56, 176, 179, 181
Cath, A. 203, 255, 259, 261, 263
Cavalcanti, M. 128, 159
Cazden, C. 45
CCELA 66, 83
Ceballos, D. and I. 176, 177
Chamberlain, N. 3
Chan, R.M.L. 197
Chapman, D. 242, 243
Cheung, J. 196
Cheung, Y. 194
Christian, D. 289
Clark, R. 128
Clyne, M. 236, 237

Subjects

For Product Safety Concerns and Information please contact our EU Authorised Representative:

Easy Access System Europe

Mustamäe tee 50

10621 Tallinn

Estonia

gpsr.requests@easproject.com

www.ingramcontent.com/pod-product-compliance
Lightning Source LLC
Chambersburg PA
CBHW080412270326
41929CB00018B/2993